No Wealth But Life

What's Gone Wrong with Healthcare

in Britain & How We Can Save the NHS

Tom Bell

To Stuart

Tom

Copyright 2023 Humanity & Integrity in Public Sector Services (HIPSS) Ltd.

Edition 1.2, revised 04-04-2024, first published 05-07-2023.

ISBN: 9798397292146

It is apparently not big, clever, or even legal, to reproduce, duplicate, transmit, or record any part of this publication, in either electronic means or printed format, unless of course you ask the publisher nicely for permission first! Contact details can be found at the end of this book.

For those with good memories who read my previous book, *Lions, Liars, Donkeys and Penguins – The Killing of Alison*, you may recognise some of the passages in this text. I hope you find the ninety-five percent of it that will be new to you as good as you told me the previous book was.

"The most exciting breakthroughs of the 21st Century will not occur because of technology, but because of an expanding concept of what it means to be human."

John Naisbitt

Contents

CONTENTS	4
FOREWORD	9
INTRODUCTION	16
PART I:	22
WHAT IS A HEALTHY NATION?	22
Chapter 1: The envy of less happier lands?	23
Chapter 2: How would you like to be remembered?	27
Chapter 3: All aboard the hamster wheel	34
Chapter 4: Public Health	44
Chapter 5: It could be you, it just probably won't be!	57
PART II:	68
A CRISIS IN SOCIAL CARE OR A SOCIETY IN CRISIS?	68
Chapter 6: Does society exist?	69
Chapter 7: Social Care	72
Chapter 8: Sybil	79
Chapter 9: The outsourcing of old age	85
Chapter 10: Let's go Dutch!	90

Chapter 11: Can Social Work, work?   94

PART III: 101

THE NHS   101

Chapter 12: What is the purpose of the NHS?   102

Chapter 13: What is the NHS?   106

Chapter 14: The Doctor will see you now, briefly…   119

Chapter 15: A ride in the ambulance   139

Chapter 16: The heroes at the hospital   145

Chapter 17: Sane in a crazy world   158

PART IV: 172

BEHIND THE CURTAIN   172

Chapter 18: Never meet your heroes   173

Chapter 19: Fit and proper   180

Chapter 20: The tragic folly of Foundation Trusts   186

Chapter 21: Leadership & management in the NHS   195

Chapter 22: Oil and water, technology and the NHS   212

Chapter 23: Proactive innovators unwelcome   222

PART V: 234

WHY ISN'T HEALTHCARE LEARNING FROM ITS MISTAKES? 234

Chapter 24: Predictable avoidable tragedies 235

Chapter 25: Asking the wrong questions 247

Chapter 26: Why don't more people simply speak up? 254

Chapter 27: The incurious culture at the Countess 260

Chapter 28: The treatment of whistleblowers 271

Chapter 29: Why regulation doesn't work... 283

Chapter 30: Advisors & thinktanks 294

PART VI: 306

THE ROLE OF CHARITY 306

Chapter 31: Taken for granted 307

Chapter 32: Picking up the pieces 311

PART VIII: 325

SAFE IN WHOSE HANDS? 325

Chapter 33: If Carlsberg did healthcare 326

Chapter 34: Learning from the private sector 331

Chapter 35: The vital role of the press 337

Chapter 36: Healthcare is a political football 344

Chapter 37: Has the NHS been set up to fail? 349

Chapter 38: The rise and role of private healthcare	361
Chapter 39: Lessons from history	373
Chapter 40: Too important to fail, too big to fix	379

PART IX: 386

HOPE IS NOT A PLAN 386

Chapter 41: So, what can be done?	387
Chapter 42: Start with purpose	390
Chapter 43: A National Health and Care Service	394
Chapter 44: Get a grip on Primary Care	396
Chapter 45: Centralise processes to create consistency	401
Chapter 46: Decentralise oversight and accountability	405
Chapter 47: Implement consistent systemwide technology	409
Chapter 48: Trash the targets	413
Chapter 49: Mandatory training for leaders & managers	420
Chapter 50: Attract, recruit, value and retain	424
Chapter 51: Scrap the Care Quality Commission	428
Chapter 52: Remove Public Relations from the NHS	431
Chapter 53: Complete transparency and openness	435
Epilogue: Can Britain be a model for a better world?	438

| ACKNOWLEDGEMENTS | 441 |
| ABOUT THE AUTHOR | 444 |

Foreword

"There is no wealth but life. Life, including all its powers of love, of joy, and of admiration. That country is the richest which nourishes the greatest numbers of noble and happy human beings; that man is richest, who, having perfected the functions of his own life to the utmost, has also the widest helpful influence, both personal, and by means of his possessions, over the lives of others."

John Ruskin; Unto This Last

When John Ruskin penned what many regard as his most impassioned, insightful, and timelessly relevant thoughts in 1860 as part of a series of four separately published essays, he could have been writing the motivational opening of a manifesto for the creation of a new national health and care service. Perhaps even a health and care service that would be accessible by all within society who needed its help, a service collectively and mostly willingly funded by all those who could afford to contribute what they were able toward its upkeep. The four essays Ruskin wrote were ultimately published as one book entitled Unto This Last in 1862. A book many regard as his most important and one that has become an enduring ode to the nemesis of neoliberalism, fairness. The impact of the sentiment and observations contained in the original essays Ruskin wrote and the book they became have been, and continue to be, globally significant and influential. Mahatma Gandhi is perhaps the most famous of the numerous instigators of sizeable and historically important socially progressive change, said to have been greatly influenced by Ruskin's work. The thought-provoking writing of John Kenneth Galbraith, which boldly challenged the self-centric individualistic materially fuelled ambition dominating 20th Century American society, also reflects Ruskin's ideologies. And the founding egalitarian thinking, the ambitions, and original policies of the Labour Party of the early 1900's that eventually led to the launch of the NHS in 1948, were significantly influenced by the thinking that Ruskin expressed in his writing. How things have changed!

Ruskin was the only son and child of a wealthy trader, a wine and sherry importer whose business ultimately grew to become part of one of the world's largest drinks empires. I think it's safe to assume the young John Ruskin would have wanted for nothing materially. And though the working-class chip that sits proudly on my shoulder has made me naturally wary of the observations and theories espoused by members of the more comfortable privileged classes, it is after all easy to talk about the insignificance of money when you have plenty and have never wanted for it, I have warmed to Ruskin. He was undoubtedly a talented and incredibly intelligent polymath who was unafraid to express views that rubbed up sharply against those of his wealthy and entitled peer group. The conclusion he so eloquently held aloft that there is no wealth but life, has not only stood the test of time and constant unrelenting challenge from the facile and the fleeting, but it has also I believe, become even more relevant in these times.

I think it is a further mark of genius that in three prescient, poignant sentences, Ruskin not only reminds us of what truly matters most to each and every one of us, he also alludes to what the very purpose of a nation and therefore the responsibility and ultimate role of its government should be. And in doing so highlights the only really meaningful yardstick by which governments should be measured. His thinking that the country that is richest is the one which nourishes the greatest numbers of noble and happy human beings predates the creation of the now famous world happiness index by a hundred and fifty years. The purpose of government as viewed by those in government is inextricably linked to the health and wellbeing of a nation and is something I will allude to throughout this book. Suffice to note at this point that the unrelenting focus on economic growth which stubbornly dominates political debate and continues to characterize the ambition of nearly all developed and developing economies and mainstream politics, is proving increasingly destructive to our physical and mental health as well as the very planet we depend upon for survival and the communities many of us live in.

Surely, it must be self-evident to all but the most ardent wilfully blind advocates of capitalism by now, that looking through the narrow lens of GDP, Gross Domestic Product to give its full name, to assess and judge the success of a country and the standing, prosperity, and wellbeing of its citizens, provides only a partial and distorted glimpse of what truly flourishing might mean for each and every one of us. Focusing on the creation of material wealth as the sole surrogate for progress will only ever give the viewer a narrow, uninformed, unintelligent, and increasingly irrelevant perspective through which to interpret what really matters to us. We are an impassioned soulful species that is the product of over four billion years of evolution and whose brain is widely regarded as the most complex mechanism in the known universe. We can and must do better than assessing our own and each other's lives and accomplishments by measuring how much crap for landfill we bought and sold each other last month.

If living our best life is to accept the role in the rat race we are harnessed to, escaping its inherent and increasing anxieties by lounging in our onesies sat in front the largest flat screen high-definition television, we can safely fix onto the wall of our front room without it collapsing, watching endless parades of hapless human holograms strutting across the horizonless landscape of reality TV. Spending our free time around each other but not with each other as we anxiously count our likes and chase our losses and dopamine hits, spinning virtual wheels and throwing online dice, or scrolling, and scrolling, and scrolling, in a semi-present passive state through kitten videos, sharing memes, meal pictures, and worse, on social media. Waiting for Jeff Bezos to deliver this year's essential superhero or cartoon character costumes and masks for the children, made lovingly from single use plastic manufactured in sweat shops using cheap labour, shipped from China on vessels registered under flags of convenience running on even cheaper labour. Standing by and sometimes cheering on as the next generation of young adult's pout suggestively into camera phones on the beginning of their journey through the angst-ridden chambers of cyberspace into a state of misinformed neurosis and sexualised body image issues. And as we enjoy another ready-made meal of super-sized junk food derived from unsustainable sources, delivered to our door in polystyrene tubs by service workers on zero hours contracts driving carbon spewing climate killers, to whom the ideas of home ownership, pensions, and a comfortable retirement are a fantasy, then perhaps the dream of our best life needs revising.

Work, strive, spend, consume, post, pollute, regret, sleep, repeat. The most precious resource any of us has is our attention and our minds have become a battleground for corporate marketing departments desperate to persuade us to buy things we don't need with money we don't have to impress people we don't know and will never meet. Great swathes of society have been sleepwalked by savvy unprincipled marketing into a state of merely existing, neither flourishing, nor even recognising its absence from their lives. Our willingness to act in our own self-interest has been exploited and made us collectively stupid. If we are an experiment in a Petri dish being observed by a race of hyper-logical aliens, we will have succeeded in entertaining and confusing the feck out of them. If we were as obsessed with the production of knowledge as we are with the production of shite we would be in a very different place. GDP has affected our education system at every level.

If there is a flaw in Ruskin's statement, it only becomes clear when viewing it through modern western eyes, and it is the implication that a person can only help and be in a position to help others once they have perfected the functions of their own life. But the view Ruskin expressed was a pragmatic and entirely understandable perspective from someone living in an age in which the average life expectancy was around 40yrs old, a society in which grinding poverty and scarcity were the norm. The Victorian era is widely regarded as an age of increasing, visible, and hugely harmful inequality, think of it as the neoliberal version of the renaissance. A polarized period of intrinsic social injustices that offered Charles Dickens more than enough ready material at hand to create the timeless, insightful, and disturbing accounts in which he so skilfully highlighted the unfairness of everyday life for the masses. Though there are some worrying similarities with the era we now live in, the Victorian era was in short, another time, one in which sizeable charitable acts and philanthropic activity could only ever be the preserve of the wealthy and entitled. In many developed societies it is now widely thought that the helping of others can be both hugely beneficial for the mental and physical health and wellbeing of those who volunteer as well as enormously useful for the individuals and communities they serve. However, this activity depends entirely on citizens having the available capacity and resources, time, funds, and abilities, to undertake such activities. More, much more, on the role of charity later.

For any country, to have an effective health and care system that supports and maintains a healthy population, that nation must firstly seek to develop a shared understanding of what a good life can look like, in all its forms, and how to define what a healthy population means in practice. Ideally as defined by its citizens, not solely the entrepreneurs, the marketplace, its politicians, or academics. Having a meaningful vision of what good might look like must be the viewing point from which nations and governments assess policies and tailor the goals of their public health and healthcare services to achieve that vision. If Ruskin was right, then the primary purpose of a civilized nation's government should be to create the conditions in which all its citizens can live a good life, as defined by them. The state of a nation's healthcare system and its wider public services are a direct reflection of the state of its society and the priorities of its government and its citizens. If this seems a touch philosophical, let me try and paint a picture to explain what I mean.

If those tasked with governing a nation see their primary purpose as creating economic growth and increasing levels of wealth to fuel further consumption and drive the economic circle of productivity and consumerism ever higher, then it could be reasonably argued that the energies of that country are focused on making money, not the health and wellbeing of its citizens. There are many who will say that the use of economic measures is merely a surrogate. They point out that a booming economy is good for us all in every respect, therefore they say a healthy economy correlates with a physically healthy and mentally happy country. But the continual and messy unravelling case study of America, once the worlds poster child for what capitalism, the free market, and unbridled consumerism could achieve, yet now with its incredible inequality of incomes, poor health outcomes, low life expectancy, and lack of opportunity for many, continues to blow an ever larger increasingly and undeniably visible hole in the notion that a financially healthy national economy equates to a healthy nation in the wider sense. Infant mortality rates in the United States are more than double those of many other allegedly less developed countries. It is a myth that the rising tide lifts all the boats.

In fact, even calling the United States an advanced society seems increasingly like an oxymoron. Can anyone legitimately claim that a country in which a significant proportion of the population does not have access to healthcare, a country in which the largest contributor to personal bankruptcy is paying medical bills, a country in which too many of the unborn are needlessly and avoidably deprived of life before it has even begun, and a country that spent over eight hundred billion dollars of taxpayers money on military expenditure in 2021, is an advanced society that prioritizes the health and wellbeing of its citizens? Wealthy yes, equitable, most definitely not. Brutish, uncaring, desensitized, and wilfully blind to its own shortcomings would seem more appropriate descriptors. The USA offers a useful vision of hell for anyone who believes free markets will provide citizen centred health and care services to all those who need them, when they need them, regardless of their ability to pay.

And in relation to the largest economically generated elephant sitting in all our front rooms, climate change, I think most people living in developed countries if they were given the option, would rather have a smaller pension pot, less expendable income, and reduced levels of consumption, if it meant they and their loved ones could still have a planet to live on. Growing the economy infinitely is a fool's errand. Wealth does not always equal health and unfettered free enterprise is proving detrimental to too many, physically and mentally.

Similarly, if the government of a nation views its priorities through a predominantly defensive or aggressive military lens, it will spend a disproportionate amount of public funds on arms and military spending and devote its political attention to securing its place at the top table of countries everyone else should be afraid of and avoid upsetting. Russia spends a huge amount of public money on arms and around half the European average on the health and care of its citizens. According to pre-pandemic data in 2019, average life expectancy in Russia stood at just over 73yrs, almost 10% less than in many of its neighbours in Europe. And Saudi Arabia's spending on arms as a proportion of its economy versus its spending on health and care, makes even Russia's look positively citizen centric. Citizen centric is as citizen centric does and conversations about the health and care priorities of a nation are only meaningful when seen in a wider context.

Throughout this book I will draw on the well-proven notion that meaningful and lasting improvement can only begin with understanding. If we, you, and I, genuinely want health and care services that work superbly well for the people they serve as well as the people who work in them, and in case you are wondering, you won't get one without the other, then its purpose must be clear. In the fifty-two years I have lived in the UK, I don't ever recall this country having a serious conversation about the purpose of government, or the purpose of the NHS, or of health and care services. We had a now infamous and incredibly fractious debate about whether we should remain in something called the European Union, which caused a great deal of tension and angst, much of which still exists. Yet we haven't had a grown-up discussion about the very purpose and responsibilities of government or the future of the nation's health and care system. A system that by any standard was not created or designed to meet the needs of the world it now finds itself in. If we looked at our present situation through the eyes of Maslow, we might say the NHS was developed to meet the needs of a society that was largely based in the bottom half of the hierarchy of needs. But now most Western societies and the individuals within them increasingly occupy the upper tiers of that hierarchy. The basic needs of many are largely satisfied, and for better or worse we seek self-actualization and self-expression through a myriad of means, physical, and virtual.

If you are reading this book as a citizen of the UK, don't you find it strange that we devoted time, money, emotional energy, passion and often anger, to a debate about a largely opaque institution, some people in Brussels most of us had never met and didn't know, and a series of issues few of us understood, yet we've never made time to talk meaningfully about the primary purpose of government itself or the future of our nation's beloved NHS and health and care services. I do, and I think it's about time we had one.

As well as recognising that the NHS was not created to meet all the demands the modern world is placing on it, the wider premise of this book is that a nation's health and care service cannot be looked at meaningfully in isolation. Any useful conversation about a nation's health and care service must by necessity also be a conversation about the state of that nation itself and the priorities of those who govern it and who live in it. Talk of having a brilliant health and care service in the context of a breaking society is like arguing which store to buy new living room furniture from while the roof of your home is on fire. No country can reasonably expect to have a functioning health and care service and a healthy population if that service is set in an increasingly dysfunctional and inequitable society. I think this is a premise that would be endorsed by Ruskin, Gandhi, Galbraith, and of course Nye Bevan himself, amongst many others. But that might be promoting my thinking into some overly lofty company and I'm only peeking over the shoulders of giants.

Introduction

"As the true method of knowledge is experiment, the true faculty of knowing must be the faculty which experiences. This faculty I treat of."

William Blake

A more modern version of Blakes aphorism would be that experience is the best teacher, but the fees are high. Blake believed experience was the best, perhaps only truly meaningful school. As an expert by experience, it's been heartening for me to see a growing awareness of the value people with lived experience can bring to public services including health and care services in recent years. Though the worth of our insights are often ignored by those with an academic and theoretical understanding of the matters at hand, our knowledge has cost much more than the price of a student loan. There are many of us, too many, whose understanding of the significant challenges facing health and care services has been shaped on the pitch, not from the comfortable insulated view of the executive box. I wonder, is it even possible to be a true expert without experience?

It is my own and other's experiences that led me to write this book. It isn't the book I originally set out to write. It's the book I realised needed writing as I tried to write the book that I thought I was going to. Life can be like that can't it. And anyway, the book I was going to write would have been much less interesting than this one.

My name is Tom Bell. I've been inseparably entwined with the NHS for as long as I've been alive. I was born into a family embedded in it and have worked closely in and around it myself for the last decade. I've lived it, loved it, and hated it. My family and I are also the unwilling and unashamed victims of a tragic and deeply painful ongoing injustice with its roots in the NHS. We have lived each day of the last three decades bearing a largely hidden but still open, unhealed, and painful wound. The tainting fruit of knowledge I possess and offer to you in this book is the product of bitter experience. I'm not the kind of person many might expect to author an insightful hard-hitting book about Britain's National Health Service. You might tell me after you've read it that I didn't succeed in that, but I've a strong gut feeling you won't. Nor am I an expert in the traditional academic sense, or a particularly well-known figure in healthcare circles.

I'm unexceptional. I have a juvenile criminal record. I was kicked out of home on my sixteenth birthday, I walked out of school the following day and was told I wouldn't be welcome back. I played the guitar badly in a punk band and suffered a mental breakdown at the age of eighteen before succumbing to the simple misguided certainty held out to me by evangelical Christianity. I'm now a devout atheist. I subscribe to the Muhammad Ali school of thinking which suggests that if you meet a person aged fifty who holds the same views they held when they were twenty, then you've just met someone who has wasted thirty years of their life. Amen to that!

In 2015 I sacrificed a financially promising if potentially personally unfulfilling management career in the NHS after whistleblowing on what I saw as the unsafe actions of directors in the NHS Trust I was working for. I now supply specialist training and consultancy services in the area of wilful blindness and ethical fading in health and care organisations. I help people understand what these common and naturally occurring phenomena are and the impact they have. How they arise, how they shape our behaviours, responses, actions, and thinking, how their presence reinforces and is reinforced by the organisational cultures we work in and around, and how to identify and address them. It's a unique and challenging business model that relies upon me convincing people who would often prefer not to listen to me that I have something useful and ultimately beneficial to tell them that's worth paying me for. As well as an aspiring author, trainer, and speaker, I have contributed to numerous national inquiries and reports relating to public services, including the justice system and the implementation of standards for NHS directors, the Kark Review as it became known. In 2020 I published a book called Lions, Liars, Donkeys and Penguins - The Killing of Alison. The book is a true story of the events surrounding the suicide of my sister after a period of abuse in an NHS mental health hospital and the coordinated cover-up that then followed it.

In the summer of 1987, my sister Alison became seriously mentally ill. It would be right to note that my family has been susceptible to mental illness, nature and nurture have both been hard at work and our upbringing and that of our parents before us was challenging. The credit account of our mental health has been eroded by compound interest. Alison's mental health fluctuated in her late teens. At the age of 21 she displayed signs of serious psychosis and paranoid schizophrenia and was sectioned, forcibly admitted, to a mental health hospital called Garlands on the outskirts of Carlisle. The hospital was situated a few miles outside the city centre and twenty miles from our home in Penrith. Upon her admission into what we now know was a decrepit, decaying, and deeply dysfunctional former Victorian asylum, Alison became the focus of an older male nurse's attention. He groomed her before exploiting her for sex on multiple occasions on the hospital premises. Though we are told the sex was consensual, Alison was extremely mentally ill and incredibly vulnerable. The acts committed upon her were clearly inappropriate as well as illegal. Today they would most likely be classed as statutory rape. Behind the closed doors and the even more tightly closed culture, hidden from scrutiny, and cunningly shielded from those who loved her, my sister endured a crisis pregnancy as a direct result of the illegal acts committed against her. In their efforts to then cover up what had happened, Alison was persuaded into a hastily arranged abortion by her abuser, Robert Scott-Buccleuch, who was aided in his efforts to hide his crimes by a Dr T. M. Singh, the Consultant Psychiatrist entrusted with Alison's wellbeing and mental recovery. Alison never truly recovered from these events. She stepped in front of a train on Friday December 13th, 1991. The date was around what would have been the third birthday of her aborted child. Research has shown that such anniversaries can be potent trigger points for women with pre-existing mental health conditions who have experienced abortion.

I love the NHS. More accurately, I love what I think it could and should be, not what it has become. My family has an incredibly proud history of working in publicly funded health and care services. My Great Uncle was a public health official in Gateshead who dealt with one of the last Cholera outbreaks in Britain. My Mum trained as a nurse at the then globally respected Edinburgh Royal Teaching Hospital. My Gran and my Aunty also trained as nurses, becoming Ward Sisters, Matrons, and Health Visitors. And this year my half-cousin Sue has just retired after thirty-six years as a paediatric nurse in the NHS. If I include my meagre five years in middle management, my family have well over a hundred and twenty years of combined employment experience in the NHS between us. I am a passionate advocate for effective public services. If there is a political flag I would stand under, it would be the flag of fairness. If you want to call that naïve or socialist, that's fine, but I would ask you to note that the worlds happiest countries and communities, are also the worlds fairest. I truly believe that the provision of universal health and care which is free at the point of use is the most tangible and wonderful example of what collective responsibility and genuine civilization can look like in practice. For me, the concept of a National Health Service is far greater than merely a national icon or an expression of Britishness, it is the physical and visceral manifestation of humanity at its very finest.

When I was younger and my mind was more like a sponge in the sense that it soaked things up easily and less like a sponge in terms of its constant forgetful fuzziness, I recall sitting cross-legged with the other children on the dusty worn parquet floors of the classrooms at Brunswick Road Infants School in Penrith. Our teacher, whose face, curly hair, and ample bosom is in my mind's eye but whose name escapes me, would encourage us to dutifully memorize and recall spurious facts about the wonders of the world, ancient and modern, and recite the dates of memorable historical events. On our quasi-educational journey to becoming compliant unquestioning citizens and consumers, my fellow pupils and I were told about the incredible architectural and mechanical achievements of the many great kingdoms and ancient empires that had gone before. In recent years I have begun wondering why when we talk and are taught about humanity's greatest achievements, we seldom give enough time to talk about the things that really make a difference to the majority? Though it may not be a physical achievement in the built sense, for me, the establishing of collective responsibility for the provision of health and care to all who need it, is without doubt humanity's greatest achievement. I'm not arsed about a parade to celebrate the crowning of a King, but I'd throw a good street party to celebrate seventy-five years of the NHS.

Britain's love of the NHS is tied to the power of the idea it embodies and the peace of mind it offers. Its very existence and its promise, if not always its delivery, taps into the deepest of our evolutionary needs to belong, to matter, to feel safe and cared for when we are at our most vulnerable, to partake of something shared and act collaboratively in pursuit of a common good. The idea of the NHS does not exist as a single edifice, it has become deeply embedded in our national psyche, like a shared unspoken value, part of what Britain and being British is, and part of who we in this country want to feel we are. For me, the inherent value it places on life and the equity of access it strives to provide is the most valid and meaningful indicator of what a true civilization should look to achieve. The construction of the Pyramids, the building of Mayan cities, the Sistine Chapel, the Taj Mahal, might have given their designers, creators, and funders a grandiose sense of purpose and perhaps some of their citizens a sense of pride, but I don't imagine their creation extended anyone's life expectancy, quite the opposite. The line between misguided egotistical folly built on the blood and sweat of peasant labour, and a wonder of the world, may be finer and more nuanced than we have been led to believe. I wonder if the populations of Egypt and India, or the dispossessed diaspora that built the football stadiums in Qatar, would rather have free unlimited access to healthcare, or the occasional view of a globally recognised postcard friendly icon?

When the world-renowned 20th century anthropologist Margaret Mead was asked what she considered to be the first signs of civilization, she is said to have replied that in her opinion it was at the point in our history when the first broken femurs, thigh bones, were healed in our ancestors. Mead went on to explain that in the animal kingdom a broken femur is almost certainly a death sentence by infection, starvation, or predation. She suggested that where evidence of the first healed broken femurs were being discovered in the remains of our distant ancestors, this was a sign that the subject had not only been carried to safety, but also protected and then tended to until their broken leg mended, and they had recovered. Mead was defining civilization as our willingness and capacity to demonstrate care for one another.

Civilization, true civilization, doesn't look like and cannot be embodied in things, large and splendid icons, grand statements, tacky branded trinkets, or the size of a nation's economy. Objects, shapes, rituals, buildings, monuments, temples, a long wall, a tapestry, a tomb, or a monarchy. Many of the dynasties and empires we casually refer to as civilizations, ancient and modern, were and still are guilty of meting out great cruelty and injustice upon large numbers of the people who happened to be born within their borders, who fell under their rule, or who stand in the way of their ideologies. True civilization is about how we as people connect, cooperate, collaborate, interact with, and value each other, how we acknowledge and respect each other, and how we treat and care for one another. Better a dry morsel in quiet peace than a house full of feasting with strife. My bible reading sessions weren't a total waste of time.

Finally, before we get into the body of this book, I will offer my apologies in advance if you find some of my humour or language distasteful. I wanted to be true to myself in this book and I hope that as you begin to see and perhaps partially comprehend if not understand what I and my family have been through, you might make allowances for my irreverence. I haven't set out to offend, but I've earned the right to say what I think and say it as I think fit. I've found humour is a great coping mechanism and I've had my fill of dry tomes, books, reports, public inquiries, written in polite or overly academic language that weave and dance their way around the issues. You can bet your last coin that if I had been allowed to write any of the inquiry reports referred to later in this book, they would read very differently...

PART I:

What is a Healthy Nation?

Chapter 1: The envy of less happier lands?

This royal throne of kings, this sceptred isle,
This earth of majesty, this seat of Mars,
This other Eden, demi-paradise,
This fortress built by Nature for herself,
Against infection and the hand of war,
This happy breed of men, this little world,
This precious stone set in the silver sea,
Which serves it in the office of a wall,
Or as a moat defensive to a house,
Against the envy of less happier lands,
This blessed plot, this earth, this realm, this England.

William Shakespeare; Richard II

Great Britain, Grande Bretagne, Rule Britannia. Were Shakespeare to be reborn, hopefully in one of the NHS hospitals with a safe maternity unit, would he grow up to write these same words again? Those of an unquestioningly patriotic disposition toward the UK should skip this chapter. Great Britain is no longer truly great, or the envy of less happier lands. Perhaps it never really was. The UK is the remnant of an empire whose significant wealth and global prestige has been built on battle, blood, conquest, sweat, enterprise, ingenuity, exploitation, and no shortage of abject human misery. When the words of the iconic, ironic, and patriotic sing along, Rule Britannia were being penned almost three-hundred-years ago, a ditty still sung alongside Land of Hope and Glory at the finale of the Proms each year, Britain was one of the most active slave trading nations on the face of the earth. Its insouciance toward humanity exceeded only marginally by Portugal. And in truth, the forced transport of slaves and their subsequent exploitation was to the privileged entitled and ruling classes of the time, merely a logical extension to the treatment of their own lower classes.

The indentured conditions of the poor and disenfranchised who worked in many of Britain's coalmines, especially those in Scotland that were owned by the English nobility, were a legitimized form of slavery in all but name. Whilst the wilfully blind middle and upper classes might have found it rousing to sing that Britons never, never, never would be slaves, in reality many Britons already were. Slavery and exploitation have never been selective. In 1845 as a direct result of seeing the horrendous conditions in which the English working classes lived and worked in Manchester in the early Nineteenth Century, Friedrich Engels published his seminal and shocking work *The Condition of the Working Class in England*. The book had a huge influence on the thinking of Karl Marx and the development of what became known as Marxism. The communist manifesto itself, the literary blue touch paper that lit the flames of some of the most seismic radical global socio-political bonfires in recent history, was conceived, created, and written by Karl Marx and Friedrich Engels. If British entrepreneurialism created the steam engine and gave birth to the industrial revolution, unrestrained amoral British capitalist greed supplied the narrative that fuelled the creation of communism. Britain is a nation with an incredible and interesting past and an uncertain future. We have a lot to dwell on and still more to work out.

In recent times the collective mental health of our country has been so battered by the artificially generated demands of modern-day life that this sceptred isle is now one of the few nations on Earth that boasts a Minister for Suicide Prevention; and that was before the pandemic and cost-of-living crisis! It's a staggering state of affairs that things have gotten so undeniably bad for some amongst this happy breed, that we have a minister whose job it is to stop us killing ourselves. Can you get your head around that? We have more foodbanks and charities per capita than any other country in mainland Europe. The certainty of constant improvement and a better future that was so forcefully sold to us and that we once took for granted, has evaporated. We are the birthplace in which the great railways of the world were first created, yet now we seem unable to even run them on time.

It increasingly feels as if the very physical and emotional infrastructure of Britain is eroding. Our public services are crumbling and imploding around us. The institutions of the state are morally bankrupt. Parliament is an amoral muddy pool of mendacity, filled with vacuous self-serving bottom feeders more interested in their second incomes than their constituents' concerns. Our elections are tampered with by foreign powers while the House of Lords plays host to the offspring of Russian Oligarchs and former KGB officers. The venal and corrupt occupy and abuse the offices of power they hold and think nothing of plundering the public purse in the midst of a global pandemic for their own gain. The democracy we were once told we could be so proud of is openly, brazenly, self-interestedly, and unashamedly rotting to its core. So much so that Roberto Saviano, a journalist, screenwriter, and one of the world's leading authorities on the mafia cited the UK as one of the countries and economies most open to corruption and bribery. And even before the arrest and eventual prosecution of the serial rapist David Carrick in January 2023, less than one in ten women had full faith in our Police and Crown Prosecution Services.

But what we on this island of hope and glory do remain genuinely great at, the arena in which we shine and excel, the craft we seem to have perfected, is the art of telling ourselves and every other nation how great we are at everything. The land of smoke and mirrors is most definitely a great and glorious public relations triumph. Which other nation would have the chutzpah to strut the global stage so visibly when its own arse is showing through the threadbare seat of its pants and the very developments it brought to the rest of the world are falling into decay within its own boundaries? We are like the child that's been moved to a new school who tells everyone that the tired decrepit flat they are living in is just a temporary second home, and their dad is never around to pick them up from the playground because they are working abroad on an important and well-paid adventure, when in reality, they are serving a sentence in Millom Prison for petty theft.

In the course of my life and work I have travelled the length and breadth of the United Kingdom and though there is undoubtedly a great deal to be proud of, to be curious about, to marvel at, and to celebrate, there is also a great deal to feel sad about. Our past successes are no guarantee of our future flourishing. And whatever history, glorious and otherwise, we might have will not heal the ills that currently beset us. Nostalgia will not pay the bills. An uneven economy and an increasingly unjust society is eroding our humanity, and a booming economy will not make us whole.

But what might greatness and great look like if we were to define them now? How should the greatness of a nation, a society, a civilization be defined in the 21st century, and by whom? If a nations ambition is a reflection and therefore an extension of the ambitions of its people, shall we continue to stoke the perception of greatness at the individual level as greed, indifference, striving, and the constant selfish insatiable appetite for more and more material growth? Or can we begin to value kindness, tolerance, patience, curiosity, understanding, and emotional intelligence, over excess and affluence? Is a great nation a healthy nation and if so, what might a healthy population look like? Is it an absolute measure, a relative measure, and again, who decides? Presumably, a nation's health is nothing more than the aggregate sum of the health, wellness, and wellbeing of all its citizens. And our health and wellbeing and how we feel about it is as unique as our fingerprints and DNA. If there is no wealth but life, and the purpose of our lives is for each one of us to decide, then the only legitimate role of the state and its institutions is to create the conditions in which options, choice, and opportunity are available to all and in which we can be healthy and well enough to capitalise on them.

Chapter 2: How would you like to be remembered?

"Wealth is not without its advantages and the case to the contrary although it has often been made has never proved widely persuasive. But beyond doubt, wealth is the relentless enemy of understanding. The poor man has always a precise view of his problem and its remedy: he hasn't enough, and he needs more. The rich man can assume or imagine a much greater variety of ills and he will be correspondingly less certain of their remedy. Also, until he learns to live with his wealth, he will have a well-observed tendency to put it to the wrong purposes or otherwise to make himself foolish."

J K Galbraith; The Affluent Society

Here lies Tom, he increased the nation's Gross Domestic Product. Now that would be a funeral eulogy worth forgetting, wouldn't it? I hope to never attend anyone's earthly farewell where the words, they increased GDP are offered from the pulpit or the graveside, or worse still carved into the deceased's headstone. In a world where accounting for everything has become the norm, and in which politicians weaponize statistics as they vie for prestige with each other and their international counterparts, what can be measured is managed and then in turn made to matter by a 24hr news media hungry for content. But as Einstein himself observed and as every non-neoliberal knows to the very core of their being, the things that truly matter to each of us cannot be measured; contentment, fulfilment, joy, love. If in the so-called developed economies, we still see the value we create in life and the legacies we leave as purely material, then we have failed, spectacularly.

The Bank of England defines GDP, Gross Domestic Product, as the measure of the size and health of a country's economy over a period of time, usually recorded for each quarter or a year. The figure is used to compare and contrast the size of economies in different countries and at different points in time. GDP is slightly different to its marginally less useful predecessor GNP (Gross National Product) and to confuse matters further there are several ways of calculating a nations GDP. These include using the total value of goods and services produced, the collective value of everyone's income, or the total amount that everyone in the country has spent. This latter option is the most widely accepted variation and includes household spending, investment by businesses, government spending, and net exports.

The fallacy that lies at the heart of constantly measuring GDP is the assumption that a wealthy growing economy in which the total amount of cash is increasing can only be a good thing. But the dream of the benevolent warm inviting and ever-rising economic tide that was cunningly mis-sold to us as the means by which we could all become fulfilled, has not lifted all the boats. It has merely heightened the water line, leaving many struggling for air and making those who are treading water work ever harder just to stay afloat. The rationale for focusing on GDP as a suitable surrogate for a more meaningful measure, is that we all somehow benefit, that money, wealth, wellbeing, and the contentment of inclusive conspicuous consumption gradually trickles through all parts of society and eventually the rising water lifts us all. But I think it's obvious by now that it's not the creation of wealth that is the issue, it is the distribution of wealth and how we define it. Ask any shopper in Primark if they would willingly become disabled in exchange for a wardrobe of Armani clothes and a branded wheelchair. Many of us take our health and wellbeing for granted without realising that to be alive and to be healthy and curious is the greatest form of wealth.

Focusing on growing GDP seems a bit like creating a huge pile of food on a table without thinking of how people are going to get to it. It's okay to say you've grown the pile of tucker and increased the range of delicacies, but if most of the people only get to view it through the window then it's not a whole lot of use. The great theory of the rising tide would work if the small details of human greed and self-interest didn't get in the way. Safe to say the theory of trickle-down economics is a busted flush. In a world of limited resources, the idea of meeting everyone's artificially generated material and emotional needs through constant growth is not a sustainable solution. It doesn't take a genius to work out that there must be a limit to material growth. Resources are finite and at some stage you will reach the end of the ruler. The illusion we are under in developed countries is that the end of traditional economic growth will somehow mean the end of everything, that it will erode our wellbeing and threaten the things we cherish, in many cases without knowing why we cherish them. The irony being that the continuation of unrestrained growth will lead to the destruction of the very planet we live on. Its curtailment may mean the end of somethings, but it could also be the beginning of a great many more.

Most traditional economists, whose knowledge and ideas were shaped by the esteemed economic thinkers of the past for whom the economic context of their cogitations was significantly different, have been taught to equate the growth of a nation's economy with the wider wellbeing of all those within it. And in fairness, in the absence of other readily available measures, and in times when truly grinding destitution and ill health were accepted facets of life for many, the notion of economic growth and trickle-down wealth creation as a means of lifting large numbers of people out of unimaginable poverty, had some merit, though its benefits were seldom distributed to the masses without objection. But now, the use of GDP in relatively wealthy and developed nations as a useful correlator with the health and wellbeing of the citizens and communities in those same nations, looks more and more like an anachronism whose time has passed. Can GDP really be viewed as a helpful measure when it combines the enormous profits generated by energy corporations and online gambling companies with the increasingly unmanageable utility bills and debts being accrued by their consumers. Our physical and mental health is being eroded and deteriorating as a direct result of a rise in the economic measures that we were told would serve us. The focus on GDP is like thinking you can teach people to fly by throwing them out of a top floor window. Sure, they'll get to spend some time in mid-air, but their excitement and memories of the experience will be short lived.

Great Britain, the birthplace of the industrial revolution has long been held aloft and in-turn viewed by less industrialised countries as one of the most affluent and egalitarian nations on earth. There is no denying that in overall material terms, the UK is an incredible success. In 2021, the UK's economy was the world's fifth largest, or the fifth wealthiest as some might call it. But this matters little to the people with no access to the banquet. The Trussell Trust is a fairly new charity based in the UK. It was founded with a small legacy in 1997 to help children sleeping rough at the Central Railway Station in Bulgaria. The focus of its activity is now by shameful necessity much closer to home. At the last count, the charity was running twelve hundred food banks across the UK. Its presence on the ground and in the media has come to highlight the sharp edge of life for many. Its very existence, like that of a Minister for Suicide, embodies the current sorry inequitable state of Britain. In 2021/22, the Trussell Trust found themselves dealing with an unprecedented increase in demand for their services distributing over 2.1M food parcels. A figure they expect to significantly exceed in 2022/23. The use of foodbanks across Britain has risen steadily since the start of the millennium. This should shock us all. The rising tide has worked for a few, but it is leaving many more behind in its wake. GDP is a useless tool for the citizens of any nation who want to hold their government to account for implementing policies that help the majority of the population. Here are just four of the very many reasons why we should stop focusing on GDP and material wealth creation as a meaningful surrogate for our collective health and wellbeing.

Firstly, and most importantly, this precious world we live on, a planet with a delicately balanced eco-system that has been over four and a half billion years in the making, cries out for long-term thinking. GDP is an inherently short-sighted measure. As well as ignoring the interconnectedness and interdependence of global trade, GDP ignores the undeniable environmental interconnectedness of the world we live in and the entire planetary eco-system we depend upon. Using GDP as a measure of progress not only facilitates and encourages the endless production and consumption of more and more stuff with which to fill our homes and surround ourselves, but it enables those countries who are growing their economy by cutting down and exporting the worlds rainforests or producing copious amounts of fossil fuels, to call themselves and be upheld by others as successful growing economies based on their trade in these self-destructive goods. That's like rewarding someone for their physical prowess because they have mastered the art of hopping while kicking themselves in the nuts. They may have excellent balance, dexterity, and calf muscles, but they will have caused irreparable long-term damage and destroyed their ability to reproduce.

Secondly, it's no secret that the global economy is like a pack of perfectly interspaced dominos, only able to stand upright if all remain still in precisely their allotted positions. In a hyper-connected and many would argue increasingly volatile economy, trying to focus on the growth of GDP in a single country is like trying to control the weather in one garden on the street; its futile, increasingly impossible and it can't be done with any real control or constancy. Most readers will be able to recall the global banking crisis that unfolded in 2007 in which an under-regulated and out of control sub-prime mortgage market in America crashed the economy of almost every country on the planet. Unsecured overvalued debt in America created panic queues outside building societies on every high street in the UK. The global economy is now so interconnected that problems in one area inevitably cause issues for everyone. My wife Debbie and I had nothing to do with the sub-prime housing market in the USA, but we both lost our jobs as a direct result of it. Nor did we have a hand in starting the war in Ukraine, but the cost of living, our energy bills and the price of goods and services has risen substantially, and our expendable income has suffered.

Then there is the largely unacknowledged but hugely significant opportunity cost that focusing on GDP has created. The constant spotlight on GDP has diverted all our attention, the policy makers, pundits, and the press, some might say deliberately, if not conveniently, to the exclusion of the things that really matter to each of us; our health and well-being and the health and wellbeing of those we love and care about; our relationships with each other; the quality and depth of our education; the agility of our minds; the strength of our communities and ultimately the quality of our lives and our personal happiness and contentment. Focusing on GDP has allowed successive governments to ride on the back of global growth while glossing over gaping iniquitous social and environmental failures. Should we elect governments to increase GDP or to create fairer, more fair, inclusive, and sustainable societies for us all; it's time to acknowledge that these two things are seldom sides of the same coin.

Lastly there is the obvious flaw in GDP that encourages the inclusion of the cost of social failure and misery while ignoring its impact on humanity. In one of the shortest most poignant speeches I feel he ever made, the ageing yet still incredibly sparky social observer and activist Noam Chomsky, neatly dismantled the myth of GDP to a group of students when he quoted the former Brazilian Head of State General Emilio Medici. Describing the Brazilian economy in 1971, Medici had said, *the economy is doing fine, but the people aren't*. The truism within this statement is supported by Joseph Stiglitz, the former senior vice president and chief economist of the World Bank and winner of the Nobel Prize for Economics in 2001. His book, Globalization and its Discontents, pokes more holes in the fallacy of GDP as a meaningful measure of anything useful, than gaps in a tea strainer. Stiglitz points out that the United States has the words largest prison population housing up to ten times the number of people per capita in prison than many other developed nations. The prison population of the United States in 2022 was said to be approx. 1.5million, a figure which some say is a significant underestimate. This means the USA spends more in total and per capita on the incarceration of its citizens than any other country in the world. The substantial annual cost of around $60B that it takes to fund the prison system in the USA offers a classic example of failure demand in the truest sense. Yet the cost of running these prisons is counted within America's GDP as part of government spending. Spending on health and care in the United States, a substantial chunk of which is propped up by household debt and no small amount of personal bankruptcies, a cost that would be supported through public funding and government spending in many other countries, is also reflected in the USA's GDP. Spending on healthcare now accounts for one fifth of America's entire GDP. In short, the proxy measure of success that is GDP rewards countries that create massive structural failures at the societal and individual level and holds them aloft as raging economic successes, based in large part on the cost of dealing with their own self-inflicted wounds. This is the madness of GDP laid bare.

Few would deny that a functioning economy in tandem with adequate infrastructure is an important foundation on which to build an equitable society. I have visited numerous countries in which many of the citizens would give their eye teeth and more to live in communities where they could access the most basic of needs; clean water, sanitation, healthcare, and perhaps a smattering of democracy on a good day. And it may seem decidedly Western and self-indulgent to imagine a world that measures wellbeing beyond economic measures. But a constant unrelenting incessant obsession on economic growth and increasing each nations GDP provides a textbook example of where being able to measure something has caused successive, if not successful governments, to chase a target while missing the point for the majority of the citizens they were elected by and are supposed to serve.

Debbie and I were in India in 2017, we were celebrating thirty years of marriage as the country was celebrating its 70th year of independence. Extreme, grinding, heart rending, soul crushing, debilitating poverty, was everywhere, in the country villages, along every road, at every major rail intersection, and in the swelling smelling corrugated slums of Mumbai and New Delhi. Yet many of the people we met, the tour guides, the van drivers, the villagers, the tuk-tuk operators, the hotel porters, the young people at the newly built mall, were incredibly excited by the fact that the size of their economy would soon overtake the UK's. Their political leaders are selling them the same myth that unrestrained economic activity and enterprise will lift them all from poverty. The last time I looked, India had well over a hundred billionaires, but the gap between the haves and have nots is wider than any chasm imaginable. India's economy may be booming, but not everyone will benefit.

In November 2022, the population of Planet Earth officially reached and passed eight billion people. This beautiful and mysterious spinning rock we call home cannot endlessly accommodate our insatiable desire for more and more things. The next stage of humanity's development and of our perception of what defines a civilization must move beyond the narrow and self-destructive lens of production, consumption, and GDP. We need to measure the health of our continents, countries, regions, communities, and our own lives and wellbeing using radically different criteria than the metrics of money and materialism that are destroying our planet and eroding our mental and physical health.

Chapter 3: All aboard the hamster wheel

"A great city is not to be confounded with a populous one."

Aristotle

Whenever I visit London, I'm struck by its pace. I am that mildly annoying Northerner, ready to make conversation with anyone in the station waiting room or on the train who is near and unwitting enough to make eye contact with me. It was Victor Borge who said a smile is the shortest distance between two people and I smile optimistically at my fellow passengers as we disembark onto the frenetic platform of Euston Station, spilling like prisoners liberated from our captor, everyone seems in such a hurry. Central London is full of people walking briskly, running for buses and tube trains like hamsters trapped on the endless ever-rotating wheel of global productivity and consumption. Whether the things they are running to make or create and the meetings they are attending will add any lasting value to them or the wider world, and whether the things they will buy with the money they make will bring them fulfilment, does not seem up for conversation.

Charles Handy's prediction that large parts of the world's economy and its means of production would be sustained by our desire for what he called Chindogu goods, the novel, the utterly unnecessary, and largely useless if at times strangely gratifying products that fill the webpages of many retailers and hog the shelves of our homes, has come to pass. On the corner of my desk sits a small plastic model of Darth Vader, when I press the yellow button at its base it emits one of half a dozen preloaded phrases. It has a Velcro strip on the underside in case I decide to mount it on the dashboard of my car. I've had it for at least fifteen years; essential, no; recyclable, probably not; a productive use of batteries, definitely not; but novel, yes. I wonder if the people who made it somewhere on a sprawling industrial estate in China gained pleasure, fulfilment, or just felt confused about the ultimate purpose of what they were producing and why. Maybe they were just grateful they were in some form of paid employment. Eagerly awaiting the day when they would have enough expendable income to afford their very own talking Star Wars figurine. Capitalism does not judge its success by the meaning its servants take from their participation in its dance, or the lasting value of its output. Do not underestimate the power of the dark side.

In this era of nakedly uncaring unrestrained capitalism, increasing financial austerity and spiralling living costs, self-preservation, survival in the short-term is of course the entirely understandable and noble goal of many who are having to run fast just to stand still or at least slow their descent into debt. The pace of the people sprinting around London like racing rats reminds me of the breakneck speed with which my Mum used to walk everywhere when I was a child. She was working and bringing up three young children as a single parent and had little time for relaxation or the headspace to afford herself the luxury of long-term thinking. The bills had to be paid, food had to be bought each week, and my two sisters and I had to be fed, clothed, and shod. The exceptionally focused behaviour of my Mum and the time poverty she endured were the products of unforeseen and unfortunate circumstance, but now it seems this unrelenting level of activity is the norm for many. My Mum was an amazingly dependable if emotionally incredibly complex machine who sacrificed a great deal so her children could achieve their aspirations and enjoy a better quality of life. Such was the pace at which she used to do things that if I didn't know better, I'd have said she was taking speed. The mind of the machine that was my Mum, has ultimately and perhaps not unexpectedly suffered. But to be immersed in a city whose citizens in their efforts to tread water and survive, appear to be displaying the same frantic urgency my Mum once did, seems strange and unnatural to me. Visiting London feels as if I'm witnessing an experiment in the destruction of wellbeing and the creation of mental illness in which the unknowing participants are subjected to ever increasing levels of anxiety and stress. People stare ahead as they walk quickly past the homeless ex-servicemen and the swarthy outstretched arms and lived-in faces of the destitute and the exploited, their hands reaching out like waving anemone into the shifting currents of passers-by, in search of a coin and perhaps some acknowledgement. Instead, people give their attention to phone screens, pressing their earbuds in deeper as they pass and are passed by the endless parade of advertising hoardings and promotional banners that wrap the city's buses and taxis in consumerisms never-ending battle for our attention. The genuinely needy cannot hope to compete for our attention with the legitimised begging of the billboards and branded buses. But do any of us really need the newest earbuds for our smartphone or the latest game for our PlayStations more than the beggar in the street needs a meal and acknowledgement of their existence. Do we need shiny things more than we need to reconnect with our own humanity? Capitalism, GDP, and their cunning handmaid marketing have made monsters of us all.

It seems as if the promise and possibility of the better life that those of my generation were told was our rightful inheritance to claim if we worked and were canny with our cash, has been taken away from Generations Y and X. The promise did not benignly slip away as if it were the inevitable victim of a change in circumstances, or an extraneous trivial item on a meeting agenda that was dropped to allow more pressing issues to be discussed. It has been stolen. Slowly, steadily, deliberately, and in plain sight of us all. There are some glimmers of hope and offers of jam tomorrow such as the long-awaited arrival of a four-day week in some quarters, which will doubtless be good for some. But for the many millions working in small businesses and the service industry, it will probably remain a pipedream. And for others a four-day week will merely be an opportunity to spend their newly liberated hours working in a second job elsewhere, as the speed and stamina needed to stay on the hamster wheel continues to increase.

In the hands of the marketers:

"If I hadn't seen such riche's I could live with being poor."

James; Sit Down

The cynics definition of marketing is of a profession that survives by selling things to people they dont need with money they dont have to impress people they dont know or like. We are strange creatures! What's good for the high rollers and the treasury is not always good for you, me, or the planet. In recent years I've become reticent to reply when asked about my qualifications. The reason being that my first degree was in Marketing, I was a Chartered Marketer for twenty years and the first member of the Institute of Marketing in Cumbria to gain chartered status. I was mildly aware of marketings negative connotations, but I was a wilfully blind purist who preferred to see only its upside. I've always despised the WOMBAT, waste of money balloons and t-shirts approach to marketing which has somehow come to represent the common view of marketing. WOMBAT marketing relies on fluff and public relations to peddle myths and sell polished turds; we can all think of a product or service we were enticed to buy with a slick promotional campaign that promised the earth, but which then disappointed, broke, or malfunctioned on its first outing. Our landfill sites are full to the brim of such WOMBAT inspired purchases. I decided I wanted to learn about marketing when I was a young salesperson, I naively believed that genuine marketing was a noble bridge between the consumers in the marketplace and the organisations that were trying to serve their needs. The centre of a virtuous circle in which consumers got what they wanted and needed, and companies became increasingly successful and more profitable as they became more adept at supplying what the market wanted and needed. That was marketing in its ideal form. But that was many years ago now, the internet was just finding its feet, talk of climate change was rare in most social circles, and the tsunami of mental health that has now engulfed western society was a distant dot on the horizon. Though I was incredibly proud at the time, I've since become increasingly aware of the role unprincipled increasingly pervasive and invasive marketing is playing in trashing our planet and destroying our wellbeing and mental health.

The simplistically explicit and at times politically incorrect advertising messages that companies once relied upon to sell their goods and services, are now a thing of the past. This is the age of sophisticated behavioural insight driven marketing, where data about our purchases and preferences, our likes and dislikes, and information about the webpages we visit and the physical places we go, is interpreted by algorithms, moving faster around hyperspace than our minds could process it. Marketings ultimate dream of being able to identify the needs of a market segment consisting of a single individual has become a reality. Modern marketing is now firmly in the hands of the behavioural scientists whose use of data has moved beyond merely selling us more stuff to feeding our prejudices and shaping our opinions. And the clever ones know how to press our buttons. Our need for acceptance, yours, and mine, remains one of our most basic human needs. As a former marketer I can say with certainty that organisations of every type collectively spend billions, around forty billion each year in the UK alone, promoting products and services to us by tapping into this most basic of our needs. The global market for advertising is currently worth around one and a half trillion dollars of which digital media now accounts for almost half. Despite the lame protestations from industries such as gambling that there is no evidence their advertising influences people's purchase decisions or behaviors, I think it's safe to say these same companies wouldn't spend such sums if they weren't going to benefit. The cosmetics company Loreal spent twelve billion euros in 2022 persuading the world that its products were essential to their self-worth. If the penny finally dropped that each and every one of us is enough and perfectly imperfect as we are, Loreal would most likely go out of business.

Comparison is said to be the enemy of happiness and contentment, so modern marketing relies on creating emotional dissonance in consumers, attempting to build a sense of dissatisfaction in each of us between where we think we are in our lives at any point in time, and the desired state we are told we should be aspiring to, a desired state that the consumption, use, or ownership of a particular product or service promises to help us reach. The concept of branding itself has shifted from its original purpose as a basic indicator of a products quality, to a means of appealing to our innate desire to feel part of something shared, something we can identify with that transcends the sense of isolation many people in modern societies feel. Our need as people to belong to something bigger than ourselves is incredibly deeply rooted. Many psychologists believe that the absence of a sense of belonging is linked to the emergence of significant mental health problems including anxiety, depression, and self-harm. When people feel they don't fit in or are shunned, it can have such an impact on their state of mind that it can also lead to physical symptoms including raised blood pressure, reduced appetite, and loss of libido. I have the T-shirts. Marketing offers us an endless tunnel through which to chase a sense of belonging. We can eat certain things, drink certain drinks, be seen in the right places, buy the right products, and wear the right clothes, and if these have the right label, we can then become an accepted and sometimes even a respected part of the tribes of our choosing. Products are manufactured with built in obsolescence and aspirational brands create a sense of angst and dissatisfaction with our lives and our lot and then sell us their placebo solution that satisfices until the next time, and the next, and the next.

In developed societies in which the basic needs of survival for most are met, for the economies of such countries continue to grow they depend on increased consumption of largely unnecessary if often enjoyable goods and services. In Reasons to Stay Alive, the author Matt Haig sums this production of dissonance up as follows:

"The world is increasingly designed to depress us. Happiness isn't very good for the economy. If we were happy with what we had, why would we need more? How do you sell an anti-ageing moisturiser? You make someone worry about ageing. How do you get people to vote for a political party? You make them worry about immigration. How do you get them to buy insurance? By making them worry about everything. How do you get them to have plastic surgery? By highlighting their physical flaws. How do you get them to watch a TV show? By making them worry about missing out. How do you get them to buy a new smartphone? By making them feel like they are being left behind. To be calm becomes a kind of revolutionary act. To be happy with your own non-upgraded existence. To be comfortable with our messy, human selves, would not be good for business."

Our need to belong and our evolved propensity to mimic and follow mean that as a species we are incredibly ill-equipped to engage in the street fight for our attention that many of us aren't even aware we are in, a fight that certainly isn't fair. Estimates of the number of messages we are exposed to daily varies from a few hundred to over ten thousand, and research suggests the average person has over six thousand thoughts each day. We are exposed to more information in a day than many of our ancestors from less than two decades ago were subjected to in a lifetime. In the age we live in our attention has without doubt become the most sought-after asset and the most precious resource we have. Research suggests that our attention spans are eroding as we are literally bombarded with advertising messages from companies trying to convince us that we need what they are selling and influencers trying to bring us into their tribe.

I'm gonna take my problem to the United Nations:

The World Health Organisation sits under the umbrella of the United Nations. The WHO's stated aim *is the attainment by all peoples of the highest possible levels of health*. A worthy if somewhat vaguely aspirational mission statement. And in a financially austere, polarized

39

post-truth world of nations riven with increasing economic inequality, community poverty, growing social incoherency, political upheaval, institutional mistrust, military conflict, resource scarcity, and climate change, the WHO's ambition to transform physical and mental health globally, is as wildly ambitious as it worthy.

Transforming Mental Health for all, published in 2022, is the latest report on the state of the world's mental health produced by the World Health Organisation. I had been pleased but mildly depressed by the honesty in the report in which the WHO acknowledged that little had changed in the twenty years since the publication of their previous report entitled *Mental Health: New Understanding, New Hope*. The latest report had been developed under the guidance of Dr Devora Kestel, the WHO director for mental health and substance abuse. I reached out to Dr Kestel's office because I wanted to understand the WHOs view on the continued use of GDP as a meaningful measure of national success. She kindly responded to my request and directed me to one of the report's contributors, and I soon found myself on a video call with a representative of the World Health Organisation based in the Middle East. A clearly impassioned individual with decades of experience behind them, the first thing they explained to me was that if the video link went down, it would be due to a power cut. A humbling reminder of the infrastructure that we in the west so often take for granted.

We started to talk, and I said I was puzzled by the absence of references in the WHOs report to the role of materialism, consumerism, neoliberalism, and marketings role in creating dissatisfaction and dissonance, as obvious sources of increased anxiety in society and leading contributors to the globally acknowledged rise in mental illness the report referred to. My surprise at the exclusion of what I felt were significant factors was met with equal surprise that they should be referenced, and I was asked if I was able to cite any academic research to support my theory that the rise of the neoliberal agenda, unbridled consumerism, and amoral marketing might be damaging to our health and wellbeing. Though the answer I gave to the question was a resounding yes, I can cite half a dozen internationally respected and published sources staring at me from the bookshelf in my loft, Galbraith, Handy, and Klein among them, it surprised me that an experienced figure in the WHO would even ask for evidence to support a proposition which many including myself, would see as a blisteringly obvious one. Was I really being asked if there was a link between the dissonance creating goals of unprincipled capitalism and pervasive marketing, and the steep rises in mental illness in developed economies. Surely, I thought, any reasonable person would be surprised if there wasn't a link.

The WHO's apparent wilful blindness to the role consumerism is playing in eroding the mental health of developed nations, may be due to the World Health Organisation being part of the United Nations. The UN also hosts the World Bank and works in close partnership with the World Trade Organisation. The UN website says it is working to ensure that developing countries can benefit equally from a globalized economy. This seems like just another way of saying, "*We see the solution to the world's challenges as being more and more trade*" and is in many respects merely a rephrasing of the now tired and soundly disproven theory that a rising economic tide will lift all the boats. With the UN's stated mission being to encourage and ease global trade as the means to increase global wellbeing, I suppose the WHO would be on shaky territory were it to admit that the unbridled rise of consumerism and the unfettered release of marketing were having a harmful effect on the collective physical and mental wellbeing of societies in many nations. But it feels like a sad vision of a *developed future* in which the promised land is a materialistic hell in which young people are prepared to shoot each other in the local branch of Foot Locker to get their hands on the latest pair of Nike Air Jordan's. If there could be a more pointless waste of young human life, I am yet to imagine it.

I spent a couple of months in Nigeria in my teenage years, over three decades ago. My dad was a brewer and brewing beer was then the country's fastest growing industry. Alcohol and tobacco were extensively advertised and fairly cheap to buy. Nigeria has been incredibly slow to reform its alcohol and tobacco advertising laws and the legacy of their unrestricted promotion is now coming home to roost in rising levels of alcoholism and some of the highest cancer mortality rates in the world. Poverty is undoubtedly a determining factor in mental wellbeing, and alleviating people from poverty should be a priority for all nations, but unfettered free trade and health are not always comfortable bedfellows. The short-term needs of capitalism are often at odds with our health and wellbeing. And after all, the problem has never been absolute poverty, it is the distribution of wealth that remains the greatest challenge.

In a thinly disguised version of name and shame, the WHOs report on the world's mental health focuses on the amount each nation commits to its mental health budgets. This seems an incredibly limited view to take. It does not identify or address the systemic causes of a great deal of the world's mental illness. America spends a greater proportion of its total GDP on healthcare than any other nation by a country mile, but that doesn't necessarily make it worthy of a pat on the back. The answer is not to throw more money and resources into dealing with the symptoms, the problems individuals and communities are facing, this will only increase the health systems capacity to accommodate the externalized misery that neoliberal corporation's benefit from creating. As long as the WHO's vision stays subservient to the largely economic goals of its masters in the UN, its role will be to continue to serve as a wilfully blind apologist for the harm neoliberalism creates. If the planet has not finally tired of us, if we make it through the next pandemic, if we have defeated the robots and survived AI, and if we have not blown each other to oblivion, then we can expect another vaguely titled ineffective navel gazing report from the WHO in 2042, which once again acknowledges that the previous report achieved little if anything while dancing around the many large and obviously destructive elephants in the room.

And here lies the contradiction of using Gross Domestic Product as a meaningful measure of assessing our collective wellbeing and development as a society. GDP is a purely financial and commercially oriented figure that grows and thrives in a marketing-controlled climate of personal and collectively reinforced dissonance and dissatisfaction in which contentment, happiness, and fulfilment will only be ours once we buy that next thing on our shopping list. Our souls are captive to the desires created by soulless corporations.

We have allowed the economists, advertisers, and marketers to distort our view of our own health, physical and mental, to see it not as a worthy cherished end in its own right and an endlessly superior measure of our humanity than GDP, but merely an enabling factor that allows us to consume. In production driven neoliberal societies citizens are seen as nothing more than the foundation on which a vapid brand fueled economy can be created. Inherently valueless blank pages for whom the true story of our purpose can only be discovered, written, and read out loud through an endless series of commercial interactions designed to both satisfy and stimulate the immense and unrelenting weight of the dissonance we are made to carry. The future of humanity and the precious planet we have been gifted teeters on the precipice, but our fear of missing out prevails as we collectively stamp ever harder on the gas pedal of productivity, in search of the prosperity and fulfilment it will surely provide. We choke on the fumes we are generating while lionizing, celebrating the architects, advocates, and ambassadors of our demise. We have become addicted, trapped, our behaviours, responses, actions, and thinking, enslaved to a higher power as we try to search for meaning, travelling in a direction that was set for us by others to serve their needs. Our worth has become inextricably linked to our economic activity and our financial ability to feed our artificially stimulated appetite for materialism and the insatiable dopamine fixes it provides. Our identities are proven through production and consumption. Cash is our earthly King, the God of GDP is globally omnipresent and omnipotent, and we are all enrolled to serve. We don't appear to recognise, value, or attempt to educate thinkers in the way we laud, defer to and train economists and financiers. Aren't we all worth more than this?

Chapter 4: **Public Health**

Twas a dangerous cliff, as they freely confessed, though to walk near its crest was so pleasant; But over its terrible edge there had slipped a duke, and full many a peasant. The people said something would have to be done, but their projects did not at all tally. Some said, "Put a fence 'round the edge of the cliff," some, "An ambulance down in the valley."

The lament of the crowd was profound and was loud, as their hearts overflowed with their pity; but the cry for the ambulance carried the day as it spread through the neighbouring city. A collection was made, to accumulate aid, and the dwellers in highway and alley, gave dollars or cents - not to furnish a fence – but an ambulance down in the valley.

"For the cliff is all right if you're careful," they said; "And if folks ever slip and are dropping, it isn't the slipping that hurts them so much as the shock down below - when they're stopping." So, for years (we have heard), as these mishaps occurred, quick forth would the rescuers sally, to pick up the victims who fell from the cliff, with the ambulance down in the valley.

Said one, to his peers, "It's a marvel to me that you'd give so much greater attention, to repairing results than to curing the cause; you had much better aim at prevention. For the mischief, of course, should be stopped at its source, come, neighbours and friends, let us rally, it is far better sense to rely on a fence, than an ambulance down in the valley."

"He is wrong in his head," the majority said; "He would end all our earnest endeavour. He's a man who would shirk his responsible work, but we will support it forever. Aren't we picking up all, just as fast as they fall, and giving them care liberally? A superfluous fence is of no consequence if the ambulance works in the valley."

The story looks queer as we've written it here, but things oft occur that are stranger; more humane, we assert, than to succour the hurt is the plan of removing the danger. The best possible course is to safeguard the source; attend to things rationally. Yes, build up the fence and let us dispense, with the ambulance down in the valley.

Joseph Malins; The Ambulance Down in the Valley

The sentiment Malins expresses in his oft quoted poem about the benefits of prevention versus cure feels largely logical on many levels, but before we go any further it's worth noting Malins was a passionate temperance activist who was staunchly opposed to the sale and consumption of alcohol, so his idea of prevention was probably a touch Stalinist for comfort. And there is a fine line between prevention, protection, and the restriction of choice. Relaxing in my garden with a decent cigar and a glass of port is my idea of heaven, I have no intention of letting any do-gooding policy maker rob me of this pleasure soon.

But what is Public Health and what is the point of it? Public Health is defined as the science and art of preventing disease, prolonging life, and promoting health through the organised efforts and informed choices of society, organisations, public and private, communities and individuals. Analysing the determinants of health of a population and the threats it faces is the basis for public health. The Royal Society for Public Health in London is the oldest public health agency in the world. It was founded in 1856, partly as a response to the rapid urbanisation of Britain that had occurred and the challenges this presented such as the need for sanitation, and in part as a result of the scientific advances that were being made in the understanding and treatment of infectious diseases. It's also worth noting that if disease had remained the preserve of the lower classes, little would have been done.

You may have heard the term, public health, and some of you may even be familiar with or come across and heard of a publicly funded organisation called Public Health England. Its stated mission was *to protect and improve the nation's health and wellbeing and reduce health inequalities*; who doesn't love a good old fashioned, and in this case, insanely ill-informed mission statement. Talk about a meaningless moon shot. In 2021 Public Health England was disbanded and its functions divided between three organisations. Some were handed over to NHS England, with the remaining bulk of its work being divided between two newly formed successor organisations. The sexily titled Office for Health Improvement and Disparities which is tasked with making us all healthier and reducing any disparities in health and wellbeing that might exist between the various sections of UK society; no pressure there then! And the UK Health Security Agency whose remit includes biosecurity, preventing the introduction and transmission of harmful diseases and organisms, and coordinating the nations response to future pandemics. Yes, there will be more global pandemics and yes there is no shortage of irony that an agency created under a Conservative Government will protect the UK from potentially harmful parasitic organisms. It's like Satan offering courses in fire-protection and burn wounds management.

The home countries still have their own dedicated public health functions. At the time of writing Northern Ireland has a Public Health Agency who's stated purpose is to *protect and improve the health and social wellbeing of our population and reduce health inequalities through strong partnerships with individuals, communities and other key public, private and voluntary organisations.* Rolls off the tongue doesn't it. The opening gambit from Public Health Scotland's vision statement says it is *working towards a Scotland where everybody thrives*, a wonderful and classic example of a waffly self-perpetuating public sector goal which can never be achieved, and which thus ensures longevity for the organisation it belongs to. And Public Health Wales is no less nobly *working to achieve a healthier future for Wales*. I'm willing to place bets on the latter two of these lofty vision statements being generated by the same public relations or marketing agency.

What could be a more worthy cause than safeguarding the public's health I hear you say. After all, public health related activities were around long before the time of the Roman Empire. The Romans in turn recognised the significant links between basic hygiene and the spread of communicable diseases long before other nations. They understood the importance of establishing and maintaining the infrastructure needed to ensure clean water supplies were available to the entire population; no water meters in ancient Rome, the city still supplies free drinking water to all who need it. The sewage system of ancient Rome was said to be so far ahead of its time that nothing was built to match it for a further fifteen hundred years. Here in the UK, public health became an officially important topic in the nineteenth century when the Public Health Act of 1848 was passed having been grudgingly given the go ahead on the pretext of its proponents that it would reduce the reliance of the poor on the state and the more well off. It was felt that the wealthy should be able to work the lower classes to their bones and into an early grave without suffering the indignity of walking past their stooped begging fleshless frames or seeing their deceased diseased corpses lying in the street.

In the UK, the notion of proactively actively seeking to understand what determines the public's health, of monitoring, managing, and then seeking to improve the nation's wellbeing, was born in the Victorian era. This was a time when infrastructure was poor or non-existent, the sewerage network we now take for granted was not yet in place, outbreaks of cholera were common, and children were employed in dangerous work in factories. The average life expectancy of approx. 40yrs was half of what it is today. Behind the costumes of every finely filmed and exquisitely produced Victorian period drama is an untold ocean of human misery and indignity. The quality of life for the majority of the lower classes in Victorian Britain was horrendous.

In this not-so-distant past, people from all walks of life and of all classes were suffering with poor health and dying needless premature deaths for the want of clean water, better hygiene, and a basic knowledge of disease transmission. The ladies of the upper middle classes were unknowingly poisoning themselves with the ammonia, arsenic, belladonna, lead, and mercury contained in the lotions they bathed in and plastered on their faces in pursuit of the ultimate alabaster complexion, while the working class were dying from an absence of compassion and the poverty of choices they were faced with. If you were unfortunate enough to be born into the ranks of the working class in 19th century England and made it to adulthood, your life chances sat on a continuum which ranged from survival at best to living hell at worst. You could work in generally horrific conditions above and below ground, you could emigrate as millions did in search of better lives, or perhaps accept destitution and face the shame of the poorhouse, or you could step outside the law and risk transportation, imprisonment, or even death by hanging. Though their political motives for acting may have been mixed, against this backdrop of ignorance and insouciance few would argue there wasn't a clear and pressing case for government to take an active role in improving the public's health. In 1958 John Kenneth Galbraith saw that more people were dying in the United States of too much food than of too little. The UK now has the highest levels of obesity in Europe with more than one in four adults classed as obese and nearly two out of three overweight. The challenges facing the public's health now could never have been imagined by our great, great, grandparents.

Are we what we eat?

I had to laugh, the meeting was dominated by overweight middle-class ladies. It wasn't a special occasion, but along with the coffees and teas there was a plate of biscuits, some slices of cake and a box of Cadbury's Heroes on the table. The topic on the agenda was a discussion about dealing with obesity and diabetes in Copeland, a district in West Cumbria which in 2017 had some of the highest levels of obesity in the UK. Labelled by the press as the fattest local authority area in England and coupled with its persistent pockets of deprivation, it had become the focus of attention for the NHS and the local authority public health teams who had come together to discuss how to address the issue. *"It's the easy access to fast food I blame"*, commented one of the attendees as she reached for another chocolate. *"And it's not just fast food"* says another, *"it's the rubbish they buy to at eat at home, Pot Noodles and the like"*, before going on to tell the meeting that in her day people knew how to cook their own meals and of how her mum was apparently a dab-hand in the kitchen. You couldn't write the script I thought as I sat on my hands trying to keep my trap shut. The head chimp at this particular publicly funded tea-party then stated firmly in that authoritative no-nonsense way that always makes my working-class hackles rise, that what families in deprived neighbourhoods need is better nutritional education, as she pushed her cake plate aside. There were traces of crumbs on the side of her face and you could have parked a pint glass and an ashtray on the shelf of her backside.

Most of the ladies are wearing nice neck scarves, bought I'm guessing from M&S or Debenhams, probably not Primark. Apparently wearing a neck scarf takes the focus from your neckline and reduces the visibility of double, triple or even quadruple chins. Draped in the right way I am told they can even shift attention from other unflattering areas of the body. I am convinced scarf sales would plummet irretrievably and manufacturers fall like lemmings off the edge of a financial cliff, without the middle-class ladies of the NHS and the public sector to wear them. It may seem as if I'm making fun of the people I was in the meeting with, but I think it's important to hold a mirror up to the people in our public services, sometimes literally, to allow them to see the absurdity of their position. They don't live in or anywhere near the deprived neighbourhoods they have assumed are the problem and for which they are being so handsomely paid *to analyse and fix*. Nobody in the room is talking about the rapid growth of the online fast-food sector, and the massive amounts being spent on advertising by the companies driving this growth. The people in the room aren't subject to the same social forces or inherited contexts that have influenced and shaped the behaviour of the people and communities they are talking about. And the assumption that everyone who is obese is from a deprived neighbourhood who just needs to be told about nutrition is so old hat that it's positively threadbare. I ask myself, are these even the right people to be looking at this issue,? I wonder if anyone has studied the BMI of managers in the public sector?

According to analysis undertaken by Diabetes UK, the number of people living with diabetes in Britain now exceeds five million with a further two and a half million at considerable risk of developing type 2 diabetes. In March 2022, NHS England said that dealing with diabetes in all its forms accounts for around ten billion pounds of its budget each year. The British Heart Foundation lists obesity as a leading cause of heart and circulatory diseases like heart attacks, strokes, and vascular dementia. The annual cost to the NHS of dealing with cardiovascular disease is estimated at a mere seven and a half billion pounds. Over the next 20 years, the number of obese adults in the country is forecast to soar to twenty-six million people.

Meanwhile thanks to the efforts of Katy Perry, Snoop Dogg, and anyone else prepared to sell their soul in exchange for increasing the worldwide prevalence of obesity, diabetes and heart disease, the market value of foodservice deliveries in the UK is forecast to rise to almost fifteen billion pounds by 2025. According to Statista, in the two-year period between 2019 and 2021 the average annual spend per person on takeaway food from restaurants in Britain rose by almost fifty percent from £450 to just under £650. The global value of the fast-food delivery industry has more than tripled since 2017 and now exceeds a hundred and fifty billion dollars annually. In certain countries the size of the market doubled during the pandemic. The fast-food delivery industry spends more on advertising and promoting itself than any public health campaign to encourage healthy eating could ever dream of. The industry is thought to spend around five billion dollars globally of which around two hundred million was spent in the UK. The advertising budget for McDonalds in the UK alone in the years before the pandemic exceeded England's entire public health advertising budget. In 2022, Just Eat spent almost three quarters of a billion euros on advertising worldwide. Apart from the odd one that might find its way into a meal, the fast-food industry does not give a rat's arse about the public's health. Their business model and marketing strategies are built on growing their share of an ever-larger generic marketplace and increasing the frequency of purchase.

Is the Public Health function still relevant?

Now more than ever. But not in its current form. The inconvenient pollution emitted by the modes of transport used in the nineteenth century was horseshit, injurious only through the slap that might be received for unwittingly tramping it over the threshold, not lethal to health in the same way the toxic-laden fumes full of poisonous particles emitted by most cars today are. According to the World Health Organisation air pollution poses one of the greatest environmental risks to health. In 2019 an estimated 4.2 million premature deaths occurred globally due to air pollution. This staggering figure means that every two years, more people's lives are ended prematurely than the entire number of people who died from Covid-19 in the three years since its outbreak. Carbon emissions are estimated to have risen by 1.3 percent in 2022.

In December 2020, in what is thought to have been the first such ruling made in the world, Southwark Coroners Court concluded that air pollution had made a material contribution to the death of nine-year-old Ella Adoo-Kissi-Debrah. In his summing up the coroner said Ella had been exposed to excessive levels of pollution and highlighted the high levels of nitrogen dioxide which were above World Health Organisation and European Union guidelines. Ella who lived in Lewisham in south-east London died in 2013 following an asthma attack. It emerged during the inquest that she had experienced multiple seizures and been admitted to hospital twenty-seven times in the three years preceding her death. The coroners ruling was seen by many as a landmark decision. The question remains, how many more children and vulnerable adults with respiratory conditions have already been harmed or died without the presence or role of harmful manufactured pollutants being acknowledged?

Britain is not alone amongst its recently estranged European neighbours. The European Environment Agency says children across Europe are being failed in relation to the continents' management of air pollution. EEA research claims nearly all children under the age of 18 in Europe are regularly exposed to air that falls below a healthy standard and says that at least twelve hundred children die each year as a direct result. Children are extremely vulnerable to polluted air, the damage that excessive exposure can cause at an early age can lead to permanent physical damage and is thought to affect long-term brain development.

In the face of the evidence and information that is widely available in our hyperconnected world, there should be a place at the very head of the table for the public health function. Yet rather than being strengthened to meet the new physical and mental challenges of our times, the Public Health functions of today have become the very definition of pissing in the wind. Little more than pyrrhic gestures, token saplings of decency planted in the path of amoral neoliberalism's stampede. Though the public health function of every country and each local authority in the UK basks in the lofty aspirations of a disjoined unachievable vision statement, a dream as we realists like to call it, such statements generally being the product of upper-middle-class minds whose only experience of inequalities is the shame of having to buy a used car or keep their iPhone for more than two years, the real purpose of public health has become the picker up of pieces and sweeper up of the messes created by poor policies, and private sector profiteering. If your mission is truly to improve the nation's health and wellbeing and reduce health inequalities, then your work must begin with earnest efforts to identify and understand the causes of demand, and actively challenge the things that lead to the absence and erosion of people's health, their wellbeing, and the populations health equality. The health of its citizens should be a governments greatest priority.

I corresponded with the public health functions of each of the UK's four home countries, and they are by their own admission, albeit expressed in varying degrees of candour, largely impotent when it comes to challenging, shaping, and influencing policy and commercial activity. It is, as was explained to me, *not in their remit to challenge*. They rarely proactively seek to name the causes of problems relating to the nation's health and wellbeing, though they are often asked and in some cases required to offer their views on policy. But they have no real teeth, no power to veto or pause. They seem very much under the control of the government of the day and its prevailing ideologies, rather than outside and able to challenge and influence from an informed position. Public health functions should not be the impartial servants of government in relation to the health and wellbeing of the citizens who ultimately pay their wages. Their function should be that of strong empowered advocates who stand up for the entire nation's health.

Unfortunately, public health in the UK has a habit of following rather than leading. It was researchers from the medical field who first raised concerns about the health impacts of smoking in 1950. The UK government then acknowledged a link between smoking and cancer in 1957, yet no meaningful public health intervention occurred for decades. The first national strategy on tobacco wasn't published until 1998, over forty years after the link between smoking and lung cancer had been recognised by government. The tobacco lobby was embedded in government and the taxes raised through levies on tobacco were significant. The tail of vested commercial interests was wagging the dog of our collective health and wellbeing. And continues to do so. Jamie Oliver has arguably done more for the health and life expectancy of Britain's children in recent years than Public Health England and Marcus Rashford more to highlight and alleviate the nutritional impact of poverty.

In November 2022, the senior coroner for Rochdale Borough Joanne Kearsley, concluded that the death of two-year-old Awaab Ishak was due to a respiratory condition brought on by extensive mould in the flat in which he lived with his parents. In her summing up at the end of the inquest into Awaab's death, she said, *"I'm sure I'm not alone in having thought, how does this happen? How, in the UK in 2020, does a two-year-old child die from exposure to mould in his home?"*. The property that caused Awaab's death in December 2020 was owned by Rochdale Boroughwide Housing. The presence and prevalence of mould had been reported to the housing company three years previously in 2017.

Commenting on the case, Dr Camilla Kingdon, president of the Royal College of Paediatrics and Child Health said, *"Increasing evidence suggests a rising number of families are living in poor-quality accommodation, with detrimental impacts on children's health. "Cold and damp housing conditions can lead to increased risk of asthma, respiratory infections, slower cognitive development, and higher risk of disability, mental health problems in children."* Awaab's death begs the question, if all the money taxpayers have spent on funding regional and national public health functions has not even brought this country to the point where we can ensure children and adults are housed in properties that are safe to live in, what has been the point of it?

The annual report and accounts of Rochdale Boroughwide Housing for the year ending March 2021, the year in which Awaab died, are awash with all the usual platitudes and meaningless statements. *"We will prioritise the areas for improvement to ensure we are providing good quality core services that deliver value for money for our customers...yada, yada, yada."* And in what must be the cruellest of ironies, one of the housing associations board members was also the chief executive of a children's hospice.

Less than three years after a coroner concluded pollution had materially contributed to a nine-year-old girls' death, the Conservative Party is trying to scrap former EU guidance designed to ensure that governments are transparent about how they plan to reduce harmful air pollution. Where are the voices of indignation and outrage from our national and local Public Health Functions? The growth in deaths attributable to antibiotic resistance and drug resistant infections has been called the climate crisis of medicine and in his review of antimicrobial resistance (AMR) published in 2016, Jim O'Neill estimated that global mortality rates from AMR could exceed deaths from cancer by 2050. Yet, despite unrefuted evidence that the routine use of antibiotics leads to reduced resistance in both the animals they are given to and the people who consume them, we are still importing and consuming products from meat producing companies who treat their animals with antibiotics. Why aren't our public health functions empowered and able to talk openly about this issue and educate resellers and consumers? On a less contentious note, a 2021 global study of bike helmet use involving over sixty thousand cyclists found that wearing a helmet on a pushbike can reduce the likelihood of suffering a serious head injury by almost seventy percent. The compulsory wearing of bike helmets would save hundreds of young and adult lives every year. Is it acceptable that in the face of such an obvious win as the wearing of bike helmets, none of the leaders of our many public health departments and functions have put their heads above the parapet and made something happen? The public health function in the UK in its present format is of less use than a chocolate fireguard.

The externalising of costs:

In business, the practice of offsetting the true costs of production, are often referred to as externalising. Put simply, if a company can produce goods and services without paying for an element of the true overall costs associated with that activity, then most will do so. A good current example of the eternalising of costs in practice are the many profitable companies operating in the UK whose business models are to some degree reliant on their employees being able to claim benefits from the state. The organisations relying on this business model are amongst some of the largest and most profitable in the world. They include supermarkets, global retail giants, and household names in the fast-food and service sectors. Publicly funded benefits are used to supplement the low wages many employees working in the private sector are paid. Private commercial organisations in the UK can rely on the presence of a publicly funded national health service to keep their employees in good shape. The availability of the NHS as a *free provider of employee healthcare* has been used to help attract many a company to these shores. Low wages and the absence of overheads associated with healthcare insurance allow companies to keep their costs low and their profits high. Not all of which they pay tax on in the countries in which they generate them. In 2021/22, the profits of the UK's leading supermarkets reached record levels, collectively exceeding four billion pounds. It would seem paying low wages and letting the taxpayer pick up the difference makes a great deal of commercial sense. And if your employees are forced to use the local foodbank because they can't afford to shop in the same stores they work in, then that's not your problem, it's just market forces at work. A considerable proportion of what are termed food-insecure households have someone in paid work; a job is no longer an adequate defence against hunger and poverty.

For an even clearer example of the principle of externalising costs, look no further than the current environmental climate crisis we exist in. It is the most obvious result of the impact of externalised costs. Climate change and the destruction of habitat and wildlife on land and at sea are the collective result of individuals and corporations externalising the genuine cost of their operations, not always directly onto the public purse, but onto nature, the planet, and ultimately humanity itself.

There are presently an estimated one and half billion vehicles in use across the planet. To the best of anyone's knowledge, not one of the world's largest and hugely profitable car manufacturers, the same companies that have produced the hundreds of millions of diesel and petrol cars, vans and wagons that clog our streets and highways and choke our atmosphere, has ever been forced to contribute any of its revenues to a fund supporting climate change, or to a hospital specialising in respiratory diseases, or providing surgery to crash victims. There are no meaningful financial penalties for selling products that make people morbidly obese and lead to heart-failure, or for supplying addictive online gambling services that leave a trail of desperation in their wake. The largest fishing ships scour the world's oceans in their search for ever larger catches, damaging eco-systems, and destroying the livelihoods of small subsistence fishing communities with relative impunity. And as much as I enjoyed working for Carlsberg, I was always aware that our most loyal and profitable customers ran the greatest risk of a premature death. Many of the largest most lucrative accounts the company held were in some of the UK's most deprived areas. The marketplace has no conscience and commerce spares little thought for the wider consequences of its actions.

Of course, some of the more obviously harmful industry sectors like alcohol and tobacco are subjected to significantly higher tax levels, or more accurately their customers are subjected to significant amounts of tax which could be viewed as offsetting the potentially negative consequences of consuming their products. But though the use of their products and services may be taxed heavily, the producers, distributors, and resellers of alcohol and tobacco make significant profits. They don't pay the hospital or rehabilitation bills for over indulgers and alcoholics from their own revenues, or the costs of expensive cancer treatments from their reserves. Nor do the fast-food chains who will now happily feed your obesity and raise your blood pressure while you order and eat your burger of choice in bed, pay to reinstate the huge tracts of rainforest that are stripped of vegetation and wildlife to support the growth of soya crops to raise poultry and cattle for meat so we can indulge our insatiable appetite for cheap fast food. When I visit Doncaster, a town where over 70 percent of adults are classed as overweight or obese, I realise the well intentioned, if generally misguided, but almost always well-paid people running public health campaigns, the eat more fruit and get off the couch brigade, are presently pissing their efforts and our taxes away in the wind.

Activist authors, activist being the term used by the media to describe anyone who has become aware of and been prepared to call out the collective insanity gripping our epoch and get off their arse in an attempt to do something about it, such as George Monbiot, Naomi Klein, and interest groups like Greenpeace, have been trying to get the message across about the true cost of fast food and its associated environmental destruction and negative health impacts for decades now. In 2013 the author David Robinson Simon estimated that the subsequent healthcare costs associated with the sale of each Big Mac in the United States amounted to almost six dollars per burger.

The drive to create and supply more and more products for sale in competitive marketplaces with increasingly squeezed profit margins underpins a great deal of the damage we see being done to our planet and we, the people who live on it. Externalising costs is of course made much easier when those costs are geographically distant or unquantifiable. What is the cost of a lost acre of the Amazon Rainforest, or of a child suffering with respiratory problems caused by urban pollution, or of a damaged coral reef, of a village underwater in Pakistan, of someone becoming a Type1 diabetic, or of someone taking their own life after gambling addiction has led them into debt, destitution, and ultimately despair?

The function of public health matters more than ever, but not as it is undertaken and undermined now. The stated mission of what was Public Health England, to improve the nation's health and wellbeing, should surely be the entire mission of wider government, shouldn't it?

Chapter 5: **It could be you, it just probably won't be!**

"In Gambling, the many must lose in order that the few may win."

George Bernard Shaw

In 2005, under Tony Blair's Labour government, online gambling and gaming was legalised under the terms of a revised gambling act. In the same year, a new oversight and licencing body called the Gambling Commission was created as the governments appointed regulator tasked with overseeing the UK's newly emboldened unharnessed gambling sector. Two years later the first iPhone was released, followed a year later by the launch of the first Google Android phone. The rest as they say, for better or worse, is history. Each of us now had more computing power in our hands than previous NASA space missions. The market for phone applications exploded and the Apple inspired phrase, *there's an app for that*, became ubiquitous. Any hope that the UK's newly invigorated gambling industry might respect the notion of moderation in all things, was quickly blown apart by the proliferation of smartphones, tablets, and easy to use applications. The gambling industry collectively realised that this new hyperconnected world had not only rendered the Gambling Commission and its now outdated legislative frameworks and guidance, largely impotent, it also presented incredible commercial opportunities. In the absence of digitally informed regulation and oversight the online gambling industries time had well and truly arrived and just as austerity kicked in and personal finances became stretched and fragile, the beast of online gambling, which thrives in times of need, was unleashed with a vengeance.

Since then, the growth of online gambling and gaming globally and in the UK has been nothing short of a wild west gold rush for its pioneers. One which has created an epidemic of debt and misery for the vulnerable it has chewed up and spat out in its relentless commercially amoral pursuit of profit. Global estimates of the personal levels of debt incurred through online gambling were approaching half a trillion dollars in 2016 and are expected to exceed a trillion dollars by 2030. Tens of billions of this enormous sum will doubtless come from the current accounts, savings, personal loans, family, friends, and legal and illegal credit lines available to gamblers in the UK. Gambling is not the noble entrepreneurial art of wealth creation with the aim of generating collective wealth and wider benefit. The profits gambling companies make are merely the flip side of the losses they create. It is a zero-sum game in which there will only ever be one winner. I was warned off gambling as a youngster with the admonition that it was a mugs game, that the only bet that's sure is that the house always wins in the long run, and I would never see a bookie riding a bicycle. Today's globally omnipresent online bookies and corporate executives are more likely to be seen disembarking from private jets than peddling pushbikes.

Their names are known to most of us. Their logos are everywhere, on our television screens, plastered across the shirts of our favourite football teams, and popping up constantly in our email inboxes and on our social media feeds. Paddy-Power, Betfair, and PokerStars, now all part of Flutter Entertainment, Bet365, Sky Betting & Gaming, 32Red, Betway, Stake, Betfred, and of course all the traditional high-street betting brands such as William Hill, part of 888 Holdings, and Ladbrokes, owned by Entain, now have an online offer to supplement their already significant retail presence. The advertising and promotional budgets of these societal bloodsuckers are enormous. In 2022 the combined annual marketing spend of gambling companies in the UK alone was estimated at almost one and half billion pounds of which less than a quarter is thought to be spent on television advertising. An amount which on its own is still three times the combined annual television advertising spend of cereal brands. The irony of watching adverts promoting Virgin Bet in which the central character was a vampire while the Virgin brand was being paid from the public purse to run mental health and care services should not be wasted on anyone. Virgin exited the health and care sector in December 2021, its business was acquired by a private equity group called Twenty20 Capital and has been rebadged as HCRG Care Group. The groups website says it looks for high return opportunities across a broad range of situations. I guess that translates to, anything where significant bucks can be made.

On April 27th, 2023, eighteen years after the Labour government had further raised the lid on Pandora's destructive box of gambling, and under increasing pressure from groups concerned with the explosion of online activity, the increases in addiction, the insouciant behaviour of the industry, and the increasingly obvious detrimental social impacts gambling was causing, a new white paper was published by the UK Governments

Department for Culture, Media & Sport. Entitled, *High Stakes: gambling reform for the digital age*, the paper had the stated aim of making gambling legislation fit for the digitally enabled smartphone dominated world we now live in and proposed a number of revisions to the regulation of the gambling industry which it said were designed to safeguard customers. These measures included the lowering of betting limits on slot machines, caps on losses, personal affordability checks, stake limits for online games, and a levy on the profits of gambling companies to fund research and education in relation to the harm gambling causes. The paper also contained some proposed tweaks about how the industry should be allowed to promote itself so as to not be too visible or appealing to its future victims, I mean younger consumers. Gambling companies are no longer allowed to use former sports stars or influential celebrities who might appeal to young people to promote their products, and in a separate move the Premier League has announced its member clubs will no longer be able to sport gambling brand logos on the front of their shirts from 2026. The Sky-Bet sponsored English Football League Championship is unsurprisingly, not planning any such ban. Whilst seen as a step in the right direction, overall, the recommendations contained in the 2023 white paper are far from the radical intervention and industry overhaul most impartial observers and mental health professionals argue was needed.

The paper was seen by many as a missed opportunity and a fudge. It has been criticised by the mental health profession and the charities who pick up the pieces and deal with the financial and mental aftermath gambling creates, for not going far enough. More worryingly, and as if to affirm the view that pressure groups and mental health professionals were expressing, the paper was broadly welcomed by the industry itself. At close of play on 28th April 2023, the share price of Flutter Entertainment PLC, formerly Paddy Power and one of the largest online gambling companies with significant interests in the UK market, had risen. At the time of writing Flutter Entertainments share price stands at 16.725, close to a five-year high and around eight percent higher than the date of the white papers, publication. Shares in Entain, a gambling corporation based in the tax haven of the Isle of Man also rose on 28th April. Entain owns brands such as Coral, Eurobet, Foxy Bingo, and Ladbrokes and processed over fourteen billion pounds in sports wagers in 2022. You can bet your bottom dollar that if the legislation had been worth the paper it was written on, shares in Entain and Flutter would have fallen. But the marketplace tends to have a better nose than the public sector and its policy makers when it comes to smelling the implications and opportunities change brings. Operators in the gambling marketplace know that the recommendations contained in the white paper, will not dent their ambitions or their profits any time soon. The white paper which was sold to the public and pundits as the biggest shake-up of regulation in the UK's gambling industry for twenty years, has turned out to be a sticking plaster to heal a flesh-eating virus. Profit has once again been placed before people. It is no secret that the door of many an MPs office has been widely opened to lobbyists working on behalf of the gambling and gaming sector. Politics and gambling, could there be a better suited partnership of self-serving interests? I wonder, was it realistic for any of us to expect anything other than a fudge in 21st century Britain? As I've got older and lost my illusions, I find myself increasingly asking, how did we get here?

Shortly after the publication of the paper on gambling, an article in the Guardian from Sunday 21st May 2023, reported that Entain, owner of the Ladbrokes brand was engaging in underhanded lobbying designed to curtail the papers recommendations. The company was surreptitiously funding a campaign to encourage people who enjoyed a flutter, to write to their MPs and complain about proposed changes contained in the much anticipated, and long overdue white paper. Entain had brought together some of its customers to form a user-group they called the Players Panel, effectively a front for Entain's lobbying, who claimed to stand for the interests of ordinary gamblers. A look at the Players Panel website reveals a carefully chosen cross section of everyday people with broad appeal who are all concerned about the potential impact on their hobby of choice that any revisions to gambling in the UK might have. The Players Panel says its purpose is to bring the voices of people who actually gamble and bet into the debate on the future of digital entertainment and gaming. There is Andy from Wakefield, Ken from Newcastle, and Sally and Terry from Yeovil who say that for them, having a bet is just part of everyday life and that they gamble regularly, responsibly, and within their financial limits. Sally and Terry also suggest that if legislation becomes too draconian, they may be forced to shift their gambling activity into the underground economy. This is one of the stock responses the gambling industry regularly throws back at its critics when it is threatened with more regulation. The industry argues that it's better to allow people to gamble in the marketplace as it stands, rather than driving them away into an even more unregulated gambling arena. A report conveniently commissioned by the Betting and Gaming Council and supported by William Hill and Entain from the global consultancy firm PWC in 2021, just as the threat of revised legislation was approaching, looked for, and surprise, surprise, found evidence to support the theory that the black market posed a threat to the UK's gambling industry. The market they say, is safer in their hands.

In fairness to Entain and its Players Panel of cuddly cut-out characters, there is no denying that the views of responsible gamblers, which represents the largest albeit least profitable sector of the industry's target market, should have been sought and harnessed long before the white paper was published, and its recommendations made public. But governments of whatever hue have never been good at listening to their citizens in general so Britain's responsible gamblers should not take this slight too personally. And if Entain had genuinely wanted the views of its users to be heard it would have created a forum for sharing views and ideas in a much more open and transparent fashion, much earlier in the process. Instead, its Players Panel emailed members offering ready-made templates for letters they could adopt, adapt, and send to their respective MPs outlining their objections. The templates contained messages framing the proposed legislation as, *"a massive infringement on my personal liberty"*, and *"It isn't fair, it isn't right, and it isn't British"*. For the record, fairness, rightness, and Britishness, have not belonged in the same sentence for quite some time now. This behind-the-scenes skulduggery was being coordinated by Entain despite its Danish chief executive, Jette Nygaard-Andersen, surely an anagram of something interesting in at least three languages, publicly welcoming any proposals the paper might bring and the advent of, in her own words, *"a robust regulatory framework that is fit for the digital age"*. Its more than mildly amusing that an organisation based in an offshore tax haven led by a Danish national was encouraging its customers to tell elected MPs sitting in the UK Houses of Parliament, what was and wasn't fair, right, or British. Entain refused to say how much funding it provided to the Players Panel and whether any of its staff were involved in creating the campaign and generating the letter templates. That's normally corporate speak for, of course we did but we won't admit it until you can prove it.

Research into the stimulus and the emotions gamblers experience during play, especially after winning, reveals an experience not unlike drug use, which leads to compulsive behaviour and addiction in constant pursuit of the next emotional high. And it is common knowledge that a disproportionately large amount of online gambling company profits, are generated by a small but steadily and significantly growing pool of problem and at risk, gamblers. Research commissioned by Gamble Aware and published by the University of Liverpool in 2021 suggests that eighty-six percent of online betting profits are generated by just five percent of customers. Estimates of the number of adult problem gamblers in the UK varies. Figures from Public Health England in 2020 suggested around two hundred and fifty thousand people were problem gamblers with a further two million classified as *at-risk gamblers*, those who may become problem gamblers. The rapacious owners of online gambling sites are not overly interested if even aware of the mental wellbeing of their customers, the state of their household finances, their marriages, relationships, or ability to pay their rents, their rising mortgages, rocketing utility bills, and cost of living. They are only interested in their customer's ability to pay their debts. It's just business, we can't be held accountable for people's personal choices they say, however much we might have spent on influencing them. Intervention and restriction would be undemocratic they argue.

The immense wealth that online gambling has created for those at the top of the food-chain is staggering while the tax revenues it has created for the UK public purse have been feeble in comparison. Many companies operating online gambling services to consumers in the UK are not even based in the country. Some have opted for legislatively preferential locations such as the Isle of Man and Gibraltar. Denise Coates, the founder of Bet365, which is still based in and pays tax in the UK, is thought to have a personal net worth in excess of twelve billion pounds and growing. The company she runs reportedly has over six million customers drawn from over two hundred countries. In the year ending March 2022, Denise's salary was just £213.4million, down from the previous year's salary of £422million, on top of which she had then received a further small dividend, a mere £48million. Perhaps she could see into the future and was quietly squireling some money away to pay the energy bills. Large mansions do take such a lot of heating you know.

Supporters of Denise, who was awarded a CBE in 2012, and named one of the most respected businesspeople in the UK by the Sunday Times, cite her organisations significant charitable donations and her personal tax contributions as evidence of her overall decency and integrity. And it would only be right to point out that the recipient of these donations, the humbly named Denise Coates Foundation, does indeed receive a generous injection of cash each year and has done so since 2012. The charity vaguely states it aim as being to promote charitable purposes anywhere in the world, for the public benefit; irony doesn't quite meet the explanatory requirements for such an obvious contradiction. And I suppose it's more acceptable than saying its purpose is to act as a veneer of decency behind which lurks one of the most socially destructive commercial activities of the modern era. In 2022 the Denise Coates Foundation received a further one hundred million pounds. Most impressive and clearly an indicator of Denise's fine and generous character I hear you say. However, a recent look at the charity's assets and latest accounts reveal it was sitting on funds of almost seven hundred million pounds, of which it spent around three percent in the same year on charitable activities, probably less than the interest receivable on amounts of such size. Charitable is as charitable does. Ms Coates appears to be relying on the significant donations, which are doubtless offset against tax, to a charity of which she and her relatives were founding trustees, to create the perception of a socially responsible modern-day enterprise led by a philanthropic entrepreneur.

Yet it's difficult to reconcile her unwillingness to spend the significant funds her charity is sitting on, with her organisations persistent marketing efforts to encourage punters to spend money they often can't spare to support their gambling habit. Bet365 and its various international trading arms have been chastised by gambling regulators in various countries over the years for breaching numerous laws and codes of conduct. In 2018 the company faced criticism over its practice of running adverts that encouraged gamblers to place ad-hoc bets in-play during sporting events. Ray Winstone, perhaps the world's most famous homespun cockney since Barbara Windsor died, became the annoyingly omnipresent face of a mildly irritating but incredibly pervasive multi-channel advertising campaign. The purpose of which was to encourage punters to get into the habit of placing spontaneous in-play bets on an ever-increasing range of variables. Who would score the next goal, who would get the next corner, how would the next goal be scored, how many red and yellow cards would the referee issue during the game, the list went on. The number of in-play bets amassed, and the profits duly rolled in. For those with a gambling problem, the development of in-play betting was akin to peddling crystal meth to drug addicts. Like stealing candy from a baby, a lot of candy, from a lot of babies, all at the same time. It's sometimes difficult to remember that the internet can also be a force for tremendous good.

With her organisation being based in the UK and with her consistently ranking near the top of the list of largest individual contributors to the UK's tax-coffers, it feels like Denise Coates and Bet365 are trying to disguise the fact that they are at heart, an insatiably hungry and ruthlessly focused Great White Commercial Shark that makes it living feasting on the financial misfortunes of its customers. And the more significant their customers misfortunes, the greater their gains. You can plaster as much make-up on the predatory fish as you wish, but it still needs to make its living by devouring the finite finances of those unfortunate enough to be in its path. The options and choices that have been made available to the online gambling community over recent years, the numerous ways in which they can be enticed to wager their money, are mind-boggling. The companies that succeed in the gaming market are incredibly astute when it comes to gaining new customers and then getting the most out of those who can afford it least. As well as a seemingly inexhaustible number of gambling permutations and in-play options, online gambling companies use sophisticated algorithms and personally targeted advertising messages to persuade their customers to place a bet and roll the dice. Some free spins, game credits, introductory offers. Go on, you never know, it could be you.

The reality of course is that for most of the residents in communities across Britain, that someone knocking on the door is more likely to be the property owner or the bailiff than the Peoples Postcode Lottery. It seems the opportunities for gaining financial security and social inclusion through work, enterprise, industry, have been replaced by onscreen games of chance aimed at the poorest and most vulnerable. The fall of the wall and the victory of capitalism has shifted us from an ethos of collective wealth creation, however poorly distributed it may have been, to an era of individual money-making. Why are we dishing out honours to people who are merely making money rather than generating financial and social wealth? Is it a fitting legacy for the children of Britain's industrial infantry, the unsung heroes who risked and all too often sacrificed their lives for a pittance digging out the black gold that fueled the Industrial Revolution and originally made Britain Great, that whatever wealth was left in their communities is being systematically drained from them in the pursuit of profit?

Who picks up the pieces?

It is thought that between five hundred and a thousand people who take their own lives each year in the UK do so because of their involvement in gambling. In March 2019 fifty-one people were killed by a gunman who attacked the Al Noor Mosque in Christchurch New Zealand. Within days the New Zealand government led by Jacinda Ahern, proposed the introduction of sweeping radical changes to the country's gun laws. And within weeks of the tragedy occurring, all military style semi-automatic weapons and assault rifles were banned, even owning the parts to construct such weapons was made illegal. Ahern was widely praised and hugely respected for acting so decisively to address what had clearly become a problem. Yet at the same time I feel sure many of us were looking at the sorry excuse for politicians we are stuck with and sighing in the knowledge that we could never expect such principled and courageous decision making from the dross that presently occupies the UK Parliament. In terms of lives lost, mental health damaged, and family and communities destroyed, the unleashing of online gambling that enables people to place bets on outcomes, individuals, teams, and sports, they were previously unaware even existed, has been the equivalent of granting access to automatic weapons in a society ill-equipped to deal with the consequences.

Did you know Finland's national game is called Pesapallo, and you can bet on it from the comfort of your armchair without knowing a thing about it. Or if you prefer you can lose your shirt while out walking by placing bets on games of Australian Football, or Shinty, or Soccer in the Paraguayan Premier Division. You can even place a wager on the weather. And if you are bored of betting on the Gee-Gees or your race meeting is cancelled, you can place a bet on who you think could win an Oscar, a Bafta, or a Grammy this year. But even in the face of this obvious explosion of options and the self-evident personal and collective social harms the proliferation of gambling has created, the UK government's response is to pontificate, ponder, listen to the lobbyists who represent the views of the unelected and invisible, and then tinker. Why, oh why, oh why, do we still believe government ministers who say they are serious about dealing with issues when at the same time they are creating the conditions in which these issues will so obviously thrive? Shouldn't the primary purpose of any government and its elected officials be to protect its citizens from predictable and avoidable harm? Why does it take the efforts of volunteers and the families of victims to address the issues that corporately interested policy shapers and inept amoral politicians create?

Gambling increases significantly in times of scarcity and want. It plays upon desperation and despite its protestations to the contrary, it relies heavily on addiction for its profits. When it's fun, it's fun, but when it's not, it's really, really, not. It creates angst, crime, mental illness, isolation, separation, divorce, and of course bankruptcy and ultimately destitution and desperation. In the industries ongoing efforts to ingratiate and embed gambling into society as a normal part of everyday life we have seen it increasingly turn to sponsoring peak time television. Soap operas like Emmerdale and high profile shows such as *I'm a Celebrity Get Me Out of Here* presented by everyone's favourite Geordie drink driver and his sidekick Dec, offer gambling firms the perfect family friendly advertising platforms from which to normalize gambling. By placing themselves alongside these well-known acceptable brands and celebrity faces they are attempting to hide the darker harmful side of their character. At the very least an activity as potentially addictive and harmful as gambling should not be allowed to promote itself in any way, shape, or form. Tobacco advertising has been banned in the UK for decades now. Gambling should be forced to follow suit, it's a no brainer.

The cost of the personal tragedies that the unchecked and unprincipled growth of online gambling has created, remains beyond measure. And the wider societal problems it has exacerbated and the failure demand it has generated, of which the burden of dealing with falls upon families, the public purse, the NHS, and charities is huge. I wonder if future generations will view the gambling barons as we now view slavers? If one day, we will rescind the honours given to those who made fortunes from such socially spurious and mentally harmful enterprises. And I wonder if Jette or Denise might know what the odds on that would be?

PART II:

A Crisis in Social Care or a Society in Crisis?

Chapter 6: Does society exist?

"I think we have gone through a period when too many children and people have been given to understand 'I have a problem, it is the Government's job to cope with it!' or 'I have a problem, I will go and get a grant to cope with it!' 'I am homeless, the Government must house me!' and so they are casting their problems on society and who is society? There is no such thing! There are individual men and women and there are families, and no government can do anything except through people and people look to themselves first."

Margaret Thatcher; 1987 interview for Woman's Own

"It takes a village to raise a child."

African proverb

Thatcher's infamous much quoted and oft maligned proclamation was a small part of a lengthier interview with Woman's Own, not a magazine that many in 1987 would associate with the rise of neoliberalism and uncaring capitalism. It has since been used as a soundbite to distance her from decency, not a difficult task I'll grant you, as a neoliberal appeal to the fortunate on whom the economic sun is shining, and to those who still labour under the illusion that people get what they deserve in this life and the next. Behavioural scientists refer to this illusion as just world hypothesis and you will often hear people innocently proclaiming that everything happens for a reason and good things happen to good people. The inherent assumption within this thoughtless statement is that people who experience difficulties somehow deserve them. We attribute people's conditions and status to their actions alone, and we trust that there is a universal order of things which means those in the gutter are getting their just deserts while those being waited on in stately mansions are somehow worthy of their opulent existence. On a simpler level I think it also suits us to look away from others misfortune because once we acknowledge their situation, we open ourselves up to feeling empathy and then experience guilt for not acting. Our ignorance, wilful or otherwise, is bliss. Charity begins at home we think as we check the value of our investments online.

Immediately after stating there was no such thing as society, in the interview with Woman's Own, Thatcher went on to say, *there is a living tapestry of men and women and people, and the beauty of that tapestry and the quality of our lives will depend upon how much each of us is prepared to take responsibility for ourselves and each of us prepared to turn round and help by our own efforts those who are unfortunate*. It's almost poetic isn't it. And somewhat confusing because Mrs T's talk of a tapestry of life sounds on the face of it, dare I say, rather like most people's idea of a reasonably well functioning society. But only an experienced politician would be able to appear to say there was no such thing as society and then go on to describe the neoliberalists version of it in such appealing poetic terms. On closer inspection Thatcher is almost echoing Ruskin when she talks about the degree to which we are prepared to take responsibility for each other. Yet as with everything context is key, and though the sentiment Thatcher expressed so eloquently might have seemed benign, even generous had it been voiced in Victorian times, it was in reality just a more acceptable way of restating the neoliberal dog eat dog philosophy of life which is that its every person for themselves and the sharing of whatever we manage to claim as our own is entirely optional. As if the inherent interdependence we all rely on can be ignored. Even those at the top of the pile need and rely upon the rest of us, even if it's only to stand on. It's a shame that as Thatcher, who clearly had no lived understanding of the damage unchecked capitalism could cause, was euphemistically rebranding society as a beautiful tapestry, her government were enthusiastically swinging a wrecking ball through the bricks and mortar it was hanging on. The beauty of any tapestry is only evident when it is hung in a straight line on an even upright wall. The job of a just government is to build, maintain, house, and cherish that wall. True democracy can only exist in an economically equitable society.

The word society is thought to come from the old French word, societe, meaning company and the word social from the Latin word socius meaning friend and socii meaning allies. As well as talking utter bollocks Thatcher was effectively offering a clever soundbite to the middle-class readers of Woman's Own, who in the wake of recent inner-city riots and social unrest and with unemployment near three million, needed reassuring that Maggie wasn't going to give more of their hard-earned income-tax to the poor. They needn't have worried, shortly after Thatcher's protestation that there was no such thing as society, she oversaw the introduction of a new tax on individuals and households called the community charge, or poll tax as it became more widely known. The word community is derived from the Latin communitas, meaning common, public, shared by all or many. Sounds a lot like society doesn't it? Thatcher was just as happy to employ the warm word *community*, as she was happy to denigrate its older sibling *society*, when it suited her political ends. She was a dyed in the wool neoliberal who preferred to use opaque words like, people, Britain, and phrases such as, men and women, our people, our nation, our country, in place of openly talking about or explicitly referring to the existence of society. To refer to society would have been to acknowledge our collective and undeniable if presently somewhat unequal interdependence.

Whether or not each of us believes society exists and to what extent we believe it, is largely a matter of individual perception and personal experience. What we see largely depends on where we stand and sometimes depends on what we are prepared to see. I believe society is not only all around us, but we are like the cars in a traffic jam, a part of it as well as sometimes frustrated unwitting participants in it and observers of it. There is an old Ethiopian proverb that says fish discover water last. It's a useful reminder that we accept and take for granted the environment we exist in. Like fish who can only ever understand the existence and importance of water when they are taken out of it and who until that point know nothing else and have no other reality or context to compare their existence in water with, we are within and part of society whether we know it and like it or not. The human species has only survived and thrived because our primate ancestors learned out of necessity to collaborate and cooperate. We may choose to what degree we embed ourselves within it but to deny the existence of society and community, is to deny the very roots of our evolution and of who we are. Without people, without each other, we are nothing.

Chapter 7: **Social Care**

"There are only four kinds of people in the world. Those who have been caregivers. Those who are currently caregivers. Those who will be caregivers, and those who will need a caregiver."

Rosalynn Carter; activist, writer, former first lady

What springs to mind when you hear the words social care? Do you think of care homes, gods waiting rooms, sheltered housing complexes, and assisted living? Or perhaps the care and day centres provided by local authorities for adults, children, and those with learning disabilities? Maybe you think of the underpaid overstretched army of care workers providing domiciliary care, visiting the elderly and infirm each day to clean, dress, feed, and care for them? Or do you think of social care as social work and that shadowy species known as the social worker who straddles our perceptual boundaries between fearless principled do-gooder and scatter-brained interfering bureaucrat. Pilloried as ill-equipped and inept when things go wrong but who gain no recognition when things do not. However you think about it you will more than likely recall at least some of the many headlines, local, regional, and national, about the crisis in social care that media channels of every format and flavour are dining on amply; *Social Care in Crisis*, the Big Issue May 2023, *Ignoring the Social Care crisis will worsen the already broken system*, UNISON press release April 2023; *Edinburgh Health and Social Care boss to step down amidst crisis*, Edinburgh Live May 2023; *The adult social care crisis in the UK*, Warrington Guardian April 2023; *State of social care a tragedy*, Evening Standard Jan 2023; *Hundreds of thousands of older people in England are having to endure chronic pain, anxiety and unmet support needs owing to the worsening shortage of social care staff and care home beds*, The Guardian March 2023; *BMA warns of social care crisis as current system is deeply flawed and in need of urgent reform*, BMA press release June 2022; *Tories "crisis, cash, repeat" approach to social care blasted by experts*, Mirror, March 2023.

Things got so bad for social care that in September 2022, even the largely Conservative dominated County Councils Network warned its own government that it was in crisis. Sometimes the press are rightly accused of making something out of nothing, on this occasion they have been woefully slow to the party. Social care in Britain, just like the NHS, has been seriously challenged and its crisis has been developing predictably, irresistibly, and very obviously for at least fifteen years. It is in its present state, well and truly fubared. There are currently over a hundred and sixty thousand vacancies in the social care sector and rising. This is a vacancy proportion of the social care workforce which exceeds that of the much more widely publicised recruitment and retention crisis that is debilitating the NHS.

A search to define social care on Wikipedia's global site is rather confusingly redirected to social work, which is described as an academic discipline and practice-based profession concerned with meeting the basic needs of individuals, families, groups, communities, and society as a whole to enhance their individual and collective well-being. The English version of social care has its own unique page on Wikipedia, of course it would wouldn't it, and is defined as the provision of social work, personal care, protection, or social support services to children or adults in need or at risk, or adults with needs arising from illness, disability, old age, or poverty. In England it is the local authorities, councils, who have a duty to assess people in terms of whether they meet these criteria and are eligible for help. It appears to be an incredibly broad field which is open to varying definitions and interpretations.

NHS England defines Social Care as being about *providing physical, emotional, and social support to help people live their lives. For various reasons and at different stages in their lives, some people need support to develop and maintain their independence, dignity, and control. Social care supplies a whole range of services to support adults and older people.* I think this is a useful description of Social Care as it implies social care is more about maintaining and preserving the health and wellbeing of its service users than social work, which feels much more overtly like a societal failure demand service.

Data from 2022 estimates there to be approx. seventeen thousand care homes in the UK. Of these twelve thousand are residential care homes and five thousand are nursing homes. The key difference between the two being that nursing homes offer greater clinical capacity for residents requiring more intensive medical care and usually retain a full-time qualified nursing presence on-site. Though all homes have to register and are subject to inspection and rating by the Care Quality Commission, nursing homes are registered and regulated slightly differently. Between them they house almost half a million people. That's the entire resident population of Cumbria. According to the Alzheimer's Society, around seventy percent of care home and nursing home residents have dementia or severe memory problems.

Skills for Care, a registered charity which claims to be the strategic workforce development body allegedly responsible for planning adult social care in England, clearly a task they have taken every bit as seriously as NHS England, estimates that the total number of people employed in the UK's residential care homes is three quarters of a million. That amount is thought to be almost equalled by the number of carers supplying publicly and privately funded domiciliary care to people in their own homes. Skills for Care predicts that the care sector may need a further four hundred and eighty thousand people by 2035 if it is to keep pace with demand. They point out that while vacancy rates and demand are growing, the number of people in the workforce has shrunk in recent years by almost fifty thousand. The turnover rate of staff in the social care sector is nothing short of staggering at almost thirty percent and the average pay for an experienced social care worker is a pound an hour less than a newly employed inexperienced healthcare assistant in the NHS. The industry offers little in the way of pensions or personal development, has a high proportion of employees on zero hours contracts, and pays its staff peanuts with many reportedly paid less than the living wage. It's difficult to know why social care struggles to recruit and keep staff, isn't it?

Skills for Care, an official partner to the Department of Health and Social Care, advocates that care staff should be paid more, an obvious sentiment most would agree with and which many have been saying for decades. But in their twenty-two years of existence Skills for Care appears to have been less use than a chocolate fireguard and has done little other than pontificate about the issue. The care home sector consists of a disparate collection of largely private companies who say they are not paid enough by local authorities to make ends meet and therefore cannot possibly afford to pay their staff more. Skills for Care have no such funding problems, their senior staff pay and pension contributions for the leadership team and trustees in 2022 was just over one and a half million pounds. An increase of two hundred and fifty thousand pounds on the previous year.

There are presently as many people working in social care in the UK as there are in the NHS. 1.2 million full time equivalent roles are filled by approx. 1.5 million people. If all its disjoined services were placed under one employment roof, social care would be the largest employer in the country and the tenth largest organisational workforce in the world. If social care and NHS services were combined, now there's a crazy yet entirely logical thought, one I will touch on later, the total workforce would leapfrog that of the Chinese army, sitting behind only India and America's department of Defence as the third largest workforce on the planet. And if we're really going to go hard or go home, then let's add on the many hundreds of thousands of people employed by charities across the UK, and the volunteers who give their time and energy for no financial return. Without the efforts of these largely unseen resources, a great deal of what is thought to be the responsibility of the public sector, and for which it is only too ready to claim the credit, would quite simply not happen or be possible. Providers of social care services from the public, private, and voluntary sectors all report that recruitment and staff retention is an increasing problem and the predicted shortfall in social care staff will increase significantly as demand rises and the labour market tightens.

The importance of unpaid carers:

For five years I held an unpaid role as the Chair and Trustee of a local carer's charity here in the Eden Valley in Cumbria. Eden Carer's is a small charity based in Penrith. It was set-up around the turn of the millennium with the mission of offering support to the many unpaid carers in the area, children, and adults. The charities stated role is to help unpaid carers in the local community by providing support and information. Its largest source of revenue was a contract it held with the local council to provide personal assessments for unpaid carers. All carers in the UK, young and old, are legally entitled to an assessment of their needs to help them understand and obtain whatever support they might be entitled to. Health and care professionals who might work or interact with someone who is a carer such as their GP, an occupational therapist, or a nurse working in a community setting, are obliged, in theory, to inform carers of this right.

Though they are officially a charity, the main service Eden Carer's provided were the statutory carer assessments, enshrined in law and funded through the local authority. It's a service most councils used to undertake themselves, but in the never-ending drive to cut costs councils have found it cheaper to outsource this requirement to independent, often charitable, or semi-charitable providers. This practice enables local authorities to provide some of the statutory services they are legally obliged to offer using low paid staff while also relying on the goodwill of charities and the people who donate to them to cover any difference between what the service costs to provide in reality and what councils give to the third sector organisations they commission, to provide them. Staff benefit's and pay in the voluntary sector are significantly less than in the public sector and third sector chief executives who rely on these public funding streams are often more willing and less able to refuse the constant demands from their overlords to provide more activity for less money. The increased reliance of charities on their public sector grant givers creates dependency and an imbalance in the relationship. Many charities simply cannot afford to refuse funding even when it comes with layer upon layer of conditions and arbitrary requirements and becomes culturally toxic. Each time that contracts to supply such services come up for renewal, councils typically invite contractors to take part in a competitive bidding process in which the council demand more and more services for less and less money. Few if any councils would admit this, but they ultimately squeeze their voluntary sector contractors so hard that they rely on these organisations cross subsidising their contractual activity using their other available resources, such as the grants they receive from other bodies, the charitable donations they gather from the public, and any reserves the charity has managed to build up over the years.

Across the UK there are an estimated 10.6 million people providing unpaid care, within their immediate and related family settings, to their friends, and to neighbours and people in their communities. Feel free at this point to raise a rigid middle finger to Thatcher. The number of unpaid carers has risen steadily as the population has aged and medical improvements have enabled people with multiple conditions to live longer. For some years now, the charity, Carers UK, has produced an annual report entitled *State of Caring – A snapshot of unpaid care in the UK*. The results of the 2022 survey make interesting and engaging reading. Many of the comments from carers quoted in the report paint a picture of people who are giving a great deal of themselves to keep those they care about afloat; often at great emotional and financial cost. In some instances, carers have had to give up their homes, sell cars, or drop out of University to deal with the cost of greed crisis to continue in their role as unpaid carers. Three out of five carers don't feel they are supported in ways that take their own access to education, employment, relationships, and health and wellbeing support into account and less than one in ten thought they were equally recognised, and their goals and aspirations respected.

The Carers Trust, a charity that works with carers organisations across all four of the UK home countries with a mission to improve services for unpaid carers, unambiguously states on the front page of its website that, *Unpaid carers in the UK have told us that they feel ignored by successive governments*. The Carers Trust provides administrative support services to the current All Party Parliamentary Group for Young Carers and Young Adult Carers. It notes that the present delays in accessing NHS services and treatment, coupled with growing demand for and pressure on social care services, has had a significant impact on both carers and the cared for. Evidence available prior to the pandemic showed that carers typically suffer with poorer health, and a higher proportion of carers than the average experience mental and physical health problems.

How should we here in the UK view the presence of such a large number of people employed, if not all remunerated, in the business of picking up the pieces and cleaning up the mess that the fragile disjoined structures of modern society and our own inherent frail humanity have created. Are the vast numbers of publicly, privately, and charitably funded people employed in the service of what could be interpreted as social failure demand, a statistic to be worn like a badge of honour, a medal to parade on the global stage that shows how much we care. Or is it a mark of shame and abject failure that we have encouraged and nurtured individual self-interested greed and indifference while allowing so much entirely predictable if not avoidable need to develop around us, to grow unchecked and unaddressed.

In June 2023, the Fabian Society, Britain's oldest and unashamedly socialist think tank, published a report called, *Support Guaranteed – The roadmap to a National Care Service*. The report was commissioned by UNISON and supported by the current Shadow Health and Care Secretary Wes Streeting, a Labour MP who reportedly received funding from the gambling industry. Ten free spins a day for unpaid carers and people working in care homes, you can see it now. The gist of the report produced by the Fabian Society is the creation of a national care service that would loosely mirror the National Health Service. The report suggests the core purpose of a social care service should be to give people the support to live the life they want, in the home they want, doing the things they want, with the people they want. The business case and rationale for spending more on social care services, is that better social care services will reduce pressure on the NHS. An initial and seemingly logical if untested optimistic argument. But as most impartial observers would agree, the creation of a public service often leads to and reveals greater levels of previously latent demand. Which in itself is not a bad thing, but it's something I think we all need to be aware of and much more upfront about. Why should a civilized society need to dress-up the creation of services designed with a humane purpose, behind an economically driven argument? It would be just as true to note that an increase in the provision of private services can drive up a nations GDP and its headline economic growth. But it's also a fact that such headline growth would be gained at the expense of the majority of citizens and to the detriment of the communities that make up the society we all live in. But what should take priority, our health or our wealth? It's a tragic reflection on our times that the present state of our political awareness and debate still seems such a long way from politicians being unashamed to say that something needs to be done for no other reason than because it's the right thing to do. Though I think the creation of a national care service would be a good thing, in my view it should only be viewed as a stepping-stone toward joining the NHS and Social Care together under one roof, an idea I propose as one of the recommendations at the end of this book.

Chapter 8: **Sybil**

"Oh yeah, life goes on, long after the thrill of living is gone."

John Mellencamp; Jack & Diane

Sybil will be a hundred years old this year. She and her beloved husband John had been one of our constant neighbours since Debbie and I first moved to Newlands Place over thirty-years ago. They lived in Newlands House, a blockish but charming old white farmhouse Johns parents had originally lived in and whose beautifully maintained Clematis laden sandstone walled garden Debbie and I looked out on from our bedroom window. An oasis of calm and contentment, beautifully and religiously maintained with a meticulously mown striped lawn, perfect blooming borders of every colour flanked by thriving voluminous shrubs, all centred around a small deep marble pond containing half a dozen Golden Tench, watched over by the life size statue of the Venus de Milo John had bought Sybil for her fortieth birthday, and a silver birch tree which brimmed with birds queuing up for a turn on one of the many feeding stations hanging from its lower branches. I always felt slightly guilty taking so much pleasure from looking over someone else's garden. As if I was stealing a benefit that someone else had worked to create.

John and Sybil were an unassuming part of Penrith folklore. They had met and courted each other as childhood sweethearts during the Second World War, only marrying once John had returned home from service. Sybil had wanted to marry John before he left for Europe, but he insisted he did not want to make her a widow at such a young age. On the one occasion John talked about his time in the armed forces, he told of how he had landed at a place called Normandy, then ended up in what he understatedly described as a *tight spot* near a place called Arnhem, and after that of being one of the first Allied Soldiers to drive over the River Rhine into Germany before meeting what he described as smiling but frighteningly battle toughened Russian troops in the German town of Osnabrück. He recalled how happy the Russian soldiers had been to meet the Allied forces and how each of the Russian soldiers' forearms, from the wrist to the elbow, were encased in the watches of the Nazis they had killed or found dead. John's final task in Europe was to help in the cleaning up of the concentration camp at Belsen, an act that I think shaped him profoundly. Though he loved to be around them and they around him, John said he would not choose to bring children into this world. His use of the phrase tight spot to describe Arnhem, a place widely associated with some of the most ferocious fighting of World War Two, was indicative of his humility.

John saw no glory in war and when he returned home to Penrith, he married Sybil and assumed his old job as a butcher at the local Co-Op. He retired from the same job at the age of sixty-five and loved nothing more than to use his free time to make things for other people out of scrap wood; birdhouses, plant containers, and even a felt lined coffin for our three-legged diabetic cat Mischief who died at the grand old age of twenty-three. He had started to make the coffin when Mischief first became ill some years earlier and had kept it in a safe place until it was needed. John is quite possibly the kindest and most thoughtful generous person I have ever known. On sunny afternoons he would relax with Sybil in the garden he was so proud of, with a good cigar and a glass of single malt whisky while Sybil nursed a Tia Maria. The annual evening at John and Sybils that we would be invited to each Christmas holiday, was always a life affirming occasion. Debbie and I often say to each other that if we become half the people John and Sybil were, we will be in a good place. Immaculately dressed and manicured, with straight black lines up the back of her stockings, Sybil would greet us at the door, and John, in crisp white shirt and tie, the same ones he wore under his overalls, would be the perfect host. Nothing was too much trouble. Debbie would eat as many of the sandwiches and savouries as she could, while I hoovered up the cream cakes and pastries until I was fit to burst. Everything was home made. Then after a few gins and tonics that had a great deal more gin than tonic, John would offer to walk us all of the ten yards to our front door to make sure we got home safely. Not only was he able to remain upright and compus mentis after drinking half a bottle of single malt, but he would also without fail, get up at six thirty the following morning to go and feed the few sheep he still kept in a field on the edge of town. Even the garden birds liked him. There was a male Blackbird who would regularly follow him with its head cocked curiously, expectantly, into the farmhouse kitchen in search of raisins, and a Robin that ate from his hand. "Be more John", or "what would John do", have become Debbie's go to phrases if I am being overly selfish, or unwelcoming. I'm doing my best, but the birds aren't eating out my hand yet.

On the 13th of February 2021, after a short spell of illness John passed away in the home he had lived in with Sybil for more than sixty years. Debbie and I were there as the brightly sparkling glint that had lived in his eyes for as long as we had known him, finally disappeared. He was ninety-six and up until two years previously had still been sawing up waste wood with a blunt old handsaw and cutting the grass with an incredibly bulky and very ancient steel lawnmower. One which was so heavy and hard to manoeuvre I refused to use it when he finally if begrudgingly allowed me to take over his grass-cutting duties, not before complaining he had just had the blades sharpened at a cost of sixty pounds. The doctor who had been called out to see John when he became ill, told him that if he didn't get to a hospital he would die. John hated hospitals and despite the doctors expletive laden impassioned admonitions, he remained adamant that he was going nowhere and would not leave Sybils side. When he passed away less than a week later, he and Sybil had been married for over seventy-five years. I have a photo of them smiling broadly on their seventy fifth wedding anniversary the previous November. In it they are standing holding onto each other in the dining room, as much if not more in love than they had ever been. A congratulatory card they received from the Queen standing proudly on the polished round mahogany table that held the middle of the room and which always had a fully laden vase of flowers on it.

Sybil's health deteriorated quickly after John's death. She couldn't cope physically in the home they had shared for so long. When John had been alive, he had helped her climb the steep stairs that led to the bathroom and to bed and was always on hand and willing to do whatever needed doing. John's death had unanchored Sybil, she was left utterly bereft of his presence, his unwavering attention, and his unfailing love. After a period during which her niece and we her neighbours tried valiantly to care for and keep an eye on Sybil, it became clear more structured expert support was needed. Carers from a local company were employed to look after her during the day while Debbie and I as her nearest neighbours became the first port of call for any emergencies that occurred through the night. There were numerous occasions where we would be woken by a phone-call from the helpline handlers because Sybil had triggered the out of hours emergency alarm and was shouting that she needed help. We would leap out of bed at one, two or three in the morning only to be asked upon our frenzied pyjama sporting arrival if we would care for a gin and tonic. Sybil was incredibly lonely and would at times become extremely confused and physically disoriented. As the frequency of her falls increased it became clear that other than granting her the wish she sincerely and repeatedly expressed to be with John, the only legal long-term solution, was for Sybil to be placed in a care home.

We visit her when we can, in the care home she didn't want to go in and still doesn't want to be in on the other side of town. Of course, it's not as often as either of us feel we should. But despite the rose-tinted vision the industrial era prophets of the twentieth century offered us of a prosperous automated world in which we would all have more leisure time, the demands of modern life still stand in the way of the things that really matter. The Croft Avenue Care Home is a substantial former vicarage, tucked away in a large and well-kept garden with plentiful parking and a welcoming if mildly ostentatious stone fountain outside the main entrance. The home overlooks the town of Penrith and the ever-changing fells of the Lake District to the south and west. Like so many of the repurposed buildings that have become care homes, the property walks an endless tightrope between maintaining its old-world charm while requiring its owners and residents to work around the very same qualities which are the source of its inherent unsuitability for the new purpose it serves. When Sybil was first admitted to the care home, she would ring from her mobile phone pleading for help to get her out of there. Her phone has been taken from her now. And each time we visited, she would implore us to take her back home to Newlands House. She just wanted to lie down in the bed in the back room and fade away to be with John. She has been in the care home over a year now and though she retains the sparkle in her eye and the wonderful smile that I think first attracted John to her, she is typically stoically if unhappily resigned to her situation. But she still does not want to be where she is. She misses the man she loved and lived for, more than I dare try to express here in words, and she misses the home they made their own which as well as being their sanctuary was an island of quiet contentment and kindness that offered solace and inspiration for any who visited its shores. At night Sybil wanders the corridors of the care home, sometimes straying into her fellow resident's rooms before perching innocently on the edge of their beds for a chat. During the day she sits whenever possible in the same seat and location in the main corridor just outside the communal living room, which she says is too noisy for her. From her vantage point she can see the front door of the care home and watches as people, visitors, staff, community nurses, delivery drivers, the postie, and occasionally a paramedic or a doctor, come and go. She often forgets what day it is and who has been to see her. And when we talk, I realise that all the facts and stories that made up the fabric of her life are slowly fading from memory. Watching someone who had kept a diary for decades and whose mind had always been razor sharp, decline so obviously, is gutwrenching. The blessed life with John that Sybil enjoyed makes her current situation all the less bearable.

The last time I went to see Sybil she was sat in her usual place. The designated meeting room of the care home was being refurbished so I pulled up a chair and sat with her in the corridor. The care home was gently melting down around us as we talked about her former neighbours, what the other families from Newlands Place have been up to, the coronation of King Charles the previous weekend, our shared love of holidaying in Scotland, her upcoming hundredth birthday, which I'm not sure she is that bothered about, and of course memories of John. As we talked a smartly dressed woman in perfectly ironed beige slacks and polished black shoes, with bright eyes, a perfect smile, and not a hair out of place, and whose upright poise suggested she had attended prep school or perhaps had military parents, walked past us several times. She circled purposefully seemingly unaware of those around her, from the main living room, through the adjoining small lounge, to the dining area and kitchen, then to the toilet and back into the corridor, before entering the living room again and repeating the ritual. All the time touching things for reassurance while quietly mumbling repeated words to herself over and over again as if trying to memorise a secret code of the utmost importance. Halfway through my catch-up with Sybil one of the residents appeared on a walking frame from the door of the main living room to my right, slowly but determinedly saying that she was in search of a care attendant. Apparently, the chap next to her in the living room was desperate for the toilet and needed help to get up before he soiled himself. At the same time an elderly lady began crying loudly for help to remove the clothing she had wet while trying to go the communal toilet downstairs just to my left. When I responded to her calls and stepped toward the toilet, the door was wide open on her indignity, I averted my gaze and confidently promised that I would go and find someone. After gaining the attention of one of the cleaning staff, a few minutes later a smiling care attendant arrived to help. She quietly and reassuringly dealt with the situation, calming the chaotic waters ready for the next shower of pebbles to be thrown into them by the mischievous unpitying gremlins of old age. As my mum used to tell me, being a good nurse and carer meant not making a drama out of a crisis.

I don't know how the people who work in care homes and nursing homes and who visit the elderly and infirm in their communities every day, do the jobs they do. They kept going through Covid, many of them losing people they had become attached to. People to whom their carer was sometimes the only person they would see from day to day. An April 2023 report entitled *Bailed out and burned out? The financial impact of COVID-19 on UK care homes* published by Coventry & Warwick Business School, researchers noted that little of the support for the care home sector was dedicated to supporting staff and their health and wellbeing. Rosalynn Carter who was herself recently diagnosed with Dementia, speaking to a Senate Committee in 2011 said, *"Our nation is in need of a fundamental shift in how it values and recognises caregivers especially in view of the rapidly escalating number of older adults, many of whom live with chronic illness and disabilities"*. The staff at The Croft Avenue Care Home seem like a good bunch, drawn from almost every continent, even some from the local area, they are always welcoming and good humoured. I'm normally offered a cup of tea or coffee on my arrival, no biscuits yet but that might come. They work for a relative pittance often at unsocial times doing a difficult and vital job that I don't think I could do. When I think of the reasonably well-paid jobs I have held over the years, jobs that required me to dress as if I were important, but during the course of which I can safely say I achieved little of lasting value or great significance, it leads me back to Einstein's proclamation that the world needs people of value rather than success. When I leave the care home after visiting Sybil, I always feel incredibly humble, and increasingly sad as the smile she gives me as I'm going, a smile that says, do you have to go, lingers in my memory.

Chapter 9: The outsourcing of old age

"Things they do look awful cold, I hope I die before I get old."

Roger Daltrey; My Generation

According to the Care Homes review website, the Croft Avenue Care Home charges its occupants, if they have the means, and the taxpayer if they haven't, around thirteen hundred pounds each week. A mere sixty-five thousand pounds every year for the privilege of clinging onto the remnants of their dignity if not their sanity and certainly not their solvency in the final years of their life. In the Summer of 2022, the Croft Care Home was sold by its previous owner HC-One to another smaller but emergingly ambitious and growing care home operator called LP Healthcare. Following the pandemic and no shortage of scandal in recent years, HC-One, whose strapline is The Kind Care Company, and whose stated values are to enable people to be their best selves and live their best lives, needed to offload some of its considerable assets to balance the books and so sold a few dozen of its very many care homes, of which Croft Avenue Care Home was one. In recent years HC-Ones less than transparent corporate practices, and some of its care homes and staff behaviours, have made many headlines for all the wrong reasons. HC-One Limited is a privately owned company whose corporate parenthood can be traced to that international bastion of financial transparency the Cayman Islands. Its two directors listed as of September 2022 are a Mr D A Smith, a former bean-counter from the corporately amoral global consultancy firm Price Waterhouse Coopers, and a Mr James Walter Tugendhat, whose brother Tom vied for leadership of the Conservative Party in 2022 and who is currently the UK Minister of State for Security.

The Cayman Islands offers its resident registered companies and their directors what it politely and benignly refers to as a tax neutral location, which I think means financially carefree and accountable to none. The jurisdiction proudly boasts of having no direct personal, corporate, or property tax liabilities. It's the dream company location for all aspiring and experienced neoliberals, tax-dodgers, and commercially irresponsible ne'er-do-wells who feel entitled to profit from the provision of publicly funded services in any part of the world with impunity and without the inconvenient intrusion of transparency or accountability. HC-One says it is registered in the Cayman Islands because its owners are transnational, which roughly translated means the provision of publicly funded social care for the widows of those who risked their all to defend Britain, has been outsourced to the enterprising and the amoral of any country who feel they can make a buck from it. I imagine Dave and James are if perhaps not being their best selves, indeed living their best lives and plan to do so for some time. But I don't think Sybil is. And I'm almost sure that few if any of the staff from HC-Ones care homes will ever get to holiday in the Caribbean.

    The proud new owners of Croft Avenue Care Home in Penrith are a much smaller outfit called LP Healthcare, a private limited company registered in Lancashire. LP Healthcare is run by two apparently incredibly busy directors who between them are listed on the Companies House website as holding thirty-two corporate appointments in a variety of private companies, some active some not. Whether or not Croft Avenue Care Home has just been tossed out of the clutches of a tax avoiding frying pan in the Caribbean and into the hungry corporate flames of a greed fuelled fire in Lytham, remains to be seen, but I think I know which way the wind will blow. Perhaps now that the website for Croft Care Home has been revamped, complete with an inviting reassuring photo of a smiling elderly gentleman confidently holding an iPad, a picture clearly taken in another location, maybe its new owners might consider lowering the position of the wall-mounted soap dispenser in the downstairs toilet to enable residents to actually reach it and wash their hands. A minor hygienic detail that years of Care Quality Commission inspections have not noticed, despite the commissions former chief executive Sir David Behan being a chair and former director of HC-One for three years between 2018 and 2021. Sir David, a lifelong dyed in the wool product of panjandrumic public sector thinking and who is now the chair of Health Education England, God help us, is clearly one of life's men of success rather than one of its value adders. I mean, who wants to talk about the basic hygiene requirements of care home residents when there are strategies and business plans to be written. It remains one of life's great sources of angst for me that the bureaucrats and well-paid administrators who have overseen, been part of, and in many ways contributed to the demise of Britain's publicly funded health and care services, now sit in taxpayer funded splendour around its top table.

Mum:

I love her and have nothing but respect, admiration, sometimes awe, for the sacrifices she made for me, but I don't visit my mum as often as I should. She lives in a sheltered housing complex in Doncaster run by the Railway Housing Association, a long-established registered charity based in Darlington that owns and rents out around fifteen hundred homes. My mum, who turned ninety in April, like Sybil, does not really see any purpose in remaining alive any longer. Mum had to leave and sell the first home she ever owned when it became clear a few years ago that she could no longer manage on her own. Her mind is alive if slightly fuzzy at times, but her body is letting her down. She has an electronic chair that enables her to sit and then stand back up and needs help to dress and clean. She is entirely dependent on the generosity of her friends from the local church and the hired help of carers and cleaners ably provided by the local branch of Age UK. Part of the underpaid overstretched army of value adding individuals appeasing our collective wilfully blind consciences and keeping Britain afloat. They do a wonderful job. The small pile of money mum made from the sale of her home on St Johns Road in Doncaster is quickly dwindling as the costs of covering the rent and the rising price of care eat relentlessly into it. The recent increases in energy prices and unbridled corporate opportunism are making further dents in what little she has left.

An extremely health-conscious former nurse and a woman who brought up three children on her own with little support from the state, it grieves me that mum will have to spend almost all her savings on staying alive as her quality of life, decreases, while we the public purse will support those who have taken little responsibility for their own health and wellbeing and our healthcare services stretch to breaking point as they deal with the self-imposed physical and mental wounds we have become so good at inflicting on ourselves. When mum first moved into the sheltered housing complex there was a fulltime warden available to help and assist residents. The office is now staffed on a part-time basis for a maximum of two days a week. If mum needs something, it's often easier for her to call me and for me to then email the housing associations head office. They are generally pretty responsive, but ultimately their business model relies on them minimising their outgoings and reducing their liabilities. The first line of the Railway Housing Associations somewhat uninspiring mission as outlined on their website is, *to make best use of our resources*, which in non-corporate real-speak equates to, *we will be financially tighter than a duck's arse*. The Railway Housing Association is a financially steady if culturally unexciting and traditionally risk averse charitable organisation. I imagine they have motivational posters on the walls of head office with phrases like, *Failure is not an option, as long as you don't take any risks,* and *Follow your dreams only if they are financially viable, and you have planned thoroughly for all eventualities.* My proposal to install video calling facilities into the home to allow mum to speak more frequently with me as well as enable other residents to speak with and see their families and friends more often, was politely dismissed. Such fancy new unproven technology clearly has no place in the waiting rooms of the afterlife run by the Railway Housing Association.

I wonder, are we all destined to be couped up in care homes owned by commercially amoral offshore corporations and opportunist entrepreneurs, or to exist as dwindling shadows of our former selves in sheltered housing complexes run by frugal penny-pinching charities. Surrounded by the dying and cruelly demented. Medicated up to our eyeballs while strangers on minimum wages wipe our genitals, and clean and feed us? Kept alive like vegetables on the turn in the bottom of the fridge, neither rotten enough to be composted or good enough to be an ingredient in the next meal, because society, we, can't face having the conversation we all know we need to have, about what we really want from our final years and what a good death, a dignified death, the death of our choosing, might look like. Suicide, though an incredible and tragic waste of life and potential, when undertaken consciously is ultimately a final act of control. Will the end of each of our unique and complex journeys, and the amazing minds evolution has gifted us to guide us on them, be to fizzle out as if discarded on the pavement like the butt end of a fine cigar, waiting helplessly to burn slowly to nothing or be mercifully extinguished in the next rain shower. Is that really a fitting end to the incredible marathon of our existence we will all have run? I sometimes think we treat animals more compassionately at the end of their lives than we do our loved ones and fellow human beings.

In March 2023 a UK based think tank called the Institute for Government, whose main funder is David Sainsbury's Gatsby Foundation, published a report, yes yet another feckin report!, called *Adult Social Care, short-term support and long-term stability*. The report noted that spending on adult social care in the UK had fallen in real terms for the five years from 2010 onwards and only just bounced back to its 2010 levels in 2020. In its report the think tank, which claims to be independent; are any of them? suggests that one of the solutions to the current social care crisis is to borrow an idea from Japan and increase the levels of funding available to the sector so as to guarantee private providers of social care services a return on their investments of between six and seven percent. I find the thought that my mum and Sybil's care costs could rise so as to guarantee institutional investors a risk-free return on their funds, frankly sickening. The authors conveniently forget to note that Japan's current government debt to GDP ratio stands at an eye watering 266%, the second highest in the world and significantly more than double that of the UK which is forecast to exceed 100% by 2028. Their capitalist solution is however mildly more realistic than the current Health Secretary Steven Barclay's latest blue-sky thinking, who in a recent interview with The Telegraph suggested that the cavalry coming over the hill for social care will arrive in the form of AI and Robots. Steve, as he prefers to be known, was interviewed by The Telegraph just before a planned visit to attend a G7 Summit in guess where? That's right, Japan. Japan has an even larger present and looming social care crisis than the UK and has been investing in the development of care robots for the elderly to help fill a projected shortfall of almost four hundred thousand care workers by 2025. The upshot of all this neoliberalism and eastern promise appears to be a future in which my mum and Sybil are either made bankrupt by private equity firms or in the case of my mum is killed by a rogue robot who gets tired of being told to say please and thank you. Japan may end up having a lot more to answer for than Godzilla and Pokémon.

The word euthanasia itself comes from the Greek words *eu* meaning good and *thanatos,* death. The practice of euthanasia allowed patients to experience a better death than the painful slow undignified one that might otherwise await them. If one day I find myself on a path I know and have been told will lead to a point where my health is taken from me, a point where I am no more than a debilitated hollowed-out sad reminder of myself to others, I'd like the right to choose how I face death on my terms.

Chapter 10: **Let's go Dutch!**

"The best way to predict the future is to create it."

Alan Kay

In the Spring of 2023, I spoke with Brendan Martin, the Managing Director for Britain and Ireland of a seemingly strangely named organisation called Buurtzorg. The world Buurtzorg, pronounced, Be-yurt-zog, is Dutch word meaning neighbourhood care. Brendan has a very amenable manner, and we had a refreshingly candid and informative conversation about healthcare which extended well beyond the time we had each allocated for our meeting. The conversation flowed, it felt natural, open, unguarded, and unstuffy. The discussion evolved organically to that point in all good conversations where the many elephants in the room were outed and placed unashamedly on display. I think it's an affirming and necessary point to reach in any meaningful dialogue, when people feel comfortable in the presence of the previously unspoken and when sacred cows and taboos can be mutually and honestly acknowledged, inspected, and understood if not always agreed upon. The reason the conversation with Brendan sticks in my mind is that it was the opposite of many of the conversations I have had and tried to have with members of the established health and care hierarchy. These can be so unnatural and so corporate and guarded that I sometimes wonder if I am speaking to a fellow human. And for every person within the existing hierarchy of the healthcare system who has agreed to speak with me, there are unfortunately, for them of course, many more that won't. Those that do, with the odd notable exception, are defensive. Conversation is conducted within strict parameters. The many elephants in the room go unaddressed, verbally danced around, seldom acknowledged, or dismissed as being beyond their remit or sphere of influence. I recall speaking with the head of communications for a large NHS body who told me it was inappropriate for me to ask for their personal opinion about the value of the work they do. As far as they were concerned the polished and professionally presented corporate view contained in the annual report was the only one that mattered. What a strange existence to have I thought. But such mentally hamstrung and organizationally reliant people are in the majority. They're not bad people, they're just doing what they need to do to get by. But Brendan positively oozed humanity, openness, and the practical grasp of reality that is born only from experience. I could see why he had been hired eight years ago by Buurtzorg's founder and CEO, Jos de Blok.

I came across Buurtzorg some years ago while I was employed in the NHS. At the time I was working on a project looking at the effectiveness and efficiency of community nursing services and how they interacted with local authority run social care services. The snippets of information I gleaned about Buurtzorg and what I was told they were achieving in Holland had seemed too good to be true. But I've continued to hear their name in meetings and at conferences and I've been curious about them ever since. Prior to founding Buurtzorg, Jos de Blok was an innovation manager for a large healthcare provider in the Netherlands. A position in which he became increasingly frustrated as he found he was prevented at almost every turn from actually introducing or implementing any innovations. As someone who held the title of Telehealth Manager in an NHS Trust and who was also prevented at every turn from introducing Telehealth, it's a position I can empathise with. The presence of innovation directors, managers, and departments in public services is a surrogate for the presence of innovation itself. The default decision-making mode of risk-averse healthcare directors and senior managers, is no. The NHS has become as adept at the art of finding reasons why things should not be done as it has at dressing up words and intentions as meaningful action.

Buurtzorg started life around a kitchen table in the Netherlands over sixteen years ago and has since become internationally known and respected in its field. From humble beginnings the company has grown to employ fifteen thousand people, of which the vast majority, around nine thousand, are nurses, the value adders. The organisation provides community nursing and home care services through a largely autonomous and independently functioning network of over nine hundred self-managed teams. Each team is no larger than twelve people to enable quick decision-making and facilitate swift action. These seemingly small self-managed teams are trusted and enabled to collaboratively schedule and prioritise their own activities and arrange their own workloads. Teams conduct their own recruitment and are expected and allowed to figure out and adopt the best approaches to meet the individual needs of their clients. While they have great freedom, each team and team member are also expected to abide by a set of established ground rules which prevent the outbreak of organisational anarchy and ensure focus is maintained on each team's ultimate purpose, meeting the needs of their service users and patients. Professionals are trusted to do the jobs they were trained in and are continually developed to do, and they are encouraged to build and share the knowledge and best practice they gain from practical experience in the field. Doing what works in the interest and context of each individual service user is valued over simply doing what might be expected to be done. When faced with issues, situations and challenges that require extra or specialist support, the teams and the staff working in them can call on an extensive network of regional coaches, ask for help from other teams, or approach head office if necessary.

The role of the back-office functions in Buurtzorg is recognised as existing to serve the professionals, to support and enable the teams and individuals in the field to provide maximum value to service users. The back office also produces the performance data needed to feed the public sector beast of performance management. It does so by using custom made user-friendly technology which automatically gathers and collates the information and data that government departments, funding bodies, and ministers need. It's noteworthy that Buurtzorg has been so successful in what it does that it has had an impact on how the regulatory regime operates and what it now looks for in terms of assurance. In short, practice in the Netherlands is informing policy and oversight, the public sector tail of performance measurement is finally being wagged, by the dog. The simplifying of processes and liberating of frontline staff from the time-consuming tedium of generating reports every time they do something, is seen as key to the businesses' success. It allows the clinical and compassionate expertise within the organisation to be deployed in the service of clients rather than being expended keeping overbearing micro-managing departmental heads and directors happy.

Brendan acknowledges that Buurtzorg's use of technology as an enabler within the business is absolutely crucial to its continued success. The organisation created its own technology platform which is tailored around the purpose of the business and the people it exists to serve. Buurtzorg is structured around the logical but oft ignored principle that if you design services and systems to optimise the value you can provide to the people you serve, then you will be able to meet their needs more effectively and efficiently, for their benefit and the public purses. As well as developing its own technology platform, Buurtzorg created an intranet to enable the sharing of information and simplify communication. The platform incorporates elements of social media and teams are encouraged to communicate frequently with each other and share ideas and challenges. The platform also serves as a bulletin board for keynote messages or alerts that need speedy or regular universal and consistent distribution across the entire organisation.

Brendan shares his view that what we appear to have done with healthcare is to conflate what is an essentially simple purpose, the provision of health and care services to people who need them, with unnecessarily complex business processes. What makes Buurtzorg so effective and efficient is the constancy of purpose it maintains which drives actions and decisions at the individual, team, and organisational levels. Buurtzorg appears to have mastered the art of keeping the regulators and bureaucrats happy while minimizing the disruption to and use of its clinical resources.

Buurtzorg has adopted the principles of servant leadership and turned the traditional hierarchical top-down non-trusting model of healthcare management on its head. In doing so it has managed to provide significant savings to the public purse while simultaneously achieving previously unattainably high satisfaction ratings and improved health outcomes for its service users. Buurtzorg's employees are consistently rated as one of the most satisfied workforces in Holland. The organisations record on recruitment and retention would be the envy of every health and care provider in the UK. Buurtzorg, and the way it works, and by all accounts it works incredibly well, is living proof that health and care services don't simply need more money thrown at them to increase their capacity or be effective. More often than not, they require new thinking and approaches.

Chapter 11: Can Social Work, work?

"The true measure of a society can be found in how it treats its most vulnerable members."

Mahatma Gandhi

There is a gut-felt logic to the sentiment expressed in the phrase above attributed to Gandhi. It acknowledges the existence of society and as such stands in stark contrast to Thatcher's arrogant pronouncement that there was no such thing. But I wonder if there are two things missing from it, perhaps an elongated version that never made it into the archives. Something along the lines of, the true measure of a society can be found in how it holds itself accountable for understanding the plight of and then helping its most vulnerable, followed by a definition of society. Not quite as catchy I know. But if improvement begins with understanding, then job number one has to be to understand how people in society become vulnerable and job number two to define what we mean by society. It is more than two and a half centuries since the start of the economic explosion of the industrial revolution, and over seventy-five years since the people of Britain were promised a country fit for heroes, yet the underlying factors that have perpetuated the conditions that create vulnerability in our society remain neither widely addressed nor understood. In relation to defining society, it's my guess Gandhi was referring to the royal we, you and I, not government. If a neighbour needs help in the here and now I think most people give it without needing an official policy statement from their local authority. Good government creates the conditions in which we can flourish, and a caring society emerges from this.

I have mixed views on the value of social work and the role and effectiveness of social workers. The man from social services who came to see my mum after dad left us in the lurch was a total waste of feckin space, he got promoted. My sister Alison was spectacularly failed by her social worker. It was the kindness of strangers and the commercial ambition of a skilled entrepreneur that lifted me from homeless poverty and social exclusion. Not the efforts of the state, my probation officer, the school welfare officer, the careers service, the job centre, or the local council. The taxpayer funded do-gooder's have done little good for my family. The more recent experiences I had with them in relation to providing support for Ella, the wonderful Ukrainian refugee we hosted in 2022, did nothing to alter my perceptions.

Effective social work, where I'm sure it does exist, strikes me as akin to what I always imagined good policing to be, preventative and unobvious. Only paid attention to when things go horribly wrong but largely ignored when things are running smoothly. We may be forgiven for forgetting all the names of those who have been fatally failed, but nearly all of us recognise their faces and feel a shudder of disbelief and anger when we see them. Leiland-James Corkhill, Victoria Climbie, Peter Connelly (Baby P), Star Hobson, and Arthur Labinjo-Hughes, to name but a few. I can't help thinking sometimes if the anger we feel and that is fuelled by the media seeking someone and something to blame, anything other than neoliberalism of course, is misplaced. Are we actually angry with ourselves for letting our own collective insouciance create the conditions in which such tragedies occur? All of us are after all, part of our own communities.

The *Truth About Social Work* is a very readable short book. Published under the pseudonym of the Social Work Tutor in 2017, if at times a touch maudlin it is an insightful collection of real-life stories from people on the frontline of social work. I tried to speak with at least one practising social worker while researching this book, but each time I came close to having a meaningful conversation, they refused to get involved for fear of contravening their employer's guidance on communicating and getting into trouble for saying something politically unacceptable. One stated that as an employee of the state they did not feel it would be right for them to share their views. Faced with such responses one has to ask if it was in the defence of free speech, democracy, and a better future that millions of people paid the ultimate price? Maybe it's a good thing the fallen are not here to see the fragile acquiescent society they bought in exchange for their lives. When did we become so pusillanimous and cowed that we became afraid to speak our truths? The control over the expressing of personal views that public sector communications departments seem to exercise over employees, should be an affront to us all in a democratic society. And I regret not being able to have an in-depth conversation with a social worker because I get the sense, they are a profession that would have a lot to say and be able to bring a great deal of value and knowledge to the table in relation to a book about the nation's health and wellbeing. Undeterred, I approached Social Work England, the specialist regulator of social work and of the hundred thousand plus social workers in England since December 2019. Their response, at the eighth time of trying, was to thank me for my questions before telling me that in their role as regulator they would not be able to comment and pointing me to their latest annual report.

The annual *State of the Nation 2023* report Social Work England directed me to is little more than a bland celebration of social work including the obligatory patronising thank you to the profession, which I'm sure was a great comfort to all those social workers struggling with their utility bills. In it, the regulator of social work perhaps unsurprisingly, talks much less about the state of the nation, than the importance of social work, social workers, and of course the regulator itself and its vital role. It's a classically unquestioning, unashamedly self-serving document, which reinforces the significance and proficiency of the organisation publishing it while tacitly accepting the horrendous conditions that are creating the demand it is facing. There was a selection of carefully chosen case-studies, an assurance to all and sundry that everyone is doing a sterling job, pleasingly wrapped up in platitudinous polite language and tied neatly with ribbons and bows of appealing graphics and staged photos. I've seen it all before. Such reports are more striking for what they omit. Not a single reference to the growth and prevalence of food banks and no use of the word debt, or gambling. But it's an ill wind that blows nobody any good and for Social Work England this bounty can be found in the ten million pounds it spends on its own salary costs.

I also approached the British Association of Social Workers for an interview about the work they do and to get their take on the challenges facing them and their members. BASW represent social work and social workers rather like the RCN (Royal College of Nurses) represents the nursing profession and its members. They wished me well with my book before saying they felt unable to comment. It's a frustratingly familiarly cautious British response and a little disappointing from an organisation that says it is the independent voice of social work in the UK. However, like Social Work England, the BASW is doing alright thank you, spending approx. eighty five percent, fourteen and a half million pounds of its turnover on staff costs in 2022. So, perhaps it is genuine in its claim to be committed to building a better society, at least for its directors and employees. Cash from chaos has morphed into much more than Malcolm McLaren's mantra. What tamed toothless self-serving servile beasts our public services have become.

The 2021 census for England and Wales showed that poverty had increased. The 2022 children in need census revealed that the number of referrals to social work from schools was the highest since recording began in 2014. Data from the department of education shows over four hundred thousand children in the UK are recognised as living in need. The UK based charity Save the Children, whose work, rather like the Trussell Trust, was previously focused on the so-called poorer countries of the world, says that over four million children in the UK are thought to be living in poverty. I recall the evenings I would go with my mum as she knocked on doors in the neighbourhood collecting donations for Save the Children. She must have looked like a modern-day female Fagan using her smiling freckled child accomplice to solicit money from unsuspecting householders who were about to sit down at the tea table. We were by any measure as poor as church mice and existed as a family on an amount that was significantly under what was then referred to officially as the breadline income, now more widely known as the poverty threshold. My mum never visited a food bank, there were none. My sisters and I may have been raised in second-hand clothes, but we never went hungry. Mum's ability to bake and make something tasty from cheap ingredients and the scraps from the butchers was uncanny. It blows my mind that almost fifty years after I was a child growing up in a poor family, there are now families across Britain, Great Britain, whose finances are so stretched they cannot afford to eat properly. The nourishment of millions reliant on the charitable acts of others. That is seriously fucked up by any measure, a phrase I would like to have seen in Social Work England's *State of the Nation 2023* report. Perhaps next time.

Save the Children was originally set-up in 1919 by two sisters as part of the Fight the Famine movement which sought to address the impact on children of the horrific food shortages that plagued Europe at the end of the second world war. The organisation was not envisaged to be needed once this problem had been addressed, but over a hundred years later it is still here and more active in the UK and across the world than ever. The revised vision on the Save the Children website states their mission as making sure that children are safe healthy and learning, in the UK and around the world. My mum and I hustled our neighbours for contributions to feed and care for less fortunate children in other countries. I think it would have broken my Mum's heart to think that in the not-too-distant future, children in the UK would need their services as much as those abroad.

Against this context it seems that social work to a much greater degree than social care, and a lot like the NHS, is predominantly a failure demand service. The hapless cleaning-up contractor tasked with tidying up the complex shitty messes created by our own and capitalisms collective failings, our ignorance, our curiosity, our inescapable ageing, and infirmity, and sometimes our downright bad luck. There but by the randomness of the universe go we. I've lost friends of all ages, people I grew up and went to school with and some I shared a squat with, to drugs, alcohol, suicide, and happenstance. The finger of fate is a very fickle fucker. But everyone's needs, however they manifest or may have arisen, are thrown into the same social care bucket to be dealt with. Whether your woes were generated by an excess of tobacco and alcohol that circumstance, preference, and then addiction have led you to consume and on which you paid generous amounts of tax. Or you achieved your penury, marriage breakdown, and subsequent mental misery by indulging in too much weed and sniffing too much cocaine, on which you paid no tax but by whose sale someone still got very wealthy, you will be helped under the same taxpayer funded umbrella. Social workers, keeping busy on behalf of Columbian farmers and the Ndrangheta, and proudly sponsored by the Great British Public in partnership with Tennent's Super Strength and Imperial Tobacco.

Social work in the UK, like most of the services run by local authorities, is a notoriously uncoordinated affair whose disjoined structures and inconsistent methods are a perfectly incongruent mismatch with its vital task of picking up the human casualties created by a fragmented, necessarily selfish, and time-poor society. My perception of social workers gained from the limited experience I have had with them over the years, ranges from the utterly feckless and completely unemployable elsewhere, to a few grounded heroes who do their best to make a difference in incredibly difficult and complex circumstances. At its unfairly demanding best, social care is that passionate driven person relentlessly scooping the excess water of fate and enterprises externalities, the legal and the not, from the hull of a battered leaking rowing boat with nothing more than a plastic cup as the boat is tossed and thrown on the waves of a thundering ocean storm. At its bureaucratic worst, it is the well-dressed captain of a passing cruise liner who offers no more than directions to the nearest safe harbour after telling those in the sinking boat that it wouldn't be safe to drop the cruise liners ladders or launch their lifeboats to help them in such choppy waters. That would contravene the companies risk policies and interfere with the estimated target time of arrival at their next destination.

Unlike social care workers, the term social worker is a protected title. Is it an offence under UK law for a person to use the title of social worker unless they are registered with Social Work England or its corresponding bodies in the home countries. Social workers in England and Wales are primarily employed by the local authorities, in Scotland by social work departments and by health and social care trusts in Northern Ireland. Social workers until recently had to have a degree in social work prior to embarking on their chosen career, however in response to the recruitment and retention challenges facing every sector, the UK Government is investing fifty million pounds a year for the next two years in recruiting, training, and developing more child and family social workers. Applicants can now get experience on the job and qualify as a fully-fledged Social Worker via a Level 6 Degree Apprenticeship. Fancy that eh, the awarding of a qualification based upon real life experience, it almost feels logical doesn't it. Whatever next!

The number of qualified social workers in the UK is thought to have grown by around ten percent from just over one hundred and eleven thousand in 2012 to over a hundred and twenty-two thousand in 2022. Of these just over one hundred thousand are presently registered to practice. In summer 2018 the Guardian ran an article suggesting Social Work was the fastest-growing profession in the world. The short article which trumpeted the benefits of social work and social workers was one of a number written for The Guardian by Dr Rory Truell, then and still secretary-general of the International Federation of Social Workers. The IFSW is a rapidly growing membership organisation purporting to represent the interests of over a hundred and forty nationally based social work bodies across the globe, including the British Association of Social Workers, BASW.

The stated purpose of the IFSW as outlined on its website is for it and its members to strive for social justice, human rights, and inclusive, sustainable development through the promotion of social work best practice and engagement in international cooperation. It's a touch woolly for me but I think it translates roughly into, let's learn from each other so we can become more effective and efficient in our continuing efforts to pick up the pieces and clean up the mess created by the self-interest and greed inherent within the neoliberal experiment.

The overriding if only academically informed impression I have of why people are drawn to social work is that they see and acknowledge other people that need help in a world in which our humanity is not always sacrosanct. Then once in the system I imagine they find that the balance of the work is less about helping people than they had envisaged. Social work appears to me as a bridge of conscience straddling the chasm between what the world looks like for many in reality and how the middle class think it should look. The existence of social workers has always struck me as a conundrum. I'm still wondering whether the global growth of a publicly funded profession committed to helping dig people out of whatever shit has been thrown over them is a good thing. I think the thing that perturbs me is that a great deal of the shit that lands on people is a direct result of government policies which are created by politicians and corporate lobbyists who have no desire to understand or in most cases even engage in the process of consequential thinking in relation to their decisions. The existence of a large and increasing social work sector in a developed economy seems like a subtler more acceptable variation on our nations need for a minister of suicide. It feels a lot like the giving of toilet paper to people suffering with entirely predictable bouts of diarrhoea brought on by the continued consumption of unfit food. As urgently practical as the cries for more and nicer and thicker toilet paper might be, I can't help thinking it kind of misses the point.

PART III:

The NHS

Chapter 12: **What is the purpose of the NHS?**

"The NHS is there to improve our health and wellbeing, supporting us to keep mentally and physically well, to get better when we are ill, and when we cannot fully recover, to stay as well as we can to the end of our lives..."

The NHS Constitution

You may think that asking what the purpose of the NHS is, is so obvious a question to ask that it's foolish, perhaps not even worthy of thoughtful consideration. My challenge to you if you are curious about the validity of my question is this, gather two or three people, perhaps including yourself into any quiet setting, with their consent of course! And then in an unscripted exercise ask each person to succinctly summarize in note form what they think the broad purpose of the National Health Service is, in one or two sentences on a piece of paper without consulting each other. For the record, I have tried this on numerous occasions, and I guarantee you will not get a uniform answer or complete agreement from any two people. In fact, the conversation can become so charged, lengthy, and convoluted, that participants often decide the issue is too complex to contemplate any further. The exercise will start simply enough with comments that mirror the same stated purpose outlined in the NHS Constitution; it's there to heal people when they get ill, or it's there to help people with their physical and mental needs, or it's there to keep the nation healthy. Then someone will light the blue touch paper by saying something along the following lines, should the NHS deal with the needs of people who don't look after their own health? It's a valid question. Though most if not all our public services were originally created and have subsequently developed without a clear purpose, healthcare services remain by far the most difficult to codify because the nature of our individual wellness is not objective.

Is the purpose of a nation's publicly funded health service to pick up the pieces after someone's private cosmetic surgery has gone wrong, is it to repair the mouths of the image conscious celebrity obsessed Instagram generation after their trip to Turkey to obtain the perfect smile and bleached straightened teeth, has not gone to plan? Or is it to fix the botched surgical work of a private clinician offering legitimate non-urgent services to people who don't want to stay on the NHS waiting list for a year? Is it to save the life of the experienced mountaineer who fell three hundred feet down the side of a Lakeland fell in the middle of winter? Is it to save the life of the inexperienced over-confident tourist who also fell down the side of the same Lakeland Fell in August, while wearing flipflops, shorts and a summer vest? Is it to repair the broken heads and stitch the skin of the youngsters who drank too much and fell from an overcrowded car, or to mend the mind of the driver who now knows they should have said no. Is it to save the life of a drink or drug driver who crashed the car they stole into a wall? Is it to save the life of the young mother they hit just before they crashed? Is it to safely deliver the new-born at home or on maternity wards? Is it to provide safe and accessible pregnancy termination services? Is it to supply contraceptives to the sexually active young without their parent's consent? Is it to extract the foreign objects unwittingly inserted too far into an orifice by the curious or the kinky? Is it to provide expensive intensive and complex surgery and organ transplants to tax dodgers or the families and loved ones of tax exiles? Is it to help free the minds of those enmeshed in an ever-tightening net of gambling addiction? Is it to offer counselling and liver transplants to the alcohol dependent? Is it to sign a form that legitimizes someone's time off work? Is it to help those addicted to tobacco? Is it to deal with the rising tide of diabetes that is accompanying our ever-increasing levels of obesity? Is it to provide mental health support to the employees of companies who push their workers too hard in pursuit of targets and profit for their shareholders? Is it to prop-up the battered self-esteem of the people in poverty who cannot buy the things they are told they need to make them happy, those who feel they aren't worth it because they can't afford it, who aren't accepted, who aren't part of one of the branded tribes of our time that give meaning to their members. Is it to mend the middle-aged motorcyclist who is sure the bend wasn't that severe the last time they rode it when they were 23 years old. Is it to replace the knees and hips of ageing hill walkers who were advised by their GP to get outdoors and keep active? Is it to rehabilitate those injured in combat? Is it to massage the torn muscles of aspiring amateur athletes or resuscitate over-enthusiastic park runners? Is it to solve the suicidal ideations of a struggling foreign student? Is it to pump the stomachs and bandage the wrists of those suffering with severe and enduring PTSD? Is it to sew back on the severed digits of mechanics, engineers, and craftspeople who are injured in the process of making and manufacturing goods for sale? Is it to deal with the after-effects of exposure to asbestos? Is it to talk to the elderly who have lost their loved ones, or the lonely who are in despair? Is it to fix and repair football hooligans in time for their next fight? Is it to help refugees fleeing from other nations? Is it to send clinicians and medics to prop-up the under resourced and often non-existent healthcare services of Third World countries to stop the spread of the next pandemic? Is it to keep the terminally ill alive on life-support machines until all hope and resources are exhausted? Is it to pick up and transport the bodies of the dead, soothe the physical burns, and tend to the emotional scars of the wounded after a tower block has been wrapped in cheap flammable cladding? Is it to stop bad things happening to people before they occur, or is it to pick up the pieces of the inevitable messes we all collectively and individually make, after we have made them?

We here in the UK, and certainly people of my generation and younger, have simply accepted the presence of a National Health Service as a given in our lives for as long as I can recall. As the NHS celebrates its 75th anniversary, it feels like high time we had a meaningful, informed, and intelligent conversation in this country about the purpose and aims of the National Health Service. If improvement does begin with understanding, then the start of any meaningful discussion or debate about the purpose of the NHS must begin by establishing what its remit is, who its customers are, whose needs does it serve, and whose needs should it serve.

The NHS has a constitution, but does anyone know what that means and how it translates into practice? My wife and 99% of the people I know have never read the NHS constitution. And nobody I know has ever come away from an appointment with their local GP saying, my, that was a seamless patient centric experience in which I was treated with compassion, respect, and dignity, and I feel the values embodied in the NHS constitution were not only deeply understood and lived by all the staff, but they were clearly embedded in every aspect of the service user experience.

So what? Well, in simplistic organisational terms, not having a clear purpose is a poor starting point for a conversation about improvement in any organisation. The practices, structures, and methods of all public sector services should of course adapt and evolve in response to changes in the wider operating environment and conditions in society, but their purpose, if not set in stone, should be relatively constant.

Without a shared and widely understood sense of purpose, the question, *"can we fix it"*, will always remain essentially meaningless, it is an overly simplistic approach that takes no account of the context, the system and wider society that the organisation sits within. If you can't define the purpose then you can't answer the question, what does good look like, and if you can't answer that question, you are destined to flounder in the foothills forever because you never identified the mountain you should have focused on climbing. The questions serious journalists need to start asking are not, *"Can the NHS be Fixed"*, or *"Can the NHS be made Fit for the Future"* but, can a future and a society be created in which a national health service works.

Chapter 13: **What is the NHS?**

"The NHS is the nation's insurance policy. You might never need it, but you know it will be there when you do. The NHS is peace of mind."

Roy Lilley

We are told the NHS is a particularly British thing, something to rouse pride and patriotism within us, we are told it is a wonderful thing, stirring up feelings that we are blessed that we have it, and we are told it is a precious thing, worthy of heated protective debate and deserving of defence. it is THE sacred cow of the UK's public services, possibly the UK itself, a treasure we must protect from all who would do it harm. A survey by the King's Fund in Autumn 2017 showed that almost four out of five people in the UK thought the NHS was crucial to British Society and felt we must do everything we can to maintain it. The NHS is often cited as the UK's greatest, most remarkable, politically audacious, and apposite postwar achievement. Nye Bevan, the wily Welsh Labour politician widely attributed with bringing the NHS into being is credited with saying that *"the NHS will survive as long as there's folk left with the faith to fight for it"*, a phrase best repeated with a honeyed Welsh lilt for best effect. But I'm sure that Nye did not know what his NHS would become and the way the world it exists within would change around it; how could he, the internet, smartphone gambling apps, the rise of inequality and the rearing of poverty's ugly head, the growth of personal debt, online bullying, the inexorable rise of obesity and our path to unimagined levels of consumerism were all unknowns. But behind the white and blue that makes up the NHS banner, lies one of the best examples of inconsistent management and public sector incompetence in history, perhaps second only to the Church, big on the promise, not so consistent on the customer experience.

But despite the NHS being revered as Britain's most cherished asset by its citizens if not always by its government, the nation's best loved brand, an institution most UK citizens are loudly, unashamedly, and incredibly proud of, the NHS is in fact a largely fictional entity. The National Health Service does not exist in either the way it is widely perceived, represented in the media, or structured in reality. The UK's claim to possess a functioning National Health Service is only slightly more valid than Lapland's claim upon Santa. For those who still believe in Father Christmas, stop reading now. For everyone else, let me explain...

Historians of the NHS will tell you it did not appear fully formed and ready to serve at its birth in 1948. The reality is that what we now refer to as a National Health Service was initially created by scooping up the host of health and care services, Private GP Practices, Dentists, Opticians, Specialists, District Hospitals, and smaller Community Hospitals, sometimes referred to as Cottage Hospitals, that already existed in the UK, and which had been disparate and broadly independent up to that point, and then placing these under a single banner. Contracts were agreed, not without much friction and resistance, more doctors and nurses were trained and recruited, and the rest as they say, is history. The NHS was, and in many respects remains, a work in progress and an aspiration, one I believe worth fighting for.

At its onset there was no clear blueprint for the organisation, what's its purpose was, and what good would look like. Some of the projects initial opponents who felt it would place an unmanageable burden on the country's finances, were allegedly eventually swayed by the seemingly semi-logical argument that once the NHS had succeeded in improving the populations health, the need for its services would decline drastically and the costs of running it would reduce. Now there is a thought.

The NHS was officially born on 05th July 1948. For the first time in the UK, dentists, doctors, nurses, opticians, pharmacists, and their allied health professions came together under the umbrella of a National Health Service. Its first patient was a 13yr old girl called Sylvia Diggory who was treated for a kidney condition in what was then called Park Hospital in Davyhulme, Manchester. Sylvia was visited in her hospital bed that day by Aneurin Bevan who is said to have asked her if she understood the significance of the occasion and told her it was a milestone in history and the most civilized step any country had ever taken. Damn right!

On that same day, a group of newly created health boards took control of the running and management of over 90% of the 3,000 (three thousand) hospitals in the UK at that time. These newly nationalized hospitals had previously been run by a mix of charities and local authorities. On the day of the NHSs launch approx. 94% of the public had been registered with the nation's new national health service. Its budget for the first year of operation was £437 Million, around £18 Billion in 2023 terms.

In his message to the medical profession published in the British Medical Journal on July 03rd 1948, the Health Minister Aneurin Bevan said; *on July 05th we start together, the new National Health Service. It has not had an altogether trouble-free gestation! There have been understandable anxieties, inevitable in so great and novel an undertaking. Nor will there be overnight any miraculous removal of our more serious shortages of nurses and others and of modern replanned buildings and equipment. But the sooner we start, the sooner we can try together to see to these things and to secure the improvements we all want…In this comprehensive scheme – quite the most ambitious adventure in the care of national health that any country has seen – it will inevitably be you, and the other professionals with you, on whom everything depends. My job is to give you all the facilities, resources and help I can, and then to leave you alone as professional men and women to use your skill and judgement without hindrance. Let us try to develop that partnership from now on.*

That was over 75 years ago, and though we talk endlessly about the NHS here in the UK, the truth is that Britain still doesn't have a truly National Health Service, at least not in the simple functional way that most of us think of it. It's not national in that it's not nationally consistent. It's not focused on health and prevention but on illness and treatment. Nor is it truly a service. To be a service would mean it was designed around the needs of its customers, its service users. Our beloved NHS remains a patchwork quilt of organisations and entities that have been loosely stitched together and who provide a varying range of inconsistent services of mixed levels of quality from numerous locations across the UK. The supply chains of most large commercial organisations are more tightly integrated with each other's operational and technological systems than the various component parts of the NHS. My vet could access my diabetic cat's medical history fifteen years ago with more seamless ease and from more locations than I or my GP can presently access my medical records. Our pets may not share our concerns about data protection, but most of us would prioritise our own healthcare needs above those of our furry companions.

The NHS is not the same in each area of the UK in the way that a private sector franchise or tightly managed global business might be. There is no effective central leadership or management function that is entirely focused on ensuring the customers and shareholders of the NHS, namely its patients, and its employees, will encounter and benefit from the same standards and consistent experience wherever they interact with the service. There is no universally agreed vision of the NHSs purpose, and no central shared sense of what good could and should, actually look like. The UK's best loved brand is also its least consistently managed and run.

Yes, there is that ubiquitous white and blue logo, pantone 300 to be precise, and yes, people have access, in varying degrees, to a publicly funded health service that is available across the UK in different formats and from a varied range of premises, depending on where you are, what you are seeking, and when and where you access it. But it's not a nationally consistent service, in fact it is anything but. More importantly, and more worryingly, its current design and structure, which are largely accidents of history, ensure that in its present state, it can only ever be inconsistent and highly variable. Behind the NHS's simple comforting omnipresent logo, and the even more simplistic protestations of the many people from all walks of life who sing its praises, sometimes with noble intent, often with selfish self-interest and self-promotion at heart, sits a chaotically fragmented service that largely relies on the goodwill of its patient facing staff to function, despite the chaos and ineptitude routinely imposed on them from above.

When I entered the ranks of the NHS in January 2012, I made the mistake of believing I was joining the able, hearty, and highly motivated crew of a slick well-oiled, and well-led ship. Part of a globally revered fleet bound on an infinite yet purposeful quest across the restless fickle and sometimes cruel oceans of human health and wellbeing. A vessel guided on its path by an unwavering moral compass focused on an unshifting and brilliantly bright North Star. I and many others, now laugh at my naivety, but at the time I genuinely believed that if any public service would have its purpose, its processes and its procedures nailed firmly down, it would be Britain's NHS. After all I figured, there can be no more important or edifying business to be in than that of helping the ill, saving lives, and preserving health in body and mind. I also assumed that any institution that had been around for almost sixty-five years at that point would know its arse from its elbow. I couldn't have been more wrong.

I've never been the sharpest knife in the drawer. But it quickly became clear to even me that the nation's health service was not a single well-fleet. It was and remains a loosely organized collective of disparate boats, whose many over-confident ill-informed captains are all too often steering their vessels in opposite and sometimes conflicting directions. There are one or two prestige, reasonably well-led, and decently equipped yachts in amongst the flotilla, there are also many more with rusting hulls and holes beneath the waterline, and then there are all things in-between. But they are all in trouble to varying degrees. As I write this there is not one ship, one NHS Trust, amongst the fleet from which its crew are not jumping overboard at a faster rate than they can be recruited and replaced. As of June 2023, there are more than a hundred and ten thousand vacancies for NHS staff, a staggering figure which has risen consistently over the last ten years. It is a crying shame and a national disgrace that what should be the greatest vocation of our times has become such an unattractive career choice that the very future of the NHS is now at stake.

So, I hear you ask, what does this dysfunctional fleet of organisational ships look like as it lurches sporadically from crisis to crisis atop the rolling waves and ever shifting tidal currents of the public sector sea? In England there are presently two hundred and fifteen different NHS Trusts providing a range of community and acute hospital-based services sometimes called secondary services, these include accident and emergency departments, urgent care centres, minor injuries units, community nursing services, mental health, learning disabilities, and children's services, and there are a number of specialist hospital centres, sometimes called tertiary services that house expertise in fields such as oncology, paediatrics, and cardiology. Then there are fourteen different ambulance services operating across the UK, ten in England and one for each of the home countries, Northern Ireland, Scotland, and Wales. The home countries also have their own NHS structures in place which differ from England. Like the various NHS Trusts, each of the regional ambulance services has its own ways of working and its own versions of technology, a great deal of which doesn't link effectively with anyone else's technology. And then on the frontline of the NHS, there are the nine thousand or so

GP Practices, collectively known as Primary Care, who provide the first port of call for the majority of people seeking help with their health. They are the front door through which many of us enter the health and care system and from where we are then referred to other services. Then there are the Out of Hours Primary Care Services, which in most areas are run by a separate entity, and of course the NHS 111 service. There are also numerous private providers offering a range of physical and mental health services who are funded through the NHS to provide both specialist and generalist services and who pick up the slack when the NHS is struggling.

All these are in turn surrounded and overseen by an array of loose local partnerships such as GP Federations, and nebulous often opaque bodies such as the forty-two newly created Integrated Care Systems, overseen by Integrated Care Boards, whose existence was made statutory in 2022. Before these came partnerships known as Sustainability and Transformation Plan areas, which were previously called Clinical Commissioning Groups, who were supported by Commissioning Support Units and Clinical Senates, these had replaced Primary Care Networks in 2012; you get the gist! Then there are the fifteen Academic Health and Science Networks, nobody has yet worked out what they do. There is Health Education England, and NHS England, which now includes what was NHS Improvement and NHS Digital, and then there is NHS Resolution, the body tasked with picking up the pieces for the failings in the system and sorting out the rapidly increasing compensation and legal bills. Then there is the NHS Counter Fraud Authority, and NHS Business Services Authority. And then there are the official and generally ineffective busybody and monitoring bodies, the multitudes of national and local oversight and regulatory organisations, services, bodies, and committees, some with statutory powers, but with little appetite for, or experience of using them.

These do not include the many other professional membership bodies and various royal medical colleges that sit under the umbrella of the Academy of Medical Royal Colleges, Surgeons, Nursing, Midwifery, Dentists, Psychiatrists, Physicians, Radiologists, Anaesthetists, Emergency Medicine, Intensive Care, Ophthalmologists, Pharmacists, Paediatrics and Child Health, Obstetricians and Gynaecologists, and Pathologists among them. Then there are the medical unions, the British Medical Association (BMA), the Royal College of Nursing, and the Hospital Doctors Union to name but a few.

And then there are the various think tanks and special interest groups such as The King's Fund, Nuffield Trust, the NHS Confederation, and others - more on them later! And let's not even think about the Department of Health and Social Care, for now.

Then there are a host of patient interest groups and advocacy bodies such as AVMA, The Patients Association, and Healthwatch. Some are closely aligned with, funded by, and supported by various parts of the NHS, many others are not. This group of stakeholders tends to have the least access to where power lies in the health and care system and the least ability to exert influence upon the system. Well, they only represent the interests of service users after all.

And it won't surprise you to know that most of these work in splendid isolation of each other. But unlike the many well-known, and it should be noted, more efficiently run private sector franchises that dominate the global consumer landscape, each NHS related organization has its own separate ideas and practices, its own executive team and hierarchy, its own leadership and management team structures, its own local board of directors, its own organizational and operational methods, its own strategy, its own vision statement and set of stated priorities, its own set of espoused if not lived values, its own ways of doing things, and of course its own unique website. Websites which fall largely under one of four headings; useless, confusing, out of date, or all three. I should know, I studied them for over a year as part of a national project; I get all the good jobs!

Spin the wheel:

Reaching into the NHS in search of support for either yourself or a loved one is a bit like stretching out your arm into the tombola at the local village fete fundraiser, or agricultural show if you live in Cumbria. You may have paid for your entry ticket in advance through taxation, but there are no guarantees of what you are going to get when you reach into the ever-rotating lottery of varying expectations. You may never even know if what you got when you pulled your hand out the rotating cylinder of variation was the most appropriate thing in relation to your needs at that point in time. You are simply expected to take your prize from the tombola and express your gratitude that it was free to access. Of course, as we all know, free to access doesn't mean free to provide. As of 2022, the annual collective cost to UK taxpayers of funding the NHS was approx. one hundred and fifty-five billion pounds, give or take.

If you doubt the accuracy of the tombola anecdote, then I would ask you to consider some real-life examples. In 2003, my next-door neighbours and now friends of over thirty years lost their thirteen-year-old daughter to an undiagnosed brain tumour. Danielle was a bright, beautiful, intelligent young girl. It was obvious to all those around her that she possessed all the ingredients to bring something special to the world. When her family stretched their worried hand into the NHS tombola drum and took Danielle to see their local GP, the doctor they saw that day, an old and widely trusted hand and well-known member of the local community, suggested that Danielle's complaints about persistent headaches and increasing tiredness were probably psychosomatic, perhaps reflecting a desire to stay at home due to a possible undiscussed bullying issue at school. He assured them there was nothing more serious to worry about. If only that had been the case. There was no such bullying issue, but while the local GP, doubtless with good intent but subject to the same behavioural biases all humans are subject to, looked well-meaningly in the wrong direction, the cancer in Danielle's brain quickly spread. By the time it was finally discovered it had become inoperable. She and her family were horrifically and devastatingly failed by the poor service their local GP provided under the publicly funded umbrella of the NHS. The pieces of the NHS's failure were then picked-up, as they so often are, by a charitably funded organization. MacMillan Cancer Support helped Danielle and her family face the end as best as any young girl leaning over the edge of deaths precipice and at the dawn of life's potential, can. Danielle's condition could have been diagnosed and her death potentially avoided had she entered another NHS setting and seen a different clinician.

At this point you might understandably be tempted to think that this was a one off, or that things will have changed since then. It wasn't, and they haven't. My friend's wife, a wonderful engaging woman in her early forties is now living with the consequences of a recently undiagnosed cancer, which had it been caught earlier could have been treated. She does not know how long she has to live, but the prognosis is not good. She will leave a husband and two children behind. The truth of the matter is that the issues of misdiagnosis and missed diagnosis, even before the pandemic, are as prevalent as they ever have been. The pressure on GPs to rattle through their appointments in ever shorter time slots is a sure-fire recipe for increases in error. Primary Care is the term often used to describe the collective capacity of GP Practices, and the clinical capacity and medical expertise in Primary Care is not what it once was in relation to the demand it now has to meet. Primary Care in Cumbria and much of the UK is a heavy and loudly creaking door.

I've tried to remain conscious as I wrote this book and when I draw on stories such as Danielle's, that I am also subject to the same behavioural and perceptual biases as those I accuse of letting theirs cloud their judgement. But I hope this book will show I have done my homework and as much as I would genuinely like to be proved wrong, I can assure you Danielle's tragic story and its painful legacy are neither extreme nor untypical. The collective incidents of misdiagnosis and missed diagnosis that occur each day in GP Practices across the entire UK are significant, they go largely undetected and unreported, and they are often the result of inconsistencies in the way services are provided and symptoms diagnosed.

I empathise with a family or a person's desire to feel they have a relationship with a named local GP. Trust is built over time and many people feel that a GP they are familiar with can understand and interpret the context of their conditions. My mum would never see any other Doctor than her trusted Dr Corlett from the local practice on Balby Road in Doncaster. She had been his patient for thirty years since moving to South Yorkshire in the late eighties and was distraught when he finally and deservedly retired a couple of years ago. But I think we have become so wedded to the idea of the local GP that in this country many of us have confused easy local access to a named or known Doctor, with access to expertise. These things are not always, in fact they are seldom, one and the same. Give me access to the right expertise provided by a stranger or using artificial intelligence, over a fatal misdiagnosis given to me by a friendly familiar face every time. It is access to relevant expertise that patients and their families need, not merely access to premises or people. The way the NHS is currently structured places far too many barriers in front of patients and service users who need to obtain access, sometimes urgently, to up-to-date expertise and assistance.

Let me bring what I mean by this to life. In 2015 I spiralled into depression. I went to see a GP from my local practice who referred me to an NHS mental health service called First Step. The service was run by my employer at the time, the local provider of NHS mental health services in Cumbria. I asked my GP if I could access the First Step service online, you can guess the answer. He just looked at me strangely. I then asked him to share his opinion on why the NHS seemed so far behind in its adoption and use of technology. I explained that I had been accessing online education and tuition since studying with the Open University in 1998, using a dial-up modem. And I pointed out that the district of Eden in Cumbria in which I live and in which my GP is based, is the most sparsely populated rural district in England. The Eden district covers an area larger than Greater London but with a resident population of just over fifty thousand. My cycling partner and I can ride fifty kilometres on a Sunday morning and see less than a dozen vehicles, one of which is either a milk tanker or a tractor. There are a mere twenty-five people per square kilometre in Eden compared with over sixteen thousand people per square kilometre in the boroughs of Tower Hamlets and Islington. Wouldn't it make sense I suggested to my GP for the NHS to offer online access to mental health support services in England's largest most dispersed rural area in which users of health and care services often had to travel for significant distances, and generally during work hours, to access basic services. At that time, the East London NHS Foundation Trust were offering their patients access to mental health services and counselling online, but I couldn't use their services or access the expertise within their organisation because I didn't live in East London. It's times like these you realize how unnational, inconsistent, uncoordinated, fragmented, and non-patient-centric the National Health Service can be. If you don't have access to private transport in this part of the world, you are at once disadvantaged.

A failure demand service:

In short, the NHS is neither national in the true sense of the word, its more regionally variable than the UK's weather. Nor is the NHS predominantly a health service engaged in healing the inherent often unpredictable physical and mental frailties and fragilities that are part of being human. It is in large part a failure demand service, an accident fixing, social failure fixing, people failure fixing, preventable error fixing, relationship problem solving, unwise decision rectifying, reckless behaviour remedying, poor business practice amelioration, socio-economic redressing, and private sector marketing generated dissonance anxiety and stress relief fixing service. The NHS is the safety net that tries to mend people and pick up the pieces in the wake of personal tragedies, organisational self-interest, and national policy fuck ups. The NHS is a failure demand service. What do you mean by failure demand Tom, I hear you ask?

Loosely put, failure demand is a term used to describe the resources you expend as a result of addressing failures that occur elsewhere, intended, or unintended. You nip through to the kitchen to make a cuppa and drop the coffee jar which breaks and spills granules across the floor. The time you then spend cleaning up and the new jar of coffee you have to go out and buy are the resources you expended dealing with your failure to pay attention as you reached for the coffee jar. The company that comes to fix your car windscreen arrives with the wrong screen, the resources time and effort they spend fixing their mistake falls under the heading of failure demand. In other words, if things had gone as planned this activity wouldn't have been necessary. If you hadn't dropped the coffee you could have done something else with the time you spent shopping for more coffee. If the windscreen repair company had arrived with the right windscreen the first time they came, they could have then used the time of their employee to do something else. Failure demands twin is opportunity cost. Opportunity cost is the benefit we lose from having to deal with failure demand. It's the article you wanted to read but didn't have time to because you were out buying coffee. It's the profit from the windscreen your company could have sold and fitted in the time your employee was remedying his workmates mistake.

Looking at personal or organisational activity through the lens of failure demand and opportunity cost provides a helpful way of identifying the resources we use picking up the pieces from failings elsewhere. The routine levels of failure demand and the opportunity cost it creates in our health and care system and within services themselves, are immense. The quantity of resources we routinely use, the time, money, physical and emotional effort we commit to deal with the levels of failure demand created in our personal lives, the organisations we work in, and in our societies, is enormous. The justice system is a great and hugely expensive example of a publicly funded service that exists primarily to deal with the failure demand created in society. Climate change and conflict are other obvious examples of failure demand at the highest levels. Lives are lost, countries ruined, homes destroyed, and refugees displaced, because people fail to act or reach agreement by other means. That second, third, and quite possibly fourth call you had to make to your internet service provider because they did not deal with your request the first time you called them, is failure demand that eats their resources as well as yours. The existence of a sizeable charitable sector in the UK is a highly visible manifestation of the concept of failure demand. Our governments give money to aid agencies to wash the wounds of the war weary from across the world and we give our spare change to local charities to fix the problems that flawed government policy and human greed have created on our doorstep. Large parts of our economy exist to deal solely with the needs created by the largely inherent and often predictable failings our societies and the actors within them create. The corporate practice of externalising that was highlighted earlier creates a plethora of failure demand in almost every sphere of life.

Failure demand also exists at a much more personal level. If you decide you are to cool for school, to suave to use a seatbelt, perhaps to style-conscious to wear a bike helmet, and then one day you find yourself in a losing fight with the laws of physics and the forces of gravity as you smash through your windscreen or sail over the handlebars of your bike because you were too busy admiring the scenery as you meandered down Kirkstone Pass, then the best trained, most skilled, intelligently piloted, and adroit surgical hands employed in one part of the NHS will be paid to try and put you and your bonce back together at no direct expense to you. The resources the country deploys to deal with the failure demand our actions create is beyond measure. The dedicated individuals trying to heal your head and the passionate teams of highly trained people supporting them can be likened to the gifted intelligent humble servants of an over-privileged, profligate, and at times incredibly stupid master. Their task is to continually run round after their irresponsible and entitled overlord dealing with the largely preventable messes their master creates. The best brains in the country who work under the NHS banner often deal with the consequences of the stupidest actions of their fellow human beings.

So, if the UK does not really have a National Health Service, what does it have? It has a fragmented, culturally discordant, technologically disjoined, over-led, under-managed, operationally inconsistent, and highly variable illness and accident treatment failure demand fixing service. Of course, the acronym for this will never catch-on, politicians, pundits, celebrities, or the wider population, couldn't get as teary-eyed and publicly passionate about the UK's incredible FCDTDOLUMOIHVIAATFDF Service.

Some, arguably with just cause, might add underfunded to the list of words above, but the truth of the matter is that we the taxpaying public could throw unlimited resources into the National Health Service in its current format, and it would make truly little difference. We can build as many luxury liners for the fleet as we like, but we must as much as is possible choose the seas they sail upon, they must be clearly instructed to sail in the right direction, equipped to deal with the needs of their service users, and staffed by trained and able crews. This book will try to show that the NHS's problems are not fixable in isolation and that money may well be the least of the significant challenges it is really facing.

Chapter 14: The Doctor will see you now, briefly...

"Wherever the art of medicine is loved, there is also a love of humanity."

Hippocrates

A study conducted by researchers at Cambridge University and published in the British Medical Journal the BMJ in 2017, found that General Practitioners in the UK had some of the shortest patient consultation times in Europe, averaging around ten minutes each. The same research unsurprisingly noted that many GPs were unhappy with these ridiculously short and historically decreasing consultation times. The 2022 annual NHS GP Patient Survey showed patient satisfaction with GPs has also dropped, though in truth this survey is largely irrelevant. Asking a section of the population if they are happy with something that the majority have nothing to compare against, is only a small step from meaningless. The former Chair of the Royal College of General Practitioners Helen Stokes-Lampard, was unequivocal in her response to the research, saying that the more time a patient spent with their GP, the better care they got. Her observation feels as intuitively logical as gravity and is perhaps more importantly, supported by evidence from elsewhere. Patients in Sweden not only have access to more Doctors and nurses per head of population, but they also enjoy more direct consultation time with their GPs, which at around twenty minutes per appointment are double that of the UK.

Like any part of the health and care system, Primary Care is part of a much bigger picture and cannot be looked at meaningfully in isolation. The demands being placed on Primary Care are a direct result of whatever else is occurring in both society and the capacity and capability within the wider health and care system. Every part of the healthcare system has to work effectively and efficiently for any part of it to work. In Sweden, the country's public health system is widely regarded as highly effective and importantly, influential, and its community healthcare services are seen as leading lights in Europe. The public money spent on health and care provided in the community in Sweden is around one third of the total public spend on healthcare. Health outcomes in Sweden are held aloft by many including the World Health Organisation as among the best in the world. It should therefore perhaps be no surprise that life expectancy in

Sweden is almost two years more than the UK. What might surprise you is that despite its relatively high numbers of healthcare professionals and clinicians per capita, Sweden has fewer general practitioners per head of population than many other countries, including the UK. The answer to Primary Cares current woes do not lie in simply throwing more resources at it. They lie in society and the entirety of the wider healthcare system. The good news to be taken from Sweden's story, is that they weren't always this good. Change and improvement are possible if public and political will can be directed.

Dr Steve, a doctor in facts and stats:

Dr Steve Taylor is a well-known figure in healthcare circles. A widely respected GP based in Bury a former mill town in Greater Manchester, he has been practising medicine for thirty years, during which time he has also trained around sixty further GPs. A regular tweeter Steve also runs a Facebook page called NHS Facts and Stats. The page is a platform highlighting the plight of GPs and a forum for setting the record straight about the misinformation that comes from government in its effort to convince us all that their efforts to support Primary Care are succeeding. When I spoke to Steve, he had just arrived at the NHS Expo, an annual convention run jointly by NHS England and the NHS Confederation. The event is a talking shop, a gathering of the usual suspects and a forum for sharing the conventional wisdoms. The NHS Confederation is an opaque body whose purpose in life is to use public funds to lobby on behalf of all the poorly paid directors and chief executives who work so hard in the NHS, and whose selfless efforts go so egregiously unnoticed but who add so much value to the nation in exchange for their meagre salaries and even measlier pensions. If Churchill were alive today, he would surely recognise that never in the field of public service history has so much money been taken from so many by so few who have added so very little. Anyway, enough on them. Steve had decided to attend the convention to build his networks and help spread his message. He is an optimist, and will I imagine have been one of the few informed voices representing the frontline of the NHS, who were present.

Dr Steve, as you would expect from someone who runs a social media channel under the banner of sharing stats and facts, is a politically aware and unafraid blend of experience and data. A rare and valuable combination. He is under no illusions about the impact that over a decade of post-austerity conservative government has had on the healthcare system and agrees with the premise that talk of creating a world-leading health and care service is disingenuous in an increasingly sick society. We will only become a truly healthy society when people are placed before profit. He is no fan of the current health secretary Steve Barclay, or of his predecessor Jeremy Hunt, who he believes has a great deal to answer for. I agree entirely. I think the extent of the damage that has been done to Primary Care and Britain's wider health and care system during the Conservative Governments period in office will only become clear with the passage of time. Steve tells me that though the government persist in saying there are more people working in Primary Care and though they have promised to recruit and train more GPs, there are now two thousand less full-time equivalent Primary Care GPs than there were a decade ago. The number of GPs has gone down as the population and the complexity of its healthcare needs has risen. Steve explains that this might not be so catastrophic had it not been accompanied by reductions in all the other services that GPs traditionally worked with and depended upon. School nurses, of which my mum was one, are now almost non-existent. The number of health visitors, of which my aunt was one, are also significantly less in number, and the number of district nurses, who local GPs often worked closely with, has almost halved in recent years. It has in his view, become fundamentally more difficult to be a GP.

We go on to talk about the rise in demand for mental health support. Having lost a sister, a childhood best friend, an aunty, and a good neighbour to suicide, it's a subject remarkably close to my heart. Steve estimates that around one third of the demand that Primary Care is currently dealing with relates to mental health. He tells me that following the pandemic he has never dealt with so many young people, mainly in their twenties, seeking help with mental health issues. While acknowledging there are some pockets of good practice, he laments the current woeful state of NHS mental health services nationally. He may be looking through rose-coloured clinical glasses, but Steve goes on to tell me that he can remember a time when a patient referred to a mental health service would have been picked-up by that service in two weeks. To add to this are the millions of people now waiting for specialist treatment who in the absence of communication from the NHS hospital they are waiting for help from, persistently contact their GP for information and updates while they wait. Everything seems to be landing on Primary Cares doorstep.

Each GP in Primary Care now serves an average of almost two thousand three hundred patients, up from around eighteen hundred in 2012, and little if any of the public funding attached to these extra patients has found its way into GPs pockets. It has largely been used to employ a range of what are widely referred to as Allied Health Professionals, physios, podiatrists, occupational therapists, dieticians, paramedics, and Advanced Nurse Practitioners, to help Primary Care cope with demand. Steve agrees with me that the presence of these specialisms on the frontline of healthcare is a good thing from the patient perspective but feels that the increasing need placed on Primary Care still requires significantly more GPs. He points out that Primary Care is now dealing with two million more appointments a year than in 2019, yet GP pay, once viewed by many as generous, has remained almost static for over a decade, meaning it has fallen significantly in real terms. Dr Steve is clearly frustrated by the hollow promises of politicians. Each health secretary has publicly acknowledged that more GPs are needed yet has done little about it. A report commissioned by Jeremy Hunt in 2014 suggested that the UK would need around thirty-five thousand GPs by 2025 if Primary Care were to continue meeting patient need. The current number of GPs in Primary Care is around twenty-seven thousand and the government is failing spectacularly in its efforts, if they can be called that, to address the situation.

The first port of call:

I've known Lisa Drake for some years now. Lisa is a business consultant specialising in digital and online services. She provides advice to GP Practices across the UK and is also a highly experienced and incredibly knowledgeable Practice Manager. I spoke with her recently about the changes she has seen in the two decades and more she has worked in Primary Care. Lisa's mind holds a constantly evolving mix of past and present facts, data, anecdotes, and stories from the sharp end of Primary Care. When Lisa shares her thoughts, she is like a well-oiled sometimes randomly directed verbal machine gun with a magazine loaded full of frustrated insights. The first and most significant issue Lisa highlights are the simultaneous rises in both the volume and the complexity of demand that finds its way through Primary Care's front door. Britain's population has grown significantly in the last seventy-five years and though the rate of increase may be slowing, it continues to grow. And since the establishing of the NHS in 1948, our life expectancy has also risen by around thirteen years each. We now live longer and many more of us are suffering with multiple often interacting health conditions that require unprecedented levels of intensive medical attention and assistance.

Lisa tells me that when she first became a practice manager, the proportion of what could be referred to as, on the day demand, represented less than a third of a practice's daily workload. This meant GPs could commit significant amounts of their time to proactively dealing with the predictable and preventable. They retained the capacity needed to manage those patients on the practice list who needed frequent attention to prevent their conditions getting worse. Lisa estimates that on the day demand as a proportion of activity now, has increased massively to around two thirds of each GPs daily workload. This she says, coupled with an increasing mismatch between the public's expectation of how responsive their local GP Practice should be, is a large part of the problem Primary Care is presently facing. Stuck in a vicious circle of failure demand, which some observers falsely attribute as a post Covid issue, but which in reality has been building for decades. This vicious circle is creating a perpetually growing cycle of demand on Primary Care which they have neither the capacity nor capability to deal with. Unfortunately for Primary Care, it has always been the first and most visible port of call and the most accessible entry point into the NHS. Failures and delays that occur in other parts of the system such as social care, community and mental health services, and secondary care, have a habit of landing back on Primary Cares doorstep. *"I haven't had my results yet"; "Nobody has been in touch about my operation"; "I will take my own life if I don't speak to somebody soon"; "Can you tell me when I will be able to see the specialist as the pain I'm in is unbearable"; "You have to do something for me, not knowing how long I will have to wait is affecting my mental health,* are all common and entirely legitimate concerns and queries that in the absence of information and communication from other parts of the NHS, patients look to their GPs for answers to.

The Institute of General Practice Managers is an organisation formed by Practice Managers and which claims to be the representative body for all managers working within general practice in the UK. Alarmed by the behaviour of some patients, in 2021 the institute coordinated a social media campaign featuring videos recorded by its members in which they shared their experiences of the demand's patients were placing on them. In some cases, the threats they were receiving, and even on occasion, the violence they and their practice were being subjected to. The videos were spliced together and the strapline for the campaign was, *if I die it will be your fault*, a phrase which according to the Institute has become an increasingly common threat thrown at GP Practice receptionists, managers, and staff. The video contained a number of phrases used by patients to place pressure on Primary Care staff to give them what they wanted. Possibly unfairly on my part, I imagine these patients to be the usual mix of the irresponsible entitled and the sharp-elbowed middle classes who are experts at pushing themselves forward to the detriment of the rest of us. The phrases patients used in their efforts to get what they wanted included, *"I Pay your wages so give me what I want"*; *"I'm entitled to see who I want when I want"*; *"Give me what I want or I'll complain to my MP and the Care Quality Commission"*; *"Give me a fucking appointment"*; *"The doctor shouldn't be on holiday I need to speak with him"*; *"I'm going to come down there right now to sort you out"*; *"I hope all of your family die"*, and, *"I know where you live"*.

Lisa is not alone in feeling that the present unprecedented pressures of life many are facing, the worries of managing from day to day, and the expectations to cope we place on ourselves and those around us are contributing to a climate of anger, hostility, and unkindness, which simmers under the surface ready to boil over when the slightest thing goes wrong, or an unpredicted inconvenience occurs. And it's not just healthcare staff that are feeling the brunt of our increased anxieties, time poverty, and financial stress. A quick look at the websites of some private sector companies suggests that customer facing staff in every field of commerce are dealing with rising levels of anger and hostility. Earlier this year I was listening to a pre-recorded message as I waited on hold to speak with a ferry operator. The message had a reminder to callers that insulting call-handling staff would not be tolerated. I was intrigued and asked the lady who dealt with my call if she had personally experienced abuse from callers. Though she laughed while she told me, I was saddened at the stories she shared. As our collective anxieties exceed any previous levels we have experienced, we appear as a nation to have been driven by our volatile circumstances into becoming noticeably less patient, kind, and considerate.

Soaking up the pressure:

There are enormous pressures on all parts of the NHS, especially on its patient facing staff, but while resource hungry hospitals may hog the media limelight and the public's attention, Primary Care is in my view the most loudly whistling kettle on the overheating healthcare hob right now. Conversely, its fragile fragmented disparate structure means it is also the most individually and organisationally vulnerable and least well-equipped part of the entire healthcare system to cope.

I met and talked at length with hundreds of GPs when I worked for the NHS in Cumbria. My role as the local NHS Trust Stakeholder Engagement Manager involved trying to build relationships and work closely with all aspects of Primary Care, GPs, the Practice Managers who ran each local practice, and for those who worked in a large enough setting, their colleagues such as community nursing leads, district nurses, referral managers, receptionists, and IT specialists who kept each local GP Practice running. In some of the smaller rural surgeries the practice manager combined many of these roles and more; parking attendant, bouncer, and graphic designer to name a few. At that time in Cumbria, there were just over eighty separate GP Practices as well as the Out of Hours GP service which was run by an independent social enterprise called Cumbria Health on Call, or CHOC as it was commonly referred to. The CHOC Doc is on their way has a reassuring ring to it. From the many conversations I've had with GPs and Practice Managers over the years, a number of common threads appear when talking about the issues and challenges they face. GPs in smaller practices, of which there are still a great many, complain that far too much of their time is spent in managing and administrating, rather than helping patients. Their precious hours and access to the ability they spent years in training to acquire, are consumed by other activities. Keeping the regulator happy by ensuring policies, processes and procedures are in place, handling patient complaints, dealing with freedom of information requests, resolving employee disputes, and dealing with health and safety legislation. And then there's keeping abreast of the constant stream of updates, revisions to guidance, changes to patient pathways, and wordy diktats which seem to spew from the many parts of the NHS like confetti. As they juggle these demands, they have to work with clunky and distinctly non-user-friendly technology which for the most part has been designed around the bureaucratic needs of the beast of performance management, and not the convenience of its clinical users or the patients they serve. You will hear some within the NHS say Primary Care is the most technologically enabled part of the NHS, and to some degree they are right. However, the overall standard of technology adoption and use in the NHS is not high by any standard other than comparison with the neolithic era. Being held aloft as the most technologically enabled part of the NHS is rather like a thirty-year-old being applauded for qualifying to run in a one hundred metre race for the under tens. Constant comparison with the lowest common denominator is not a recipe for improvement.

What has also become clear to me over the years is the incredibly significant emotional pressure of being a GP in a small practice in present day Britain. GPs with smaller practice populations where their patients are often known to them and where GPs often live in the heart of the same communities they serve, often suffer with their own anxieties in relation to the health and wellbeing of their patients. No matter how experienced, they can find themselves carrying a significant emotional burden when things beyond their control don't go to plan. I recall one particularly passionate GP from a small practice in West Cumbria who worked relentlessly on behalf of his patients before suffering a severe mental breakdown. Before his breakdown we had spoken about the challenges facing his practice and he had given me a glimpse into the thoughts that troubled him after he had seen a patient in the eight-minute time slot he had available, knowing that he might not have done them justice. Wondering if he had missed something obvious from the previous patient he had just seen while trying to concentrate on the needs of the patient in front of him in the present moment. He shared the anxiety he would feel after referring a seriously mentally ill patient to an NHS service he knew wasn't fit for purpose and how he would often find himself acting as a counsellor for patients who had been on mental health waiting lists for months, trying to keep them afloat until they could access the specialist help they needed. He has left general practice now, taking his experience and unquestioned passion for patients with him. He is not the only one. It is little wonder that fewer and fewer trainee GPs want to become partners in a Primary Care practice, especially a small or rural practice. Who in their right mind would want to stand alone and fight the irrepressibly rising waters of health inequality in the UK today?

Consistently inconsistent:

If Primary Care is the most challenged part of the NHS, it is in no small part due to its fragile fragmented disparate structures. The largest GP Practice I worked with during my time in the NHS, provided services in West Cumbria to a registered practice population of around twenty-five thousand. Working from four locations, its two busiest facilities were in Egremont and Whitehaven. The practice consisted of half a dozen registered GP partners, and several additional GPs who were employed on a full and part-time basis. These were supported by nursing teams, health visitors, a mental health specialist, and community midwives as well as a full complement of administrative and reception staff. The practice employed a single practice manager across its sites and had its own in-house IT expert. They supplied services to every demographic imaginable. From wealthy local entrepreneurs and the many well-paid senior managers and employees linked to the Sellafield nuclear facility and its various supply chains, to the generationally inactive disengaged descendants of West Cumbria's previously prosperous industrial past who live on the council estates that fringe the town.

The county's smallest GP Practice could not have been more different to its largest. Located in a tiny building at the very heart of the little village of Glenridding which borders the shores of the beautiful Lake Ullswater, the Glenridding GP Practice boasted a registered patient population of less than a thousand. It was until only a few years ago, staffed by one full-time and one part-time GP and a straight-talking no-nonsense Practice Manager whose direct manner could be as tough and unforgiving as the Lakeland fells that kept watch over the small village in their midst. Though her directness could be unnerving to the unwary, in truth her approach made a refreshing change in a healthcare system that seems to welcome and reward those talented in the art of vague pontification and unquestioning agreement. We got on well enough that she offered me free use of the practice carpark should Debbie and I be planning any walks in the area. Car parking charges in the Lake District National Park are extortionate. The running of the Glenridding practice has since been taken over by the county's out of hours provider, CHOC, and is run on a largely remote basis using video conferencing to provide initial triage, routine appointments, and prescription services. The GPs that were there have now retired, and no permanent successors could be found to replace them. The fate of the Glenridding GP Practice mirrors that of at least a dozen other practices that existed in Cumbria less than a decade ago, and many hundreds of others in small communities across the UK.

In between the large modern multi-site GP practices of post-industrial West Cumbria and the bucolic nostalgia of a single small stone building in Glenridding, the GP Practices of Cumbria were, just as they are across the entire UK, scattered along a continuum of difference and inconsistency. Each GP Practice I found myself engaging seemed as different to its counterparts as people are to each other. Some were located in shining new modern multi-purpose health centres, found on the edges of towns, surrounded by extensive car-parking, with disabled access, spacious comfortable waiting rooms that sported large digital display screens and with a well-stocked dispensing pharmacy on site. Others were housed in splendid old Georgian buildings with front steps leading onto the pavements of busy main streets in town centres. The clinicians and staff inside practising their craft under large ornate ceiling roses in yawning rooms of cracking plaster framed with skirting boards and picture rails hidden underneath layer upon layer of peeling gloss paint, brushed thickly over the stories that must have unfolded in these incredible spacious former family homes. Beautiful buildings that now seem defaced and awkward, forced to wear a hotchpotch assortment of legally required alterations and adjustments, rails, ramps, an accessible toilet, and a lift just big enough to fit a wheelchair in. And not a car parking space to be had. Other GP Practices were almost impossible to find, hidden in residential cul-de-sacs and tucked away down quiet side streets in town centres, with cramped and constantly overcrowded reception areas, walls covered with old posters and spots of Blu Tack, and leaflet holders brimming with out-of-date patient information. In these settings a full complement of staff would often be squeezed into just a few hundred square feet that included three or four boxlike consulting rooms. Or sometimes a practice could be hidden on the edge of one of the tiny hamlets dotted around the more remote parts of the Lake District. Few were run by a single GP, typically each practice had between two to four GP Partners and most had a registered patient population of between four and twelve thousand.

Once inside the front door, lifting the lid on each GP Practice revealed as many differences in how they work as the buildings and locations in which they were housed. Some had GPs specialising in cardiology, dermatology, mental health, emergency medicine, women's health, substance misuse, or sports medicine. These were formerly known as GPs with Special Interests, now called GPs with Extended Roles. Some GPs had more than a passing personal interest in non-medical therapies. I recall an appointment I had with a GP from my own practice who encouraged me to invest in a small plot of forestland to protect my mental health. I would have if I could have afforded it. Some GPs have no hesitation referring their patients to less traditional non-NHS branded sources of support, such as encouraging patients with mental health issues to work with voluntary organisations who used the outdoors and horticulture as means of recovery. While others would never refer their patients to anything that was not NHS branded for fear of being culpable in the event that anything should go wrong. Some encouraged their patients to use applications on their smartphones to help them monitor and manage their mental and physical health. Others saw no benefit in such things, and many were blissfully unaware of the plethora of voluntary services or online options and smartphone applications even available to their patients. And I don't think any of the GP Practice Managers I worked with had a consistent role or job description. A thankless job serving many masters that I would not take if it were offered on a silver platter.

My local GP Practice:

My wife Debbie is registered with a relatively large local GP Practice called Birbeck Medical Group in Penrith. I am registered with the smaller Lakes Medical Practice, also in Penrith. We've each been patients of our respective GP Practices for around forty years, and we've outlasted every GP and member of staff either of them have had. The Birbeck Medical group presently has five GP Partners and five salaried GPs along with around ten further patient facing staff, including an advanced nurse practitioner, numerous nurses, and three healthcare assistants. These in turn are all supported by a practice pharmacist, a practice manager, two deputy practice managers, and around twenty administrative staff including receptionists, data administrators, a medicines management team, and two secretaries. Many are full-time employees, some are part-time. The Lakes Medical Practice presently has two GP Partners and two salaried GPs, some practice nurses, an advanced nurse practitioner, a phlebotomist, a wellbeing coach, and an administrative support team including a practice manager, a deputy practice manager, a safeguarding lead, numerous receptionists, and associated admin staff. They have adopted different approaches and ways of working to each other ever since Debbie and I can remember. When one started offering telephone only triage services some years ago, the other staunchly refused. One is currently rated as outstanding by the Care Quality Commission while the other is rated as good. One used to employ a GP with a special interest in mental health, but no longer does. The other has previously never seen the need to but has recently decided to employ the services of a psychiatrist for a day each week. Each has a different message and options on their answerphone. One has a Facebook page which is regularly updated, the other has a Facebook page which is almost dormant. One says it is open for extended hours on a Saturday, the other says it is not. One says that it opens at 08.00am and stays open until 6.00pm each weekday, while the other says it opens at 08.30am and closes at 6.30pm. One has a website containing a section, albeit an extremely rudimentary one, entitled Self Help, and has an established track record of working closely with local voluntary groups and third sector providers, while the other has no such content on its website and seemingly little desire to engage with any sources of support that sit outside the official NHS tent. One practice website offers a distinctly non-user-friendly online appointment booking system with a series of dropdown options that spit out the same standard reply to every query entered, *Sorry, we couldn't find any locations near this area*, helpfully accompanied by a suggestion to ring the practice. And on the various days I have been looking over each of their websites, one practice was offering online consultations while the other was not, this facility having been temporary unavailable for some time. What is the definition of temporary I wonder? And anyway, I'm sure there is no call for such patient centric digital innovation in England's most sparsely populated rural district where public transport is all but non-existent in many places, so no harm done.

In late April this year I was told by the pharmacy I collect my bi-monthly allowance of happy tablets from that I needed a review of my prescription, so one morning in early May I rang my GP Practice to arrange an appointment. After listening to a series of pre-recorded options being outlined, I keyed in the appropriate one and was directed to the practice website to submit my query using an online consultation service. Debbie also needed to call her GP Practice that morning, their phone line was engaged and there was no pre-recorded instruction to use the website. She continued to dial at regular intervals until she finally got through, at which point she was asked why she hadn't used the online booking service. Debbie didn't know her practice provided such a service, importantly she wouldn't have used it if she did. My wife is not as comfortable using technology as I am.

Despite their very many differences, what each of Debbie and I's GP Practices do have in common, along with many other GP Practices across the UK, is that they share the same postcode. They even share the same carpark and many of their patients collect their prescriptions from the same pharmacy. In fact, the truth of the matter is that both these culturally different and operationally disparate GP Practices can be found across the corridor from each other in the very same building. When I visit my GP Practice, I use the entrance at the front of the same building as Debbie does on the rare, exceedingly rare occasion, she visits her GP Practice. I walk down the corridor and turn through a door to my right, while Debbie walks down exactly the same corridor and turns through a door to her left. I sometimes wonder if there can be many more pointless or effective ways of throwing public money down the drain than by running two sets of independently managed publicly funded healthcare services from under the same roof who each appear to insist on duplicating as many resources as they can in their efforts to maintain their identity as separate GP Practices. Why have none of the incredibly well-paid managers who sit amidst the towering skyline of ivory NHS towers creating nebulous strategies and unachievable plans, failed to get to grips with such obvious and unnecessarily expensive anomalies?

Economies of scale is a dirty phrase in some circles, mainly public sector ones. It often equates to closing facilities, combining separate functions, centralising services, and of course shedding employees to reduce costs. I'm not a fan of making anyone redundant, I've got the t-shirt and it itched severely. But the universe owes none of us a living and I'm not in favour of keeping people in well-paid publicly funded roles with extensive benefits and expensive pensions for the sake of it. Doing so seems no more legitimate than condoning massive benefit fraud. Does a collection of publicly funded GPs in the same building really need two practice managers with three deputies, twelve receptionists, and dozens of support staff employed to do the same things, duplicate administrators paid to maintain separate social media pages, duplicate sets of hosting costs for separate and inconsistent websites, the managing of duplicate patient participation groups, the paying of two sets of accountancy fees, insurances, HR support services, and countless duplicate policies relating to everything from data protection to health and safety, grievance and HR procedures. If these obvious duplications could prove they were of benefit to anyone other than the people employed in unnecessary roles or to the private companies that clearly benefit from supplying multiple sets of similar professional services to each GP Practice, then I would advocate carrying on as we are. But they can't. And worse than that, these duplications are not merely wasteful, they facilitate mediocrity at best and create inefficiencies that are diverting precious finite resources from where they could be better used for the benefit of patients and wider society.

Why should the patients of one NHS funded service that sits under the same roofing joists and slates as its counterpart, not have equitable access to the same opening hours, the same levels of clinical capacity, the same necessary specialisms, the same digital resources, and the same sources of correct updated information as each other? Of course, the issue is much bigger than any anomalies that might exist in a small market town in Northern England. The real question is, why should any citizen in the UK not have equitable access to a consistent universal service from their Primary Care provider? The incredible levels of duplication that exist within the UK's Primary Care system would simply not have been allowed to continue had these same small businesses been operating in the private sector. There is no other sector of small business in the UK that has been able to resist the global pressures to consolidate and achieve economies of scale and operational consistency quite like Primary Care has. There is also no other group of small businesses in the UK whose customers would benefit more from the efficiencies that consolidation could bring, than Primary Care. Would we rather live in a society where the texture of our burgers can be guaranteed or where the quality of our medical services is consistent?

If there is one part of the inconsistency in the UK's healthcare system that epitomises the wider inconsistency of the NHS itself, it is

Primary Care. The inconsistent nature of Primary Care is its most strikingly obvious feature. Consistency may be mocked by the creative and spontaneous as the hobgoblin of small minds, but it has its place, and in the world of health and care its importance cannot be overstated. Why, in a world in which one in four of us will experience mental illness, shouldn't every patient have access to a GP Practice or health centre that houses a specialism in mental health? And if one in two of us will develop some form of cancer during our lifetime, why doesn't every Primary Care setting house a cancer specialist with access to up-to-date expertise? We possess most of the statistics which reveal the type and frequency of demand placed on our healthcare services, yet we have never purposefully designed Primary Care, the very frontline of our NHS, to align its clinical expertise with the highly predictable demands it will face. It is astounding that there has been no concerted effort by NHS England to ensure there is a match between the capacity and capability in Primary Care settings and the needs of the patients they serve. It is even more perplexing if just as unsurprising that the Care Quality Commission does not factor this meaningfully into its assessment processes or reporting.

If you were tasked with developing a national franchise supplying professional services in the private sector, you would develop and match the competences contained in your offer against the needs of your marketplace. If one in four of the small business owners who use an accountancy service need help with VAT or tax related issues, you would logically expect the accountancy firms they deal with to offer ready access to experts in these fields. The golden thread in every successful private sector franchise, be it purely a service or a product, or as is more often the case, a combination of the two, is consistency. The multi-billion valuations of the world's best-known brands all hang on this thread. Consistency in what they provide, consistency in the quality of their products and services, consistency in how they can be accessed and consistency in the expression of their values which are manifested in how they do what they do. I wonder how we the taxpaying public, the stakeholders, customers, and ultimate shareholders of all public services, have come to expect and accept such incredible inconsistencies and variation in the services we fund, levels of inconsistency and variation we would simply not expect or tolerate in the products and services we consume from the private sector?

Why is Primary Care allowed to be so inconsistent?

Were anyone to be tasked with designing Primary Care or the NHS itself, few would choose to start from where it is now. When anyone asks why Primary Care is allowed to be so inconsistent, depending on the audience the question is asked of, a plethora of answers, reasons, and excuses are offered. One of the more popular I come across is that GP Practices are their own independent businesses and therefore cannot be dictated to about how they should do what they do. Their professionalism and judgement must be respected, and they must be allowed to design and provide services in ways they believe suited to the needs of their local population. Of late as I hear this, an inanely smiling clothed monkey has started to appear in my head crashing a large well-worn and very loud clanging symbol. To me it's the lazy thinker's response which equates to, change is difficult, let's not upset the nice GPs, I don't know how that would be possible, yada, yada, yada...

Then there is the classic, one size doesn't fit all argument. A strangely fashionable and vague response which sells inconsistency and variation as somehow being positive attributes. It also flies in the face of effective and efficient service design principles which are based on the proven notion that if services are designed to meet the majority of demand, i.e., the largely predictable, then having the processes and resources in place to deal effectively and efficiently with this majority of demand, in turn frees up resources which can be used to deal with the less predictable. It's a principle that is applied to great effect in the private sector, but one which hasn't taken root in the NHS.

GP Practices may like to be, or by accidents of design and history, are commonly thought of and labelled as small independent businesses in their own right. And it is true that the many local GP Practices of all shapes and sizes that were absorbed into the NHS at its birth were largely, genuinely independent small businesses in the truest sense. But surely, after seventy-five years of living from the public purse, they should be both perceived by the public and more importantly directed, operated, and managed by the NHS as franchises, working under the NHS banner. Most modern GP Practices are not really independent self-sustaining small businesses in the strict sense. They do not have to market themselves and compete for business, though their websites would doubtless be better, and they would be far more efficient if they did, and their income streams, salaries and pensions are guaranteed from the taxpaying public purse. Yet they are managed and directed less stringently and certainly less purposefully than any other private sector franchise I am aware of. The argument that consolidating GP Practices, centralising their technology, their administration, their back-office functions, their online presences, and making their processes consistent and more efficient would somehow be an attack on their professionalism and judgement, is nonsense.

Anything that releases GPs from non-value adding activity, that improves the overall capacity and capability in Primary Care and enables it to easily shift clinical resources and specialisms from location to location to meet patient need, that enables GPs to develop specific competencies and skills, and creates opportunities for everyone employed in Primary Care to grow professionally, clinically, and strategically, would be of great benefit to the system and in turn the patients it exists to serve. Helping GPs in Primary Care to spend more time doing the things they trained to do, in ways that are more effective and efficient, with less stress and a better work life balance, will by default lead to better outcomes for patients and make Primary Care a more attractive and fulfilling career choice.

The unheeded smell of the coffee:

The problem of recruitment, retention, and capacity in Primary Care is at last starting to become more widely acknowledged. Yet it's a strange phenomenon that even though the roughly eight and a half thousand GP Practices that make up Primary Care in the UK and who between them currently handle the vast majority of interactions the British population has with the NHS each and every day, the significant issues they collectively face, issues that have been present, visible, and growing for many years, have garnered less political and press attention than the two hundred or so NHS Hospital Trusts whose struggles and challenges seem to dominate the attention of policy makers and the media.

Primary Cares journey in Cumbria's has been a canary in the cage for Primary Care across the UK for as long as I can recall. Rurality has an uncanny ability to prophesy the effects of change and the impact of policy, whether it's made or ignored. Rurality amplifies and highlights issues which may initially seem spurious to many in built up areas, including those working in the large organisations, the think tanks, and regulatory bodies shaping and dictating policy who are predominantly based in cities and urban centres. But when the jam of public services is spread thinly, it's the gaps in remote and rural locations that manifest themselves first. Public services of almost every type and description in Cumbria, especially NHS services, have persistently struggled with quality issues, financial problems, and seemingly intractable recruitment and retention challenges for longer than most care to remember. But Britain is an increasingly urban centred population, almost eighty-five percent of its citizens live in built up areas. A proportion that continues to rise steadily and which is one of the highest in the world. As a result, the needs of people living and working in the more remote and rural areas of the UK are largely ignored by politicians and political parties keen to address the concerns of people in urban areas in order to attract or maintain their share of the vote. The London centric decision-making that has come to dominate thinking, national policy, and the media, and which often has a particularly deleterious impact on places like Cumbria, shows no signs of abating.

A few years ago, I was asked to attend a forum organised by a prominent and long-established UK healthcare think tank called the Nuffield Trust. The forum was arranged to discuss the challenges facing the provision of NHS services in remote and rural settings. The event was, without any sense of the obvious potential for irony, to be hosted in central London. God forbid that those attempting to understand and shape the future of healthcare would leave their ivory towers in the big smoke, or even consider holding an event about the challenges facing healthcare in remote and rural areas, in a remote or rural area. Sitting at the forum, listening politely to the usual mix of hierarchically detached self-important people waxing lyrically about the challenges facing the provision of healthcare in the more sparsely populated regions of the UK, I couldn't help but me reminded of the stories of cultural insularity widely thought to have facilitated the demise of America's motor industry.

The story goes that after companies like Honda and Toyota had entered the North American car market in the early 1970's and even as these Japanese competitors then started to make significant inroads into it, the established hierarchy of America's car industry had remained out of touch with the threat these newcomers posed. This was because in the towns and cities these same senior executives and managers lived and worked, everyone was still driving an American made automobile. To the finance, operations, sales, and marketing executives based in Chicago, Detroit, or Michigan, the epicentres of the car industry in which almost everyone who wasn't entitled to a company car was obliged to drive an American branded vehicle, hearing concerns from the dealerships situated across the country about the rise and threat from these nascent imposters must have seemed like listening to a fairy-tale that was unfolding somewhere else. What was the problem the executives argued, everyone they knew was still driving an all-American automobile and everywhere they looked they were surrounded by American made cars. The dealers must be exaggerating, trying to get better terms, or perhaps making excuses for their falling sales volumes. The rest, as they say, is history and in 2009 after a long and socially painful decline, General Motors once the posterchild of American manufacturing, filed for bankruptcy.

I had arrived at the Nuffield Trust conference in London that morning having spent just over three hours on the train from Penrith to Euston. And my time in transit was one of the least of those attending that day. I'm fortunate that I can walk to Penrith's rail station on the Westcoast mainline from my front door in under ten minutes, five if I need to. Many of my fellow attendees had had to spend the previous night in London to ensure they would arrive at the forum on time. The Nuffield Trust is located on Cavendish Street in the heart of the capital, a half hour walk from Kings Cross and Paddington stations and a twenty-minute stroll from Euston. There are three tube stations less than a kilometre away and no shortage of London's nineteen thousand or so bus stops, are within a spit from number 59 Cavendish Street. The hosting of a forum tasked with understanding the challenges facing healthcare provision in remote and rural areas in such a location, felt beyond ironic. Trying to get people who have a choice of public transport options to understand the problems that a patient living in an isolated rural community might face when trying to access routine healthcare services, or highlighting the issue of staff travel and the massive rural opportunity cost of clinical time spent in transit, or of simply being able to get medical trainees to their places of education, is the very definition of banging your head on a wall.

The forum was chaired by the then Chief Executive of the Nuffield Trust, Nigel Edwards, a knowledgeable generally amenable chap, and an old hand in the health and care think tanking business. The aim of such healthcare think tanks appears to be to produce endless streams of expensive reports and glossy graphics which point out the bleeding obvious in a game that allows those in charge, is anyone I hear you ask, to show they are serious about understanding and unravelling the issues facing healthcare while ignoring the real elephants in the room so as not to cause offence to those in charge of the purse strings. Find me a document produced by a healthcare think tank that has achieved anything of lasting significance from the patient perspective. The primary purpose of the UK's health and care think tanks appears to be no more than ensuring their own perpetuation.

A report commissioned by NHS England published in June 2023, suggests the NHS and government have been fixated on NHS hospital and acute services for the past two decades and as a result have failed to invest in prevention and Primary Care. Why does it require a report, one which experience suggests will achieve little, to make the NHS even acknowledge the bleeding obvious. No shit Sherlock.

Chapter 15: A ride in the ambulance

"It is one of the triumphs of civilisation, as the light high bell of the ambulance sounded. Swiftly, cleanly, the ambulance sped to the hospital, having picked up instantly, humanely, some poor devil..."

Virginia Woolf; Mrs Dalloway

In early Autumn 2017 for the first time in my life I experienced severe chest pains and was taken, blue lighted, as some like to say, off to Carlisle Hospital. That morning, I had been to my local GP Practice to be inoculated against the usual nasties in preparation for a trip to India to celebrate our thirtieth wedding anniversary. I was given three injections by the practice nurse and after resting for the obligatory ten minutes in the patient waiting room, I was allowed to go home. A few hours later my chest felt as if it was shrinking in on itself, I could hardly breathe. After sliding from my seat like a reluctant sticky blancmange, I was just able to shuffle from the living room past the foot of the stairs and across the kitchen floor to reach up and unlock the front door. My sister-in-law, who was first on the scene said I looked terrible, as if I'd had the colour drained from me. An ambulance was called, and the crew arrived on scene in a matter of minutes. As they loaded me into the vehicle, I took the opportunity to undertake some unplanned research and started chatting. The driver, who looked in his mid-thirties told me he previously drove ambulances in his native Poland and had been in the UK and working for the NHS for almost a decade. His colleague was an older woman with a strong local accent I instantly recognised as Cumbrian. She had worked in the local NHS for over thirty years and when I asked her about the many change's she must have seen in that time she smiled broadly as she shook her head while gleefully telling me she was as sick as a parrot of the whole shebang and was looking forward to retirement later that year.

Initially I was driven to the nearest community hospital on the edge of Penrith. But as we pulled up outside the hospital the crew were advised that because I had reported having chest pains, I was officially in ambulance service parlance, a Category 2 response, and protocol dictated I should be taken to the nearest accident & emergency unit at Carlisle's Cumberland Infirmary. Off we trundled. As we headed up the M6 the lady who was in the back of the ambulance with me started asking questions, recording my answers and making notes using a pen and paper. I asked her why she wasn't using an iPad or something similar to which she replied that she wasn't a fan of technology and hoped not to have to use any before her imminent retirement. She said she enjoyed journeys up the motorway as the time in transit allowed her to make notes in good time. At this point, the driver joined in the conversation and said that in his opinion the use of technology in healthcare was more advanced in Poland than in the UK. He told of his surprise at joining the hallowed NHS only to find out how inefficient and technologically backward it was. His colleague groaned as if knowing what he would say, I got the feeling he took every opportunity to make the point. I sympathised with him. Having had experience working in numerous sectors before joining the NHS in 2012, I had been flabbergasted, I'm being polite, at the stone age state of technology in Britain's healthcare system. I asked the lady taking the notes how the information in them would be made available to the hospital once we arrived. She said they would be handed over to the consultant and then manually entered onto any relevant patient record systems. I asked how the ambulance crew would have gathered information about me and my symptoms and the context leading up to them if I hadn't been conscious. How would they know that what I was experiencing was possibly the result of a reaction to the inoculations I had been given that morning if I hadn't been able to communicate this to them. The simple answer I was told, is that they wouldn't have. Even if the practice nurse I had seen that day had entered the information about the vaccinations I had been given onto my patient record, the ambulance crew wouldn't have been able to access those records. I was about to ask if the information they were now capturing for use by the hospital would eventually be transferred electronically to my patient records in Primary Care, but I didn't. I think I knew the answer before I asked.

The digital infrastructure and recording systems used by each regional ambulance service are largely unique to it, they do not integrate seamlessly, if at all sometimes, with the hospital systems, of which there are many, which in turn don't integrate seamlessly with the various different systems in Primary Care. Primary Care, regional ambulance services, community services, secondary acute and specialist tertiary services, are all working to implement technology in splendid isolation of each other. Duplication of systems and effort abounds and as a result of no-one effectively being in charge or in control, no parts of the system seem able to interact seamlessly and fluently with each other. The companies that deliver parcels of non-essential stationery and gifts to businesses and homes in the UK each day would appear to have more joined up technology than NHS Ambulance Services.

I think this was my third trip in an ambulance. I don't recall much about the previous two. The first time was in the mid-nineties, I was attacked and kicked unconscious during a night out in town. My nose has never looked the same since. The second time was a couple of years after the millennium. I started fitting and was barely conscious after winning and then foolishly drinking a bottle of Aftershock at the Halloween fancy dress competition in the local pub. Debbie has never forgiven me for having to direct the attending ambulance crew through a gathering of drunken Zombies, Mummies, and Ghouls, to a spasming husband dressed as Dracula. I'm told the spattered fake blood on everyone's costumes caused great concern to the paramedics who were initially unsure what they had been called to and just who was in need of medical attention. I was sent home from the local hospital earlier that morning. Utterly ashamed of my behaviour I sent a cheque and a letter of apology to the North West Ambulance Service the following week.

In 2022, some years after my trip to Carlisle Hospital, I became involved in a project working with a small organisation called the Professional Records Standards Body. The PRSB had been commissioned to look at establishing core information standards for shared care records in the areas of pharmacy, optometry, dentistry, ambulance, and community services. I was one of five non-clinical public representatives involved in the project, voices from outside the system if you like, and I was allocated to the ambulance workstream. The ten ambulance services of England and the Welsh ambulance service are represented by the Association of Ambulance Chief Executives. The creation of AACE, as they snappily refer to themselves, was to *establish a highly visible organisation able to link with other national bodies to develop policy, and progress work programmes, in an effective and efficient way.* The AACE website goes on to say that they are ideally placed, with *all the right contacts and expertise, to help facilitate the sharing of best practice and the provision of high-level advice and guidance to any organisation involved in urgent or emergency healthcare.* No mention of patients or of seeking to improve patient care I noticed, but I thought the big-brained folks at AACE would be a useful bunch from which a layperson like me might obtain some in-depth information on how ambulance services are used. And so, the fun began.

I contacted AACE, explaining what I was doing and who I was doing it on behalf of. I asked if someone could find half an hour at a time of their choosing for a video call to help me understand the nature, the type and frequency of demand on ambulance services nationally, and how they capture and use the data. What they do, where they do it, how much of it they do, who they do it to, and why they do it. For example, what are the largest causes of demand on services, is it falls amongst the frail and elderly, hypoglycaemic fits, heart attacks, strokes, respiratory problems, road accidents, overdoses, transports from care homes, etc. They responded swiftly and signposted me to the performance reports they publish each month which are placed on their website. Ambulance services categorise and report their activity using a standard set of response time classification criteria, from C1, an immediate response to a life-threatening condition, through to C4, a non-urgent problem requiring transport to a clinical setting.

I emailed them back thanking them for their reply and explained that I was more interested in the nature of demand and not just the amounts. My thinking was that if the demand on services could be segmented into the types of need and the demographics, then the project I was involved with could prioritise which aspects of a patient medical record and what shared information would be most useful to both the ambulance crews and the healthcare professionals they handed patients to. AACE replied in June 2022 saying they would get back to me. I'm still waiting. In the absence of a meaningful response from the body purporting to have access to all the right contacts and expertise, I approached the regional and home countries ambulance services individually to see if they had a handle on their data. Some of them were responsive and incredibly helpful, the Welsh Ambulance, and the North West Ambulance Services, were the most responsive. Some simply never replied. And others were disappointingly defensive and at times clearly confused as to why someone might want such information. In my view the kind of information most private sector businesses dealing in activity much less valuable than the transport of patients would undoubtedly have at their fingertips. My many pleas for conversations were met with email responses from Communication Directors, Information Governance Officers, and Project Support Officers, suggesting I submit an official freedom of information request if I wanted such information. I also approached some international ambulance services, and it was both pleasing and incredibly frustrating that I was able to communicate and speak more easily with ambulance services in Denmark, Finland, Ireland, New Zealand, and Queensland Australia.

As well as the St John Ambulance Service which is contracted to provide some NHS funded services in certain areas, the UK is also home to twenty-one separate charitably funded Air Ambulance Services. Between them these regional charities regularly attend over one hundred missions each day. Air Ambulances UK, a national charity that exists to support the work of the UK's Air Ambulance Services, estimates the cost of each helicopter mission at just under four thousand pounds. It goes without saying that when I asked the NHS funded ambulance services that were good enough to respond and engage with me, if their patient record systems were linked to any of the various regional air ambulance services, the answer was an unambiguous no.

If the principle of marketing is correct, that the more you know about someone the more you can sell to them, then the same rule can be applied in healthcare, the more you know about your patients, the better you can treat them. What's also true as well as incredibly important in a healthcare setting is the speed at which the appropriate treatment is applied. The prompt treatment of stroke victims can be the difference between life and death. In remote and rural areas, the time a patient spends in transit before reaching a clinical setting can be significant. Why is it that for a few pounds a month a small business employing a handful of people can give its employees an application on their smartphones which subject to coverage provides them with instant access to detailed information about their contacts and customers wherever they are whenever they need it, yet the nations ambulance services cannot access our patient records? This lack of access to vital clinical information in places like Cumbria, is a genuine risk to patient safety.

What emerged from my involvement in the PRSB project, a project with what I felt was a relatively simple and laudable aim, was an understanding of just how disparate, disjoined and technologically backward England's regional ambulance services are. It's bad enough that ambulance service systems aren't equipped to communicate easily with the other parts of Britain's health and care system. But can there really be a valid reason other than ineptitude and mismanagement why the UK's ambulance services do not possess the same digital infrastructure and have one common patient record system between them? It's an absurd state of affairs. I have friends who work in both the urgent and the non-urgent patient transport sides of NHS ambulance services. The pressure call handlers experience has long been known to be a leading source of stress, and the work of ambulance crews, drivers, and paramedics, who are often the first to arrive at a scene the rest of us would run in the other direction from, is genuinely inspirational. But their ability to do their work effectively and efficiently is hampered by the absence of information they have access to and the silos they work in. Silos which the Association of Ambulance Chief Executives seem happy to perpetuate. But which of the well-paid ambulance service chief executives will be the first to say, I'm not needed?

Chapter 16: **The heroes at the hospital**

"How very little can be done under the spirit of fear."

Florence Nightingale

At the height of the Covid-19 pandemic in 2020, one of the UK's other great treasures, the wonderfully subversive cultural Zorro known as Banksy, unveiled a painting in which a young boy was depicted kneeling down, playing with a superhero nurse toy while model figures of Batman and Spiderman were left unused in the nearby toy basket. The painting was delivered to an NHS hospital in Southampton and was later sold to raise money for an NHS charity. The painting sold for over fourteen million pounds and the final sum raised, including the buyer's premium donated by the art auctioneers Christies, was over sixteen million pounds. Banksy's inspirational work was part of a swathe of Corona virus related street art that appeared in many cities and towns around the world. The Frontline Heroes of the world's health services were acknowledged, recognized, celebrated, and lionized as larger than life in a way like never before. Stunning captivating images of nurses in their blue uniforms and clinical staff in their green surgical scrubs were lovingly etched on brickwork and buildings from Vancouver to Vilnius, Melbourne to Michigan, and Paris to Pontefract. Some sported wings, others were depicted wearing Superman vests, others were shown holding the world heroically and steadily on their shoulders like the Greek God Atlas, and many were simply images of frontline staff accompanied by the words, *Thank You*.

In 2022 a survey conducted by YouGov named nursing as the top profession for their contribution to society. The British public believe nurses make the greatest contribution, followed closely by doctors. I asked my seventeen-year-old Niece recently if she would consider a career as a nurse when she leaves school. She looked at me horrified, *"Oh my god uncle Tom, I can't imagine anything worse, do you know the shit they have to deal with"*, she exclaimed as she lasered my ill-informed attempt at career guidance with a well-rehearsed look of teenage dismissive disgust. She is a bright young lady who I'm sure will end up earning a good wage in a less demanding, if less rewarding role elsewhere.

The British government pledged to boost NHS nursing numbers by fifty thousand by March 2024. But NHS workers are heading for the exit in unprecedented numbers, citing burnout, fatigue, and pay as significant factors in their decision to leave. A 2020 survey by the Royal College of Nursing found nearly three quarters of nurses said the staffing level on their latest shift had not been sufficient to meet the needs of patients safely or effectively. In 2022 NHS England sent a letter suggesting nurses increase their hours and encouraging those who were due to retire to reconsider. An article in the Times in November 2022 revealed that some NHS Trusts were paying over two-thousand pounds per shift to private sector nursing agencies. The total spent on agency staff by the NHS in 2022/23 is said to have exceeded three billion pounds. Agency nurses, some of whom earn multiples of the NHS employees they are brought in to work alongside, complain they are treated differently by their NHS colleagues who resent the amount they earn. I can't imagine why.

Estimates of the current global shortage of healthcare professionals' range upward from four to six million. Research by the World Health Organisation claims there will be a projected shortfall of ten million health workers by 2030, mostly in lower to middle income countries. A report published in March 2023 by the International Council of Nurses, claims the current worldwide shortage of nurses is of such significance that it should be viewed and treated as a global health emergency. It points out that though the problem existed prior to the pandemic, the rate of attrition in nursing is rising and the numbers of nurses saying they intend to quit the profession has risen globally to one in five. The clinical recruitment and retention challenges faced by public, private, and third sector healthcare providers in the UK are indicative of a much broader and globally significant issue. To add to what was already a challenged landscape, the World Health Organisation estimates that around two hundred thousand healthcare workers lost their lives during in the two years following the onset of the Covid-19 outbreak.

A further report released in June 2021 by those busy report writers at the Royal College of Nursing pointed out that NHS trusts had taken to recruiting people without the right qualifications to function as registered nurses, despite the risk to patients. The College criticised what it claimed as a worrying trend driven by the widespread shortage of nurses in England and published examples of advertisements posted by NHS trusts looking to fill nursing roles, including some senior positions, even if the candidate was not qualified as a nurse. One trust advertised for a matron to work in acute medicine, a managerial role usually filled by a senior nurse, stating that a qualification in nursing was not necessary. And before you ask, I don't know which NHS Trust it was so I can't tell you. We'll all just have to take our chances together!

Such is the desperate state of recruitment and retention in our beloved NHS that the UK government has for some years been imploring the captains of the fleet's ships to send raiding parties to previously unexplored shores in search of new recruits. We have somehow managed to make nursing and healthcare such undesirable vocations to our own citizens that we cannot attract, recruit, or retain the people needed to work in Britain's best loved brand and most revered national icon. One local hospital in Northern England lost nearly all its nursing assistants when Sainsbury's opened a new supermarket nearby. They were offering similar wages for stacking shelves and none of the bullying or pressure this particular hospital is known for. Rather than address the fundamental issues we have known about for decades that are driving nurses and doctors from the NHS, we are attempting to solve our problems by stealing staff from elsewhere, from developing nations who can scarce afford to lose them. It feels like a form of clinical colonialism, healthcare imperialism in which the wealthier nations of the world once again plunder their poorer neighbours for resources. The need in these countries is without doubt greater than ours but their ability to pay is not. Figures released in 2022 by the Nursing and Midwifery Council showed record numbers of overseas trained nurses are coming to work in the UK.

During recent years you will doubtless have read or heard a story from the local press about the many successful international recruitment campaigns undertaken by your local NHS Trust. These stories are fed to uninquisitive local journalists and copywriters to counter the tales of doom and gloom that are carried by the larger national media channels. The countries of origin for the new recruits to our NHS have included Kenya, Sri Lanka, Philippines, Nigeria, and Malaysia. In 2021 the governments of the UK and Kenya agreed a deal that enabled Kenyan nurses to come and work in the UK. In exchange Kenya's government would be reimbursed, apparently with a proportion of each nurse's wages, and the nurses who came here would have the chance to apply for UK citizenship. In 2022 the UK government drafted an understanding with the government of Sri Lanka to encourage and enable nurses and other healthcare professionals from Sri Lanka to work in the UK.

Life expectancy in Kenya is significantly less than in the UK at around 66yrs and infant mortality is around ten times higher than the UK at just over 31 deaths per 1,000 births. Life expectancy in Sri Lanka is significantly better than Kenya's if official statistics can be believed and infant mortality is just under double the UK's at around 6 deaths per 1,000 births. As for Nigeria, life expectancy there is one of the lowest in the world at just under 55yrs and Nigeria's infant mortality rates make Kenya look positively outstanding at a staggering 72 deaths per 1,000 births. In July 2022 media outlets in Nigeria reported the migration of Nigerian-trained nurses to the UK had intensified and increased by a whopping 68%, reaching an all-time high of 7,256 in the preceding year. The UK has subsequently stopped recruiting qualified healthcare workers from Nigeria after the World Health Organisation highlighted Nigeria as a country that needed to preserve all its medical expertise to address its own significant healthcare challenges. Would NHS Trusts and the UK government have continued to welcome health and care staff from Nigeria if they hadn't been shamed into doing so?

But when one door closes, another one opens. In August 2022, the UK government signed a deal with the government of Nepal to recruit nurses from what is widely regarded as one of the poorest and least developed countries in the world. Millions of Nepalese live in abject poverty, the economy is in tatters, and the war in Ukraine is having a negative impact on a country that relies heavily on imports. The government is short of money, desperate for foreign currency, and in no position to negotiate on strong terms. Importantly, worryingly, Nepal remains on the WHO's recruitment red list of countries that need to retain their own medical skills to serve their own citizens. The UK government has effectively kicked one of the most vulnerable countries in the world when it is already down in order to address a long-standing recruitment crisis which is largely of its own making.

How has our once hallowed NHS become such an unattractive employment option that it is unable to recruit and keep the staff it needs, that we all need, from our own shores? How have we reached a point where the future workforce of the NHS would rather replenish the pot noodle display in Sainsbury's than create a career in healthcare? And can it be right on any level that we are stealing the medically qualified from poor and developing countries, the populations of which all have lower life expectancies than the UK? This clinically colonial approach to shoring up our ailing NHS has a distinct whiff of unprincipled fuckwittery and short-sighted unsustainability around it. We are once again stealing precious resources from other regions, effectively depriving the needy and vulnerable in some of the least developed countries who would benefit most from the valuable expertise we are taking from them. And just as in the bad old days of empire, we are competing with other developed nations, Europe, and the USA, for these scarce resources. Germany, along with numerous others, is just one of a lengthy list of countries that has been proactively recruiting health and care staff from less developed nations. Around 2,000 Filipino nurses have been recruited into Germanys healthcare system in the last few years. Many more are being sought.

The report the WHO published and the so-called red list of 47 countries it produced in which Nigeria and Nepal were highlighted, was created in response to the increasing global shortage of medical staff and the burgeoning outflow of health and care professionals from countries that need them most. The WHO has been aware for some time that the combined impact of Western nations poaching health and care staff from the less well-off and less developed is having a significant impact on the ability of poorer countries to provide effective health and care services to their own citizens. Almost half of new nurses in England are now trained abroad and just two out of every five junior doctors in the NHS are UK-trained. Nursing leaders globally are calling upon high-income countries to adopt a strategic approach and invest in nurse training and retention instead of increasing their international recruitment efforts.

Welcoming the bad and the bogus:

When we import medical and clinical ability from other countries to fill the gaps in our creaking healthcare services, we have fewer guarantees of its quality. Transparency International, a global movement set up in 1995 that now works in over one hundred countries and who's stated mission is to stop corruption and promote transparency, accountability, and integrity at all levels and across all sectors of society, publishes an annual index of countries. The information they use is drawn from numerous sources including the World Bank and the World Economic Forum. The organisation collates data and then scores each nation from 0 to 100, the higher the score the less corrupt. Nigeria has consistently been ranked amongst the most corrupt countries in the world since the index was created. Having visited the country twice I wouldn't disagree. Its score as of 2021 was 24 out of a possible 100, and it sits in joint 154th place alongside Lebanon and the Central African Republic. Sri Lanka, Kenya, and the Philippines fair little better. Malaysia is the best of this bunch with a score of 48 out of a 100. Nothing to worry about there then!

In 2016 the WHO published a report that lambasted the lack of oversight and monitoring in India's health and care system. The proportion of practising genuine Doctors who were officially qualified and medically able to provide safe healthcare in some parts of India, was less than one in five. Forging a certificate that states you are medically qualified is child's play to anyone with a basic computer and a half-decent printer. And in Sri Lanka, bribing officials to obtain the qualifications needed to work in almost any field, is not uncommon. My family lived in Sri Lanka for a couple of years when it was still called Ceylon and my late father spent many years working there before eventually retiring to the island some time ago. Corruption and the arranging of bribes was an accepted and expected part of daily life. The Sri Lankan economy effectively collapsed early in 2022. Many Sri Lankans feel the country has become more corrupt over the past two decades. Its gradually declining scores on the Transparency International website and the very visible anti-corruption rioters on the streets of its capital Colombo, would suggest their belief is correct.

Here in the UK NHS Trusts have become so short of staff they are actively trying to pinch nurses from each other using expensive advertising campaigns and glossy brochures. The Cornwall Partnership NHS Foundation Trust paid for billboard advertising on Manchester's rail stations to try and tempt mental health nurses from England's rainy Northwest to the sunnier climes of the Southeast. At the same time, Lancashire Care NHS Foundation Trust was funding a recruitment drive aimed at medical staff under the title, *Lancashire. A great place to live and work*. NHS Trusts in the Northeast and Cumbria also developed websites and promotional materials aimed at enticing clinical staff from other parts of the country, and other NHS Trusts, to come and work in the area.

My mum tells me that *in her day*, to be able to say you had trained at the Edinburgh Royal was almost a guarantee of being offered whatever nursing post you applied for. She also told me that one of the things she learned from her time on the wards after she qualified, was that when a hospital wanted rid of a sub-standard or unpopular consultant, they politely encouraged them on and gave them a glowing reference. It seems little has changed. As well as welcoming non-clinical managers and directors who have been exiled from elsewhere in the UK, Cumbria's NHS has been suffering such a severe recruitment and retention crisis that it has become a magnet for the clinically bogus and the bad. Such practitioners leave a trail behind them before the evidence of their poor practice or lack of skills becomes too obvious to be ignored any longer. They then disappear from the county as mysteriously quietly and as quickly as the press releases celebrating their arrival were created and sent to the local paper. Britain imports many health and care professionals, nurses, and budding students seeking a career in medicine, from some of the most openly corrupt countries in the world. Countries in which money talks and with friends in the right places a medical qualification can be yours.

On the 28th of February 2023, Zholia Alemi was sentenced to seven years in prison. In 2018, Dr Zholia Alemi, 56, Ms. Alemi as I imagine she is now known to her fellow inmates, had been working as a psychiatrist in Cumbria, was finally exposed as a fraud who had falsified her qualifications and faked her medical ability for over 22yrs. She was only found out when she tried to forge a new will for an elderly dementia patient in her attempt to inherit their £1.3m estate. She had faked the necessary clinical qualifications and created a false letter of recommendation from a fictional job in Pakistan before finally registering as a doctor with the UK's General Medical Council (GMC). But for the efforts of an unusually dogged local reporter her charade may have continued indefinitely. The NHS Trust that employed Ms. Alemi has said little about the whole affair, the HR Director quietly moved on from her post, probably with a good wedge. The final cost of the subsequent and doubtless significant financial claims for compensation from the patients who were treated by an unqualified quack and their families and loved ones, will still be accruing. There is good reason to believe the case of Dr Alemi is not an isolated one. A healthcare system that is reduced to recruiting anyone from anywhere with a pulse is not a safe one.

The healthcare profession and the people working in and around it know these unqualified potentially dangerous individuals are present in the system, and in some cases know who they are. But for an organisation to admit it hired an unqualified if gifted forger, or someone who could afford to pay for an authentically sourced if unearned educational certificate, into a publicly funded position of trust in which they were tasked with dealing with societies most vulnerable, is no small thing. In many cases these people, if, or when they are identified, are discreetly moved along, sideways, sometimes upwards, before their presence and its consequences can be discovered.

Our people are our most important asset:

I've lost count of the times I've seen glossy brochures, or NHS websites, or how often I've heard an NHS director or chief executive say, "our people are our most important asset". It suggests employees through their status as sentient beings must be acknowledged as being at the top of a long list of other lessor assets, simply resources to be harnessed or sweated, as more corporate types might say. But the reality is that an organisation's manufacturing processes, its supply chains, bespoke software, or intellectual property might be its most valued and value producing asset. But these innate entities won't complain if they remain unacknowledged in the annual report. People like their efforts and presence to be recognised.

That people within organisations still refer to their fellows as, an important asset, feels inherently at odds with our humanity. I can understand that at some level it's a useful distinction that allows people to make decisions about restructuring and refocusing, or hiring and firing, while allowing them to remain mentally and emotionally disengaged from the consequences of their decisions. You didn't lay off and destroy the lives of a few hundred or a few thousand people, you merely rejigged your assets to meet the needs of your business. But does any organisation even exist without *its people*; perhaps some may do so in the future, but for now I think most would agree that an organisation, is its people. Perhaps, rather than glibly stating that people are their most important asset, the more appropriate mindset for leaders would be to acknowledge that they and the organisations they run are nothing without their people.

For fifteen years at least, the preeminent challenge facing NHS health and care services has been the recruitment and retention of staff, especially nurses. During my time in and around the NHS I've had many discussions about the challenges of trying to attract people to work in the NHS. Of all the conversations that have stuck in my mind there is one in particular that lifts the lid on the poor culture in the NHS and helps answers the question of how it came to this. Picture the scene if you will, as he tolerates my presence in his office, my director, who is stood looking purposefully out the window, his hands held together behind his back like Mussolini addressing an adoring crowd, pronounces in a lofty knowing tone, *"Working as a nurse in the NHS is just a job like any other to the people who do it"*. Then as a comedian misjudging his audience, he mistook my stunned silence for encouragement and in a rising increasingly oratorial voice proclaimed, *"To me in this job as a director, this is so much more than just a job; so much more. To me"*, his voice climbing steadily to the finale, *"it is about the very future of this organisation"*. It was by any stretch of the imagination an incredible feat of perceptual self-delusion, to turn the caring of patients from vocation to commodity, whilst simultaneously raising his own pen pushing and administrative acts to the status of noble deeds. Here was a man who had spent three decades kissing arses telling me he was more important than a nurse who knows what it's like to wipe one.

He had no idea when he said this that my mum, my gran, and my aunt had all been nurses. They had real skin in the game. Often serving communities they lived in and knew, sometimes forming lasting friendly professional relationships with many of their patients. They saw the hapless bureaucrats, managers and directors, self-proclaimed leaders without followers who had little knowledge of the world outside their office were a problem, not the solution. If they'd been in the room when he expressed his ill-informed opinions, he wouldn't have got out alive. Sure, not every nurse is Florence Nightingale, I understand that better than most. But despite what happened to Alison, it's still my belief most people attracted to nursing see it as a vocation and they want to serve. The overwhelming majority of nurses I have met both as a patient and during my time as a manager in the NHS are hard-working and dedicated. But of course, they are just mortals, not angels. They are prone to the same temptations and habits, good and bad, that befall employees in any setting. In most instances where they have behaved badly, sometimes incredibly harmfully, even fatally, it is generally the result of feeble characters working in bullied teams or collusive cultures that won't let them admit their mistakes. And of trying to achieve targets which detract their effort and attention from caring for patients.

The nurses I used to work with laughed at the idea that they needed new sets of values, patronisingly presented to them at expensive launch events every few years by directors who appeared to have jettisoned their own moral compasses some time ago. These same nurses told me they were under pressure covering vacant posts that managers were refusing to advertise so the Trust could save money to keep and build its reserves. Values; really?

Nurses taking their own lives:

I remember having a whizz bang idea soon after joining the NHS. My thought was that if we could access data that showed which industries created the most mental health demand on the NHS, then we could work with the local public health team to educate the businesses that operated in these sectors. Perhaps sharing best practice for good employment, and if that failed, naming and shaming them. I bounced this winning idea off one of the GPs I knew. She was a senior figure in the NHS in Cumbria at the time. She agreed with the idea in principle before telling me that the vast majority of people in employment who came to her practice looking for help with their mental health, were NHS employees and it wouldn't be a good advert for the local NHS if people knew this. I thought at the time she was exaggerating, I found out to my cost that she most certainly wasn't.

In April 2022, a local democracy reporter in Derbyshire called Eddie Bisknell ran a story highlighting the morale of staff working in the Royal Derby Hospitals Accident and Emergency Department. A leaked internal report had revealed a department in which exhaustion was rife, burnout prevailed, and sickness absence was as high as staff morale was low. Employees had been told to cry privately to avoid upsetting others.

Staff claimed the level of underqualified and inexperienced personnel in the hospital made some services unsafe. They said they felt they were losing their humanity as they were constantly pushed by managers to hit a range of performance targets. A member of staff reportedly told the internal review team that they couldn't continue, and they felt like they were drowning. Another said they were scared and worried that someone would be pushed too far.

Post pandemic research undertaken by Arizona State University suggests that talk of burnout amongst healthcare staff is in itself, inadequate. It says what many healthcare professionals and patient facing staff are actually suffering with, is a form of trauma and it likens the mental health of those who are struggling as akin to what soldiers who have engaged in battle experience. It says, *"For health care workers, it is no leap of the imagination to view the uncertainty, exhaustion, stress, grief, and lack of support as forms of complex trauma. Nor is it a leap to view the resulting dissonance, instability, avoidant coping, disorientation, and dissociation as responses to this complex trauma."*

Gemma Clay is a nurse and a clinical doctorate fellow at University Hospitals Sussex NHS Foundation Trust. In 2020 she was shortlisted as a finalist for Nurse of the Year. She has undertaken a great deal of research into the high and growing levels of stress, mental illness, and suicide amongst nurses. I spoke with Gemma in 2023 about an article she had written for the Nursing Times the previous summer in which she talked candidly about her own mental health experiences and highlighted the significant and unrelenting pressure nurses were under. I had first become aware of the issue of suicide amongst nurses after reading a piece in one of the national newspapers claiming over three hundred nurses in England and Wales had taken their own lives between 2011 and 2017. Gemma spoke openly about some of the pressures of nursing in today's NHS. In a heavily regulated profession, the practitioners of which can be struck off while those who manage and oversee them remain largely unaccountable, and in a vocation that exposes them to the extremes of the human condition, nurses can easily become trapped in an invidious and increasingly unmanageable emotional situation, which not all can see a way out of. As well as being exposed to the full spectrum of emotions while keeping tick-box happy managers at bay, many nurses and clinicians feel a toxic culture exists in which internal incident reporting systems are used as tools to threaten, sometimes to ensure silence, and sometimes to shift blame. On top of this, they are also subjected to the increasing pressure of rising living costs. Research undertaken by the Laura Hyde Foundation, a charity that seeks to ensure people working in medical services can access the mental health support they need, reported a seventy percent surge in health staff seeking help with suicidal thoughts and claimed that over two hundred and twenty nurses had attempted to take their own lives during the first year of the pandemic.

It won't surprise anyone to learn that the impact of a burnt out traumatised poorly treated workforce on a hospitals' ability to provide safe patient care, is significant.

To anyone who will listen I'm often heard sharing my amazement at how my former employer Carlsberg seemed infinitely more able to recognise and value its staff in the service of selling sugary alcoholic liquid to the masses than the NHS seems able to for people employed in what is surely the greatest vocation of our times. How did we reach a place where before the pandemic, NHS Trusts had to offer signing-up bonuses and financial incentives to get people to work for them? It's notable that many who came back to practice their craft in the fight against the pandemic were attracted by duty, altruism, and the chance to make a difference. Why did it take a global pandemic for people to understand the true value of doctors, nurses, and care staff? They have been undervalued and mismanaged by their employers for too long.

Around a quarter of NHS Trusts in England run food banks for staff. Some NHS Trusts have reported staff using sick days to avoid going to work as they can't afford the transport costs to get there. And while healthcare staff have been fighting for a pay increase, apparently the non-fungible token claps and pan banging we provided during the pandemic are not recognised as currency by energy suppliers, mortgage providers, or supermarkets, those straddling the ridge of what passes for leadership in the NHS, have been doing just fine. An article featured in the Mirror in 2021 claimed that almost three thousand senior managers in the NHS were on salaries of over one hundred and ten thousand pounds, a combined annual total of nearly four hundred million. This would be terrific value if things were going swimmingly. In January 2023 NHS England was criticized by national auditors after it emerged that a number of significant and unauthorized payoffs had been made to senior managers whose roles were no longer needed. Not a phrase you are likely to hear in relation to nurses anytime soon. Figures from the Office of National Statistics reveal corporate managers and directors have some of the lowest rates of suicide. I think for many NHS directors and senior managers who flit seamlessly from one healthcare system or Hospital Trust to another, there is no real attachment to areas or communities, it really is just a job. To most nurses, I think it will always be much more. The number of lives being lost is less than in the First World War, but it would seem nurses, and for that matter many of the frontline health and social care staff we depend on, now more than ever, are the lions of our era, led by a large and well-fed herd of donkeys.

Chapter 17: Sane in a crazy world

"The barometer of the success of any nation is the health and wellbeing of its people. We have a long way to go before we can say we are a thriving nation."

Mental Health Foundation; 2017

Two years before the outbreak of Covid-19, in 2017 a long-established charity called the Mental Health Foundation published a report called *Surviving or Thriving? The state of the UK's mental health*. The first of the three headline conclusions it reached is that Britain's current levels of good mental health were disturbingly low. The second was that the UK's collective mental health was deteriorating. The third of its cheery conclusions was that the risks of experiencing mental illness were higher for females, young adults, and those on low incomes. The positive news for me is that we over 55's apparently experience better mental health than average. In my own case I put that down to reaching an age at which I've learned what really matters in life and no longer giving a flying feck for what other people think. And it's genuinely liberating. And as well as being constantly aware that poor mental health could pull me under at the time of its choosing, I also know that I'm incredibly fortunate. Though we are not wealthy by many measures, we don't have to worry about money, yet. The small-terraced house we live in is paid for and Debbie and I aren't overly materialistic. I recall how differently we felt when we were struggling. It is undoubtedly easier to roll on the waves of life's adversities when you have some anchors.

All the available evidence, and more importantly Ruby Wax whose writing on mental health issues is both insightful and highly entertaining, suggests that Britain's emotional wellbeing and the mental health of large chunks of its population, is along with many other countries, heading for a precipice. Just like our physical health our mental health exists on a continuum. There are times I feel fit enough to cycle up a decent sized fell, and there are times I feel stretched after doing just a few miles on the flat. We aren't physically or mentally ill or healthy in an on or off black and white sense. We are always somewhere on the continuum, at one end or the other or somewhere in the middle. At times so far towards one end of it that we can't imagine being at any other point on it or able to empathise with those who are.

The quality of our lives and in large part our individual and collective wellbeing is inextricably linked to the quality of our aspirations. In November 2022, senior representatives from nineteen charities and organisations involved in suicide prevention and mental health sent an open letter to the Prime Minister. In it they pointed out that the first intervention needed to reduce mental ill health and prevent suicide would be to ensure that every household had the means to be safe and warm and with enough to eat. They then urged the Prime Minister to act with speed and compassion to tackle the root causes of destitution, to prevent suicide and stem the rise in mental ill health. Their letter is just yet another indicator of how far we have fallen, and how far we have allowed ourselves to fall. The letter was also in my view, an overly optimistic effort to secure compassion from the wealthy husband of an even wealthier woman who avoided paying tax in the UK until her reticence to contribute to the country she was living in was highlighted by the national press. Ready for Rishi, I'm not sure we ever could be.

Data from NHS England showed the number of prescriptions for antidepressants almost doubled from thirty-six million in 2008 to over seventy million in 2018; I'm one of those statistics and the tribe I'm in is growing. Post pandemic estimates suggest that between four and six million people in the UK are now using antidepressants and every ten seconds, someone in the UK calls the Samaritans. I had their number listed as a contact on my phone for a while. I can tell you from experience the service they provide to people in the eye of a mental health crisis is incredible. Mental health is a subject that's close to my heart for many reasons and there are times when I feel able to talk objectively about mental health and suicide, and times when I feel physically sick thinking about it and the impact it has on everyone involved. The following text is taken from my previous book, The Killing of Alison, it's my feeble attempt to highlight a small part of the impact a suicide has.

"I can only describe Alison's death as like a bomb going off in a small room. An emotional grenade lobbed through the unsuspecting window of the warm and homely living room of our lives. You cannot jump behind the sofa or shield your eyes from the blast. There is nowhere to hide

from the shockwaves. Suicide in a family strikes the very epicentre, the safe and treasured space of your world. Everything is thrown in the air, the ground you stood on, the things you once held true, the certainties you had, the aspirations you had, the mental lens you use to view and make sense of the world shifts irrevocably. It is truly a What the Fuck moment.

Try if you will. Close your eyes and imagine you have just been told someone close to you, dear to you, someone you love, has taken their own life without warning or notice. There is no lengthy suicide note of explanation. They did not text you with an outline of the logic leading to their decision. There was no dark brooding, obviously ominous post on Facebook. You have not had the chance to talk to them recently, but you recall the last time you did, and they seemed fine. Go on, try.

Suicide is most definitely not painless for those left behind. And who else can you blame but yourself for not seeing it coming? My family and I were largely ignorant of the potentially lethal consequences of mental illness. To talk openly of it in the eighties and early nineties was almost unacceptable. Use of the word suicide, the S word, was beyond the breaking of taboo in polite circles. People died suddenly; they didn't take their own lives. Suicide prevention training wasn't even yet a glimpse in the eyes of public health officials, charities, or government departments.

When suicide takes someone, you cannot hunt down their attacker, the assailant or drunk driver. You will not get to look your loved one's killer in the eyes across a court room, or shout at the cancer or fundraise to search for a cure into whatever malevolent medical condition is responsible. In the privacy of your own mind, you can only keep asking why. Why, why, and why, again and again. Why didn't she talk to us? Why couldn't she see how much she meant to us? Why didn't she realise things were going to get better? Why did she choose the one option that closes all the other possibilities down? And of course, why didn't I make more time for my sister, why couldn't I see it coming?".

I don't think I will ever stop guessing what thoughts were going through my sister Alison's mind when she stepped in front a train at Rotherham station. My predominant thought is that it was a last final act of control and self-determination. The only escape route she could see from the despair that the chemicals running riot in her head and the situations she had been exposed to had created. I will never know. What I do know is that my awareness and understanding about the loss of the life she could have led, becomes more acute as I get older and with each year I realise the increasing significance of her suicide.

Gambling with our mental health:

A paper published in the globally respected medical journal and world's highest-impact academic journal The Lancet, in January 2021, described the activity of gambling in the following stark terms; *Gambling involves placing something of value at risk in the hopes of gaining something of greater value...it is not an ordinary activity: it is a health harming addictive behaviour, recently recognised in the international Classification of Diseases 11th Revision and Statistical Manual of Mental Disorders, 5th Edition.* In the UK, guidelines for the treatment and management of gambling disorder are currently being developed by the National Institute for Health and Care Excellence (NICE). The article in The Lancet went on to highlight gambling as a source of potentially serious wide-ranging harms affecting families and communities. An incredibly worrying if largely self-evident statement when one realises that online gambling activities including highly addictive poker, bingo, and casino games are thought to have increased by up to six-fold amongst existing gamblers during the pandemic. With many who were struggling financially before the pandemic found to be more likely to engage in gambling during lockdown. A report published in April 2023 by the Bristol University based Personal Finance Research Centre suggests that almost twelve million adults and children in Britain may be negatively affected by someone who gambles. The cloud of Covid that propelled the uptake of online gambling has supplied a large and lucrative silver lining to the peddlers of dopamine fuelled financial risk taking who would like us all to have Las Vegas on our smartphones.

Gambling with Lives is a charity that was set-up in 2018 by people with lived experience of losing a loved-one to gambling related suicide. The charity aims to provide support to people affected by gambling and to raise awareness and understanding of gambling's all too often devastating impacts. Its co-founders Liz and Charles Ritchie lost their son Jack to gambling related suicide in 2017, he was twenty-four. A photo of Jack, looking happy, smiling, a young man with the rest of his life ahead of him is posted along with many others on the Gambling with Lives website in a gallery highlighting some of the victims of the gambling industry that have been lost to suicide. Their ages range from twenty to forty-six years old. The charity has set itself the vision of a world free from gambling related suicide and actively campaigns and develops and shares research to support its cause. In 2022 I met and spoke with Will Prochaska, the charities former CEO, now its director of strategy. Will, a former management consultant whose eyes, facial expressions, and slightly mad professor hair, exudes the intensity needed for such a purpose driven role, is under no illusions about the scale of the challenge they face and the weight and strength of their opposition. The gambling lobby is extremely well funded and incredibly well connected. But as Will reminded me, and as Margaret Mead famously observed, we should never doubt that a small group of thoughtful committed citizens can change the world; indeed, it's the only thing that ever has.

At a joint meeting of two All-Party Parliamentary Groups, the Suicide and Self Harm Prevention Group and the Gambling Related Harms Group held in November 2022, the MP Liz Twist, opened proceedings by unambiguously stating that there remains an established connection between gambling and suicide. The next speaker, Heather Wardle, an author, and reader in social sciences at Glasgow University, started her contribution by clearly restating the strong and substantial relationship between gambling and suicide. She in turn was followed by a contribution from a lady called Annie Ashton who had tragically lost her husband Luke to gambling related suicide in 2021. Annie explained that she had not even been aware her husband was gambling. She has since become a significant force for change and for good and her petition on the 38Degrees website to force the UK government to publish a revised gambling act, gained over ninety thousand signatures. It's my experience that people who have lived through an issue rather than studied it from a distance are those more likely to both understand it and in turn do something to address it. The systems current level of ignorance in relation to the harms gambling can cause is such that Annie had to hire legal representation to persuade the coroner to even look at gambling as a factor in her husband Luke's death. To become an assistant coroner or senior coroner in Britain currently requires no formal medical knowledge or mental health training. As a result, awareness and understanding of mental health issues within the UK's coronial system, is woeful.

The joint meeting of Parliamentary Interest Groups was then addressed by Dr Matt Gaskell. Matt is a consultant psychologist and clinical lead for addiction services at Leeds and York NHS Foundation Trust. He is also the clinical director of the NHS Northern Gambling Service which runs clinics in Leeds, Manchester, and Sunderland. Before you read any further, I would like to encourage you to reread the previous sentence, perhaps even dwell on it for a minute. I hope it shocks you as much as it shocks me to realise that the NHS is now running specialist clinics to deal with the fallout from the gambling industries gold rush. Neoliberalism and corporate self-interest are smashing the windows of our home, and the public sector and the public purse are then having to clean the glass up and replace the panes. I met with Dr Matt during my research for this book. Matt, like Will Prochaska from Gambling with Lives, is scathing about the disingenuous efforts the gambling companies currently engage in to encourage their customers to police and control their own behaviours. He points out that the industries calls for its customers to only engage in *responsible gambling* places the onus on problem and at-risk gamblers, to manage their own addictive behaviours and inculpates them for their increasingly uncontrollable actions. This explains Matt, creates a sense of shame in those who are addicted and therefore unable to stop voluntarily which in turn acts as a barrier to them asking for the help they need. The present self-management approach of the gambling industry does strike me as akin to drug pushers spreading a message amongst users that they really should take time out and seek to understand and manage their own behaviours and motivations to enable them to deal with their habit on their own. I'm all for personal responsibility, but this is not a level behavioural playing field and a trite message of self-determination that makes customers entirely responsible for their woes and predicaments is a hypocritical and contradictory one. Especially from an industry that spends one and a half billion pounds a year in the UK alone on analysing, influencing, driving, and nudging these very same customers behaviours to meet its own financial ends.

I may have caught Matt on a bad day, but I left our meeting under the impression that he felt he had wasted the last twenty-five years of his clinical career in mental health dealing with an ever-increasing stream of entirely avoidable failure demand, the human misery and mental illness that the rise of unchecked unprincipled capitalism has been allowed to create. He has become, unusually for an NHS employee, strident, forthright, and often outspoken in his views he is regularly trolled by representatives and supporters of the gambling lobby. He is also, in my opinion, precisely the kind of person the NHS and Britain's publicly funded health services need more of.

Studies from the USA publicised by the International Association of Suicide Prevention, IASP, during world suicide prevention week suggest that problem gamblers have the highest suicide rate of any of the known addiction disorders. A report published in 2018 by the Money and Mental Health Policy Institute, a research and advocacy body set up by every Brits favourite financial advisor and all-round champion of the economic underdog, Martin Lewis, found that people in problem debt are three times more likely to think about suicide than the rest of the population. It goes on to state that more than one hundred thousand people in debt, attempted suicide that year. That's the entire population of the City of Carlisle attempting mass suicide, and that was before the pandemic and a cost-of-living crisis. In 2022 the Money and Mental Health institute published a further policy note in which it observed that more than half of UK adults reported feeling anxious, depressed, filled with dread and unable to cope, due to concerns about their finances. It is a staggering and outrageous fact that people are literally dying from debt induced desperation and depression in one of the world's largest economies.

Suicide is already the largest killer of men under the age of forty-five in the UK. The Samaritans answer a call from someone in need every ten seconds and tragically, every ninety minutes someone takes their own life by suicide in Britain. The added weight of gambling-related debt placed upon sections of the community already laden with a toxic mix of post-austerity financial burdens and spiraling living costs is a perfect storm of despair which has stolen hope and robbed too many of the one chance we are all gifted in this life to flourish. Gambling debt is a breeze block on the backs of those already struggling to stay afloat and who are least able to carry it.

What are we doing to young people?

Research by the Royal College of Paediatrics and Child Health shows the rate of young people ending their own life has increased in the last five years. Suicide is one of the leading causes of death in children and young people between the ages of 15 and 24, with young men being three times more likely to take their own life. The research points out that the risk factors contributing to suicide are cumulative and cites deprivation and adverse childhood experiences as key ingredients in the cocktail. This paints a hellishly bleak picture of the future for the four million children said to be living in poverty in the UK and the four hundred thousand children known to social care services of whom a hundred thousand are in care. A good start in life for every child is so much more than a nice to have. It is the platform on which everything that follows is built. And by good I don't mean prosperous or affluent.

Almost one and a half million children and young people sought help from the NHS with their mental health during 2022/23, and the number of school age children being referred to specialist child and adolescent mental health services exceeded one million for the second year in a row. These included referrals for conditions including anxiety, depression, and eating disorders as well as a host of other complex psychological problems. The number of children self-harming has more than doubled in the last ten years and the UK Gambling Commission found the number of problem gamblers between the ages of eleven and sixteen had quadrupled over a two-year period. It now exceeds fifty thousand.

The neoliberal agenda and the internet have combined to unleash forces upon a world and its citizens that simply weren't equipped to deal with them, forces that may never be contained or tamed. The tragic death of fourteen-year-old Molly Russell from Harrow who took her own life in November 2017 after becoming hopelessly ensnared in a hope crushing cage of online content is undoubtedly merely one point on a continuum along which many other young people exist. In what was considered a landmark ruling, time will tell, the coroner concluded that Molly had died after suffering from the negative effects of online content. An article on the Business in the News website in the summer of 2020 claimed that three websites offering pornography regularly received more monthly traffic on their sites than Amazon or Netflix. A paper published in January 2021 linked mental illness in students with increased access to online pornography. My first exposure to pornography was in my teenage years looking at the readers wives' section in dogeared copies of Penthouse or Playboy that my older peers had discarded. I'm not even sure the content I used to get my kicks to would even make it onto a soft porn website now. It seems we have created a climate in which the extremes of the deleterious domains of life previously reserved for adulthood have become widely available to consumers of any age.

Suicide amongst students is a growing problem, and one that is thought to be under-reported by Universities keen to protect their reputations. The parents of Harry Armstrong Evans, a student who tragically killed himself in 2021 after suffering a mental health crisis, have proposed the introduction of *Harry's Law* to make Universities more transparent in acknowledging and reporting suicides. The University's wellbeing team came under scrutiny when it emerged they had not responded adequately to Harry's request for help and had deleted relevant entries regarding phone calls from Harry's mum, from their logs. Recent research suggests the average level of student debt upon graduation is now approaching fifty thousand pounds. The prospect of owning their own home for many is decreasing, and the retirement age appears to be continually reviewed and raised. The pressure to get good grades coupled with the mounting debts they seem to be accruing and an increasingly uncertain future, is surely a factor impacting on the mental wellbeing of many young students.

There is an increasing body of research linking mental health in young people to climate change. A survey of three thousand children undertaken in 2022 just before the United Nations COP 27 Climate Change Conference by the British based charity Save the Children, found that climate anxiety amongst young people was pervasive. Over two thirds of young people said they were worried about the world they would inherit, with some saying they felt powerless and scared and almost two thirds of survey respondents saying the issues of climate change and inequality were having a negative impact on their generation's mental health. Terms such as climate anxiety and eco-grief are becoming increasingly commonly used to describe the impacts on people's mental health that our destruction of the planets' eco-system is having. The mood of many young people was tapped into and summed up by the rock band Muse in the subtly titled track *We Are Fucking Fucked*, released in November 2022. The lyrics of the second verse are, "*We're at death's door, Another world war,*

Wildfires and earthquakes I foresaw, A life in crisis, A deadly virus, Tsunamis of hate are gonna find us." Love them or loathe them, you can't argue that's it's not a powerful punchy summary of the issues humankind is presently facing and that are preoccupying the minds of many young people. Climate change is the biggest physical and mental public health challenge facing us. And I've yet to meet anyone who feels the issue is being addressed satisfactorily. In a letter to the Guardian in 2022 entitled *We cannot fight depression without first tackling deprivation*, Dr Michael Peel finished his correspondence with the following. *"The surest way of exacerbating depression is taking away any hope that people have left."* In the absence of international will and in the face of the endless prevarication and procrastination that blocks the implementation of long-overdue solutions, it should be no surprise that young people feel increasingly worried and anxious about their future.

COVID-19 and the measures it led to, the lockdowns and restrictions on physical peer interaction, the closure of universities, the lack of access to green spaces, sometimes cramped living conditions, reduced income, and the increased levels of emotionally charged behaviour by both parents and siblings, have had a significant impact on the mental health and wellbeing of young people in Britain and many other countries. Homeschooling did not come easily to many parents. The divorce and separation rate rose sharply during and after the pandemic and reported incidents of domestic violence increased by a third in many countries including France, the USA and the UK. In July 202, the Mail Online ran an updated story about a rise in the quantity of prescriptions for antidepressants being given to teenagers in England. Mental health charities had told the Mail Online that they feared GPs might be prescribing drugs more freely because NHS mental health services were swamped with demand. There may be some truth in this.

NHS Mental Health Trusts, of which there are around fifty in England, are managed and constrained in ways their acute and secondary care counterparts are not. In NHS acute and emergency settings it is hard if not impossible to turn people needing urgent medical help away. Asking someone to place their severed foot in a freezer and come back in three months-time when the consultant surgeon will be free is not the *"done thing",* and if an acute hospital does overspend because demand for its services exceeds expectation, then the treasury, that's you and I, will dig it out the financial doo-doo and tell it to manage its budgets better next time. NHS mental health services, are a slightly different kettle of fish. They, implicitly and unfairly I would argue, are not expected to exceed their annual budgets and are instructed to manage any fluctuations in demand for their services by stacking and prioritizing it rather like air traffic controllers manage flights in and out of an airport. Many people suffering a severe mental health crisis are quite literally told to hang onto their broken minds and imploding emotions until there is a consultant available. And the timings of this expected intervention are often unclear, which only adds to patients' distress. Despite decades of government promises and pledges to create parity of esteem between NHS mental and physical health services, the reality is that mental health services have been starved of resources and have played second fiddle to their acute and secondary cousins for as long as anyone in the health and care system can remember.

Is it time to talk?

There are many initiatives, predominantly targeted at men, aimed at encouraging us as a nation to talk more openly and more often about our mental health. We have an annual Time to Talk Day which many leading mental health charities and NHS Trusts promote and participate in. There is also some great advice about how to start meaningful conversations, the sort of language to use, the right open-ended questions to ask, and how to create the kind of safe psychological conditions conducive to sharing. The national mental health charity MIND provides easy to understand guidance and a downloadable resource pack for people wanting to know more about Time to Talk Day and how to get involved. I understand both the benefit of being able to talk openly and the relief that being listened to can bring. I also think that anything we as individuals can do to reduce the stigma that surrounds mental health and create greater awareness and understanding should be unambiguously welcomed. And I also wonder if creating a climate in which we are all talking is part of a culture that accepts things as they are and becomes a surrogate for meaningful change. The approach reminds me of the conversation I had with the head of school when I was a governor during which I questioned his obsession with creating resilience amongst children. I was curious as to why he wasn't as obsessed with creating questioning children who were capable of critical thought and of challenging what was going on around them and being done to them, rather than dealing meekly and compliantly with whatever is thrown at them. The two things are not mutually exclusive and there is of course a balance, but I can't help thinking that if we focus too much on simply enabling people to cope with the ideologically generated shitstorm they are in by talking about it, we will lose sight of the bigger picture and learn to tolerate rather than challenge.

NHS mental health services:

The evidence shows that more unequal societies create more mental illness. The NHS is ill-equipped to deal with the flood of failure demand coming its way. There isn't a range of NHS mental health services that are widely available for much of what we need help with, in our modern lives, loss, abuse, stress, divorce, gambling debt, fear of eviction, peer pressure, climate anxiety, and loss of hope. When I've needed urgent help, I have turned to volunteers or the private sector where I paid for it from my own pocket. We can't in all fairness blame the NHS for not being able to deal with the growing list of things driving more and more of us down the road of mental illness and depression and over the cliff edge of suicide. NHS mental health services are in an unfair fight with circumstance and political ideology they were ill-equipped to get into never mind win, a situation that is unlikely to improve in the near future.

Andy Bell is the chief executive of the Centre for Mental Health. A registered charity founded almost forty years ago, they have gradually evolved into a mental health research resource and an independent not for profit thinktank. Their stated purpose is to eradicate mental health inequalities and fight injustice by changing social policy and practice. Andy is an advocate of equality in the provision of NHS mental health services and equity of access to them. As someone living in a relatively remote rural area where the availability of and access to good quality mental health services is dire, I would second his ambition. Over the years the Centre for Mental Health has been involved in a great deal of research that has consistently revealed inadequacies in the availability of mental health services to disadvantaged and marginalised communities. Our postcode is often more important to our mental health than our genetic code. Andy tells me the traditional view of the NHS as being the organisation tasked with providing the vast majority of mental health support is a simplistic one. He points out that in reality they are just part of a more complex nuanced blend of provision in which social care services are inextricably entwined. He talks to me about the value of early intervention in communities and what he refers to as assertive outreach, a concept I liken to a valued but annoying exercise buddy who rings you up to see how you are or to tell you they will be knocking on your front door in ten minutes so you can both go for a walk or a cycle ride. He is in no doubt that providing support to people where they are is not only vastly cheaper but also more clinically effective than waiting for their mental health to implode and placing them in secure units at significant cost to the public purse. In the most extreme cases Andy tells me that housing someone in a secure mental health unit can cost up to a quarter of a million pounds a year.

We discuss the frustratingly slow often non-existent adoption of technology in the NHS, and I share my long-standing belief with Andy that while NHS mental health services are underfunded, they don't help themselves as they seldom seem to spend the money they do have efficiently or effectively. I also decry the regional inconsistencies and often disjointed ways of working that seem to typify them. I explain that there doesn't seem to be any widespread agreement amongst the NHS Trusts providing mental health services across England or the home countries, as to what good actually looks like. He doesn't disagree and goes on to say he would like to see what he describes to me as a whole government approach to mental health. As he clarifies what he means by this, which to me sounds like he is advocating that the public health and wellbeing function of a nation should be paramount, I sense we are singing from the same song book, if not precisely the same song sheet.

In May 2023, the head of London's Metropolitan police force Mark Rowley, announced that from August police officers would be instructed not to attend emergency calls if they related to mental health incidents. Giving NHS health and social care services until the end of August to prepare for this change he justified the rationale by referred to an estimated ten thousand hours a month which he said police officers spend dealing with mental health issues. He went on to say the new policy would only be waived if there was a threat to life and that not dealing with mental health issues would free his officers to focus on the business of fighting crime and catching criminals. The policy, apparently borrowed from Humberside's police force, feels more like a soundbite designed to distract from the Met police forces reputational issues rather than a meaningful strategy. London's metropolitan police force employs just over thirty-two thousand officers and the idea that freeing up the time that less than one quarter of one percent of its officers use dealing with mental health issues will reduce crime in the capital city, is spurious at best. Adopting a catchily titled *Right Care Right Person* approach is all well and good if the capacity in the system in question exists. As we continue through an era in which many see the increasing prevalence of mental illness as one of the greatest health challenges facing us, wouldn't it make more sense for police forces to train their officers in how to deal with mental health related issues, instead of turning their back on people in need who cannot access the help they need from an impossibly overstretched health system. I would anticipate the future failure demand that will emerge from Mark Rowley's decision will ultimately create more work for both the health and justice systems.

It puzzles me how in the face of the growing mountains of research that organisations like the Centre for Mental Health, the Mental Health Foundation, and the Money and Mental Health Policy Institute possess and make freely available, the neoliberal machine is allowed to grind relentlessly on chewing up the mental health and wellbeing of us all and spitting out the remains as it marches like a Terminator over the skulls and carcasses of those it leaves in its wake.

PART IV:

Behind the Curtain

Chapter 18: Never meet your heroes

"Toto, I've got a feeling we're not in Kansas anymore."

Dorothy Gale; The Wizard of Oz

I really can't begin to tell you how incredibly proud I was to join the NHS. I was forty-three years old, yet I felt like a child waiting for Christmas. I called almost everyone I knew, and I didn't sleep properly for a week with excitement and anticipation. I kept revisiting the offer letter I had received confirming I had got the job. I was elated. I had such incredibly high hopes for my future. I had slept rough many times on the public bench just outside the office building where I was to be based in my new role. I had claimed my daily homeless allowance from the very same offices when they were used by the department of social services thirty years ago. Now, with the help of many others my life had turned around and I felt I had a real chance to make a positive difference. I was readying myself mentally and physically to step onto the deck of the multi-purpose sleek high performing meticulously managed and amply equipped vessel that awaited my arrival. An entity I imagined as something between the self-contained functionality and technological complexity of the Death Star, with less Darth Vader and more Martin Luther King style leadership. An enterprise with the status and working efficiency of the Ark Royal. An institution with the organizational capacity and capability of the Roman Empire at its zenith. Such was my pride at becoming part of the nation's most iconic revered institution that during the half-day induction I enthusiastically applauded the Chairman's speech. I don't recall what he said but I remember being the only one in the room clapping like a circus seal in front the fifty or so other people who were also being inducted that day. A tumbleweed moment to cherish.

The reality was that I had unwittingly clambered onto the deck of one of the most dysfunctional and poorly led tubs within the NHS fleet. Just one of many boats of differing sizes, setting its own sweet course in the most undirected flotilla of ships to ever sail on the worlds' organizational seas. This one had more than one hole in its hull, a large cast of work-shy stowaways whose purpose was unclear, and a distinctly down-beaten, jaded, and weary crew. The ship I boarded sailed under the flag of the Cumbria Partnership NHS Foundation Trust, and was steered by a decidedly duplicitous, devious, and distrustful captain. A former mental health nurse who had by all accounts risen swiftly through the ranks by kissing more arses, ticking more boxes, standing on more heads, and generally playing the game more ruthlessly and craftily than his counterparts. He had been in post almost ten years and had developed a reputation as a bully. The story was that he had inherited a rickety ship and needed to demonstrate strength in the most traditional way. People were scared of him, and a culture of secrecy prevailed in many parts of the Trust; what went on and what went wrong in the localities stayed in the localities, because those who delivered unwelcome news to the centre were not well received. He was more Darth Vader than Martin Luther King. Such was his reputation for secrecy, it was rumoured that the overtly charitable act of employing people with learning disabilities to staff the head office café, was a ploy to ensure that the many sensitive conversations occurring over coffee and cake, would not be listened to, or even viewed as being of interest by the café staff. He had clearly taken the mantra made famous by Andy Grove of Intel, that only the paranoid survive, very much to heart.

The chief executive had surrounded himself with a strange and obsequious entourage of sycophants who had clearly been promoted stratospherically beyond the limits of their ability. They were palpably significantly less astute than their leader and did not pose a threat to him or seem to possess an original thought or ounce of courage between them. A shifty slippery evasive set of expensively suited carefully manicured characters who laughed at his jokes like whipped hyenas and who wouldn't look out of place on a Crimewatch special about white-collar crime. This gaggle of sartorially savvy drains on the public purse, smartly dressed benefit cheats, were ensconced in well-equipped offices located on the first floor of head office on what was known as the million-pound corridor. This being the approximate collective sum of their combined annual salaries. They entered and exited the building to and from the carpark via a separate set of stairs, the executive staircase was out of bounds to those of lessor gods.

It may not surprise you to learn that most of this gang of gifted individuals, went on to bigger and better things within the NHS. It's reassuring to know the nation's healthcare service remains in good hands isn't it. Shortly after I boarded the good ship Cumbria NHS, the captain himself was moved up the food-chain and higher into the ivory tower, becoming chief executive of the NHS Mental Health Confederation. A grim day for users of NHS mental health services and their families. On a more serious note, I would suspect that between them the occupants of the million pound-corridor are collectively responsible for a great deal of avoidable harm and the numerous preventable deaths of more people than any suspected fugitive, criminal, murderer, or ne'er-do-well that has ever appeared on Crimewatch. We tend to view incidents of death and harm through a different lens when they are the result of decisions and acts committed by the amoral, the inept, and incompetent from within our public services. As long as they dress smartly, speak with certainty, and assure us that lessons have been learned, we forgive them anything. The number of patients who die an avoidable death in the care of the NHS each year is at least fifty times more than the fatalities of knife related crime across the UK in the same period and six times more than the number of road deaths in Britain each year. But which issue will get ministers, councillors, and mayors, more airtime, and votes?

Exactly the right, and wrong man for the job:

I should never have been offered the job I was recruited into by the Cumbria Partnership NHS Foundation Trust. It was only after I'd joined my new NHS employer that I discovered I hadn't been recruited for my capabilities, integrity, communication skills, witty repartee, or appealing personality, but for an assumed ability to be deliberately disingenuous. This revelation came to light when I overheard my boss proudly describing her new recruit, me, to her colleagues as someone who would manage the Trusts stakeholders well because I was able to say something convincingly without meaning it, as if this were somehow a positive character attribute. It was a misplaced, insulting, if with hindsight understandable and amusing assumption of my nature based solely I think on my choice of professional affiliation as a Chartered Marketer. Though I was offended at the time I take comfort from knowing that the ambitious and enthusiastic lady who hired me, was in fact a terrible judge of character. She was an experienced public relations practitioner who as well as working in senior political circles had previously worked for a small public relations firm run by a prolific paedophile. He was convicted in 2011 for a string of sex offences against young boys. The sentencing judge described him as deeply manipulative; in my experience a prerequisite for most high-flyers in the dark art of public relations and something he probably received as a compliment. Old school marketers like me are as wary and cynical about PR practitioners and spin doctors, turd polishers to give them their official title, as anyone.

But though I should never have been recruited, I remain deeply grateful I was chosen for the job I applied for. The misguided immeasurably ironic choice my new boss made to hire me that day turned out to be the catalyst for a series of events neither she nor I could ever have foreseen. The truth about the success of my job application to the NHS is that my interviewer fell into one of the classic and most widespread behavioural biases that guides much of our day-to-day decision-making. She was merely doing what countless other managers in all types of organisations in every conceivable location on the face of the planet do on any given day of the year. She was seeing the world as she was and not as it was. I imagine she interpreted my carefully chosen interview responses as cleverly constructed bullshit rather than the sincere expressing of genuine aspirations. And I think she viewed me as she viewed herself and attributed me with the characteristics she wanted to see. It's a trap we can and do all fall into from time to time, even the most cynical of us. The organisations devious intent for the role I had been offered, which was slowly but surely revealed to me over time, was only matched by my complete naivety. The role I had been hired into, the NHS Trust I had been employed by and I, were a match made in hell. But at least I can tell you now, with certainty, that growth really does come from discomfort.

I had been employed into a new middle management role in which I was to oversee a tiny but committed and as it turned out, very competent team of two. Our responsibility was to cultivate and develop relationships and build partnerships with relevant stakeholders. By stakeholders I mean other interested parties on the patch, anyone directly involved in, affected by, or with an interest in the work of the Trust. I saw the purpose of our roles as building bridges over which useful exchanges of information and insight could flow freely in both directions. The better the relationships, the stronger the bridges, the more they would be trusted and used. Good working relationships were necessary if the Trust was to understand and meet the needs of the communities, patients, and service users that its stakeholders represented.

The primary focus of mine and the team's attention were the eighty plus GP Practices spread across the county and the many hundreds of doctors, practice managers and staff that worked in them. Other important stakeholders included local patient interest groups and charitable organisations like Age-UK, the mental health charity MIND, the Alzheimer's Society, and the various Leagues of Friends charities that fundraised for each of the local hospitals. We established links with Adult Social Care, local authorities, housing associations, local health oversight bodies like Healthwatch who I'm still not sure what their purpose is, district councillors, MPs, and many, many others. For a former Chartered Marketer with a strong background in relationship building and partnership development, it was a dream job. I was being given a chance to play to my strengths in the service of the people and communities of Cumbria, the county I have lived in and loved for more years than I care to remember.

We set about our work with what I now see was a very un-public-sector level of enthusiasm and purpose. In fact, such was our work rate that it was suggested to me the team should take its feet off the pedal because we risked embarrassing others. Within months of being in post I had commissioned, co-designed, and launched the first online directory of NHS community and mental health services in the UK. I ignored the advice to slow down, and we continued apace. Stakeholders were identified, contacted, met, categorised, and most importantly, acknowledged and listened to. I insisted that every meeting a member of the team attended was logged and the key findings from it entered onto a shared database. I encouraged my colleagues to seek and extract some gold dust, any useful insight, however little, from every encounter they had; did people know which services the Trust provided, did they know how to engage with it, where did they feel the Trust could improve, what could it do that would help them in their roles, what should it do more of, what should it do less of, what did it do well that it could build on, and importantly, where did it really suck. Most of the people we engaged with welcomed the opportunity to be heard. They had not had a point of contact in the Trust before, and as it turned out, they had a lot to say, and they were not shy when it came to sharing their views.

My role required good listening skills and broad, extremely broad shoulders. It turned out that most stakeholders thought the Trust sucked in a great deal of what it did. But coming from the private sector and being an eternal optimist, I viewed this feedback as just a platform of useful insights on which improvements could be built. It still rings in my ears as one of the cheesiest American management phrases I have ever heard, but it also remains a fact that feedback really is the breakfast of champions. Feel free to spew now. When I joined the NHS, a manager told me I was the most positive person she had ever worked with. Positivity to me is about acknowledging and confronting challenges, not pretending they aren't there. Each month I compiled a written report on behalf of the team, this was shared with the chair, chief executive, directors, public governors, and many senior managers across the Trust. I also compiled and shared a more in-depth annual report which highlighted the work of the team across the year. These annual reports explored the themes we were encountering in more depth and contained observations about further areas to review and ideas for improvement drawn from all sectors of business, public, private, and voluntary. I come from the school of thinking which dictates that knowledge that only lives in one place, one person's head, one person's diary, is a missed opportunity and a commercial risk. It was my intention to always play with an open hand, to share whatever gold dust we found, and to create insightful reports that drew on the real-time information and real-world feedback we were receiving. Each report we submitted contained a mix of the good, there was praise where it was due, the bad, clearly vital when providing healthcare services, and everything in-between. I've prided myself on being a well networked individual for many years. I know from experience there is always someone somewhere who has faced and tackled the same challenges we each find ourselves grappling with at any point in time. Access to networks is access to knowledge, and time spent building networks is seldom wasted.

Most of the comments contained in the reports came from our primary audience, the doctors and practice managers working from the many GP Practices across Cumbria. The NHS trust I worked in employed about four thousand people and managed a wide range of physical and mental health services, inc. community nursing, and nine small hospitals that provided a mix of outpatient services and inpatient beds. As the first port of call for people with health needs Primary Care is the source of nearly all patient referrals into NHS services. Nationally, this amounts to tens of millions and growing, each year. GP Practices are the front desk of the NHS, the intermediaries and brokers who filter and direct, matching patient need with medical ability. This means Primary Care has a wealth of knowledge and insight about the experiences their patients received from the NHS services they are referred to. Primary Care is uniquely placed to offer a view to the wider health and care system about how the needs of its patients are being met. Many of the observations from Primary Care about the NHS Trust I was working in, were not complimentary. But they were often highly insightful, and I wanted to keep the integrity and earnestness of these views in my reporting. Even the more polemic and sometimes emotive feedback was included in our reports, and sometimes, but only with the permission of the relevant parties, the reports contained verbatim, at times stinging, but pertinent and potentially useful observations. The reports made uncomfortable reading for some. An area wide survey we conducted revealed that less than one in ten doctors and practice managers thought the Trust was responsive, and less than one in twenty thought it clearly understood their needs. This would not be good news for an organisation running a service-based business of any type, never mind one supplying healthcare.

What I hadn't foreseen was that the team and I were unwittingly moving ourselves into an invidious position by asking questions many of the Trusts senior executives had not been prepared to hear the answers to. Following the results of the survey we had undertaken with the GP Practices, I was taken aside and told to never repeat the exercise, unless I was prepared to ask only questions that would elicit positive answers. The insights we gathered and shared were not seen as precious, they were seen as unwelcome. I suppose even a sack of gold dust can be a burden if you're trying to climb out of a hole. Nor had I foreseen that one of the recommendations emerging from the inquiry into the tragic events at Mid Staffs Hospitals, would signal the end of the teams work and of my career in the NHS.

Chapter 19: **Fit and proper**

"When your values are clear, your decisions become easier."

Roy E. Disney

Following the public inquiry into the events at Mid Staffs Hospitals and the publication of Sir Robert Francis's report in 2012, of the 290 recommendations he made one of the more contentious thoughts emerging from Sir Robert's findings was the creation of something called the Fit and Proper Persons Regulation to be applied to NHS Directors. It became an accepted recommendation and officially came into force on November 27th, 2014. The idea behind the new regulation came from the private sector. In the UK as in many other countries, the senior accountable officers of any organisation in the private or voluntary sectors, chief executives, directors, chairpersons, can be barred from becoming a director of any company if they are found to be unfit to hold the post of company director. A central register of all disqualified individuals in the UK is held online at Companies House and can be easily accessed and checked by anyone. It is widely recognised as a useful way of ensuring that individuals thought unfit to be directors cannot simply move with impunity from the post of a failed director in one company to setting themselves up as the director of another.

The introduction of a Fit and Proper Persons Regulation for Directors in any part of the public sector was a new thing. To me, as a relative newcomer to the NHS and having spent most of my working life in the private sector, it seemed an entirely logical and long overdue step. The idea that errant directors of commercial companies in the private sector could be held accountable for their actions, while publicly funded directors responsible for overseeing health care services could not, feels entirely counterintuitive. In the wake of the Mid Staffs scandal, where failings in publicly funded health care services had been dominating the headlines in all sections of the media, it seemed right to bring a greater degree of accountability and transparency to the leadership and management of the National Health Service. What happened at Mid Staffs had shaken the nation and as details of what had occurred at Mid Staffs emerged, the press and public expressed increasing frustration with an unwillingness on the part of public sector executives to be held accountable for their actions. There were well-publicised examples of NHS directors leaving their employment with generous golden handshakes just as a pending investigation was about to begin. These same executives then assumed senior positions in other parts of the NHS, or other publicly funded closely related bodies. In short, there was little evidence of any personal accountability, no obvious penalties for failing, and no consistent way to ensure that directors in the nation's health service were fit for purpose.

I was not alone in welcoming the idea, many of the NHS colleagues I worked with at the time thought it was a positive step toward holding previously untouchable inept NHS executives to account. One of the flagship measures in the new legislation was that directors could be deemed unfit to hold office if they were found to be in possession of information on which they did not act. The intent of this part of the requirement was to address one of the specific failings unearthed by the Mid Staffs inquiry. What the healthcare regulator had discovered during their investigation into Mid Staffs was that the board and senior managers had been given numerous opportunities to receive, digest, and then act on both empirical data and anecdotal feedback made available to them about the issues emerging on the wards. But while the hospital board had seemed ready to welcome unfounded praise which had no basis in fact, they had chosen not to acknowledge any information they perceived as adverse or unfavourable. Lives could have been saved if they had simply been prepared to listen and it was this that the new legislation sought to remedy.

The introduction of a Fit and Proper Persons Requirement for NHS directors was welcomed by patient interest and representative groups. Many of whom had been pushing for the introduction of consistent high-quality standards of leadership across the NHS for some years. But the requirement received a mixed response from the upper ranks of the NHS. Senior executives in NHS Trusts have long suffered from a form of organisational siege mentality, something Peter Senge alludes to in his book the Fifth Discipline. In this mindset, the leaders of embattled organisations start to believe the enemy is not only out there but it's out to get them, regulators, patient interest groups, the press. All events and information are viewed and translated through a long and wary lens of paranoia, mistrust, and suspicion. The introduction of the regulation was described to me by one NHS chief executive as just another unwelcome and unnecessary ridge to climb on a growing mountain of legislation and regulation. Something else to deal with, yet another hoop to be jumped through which would eat precious time, attention, and energy. It was also viewed in some quarters with great trepidation as being another possible stick which would be held over the heads of directors by the regulator. And others saw it as a means by which they could potentially end up being held accountable for events that were largely out of their control. How could it be fair they argued that they could be held accountable for events beyond their control that occurred in locations many of them had never frequented? In the absence of clarity about how the fit and proper requirement would work and a lack of detail about the definitions referred to, many NHS boards sought legal advice regarding the implementation of the act and its implications for them personally and organizationally. For example, what might the information that directors should be acting upon look like? Should it be in written form? Would every email now have to be viewed as a potential source of adverse information that might later form part of an investigation? Or could information that should be acted upon simply take the form of informal conversations with members of staff, which a director might then find themselves being held accountable for at some future point? In this uncertain, and potentially risk laden environment, and in a world where everyone has a voice recording app on their smartphone, the directors of many NHS Trusts understandably, adopted an ultra-cautious approach to managing the possible implications of the act.

Unfortunately for me, the NHS Trust I worked for was one of those which sought advice about the implications of this new legislation; how it might affect them and how they could work around it. At that time the Trust was struggling to manage its reputation in the wake of recent high-profile and persistent attention from the national and regional press. The board had been blindsided by the tragic death of a gifted young girl called Helena Farrell who had taken her own life after being failed by the Trusts mental health services. Helena's suicide exposed significant gaps in the quality and safety of services. And things were only set to get worse in the face of the many local and national challenges the NHS was facing. Directors and the chief executive had become concerned. They were worried about the introduction of new legislation that could potentially see them being held to account for things they considered to be systemic issues, largely the result of decisions made beyond their influence.

National funding levels, a nationwide recruitment crisis, and the rising demands a rapidly ageing population was placing on healthcare services. The devious conclusion they reached about how to deal with the introduction of the fit and proper persons act, signaled the end of my career in the National Health Service.

In October 2014, one month before the act came into force, the work of my team was abruptly ceased. Our roles were deemed unnecessary, and we were peddled some bullshit about a planned restructure. We were to be moved to other jobs in the Trust. The database containing all the feedback, insights, and observations we had captured was cleansed. The directors had decided that if there was a possibility, they might be held accountable for not acting on information they had received, then the safest way for them to deal with this new risk was to get rid of the information they had and remove the means by which they could receive anything further. Think of it as a bit like welding shut your letterbox so you can't receive any bills and therefore won't be held accountable for not paying them. Or perhaps sending all your emails from a no-reply email address so that you don't have to read or acknowledge anyone's replies. Constantly transmitting, never receiving. In short the directors had decided that they couldn't be found sitting on information on which they hadn't acted if they didn't have any information. It may seem an incredibly cynical act on their part, and my personal view of their decision is not positive. But in a risk averse culture and in an operating climate where the relationship with the regulators can be adversarial and in which the press can be quick to apportion blame, it's a logical decision when viewed through the lens of organisational and self-preservation. I aired my concerns about the decision they had made with the chair, my director, the chief executive, and some of the non-executive directors, but to no avail. And that's when I reluctantly decided I had no other option but to whistleblow.

I contacted the Care Quality Commission and shared my concerns that the decision directors were taking would make services less safe. The generally accepted maxim of organisational improvement being that you can't fix what you don't know is wrong. Unfortunately for me, what I didn't know at the time is that the regulator, the Care Quality Commission, had not been given any powers to monitor the new legislation or act on any concerns relating to it. They thanked me for sharing my concerns and then depressingly explained there was nothing they or anyone could do. The whole exercise of introducing the Fit and Proper Persons Test for NHS Directors was beginning to look like a complete and utter box-ticking charade. But by now, I had told my directors what I was doing, I had shown my hand and effectively triggered the beginning of the end of my career in the NHS. It is surely one of the ultimate ironies, that a well-intentioned act developed in the wake of a national tragedy, an act designed to improve the quality of healthcare by promoting principled leadership behaviours, had effectively been scuppered by exactly the kind of unprincipled behaviour of the very same directors it was designed to influence.

Wilful blindness brought on by the summit fever of achieving Foundation Trust status, had been the root cause of what many regarded as the greatest scandal in the history of the NHS, the neglect and death of vulnerable patients in the care of a hospital. What happened at Mid Staffs Hospitals was the result of wilful blindness. Now, the NHS Trust I was working for was taking wilful blindness to another level. In their eagerness to avoid implementing recommendations designed to ensure a similar tragedy could not happen in their own Trust, directors were actively choosing ignorance, seeking to create a shield of plausible deniability.

I don't think the decision directors reached could be classed as ethical or principled in any sense. But I do view their actions as predictable risk-averse responses from people who have built careers by adapting to a system that rewards gaming. For me the incident raises the question, at what point does behaviour move from being merely a passive response, an understandable and in some respects excusable reaction to working within a bad system, to being a proactive perpetuating part of a poor system itself. What would you or I do in their shoes if we felt we had achieved significant status and income and felt it being threatened by the implementation of legislation we had no control over?

Nearly four years after the implementation of the Fit and Proper Persons Requirement for NHS Directors was introduced, Tom Kark QC was asked by the Minister of State for Health to undertake a review of its effectiveness. Since its introduction in November 2014, not one single sanction had been brought as a result of the act, and a wealth of anecdotal evidence was building-up to suggest the legislation was not achieving anything. The guidance was not being implemented consistently if at all, across the NHS, nor was it widely understood by boards of the NHS Trusts themselves, and significantly, the act still remained unenforceable by the UK's healthcare regulator, the Care Quality Commission.

The Kark review as it became known was published in November 2018 before being discussed in Parliament in early 2019. I had shared my experiences with the review team and was invited to contribute a written submission detailing what had happened to me. It is still my opinion that the Fit and Proper Persons Requirement for Directors has made some directors and senior staff in the NHS less willing to engage and listen for fear of finding and hearing things they would rather not find or hear. The act increased the prevalence of plausible deniability in senior circles of the NHS and because of this it has made some parts of the NHS health system less safe than they were before its implementation.

In March 2019, following a continued stream of press coverage and revelations of preventable deaths, failing hospitals, poor leadership, and wilful blindness in numerous NHS settings, Sir Robert Francis himself, the well-meaning architect of the legislation was forced to acknowledge that the Fit and Proper Persons Requirement for NHS Directors was itself not fit for purpose and had not been effective in protecting the public.

Chapter 20: **The tragic folly of Foundation Trusts**

"Politics is the art of looking for trouble, finding it everywhere, diagnosing it incorrectly and then applying the wrong remedies."

Groucho Marx

In the endless quest for innovative ideas about how to run the NHS, in 2001 Alan Milburn, the health secretary serving in Tony Blairs Labour government, visited a hospital in Spain. This outwardly shiny and ultra-modern facility located in the Madrid region was held aloft by policymakers as the future of publicly funded healthcare. A shining example of the effectiveness and efficiency that could be achieved if you combined the resources of the public purse to develop infrastructure, with the enterprise of the private sector to provide services. Sounds sexy doesn't it, it's having your political cake and eating it. Incidentally, have you noticed how the institutions of government in most countries spend a lot of time telling their own citizens and anyone else who will listen about how brilliant they are; the envy of the world, best in class, and world leading. These honey laden stock phrases and vacuous soundbites seem to drip from the tongues of politicos and public sector leaders like waste into a sewer. The challenge of supplying and funding effective and efficient health and care services is of course a global issue. The need to maintain the reputation of a nation's healthcare service is not solely the preoccupation of politicians in the UK. It's a headache that is shared by politicians and leaders across the planet. Any government that purports to have found a solution to this seemingly intractable problem will quickly leap to the rooftops and shout about it. By highlighting it to the rest of the world, they also heighten awareness of their successful policies amongst their own voting population. You get to look good globally and secure votes at the next election. It's a win-win.

The hospital Alan Milburn visited in Spain had been built by the Spanish National Health Service, however the day-to-day running of it had been contracted out to a private company. It was said to be more effective and efficient because the contractor was freed from many of the traditional constraints placed on nationally run hospitals and its managers were allowed to negotiate its own contract terms with staff and suppliers. The hospital was also said to be responsive to the needs of its community and engaged with a wide range of local stakeholders, including patient interest groups and voluntary organisations. Milburn was apparently impressed with the concept, and in 2002 he announced the creation of a new type of NHS organisation that would run NHS hospitals and provide NHS community and mental health services fit for the future. These new sleek shiny super-efficient bodies in waiting were to be called Foundation Trusts. Like their Spanish counterparts they would be given freedoms to exercise their own commercial decisions and invest in services as they believed fit. They were also tasked with engaging with their local community. Foundation Trust status was to be a seal of approval, a guarantee of quality, a badge of honour that each NHS Trust who earned it could wear with pride.

Foundation Trust status had to be applied for by each NHS Trust and then earned by complying with a strict set of criteria and a series of conditions relating to financial sustainability. Every individual NHS hospital, Acute Trusts, Community Services Trusts, Mental Health Trusts, and Ambulance Service Trusts were eligible to apply to become Foundation Trusts. The first ten hospitals to attain the hallowed NHS Foundation Trust status were revealed to the public in 2004. They have been a spectacular, largely invisible, and greatly misrepresented failure. In its party manifesto of 1997, Blair's Labour Party had pledged to safeguard the basic principles of the NHS and remove the top-down style of management and the wasteful costs associated with it. The creation of Foundation Trusts has taken our NHS in precisely the opposite direction and cost more lives and been responsible for more harm and more lost morale amongst NHS staff than you or I could poke a very, very large stick at.

To become a Foundation Trust each NHS organisation, be it a hospital, a group of hospitals, or group of services provided in the community, had to prove to the regulator, a newly created and distinctly opaque publicly funded body called Monitor, that they were financially savvy and responsible. To do this they had to show they were running their services efficiently by under-spending and keeping a proportion of the funds they were given to run services each year. Monitor then annually assessed the financial status of each Foundation Trust and gave it a rating based largely on how much money it had managed to withhold from the amount it had been allocated. For example, if an NHS Trust was given an annual budget of £200M to provide services in a given area, it would be expected to retain approx. £6M, or 3% of that total amount, if it wanted to keep the regulator happy. Broadly speaking, the greater the percentage of its budget that each newly created Foundation Trust could save and keep, within predefined limits, the more highly it was regarded and rated by the regulator, Monitor. Take a moment if you will, to consider the obvious flaw behind this idea; hospitals were queuing up to become part of a movement that rewarded them for stripping funds from patient facing services and then depositing these same funds to sit idly in their current accounts. It's the reverse parable of the talents in which people are rewarded for not investing their money. Creating efficiencies, making savings, and driving overheads down by predetermined amounts can work in competitive markets where it is used as a means of driving innovation and reducing costs. But trying to release unidentified nebulous efficiencies and drive down costs in the absence of competition will only lead to a reduction in the quality of the services offered, it does not create innovation.

At this point, everyone reading this who has been involved in running or who has worked in a business of any size or studied the basics of business at school will be scratching their heads and asking, did the Labour government really think asking hospitals to strip money from frontline services was a good idea? And then you might also ask, did the chief executives and directors of NHS hospitals go along with this madness? The answer is yes, and yes.

The government was wedded to the idea that if it rewarded hospitals for running services more efficiently, these same hospitals would become leaner, more enterprising, and more innovative. They would continually improve, becoming ever slicker at providing vital services with limited resources. If NHS Trusts could visibly demonstrate they were able to save money and build up their reserves, then it would finally show the electorate that the NHS could be funded within the country's means. It would have been the Valhalla of political achievements; you and I would have a picture of Tony Blair hanging over our fireplaces now. But while the chief executives of each newly appointed Foundation Trust were enmeshed in groupthink and busy singing the praises of their newly accredited organisations to the regulator, the local MP, the press, and anyone else who would listen, the reality for the service users of

Foundation Trusts and the staff working in them was vastly different. Staff were being shed and patients were being poorly served.

Asking NHS hospital chief executives and directors who were products of public sector thinking and drenched in risk adversity, to suddenly act like enterprising commercially savvy businesspeople was a fool's errand. These people were largely long servers of the institution, graduates of NHS leadership training programmes, innovation averse, hierarchical, politically aware career builders, public sector to the core. These were not questioning, curious, entrepreneurial individuals. And that's purely observation, not criticism on my part. The message these individuals had received had not been interpreted through their politically savvy ears as, become more effective and efficient, it had been interpreted as, demonstrate how you are becoming more effective and efficient. In their subsequent efforts to show the regulator they were becoming more business-like, commercially focused and streamlined, they were simply stripping resources and costs from patient facing front line services to achieve the savings they had to demonstrate to the regulator each year. The idea that systemwide organisational anorexia could be a sustainable way forward for the NHS was madness. The creation of Foundation Trusts was nothing more than a recipe for poorer patient facing services.

By 2012 almost two thirds of NHS hospitals and service providers were officially listed as achieving Foundation Trust status. An unquestioning cult of compliance had kicked in across the entire NHS and to challenge the orthodoxy of the day was not the way to secure a friction free career. I have sat in a meeting at which senior managers and clinicians agreed to cease advertising all vacant mental health posts in order to reduce the wage bill thereby enabling them to stay within the budget they had been given. Rather than risk the wrath of directors and tell them services were already dangerously under-staffed, that waiting lists for patients needing help with their mental health were rising, they said nothing. At that point in time, the area in question, Copeland in West Cumbria, had some of the highest levels of serious mental health and suicide rates in the UK. What then happened was tragic and entirely predictable. The reduced capacity in the service led to increased waiting times for patients, moderate mental health issues went untreated and escalated to become more severe, some of the remaining more experienced clinical staff left or retired as the pressure on services became unbearable, and the suicide rate in Copeland increased dramatically the following year. Unnecessary harm was inflicted on people, lives were lost, families destroyed, and the overall long-term costs to the organisation and the wider system increased. But the area managers had kept their directors and the chief executive happy, and in turn the NHS Trust had hit its financial targets and kept the Foundation Trust regulator happy.

By this stage achieving and maintaining Foundation Trust status had become a potent textbook example of a government policy that rewarded organisations for chasing a target and missing the point. The practice of knowingly running labour intensive services below capacity to keep costs down was a tactic widely used by NHS Trusts seeking Foundation status. It remains a well-used tool applied by managers in all parts of the public sector to keep costs down and operate within the unquestioned unchallenged arbitrary budgets they are allocated.

When I joined the Cumbria Partnership NHS Foundation Trust in January 2012, the organisation was in rude financial health. Sitting on tens of millions of pounds in reserves, while simultaneously offering some of the worst quality least responsive mental health services from a selection of the poorest facilities in the country. There were no plans in place as to how the Trust was going to spend the significant reserves it was sitting on. The Trust had a director of business development and strategy who had not written a strategy, in fairness he had only been in post around ten years. Importantly, directors of the Trust knew that if they invested their growing pile of reserves in buildings and new services, they would then have to increase clinical capacity and hire people to deal with demand. This would create added ongoing staff costs which would impact on finances and threaten its Foundation Trust status. The approach of financial directors in Foundation Trusts was to avoid investing in anything that would attract ongoing costs. The idea that the newly created Foundation Trusts would invest the money they had saved in new services was fundamentally flawed because the focus of the regulator was on ensuring that these same Trusts could contain and reduce their ongoing costs. The NHS at its heart is a services business, if you reduce the amounts being paid in wages you impact on the services ability to meet the needs of its service users. Your local sandwich shop, pub, taxi or delivery company can tell you this.

One of the many mistruths supporting the concept of Foundation Trusts is that they were sold to the electorate as a means by which local communities could have greater control and a larger say in how local NHS services were run and in what services should be provided. One of the criteria for becoming a Foundation Trust was that each NHS Trust had to show how it was going to develop a base of members drawn from its local population. From this base of members local governors would then be elected who could, at least in theory, represent the needs and wants of local people. The minor detail of reducing the amount that each NHS Trust would spend on frontline services for these same people was never highlighted. Most of the governors who have sat and still sit on the boards of NHS Foundation Trusts have little if any understanding of what they have been party to.

Though the Labour Government said the creation of Foundation Trusts was all about increasing citizen engagement and community control, there were never any ambitions expressed for how this should look in practice. What proportion of the communities it served should a Trust obtain as members to accurately represent the views of these communities? How often, how, and about what topics should it communicate with them to insure they were adequately informed? The NHS Foundation Trust I worked for had over twelve thousand so called members on its database, which was really nothing more than a long list of random people held on a computer, most of whom didn't know what being a member might mean, and who couldn't remember even signing up. If you left your name and address lying around or if you were a patient in one of the community hospital's you would end up on the database. A great many members had been enticed into signing up by the offer of a wallet sized card that guaranteed the holder discounts at various retailers. This promise of cheap goods was waved in front of many a prospective signatory during the half-time interval at Carlisle United home matches or in the centre of town on market days in Penrith. To bulk the membership database up and keep the regulator happy, the Trust counted its own staff as members, with or without their permission or understanding. Numerous people listed on the database were in fact, dead, uniquely placed to share insights on the quality of care they had received but unavailable for comment. The regulator never asked how the Trust was engaging with or involving its membership base in the development of services. The creation of Foundation Trusts was only ever about the money, it was never about giving people a greater say.

Amazingly, stupidly, worryingly, ultimately disastrously, yet also unsurprisingly, Monitor, the governments newly created regulator of Foundation Trusts was not responsible for assessing and overseeing the quality of the health and care services each newly accredited Foundation Trust provided. Its focus was on the finances of each Trust. The quality of services was monitored and regulated by an altogether separate organisation called the Healthcare Commission. Again, those of you with half an ounce may be scratching your head at this point and asking, in a service-based business where around half the money is spent on staff wages, how can you separate the monitoring of a hospital's finances from the quality of its services? The answer of course is you can't. But that didn't stop the Labour Government, Monitor, or the NHS from trying. The crassly thoughtless separation of these regulators, who did not work well together for fear of encroaching on each other's empires, meant that issues of reduced staff capacity and clinical capability, which were largely the product of keeping Monitor happy, were then looked at by the Healthcare Commission in isolation.

To aid in the relentless unquestioning drive to ensure all NHS ships were sailing under the banner of Foundation Trust status, another new publicly funded body called The Foundation Trust Network was created. Between 2012 and 2022, the chief executive of the FTN, now called NHS Providers, was a chap called Chris Hopson. The FTNs role was to champion and cheerlead the role of Foundation Trusts, to promote the *benefits* of membership to all NHS Trusts, and help prepare willing eligible NHS organisations to jump through the hoops and join the gang. Hopson and his colleagues had drunk the Kool-Aid in copious amounts and his praise for the concept of Foundation Trusts and the good they would achieve was unquestioning and unconstrained.

Hopson is a politically aware creature. He worked under Dr David Owen in the now defunct Social Democratic Party before moving through a range of consultancy and communications related posts in political circles and the mainstream media. He became the Communications and Marketing Director of HMRC, progressing to Customer Contact Director before taking on the role of Chief Executive at NHS Providers. He has no medical or clinical experience. He has never managed an NHS service, hospital, NHS Trust, or private health service. Yet he felt equipped to lead the charge towards what many now regard as the most ill-thought out, misguided, and misleading shake-up of NHS organisations in a generation. It seems counterintuitive that someone unelected by and ultimately unaccountable to the public, should be able to have had such a detrimental influence on the structure of our publicly funded NHS.

Even after the publication of the Francis Report in 2012, and the bright, horrific, and undeniable light it shone on how the desire to obtain Foundation Trust status had underpinned the tragedy at Mid Staffs Hospitals. Hopson and the Foundation Trust Network were unapologetic, unabashed, unmoved, and largely unavailable for comment. Mid Staffs was a one-off they and their peers argued, an unrelated series of events which should be placed on the doorstep of the hospital's board. The desire to become a Foundation Trust was a minor issue in the broader scheme of things. The FTN seemed unwilling, or was perhaps unable, to even countenance the notion that the drive to make hospitals become Foundation Trusts by pushing down costs and slashing frontline resources was a fundamentally flawed proposition. Mid-Staffs exposed the idea that Foundation Trusts could save the NHS as a hoax. The King was clearly and obviously in the altogether. But as the American political writer Upton Sinclair astutely observed, it is difficult to get any man to understand something when his salary depends on him not understanding it. Chris Hopson is now Chief Strategy Officer for NHS England.

The drive to ensure all NHS Trusts achieved Foundation Trust status continued for another five years after the Mid Staffs tragedy, albeit less zealously. The stated policy to ensure all NHS Hospitals became Foundation Trusts, quietly disappeared some years ago and the idea is now thankfully dead, for now. Some former Foundation Trusts are dropping the words from their title as they become teaching hospitals and align themselves to higher education.

No part of government, the Department of Health, the Foundation Trust Network or NHS England ever created or kept a central database or set of records to report what benefits were tangibly gained from the entire misguided adventure they had led or encouraged others to join. Nor have they ever sought to show which if any of the new and shiny

Foundation Trusts ever even used the financial freedoms they were said to possess, or to what extent they enabled their local communities to shape services in practice. What evidence is available would suggest that few if any of the Foundation Trusts used their financial freedoms to borrow from the money markets while executives of most Foundation Trusts continue to pay lip service to boards of public governors they would rather not have.

It is sad and bitterly ironic that the drive to achieve the status of becoming a Foundation Trust, a badge which had no proven benefits and many obvious pitfalls, was so readily leapt upon by experienced senior people who simply failed to think about the implications of what it was they were being asked to do or lacked the courage to challenge what it was they were being asked to do. The roots of many of the tragedies that have unfolded in the NHS over the last two decades can be traced back to the drive to ensure all NHS Trusts achieved Foundation Trust Stas.

The unthinking creation of Foundation Trusts, and the obsequious unquestioning and disastrous adoption of the concept, remains one of the murkier chapters in the history of our NHS. The consequences and impact of the Labour Governments policy to set up Foundation Trusts has never been acknowledged. The immense damage done to the NHS and its users is largely irreversible and wholly immeasurable. Its most obvious impact is in the lives avoidably lost, the countless patients harmed, and the destruction of staff morale across great swathes of the NHS. And all for what?

Chapter 21: Leadership & management in the NHS

"The intellectual yet idiot, IYI, is a production of modernity hence has been accelerating since the mid twentieth century, to reach its local supremum today, along with the broad category of people without skin-in-the-game who have been invading many walks of life."

Nassim Nicholas Taleb; Skin in the Game

The finest definition I have yet heard about what leadership is, was shared with me by a theatre director, who said *leadership is about creating the conditions in which things can happen*. I haven't heard a less waffling definition yet. As well as implying that leadership is not about micro-managing, this definition leads to at least two thoughts. Firstly, leaders are responsible for the good, the bad, and everything in-between that happens on their watch. Secondly, people at any level in an organisation have the potential to demonstrate leadership. True leadership can and does occur anywhere, and I would argue that in the NHS and many other public services it is often most prevalent the further from the official hierarchy you look.

The observation Peter Drucker famously made that culture will always eat strategy for breakfast, is probably the most proven yet most ignored leadership and management principle there is. The best-written and most deeply researched business plans and strategies will fail if the culture of the organisation is not aligned or receptive to its methods or its goals. The culture of an organisation is the real indicator of how its people will behave and of what behaviours are truly valued rather than those that are espoused or paid lip-service to. The culture of an organisation is akin to the character of a person, it sits outside the written word and manifests itself in acts and deeds; it's the reality of what is rather than the ideal that is envisaged. Open cultures, closed cultures, hierarchical cultures, anarchic cultures, creative cultures, collusive cultures, corrosive cultures, compliant cultures, toxic cultures, organisational cultures strengthen and perpetuate as they inevitably attract and retain people who fit in; birds of a feather flock together and cultural conformity prevails. Leaders set the tone, their actions, responses, their decisions, and the priorities they focus on become reflected and mimicked throughout the organisation. Organisations need senior leaders who prioritise the development of productive open cultures and who make time to visibly demonstrate their commitment in this area. Where leaders experience compliance and conformity, they should challenge, they should encourage those around them to challenge them, and question them when they don't.

If the primary purpose of leadership and management is to create the conditions in which the right things can happen, then it cannot be denied that leadership and management within the NHS and across the wider health and care landscape, has been a spectacular and incredibly costly failure. The level of inconsistency that has been tolerated and allowed to develop by successive governments, health secretaries, politicians, chief executives, directors, senior managers and regulators throughout the length and breadth of the UK's healthcare services, is genuinely amazing. But more worryingly and most importantly, it is incredibly unsafe. The NHS, whatever we think it is, lacks good quality leadership and management in the quantities we need it to possess. It is an unfortunate reality that the healthcare system is awash with chief executives, directors, senior managers, and aspiring leaders, who feel, and in many cases have been encouraged to believe, they are the leadership equivalent of fine vintage champagne parading in cut crystal glasses when in reality the fruits of their deeds would suggest they are flat warm disappointing festival lager in thin plastic cups. Many of them have little if any real skin in the game and would not get and could not keep a well-paid job in any other setting than the cosseted cosy courage free confines of public service management circles. Their mastery of the unique arts that have brought them success within the public sector, has made them unemployable elsewhere.

When I joined the NHS in a middle management position, I had to jump through hoops to prove my intellect and initiative, and then once I was employed everything possible was done to ensure I didn't use them. The NHS draws bright well-intentioned people in, asks them for their best and then reduces them to the role of useful idiots. Leave your brains and your balls in the car park and hang your moral compass on the coat hook provided. Bureaucrats, administrators, monitors, overseers, and nay sayers, are pervasive in the NHS, not leaders. The very notion of leadership in the NHS is a misnomer. My experience, which I would be the first to acknowledge is partly shaped albeit to a small degree by the isolated operating characteristics of Cumbria, is that what we call leadership in the

NHS is no more than thinly veiled fatalistic cheerleading. The overwhelming sense of impotence and stultifying lack of ambition is pervasive. The centre issues a diktat and the great and good work out how to do demonstrate if not do, just what they have been asked; few if any challenge or question and various whiteboards and Zoom meetings around the UK groan as they are inundated with PowerPoint slides containing increasingly meaningless exhortations like, *Failure is Not an Option* (I beg to differ) and *Challenge Accepted*.

The NHS has run its own leadership training academy for some years. The institution likes to promote from within. The vast majority of its directors and senior managers have never worked in any other setting and many of those occupying the most well remunerated positions of responsibility within the NHS have come through its own graduate recruitment schemes. The current Chief Executive of NHS England, Amanda Pritchard, is a product of the NHS Management Training Scheme which she entered in 1997. Her predecessor Simon Stevens also entered the NHS via the Graduate Management Training Scheme, starting his career at Shotley Bridge General Hospital. Amanda, a former healthcare official and public policy analyst, and the daughter of a bishop, is clearly a politically astute animal who understands the triumph of hope over experience or evidence. In her mid-twenties, she served as health team leader in the now infamous Prime Ministers Delivery Unit under Tony Blair. The delivery unit was the product of an incredibly destructive fad called New Public Management and a triumph of political self-delusion over reality in which the achievement of meaningless arbitrary targets was perceived and celebrated as a meaningful surrogate for real impact. Chasing the target and missing the point became the undisputed mantra for public services under the last Labour Government and has persisted since. Following her stint for the PM Amanda was then appointed as deputy chief executive of Chelsea and Westminster Hospital NHS Foundation Trust at the ripe old age of twenty-nine, before progressing ever upward. The senior ranks of NHS England and NHS Hospital Trusts across the UK are peppered with these politically astute proteges, products of the NHSs own fundamentally flawed politically servile and self-perpetuating thought processes. Amanda may be a genuinely lovely person, but she is undeniably, a continuation of the politically subservient leadership style preferred by ministers who value dealers in hope over systemic thinkers who want change and will challenge. Do not expect anything radical from Amanda!

We can do this!

Readers may recall a story that ran across the national press in the autumn of 2017 about a hapless group of senior NHS executives who were forced to chant, *"We can do this, we can do this"*, during an executive awayday. The chief executives and senior directors in question were drawn from a selection of NHS Trusts across the country who it was felt were most likely to not meet their targets for admissions in the coming winter. The Trust leaders, if they can be called that, said they were left feeling bullied and humiliated. They said they had been cajoled into chanting the phrase ever louder by a senior NHS official, someone more senior than themselves. The gathering had been attended by some NHS big hitters. Simon Stevens, the former head of the NHS, and the health secretary of the time Jeremy Hunt were said to have been present. The sixty or so Chief Executives had been collectively summoned to the NHS headmaster's office because achieving the four-hour admissions target, a symbolic and politically important goal, was thought to be under threat. According to sources from within the meeting, the group had been harangued and told they were putting patient lives at risk before then being encouraged to chant their way out of trouble. I'd love to have been there, I really think I would have pissed myself laughing.

After the story broke in the press, the cheerleader in chief, a long-serving NHS employee called Paul Watson, now known to his friends as, *He can do this Watson*, was forced to offer a public apology for any offence or upset he may have caused. But what genuinely concerns me about the whole sorry episode is not that Paul drank too much coffee that morning and fancied himself as some sort of Bob the Builder style motivational guru, I can excuse Paul for his unconventional if admittedly fun approach to motivating managers and improving performance. No, what really concerns me is that not one of the sixty highly paid executives who are tasked with running some of the UK's largest hospitals, told Paul to feck off being so stupid before twatting him squarely on the chin to a rapturous round of applause from their colleagues. Paul was not the problem. The problem was that we have created such a sycophantic obsequious servile and unchallenging culture at the very top of our precious health and care system that it is run by people who have become afraid of their own shadow.

Teams not families:

A few years ago, I visited the head offices of the Leadership Training Academy of the UK's National Health Service. The academy is situated in Leeds. I was guided into the café area to wait to be called to my meeting. As I sat drinking a Latte in the modern and very pleasantly appointed surroundings, I found myself in, I couldn't help thinking how far from the pain of patient tragedy, the stress of frontline nursing, and the realities of being bullied as a Whistleblower, this place was. There was a visual display in the café which said that joining the NHS was more like joining a family than an institution. How reassuring to the people who come here to attend courses and who work here I thought. Then I remembered the Mafia run their business like a family.

We're a team, not a family, is the headline of a slide from a PowerPoint presentation given to staff some years ago by Reed Hastings, then the Chief Executive of Netflix. The presentation was entitled *Freedom & Responsibility*. If you can make time to look for and go through the presentation on SlideShare, I think you will find its key message about Netflix being a company that sees itself as a team and not a family, very thought provoking. The messages it contains around the need for courage, curiosity, and honesty and many of the behaviours it outlines are also refreshing. The message that a company should be more like a team and less like a family was not one I used to agree with. I used to feel there was nothing inappropriate or untoward about an employer saying it wanted to be like a family, but I think I understand now that it can never be that way, and in relation to the public sector, I don't think it should be that way.

Families are characterised by a form of necessary wilful blindness that love creates. My mum is still convinced I got in with the wrong crowd when I was a youngster, her biases preclude her from acknowledging that I was the wrong crowd. Families tend to underplay, excuse, or hide wrongdoing, there are topics they don't discuss at the dinner table, Uncle Franks time in jail, Cousin Bessie's propensity for illicit substances, or Grandad's love child to another woman. Families protect their own no matter what, and loyalty within a family setting is often necessarily and unconditionally blind. These traits and behaviours are not what are needed in high functioning organisations or appropriate in publicly funded health and care services. We need teams, not families in our health and care services. The culture we need must be more like the culture of the airline industry in which people are ostracized when they don't speak out and speak up and share what went wrong, and less like the Victorian family who won't talk about anything other than those topics deemed suitable for polite discussion at the dining room table. Whether an organisation sees itself as a family or a team has an influence on how open or closed its culture is, how it deals with the presence of wrongdoing and poor practice, and importantly how it treats those who bring such matters to its attention.

The problems with encouraging employees to behave as if they are part of a family who provide each other with unconditional support no matter what, are manifold in healthcare and they manifest and multiply when things go wrong. To be collegiate is great, but the idea that the teams and departments and organisations within a healthcare system should treat each other like family members is a barrier to openness, transparency, learning and improvement. High performing teams rely on the cumulative good performance of all their members. If someone isn't up to scratch or is going through a bad period, then compassion and understanding for them should be forthcoming, and training made available where appropriate. But tolerating and accommodating deficient performance in healthcare, which equates to creating the conditions in which patient harm will occur, should not be overlooked or excused because of misplaced loyalties. Despite what my family has endured I am big on forgiveness, though I prefer to call it understanding; I think forgiving seems incredibly pompous. I'm not in favour of punishing people who make well-intentioned mistakes, we're all only human. What I'm not in favour of is hiding mistakes or helping others to hide theirs. Being paid for from the public purse is a privilege not a right.

Seek diversity of thought and positive conflict:

Baron Victor Adebowale has been Chair of the NHS Confederation since 2020. A few years ago, amidst the thick fog of what sometimes feels like our never-ending navel gazing guilt ridden journey into political correctness, Lord V made the mildly contentious point that what boards and senior leadership teams really needed to ensure their success was not diversity of skin colour, it was diversity of thought. Amen to that Victor. If only the NHS Confederation could also take it to heart. As a pallid white middle-aged man with grey hair, I welcomed his comment. It was an observation I would happily have made had I felt able to. One look at the UK's shortest serving chancellor Kwasi Kwarteng makes a model mockery of ill-fated attempts to achieve diversity on the basis of skin colour. Black, White, Boris, Kwasi, Truss, ineptitude and ingenuity have neither pigment nor gender.

In his critically acclaimed 2002 book, *The Rise of the Creative Class,* the author Richard Florida highlighted the pivotal role of diversity, true diversity, in the creation and development of a wide range of innovations, increased productivity and profitability within a range of organisations, as well as the wider establishing of tolerance and cohesion in communities. The book doesn't shy away from the very real conundrum of striking the balance between hiring and harnessing the talents of creative people while ensuring the corporate culture doesn't implode. And while it's tempting to talk of the successes diverse thinking has generated, it's also worth noting that a great many organisations who believed diversity would be the answer to their problems, have paid a heavy price for failing to understand how best to incorporate divergent thinkers into their organisational cultures and operational structures. The so-called Great Resignation that swept the USA in 2021, precipitated by Covid-19, seemed to bring the mismatch between self-serving inflexible corporate cultures and the aspirations of their employees to a head. The phenomenon has parallels with the NHS's poor treatment of its employees and the retention and recruitment crisis this in turn has created.

General Paton, a leader operating in a notoriously hierarchical setting, said that when everyone in the room is thinking the same then some people are not thinking. Alfred Sloan, the legendary and much quoted former President, Chairman and Chief Executive of General Motors during its halcyon years of growth and market dominance was reputed to propose halting any meeting at which everyone was in agreement. He would ask the participants to give themselves time to develop disagreement to gain a greater understanding of whatever decision they engaged in making was really all about, before reconvening at a later date. He actively sought to develop disagreement to ensure the best and most informed decisions could be made. His meeting styles and reputation for making good decisions became the stuff of corporate folklore because of his explicit desire to generate and harness conflicting views. And it's a style many of the world's most notable entrepreneurs have replicated and refined. I imagine Alfred would have lasted less than five minutes in the upper tiers of the NHS. I think his mind would have snapped had he been forced to deal with the sycophancy and groupthink that typifies so many NHS senior management meetings. *"What's that you say Alfred, you think we should disagree, yes of course we agree that we should disagree, now if you could just tell us what you would like us to disagree about"*. I can visualize him running headlong through the closest fire exit or leaping out the nearest window to resist the overpowering urge he would doubtless have felt to throttle someone, perhaps more than just one.

The founders of Google, Larry Page and Sergey Brin, attribute a good deal of the company's success to its ability to safely accommodate and harness positive conflict. Andy Grove the founder of Intel implemented the mantra of listen, challenge, then commit. Good leaders welcome and stimulate positive conflict. Unquestioning agreement is a sure sign of a culturally fragile organisation. From Patton to Sloan, Grove to Brin, Page and Pichai, Eno to Ogilvy, Gates to Nadella, Jobs to Cook, Branson, Knight, Bezos, Hastings and of course Musk, successful business leaders actively look for and develop alternative views and diversity of thought. We may not always agree with their business models or their politics, but we can't deny their ability to identify and seize opportunities, or to innovate and harness diverse ideas and resources in the pursuit of success.

The wilful blindness which lies at the heart of many of the challenges facing the NHS and which sits just beneath the surface of the many tragedies that have unfolded in health and care recently, thrives when birds of a feather flock together. These people inevitably end-up reinforcing each other's world views, prejudices, biases, and blind spots. Diverse types of people as well as a different type of leadership, management, and personal development are required. Healthcare organisations need leaders at every level who will take the opportunities given to them to speak up. Who proactively look to create psychologically safe conditions in their departments, teams, and specialties, in which people feel truly valued, trusted, and able to speak up freely, confidently, and safely. When managers and leaders are overly focused on chasing multiple targets and ticking a constantly changing stream of regulatory boxes, it blindsides them, their organisations, and their people, to the ever-present sources of risk that lurk in the shady spots of every organisation.

It remains a truth that fighting and tragedy emerge from the avoidance of positive conflict. Anyone who has been married as long as I have, knows this to be true. When we feel unable or avoid saying what we think we need to say, asking the questions we want to ask, or talking about the things we think are important, we store up our concerns and tensions and become increasingly resentful. Purposeful conflict is healthy, and well-intentioned challenge is good. It's often in the middle of exchanging conflicting views and challenging conventional wisdoms, that remarkable things occur. Fighting isn't always made obvious by its existence but in whatever form it takes it is destructive, and it comes about when positive conflict has not been allowed to surface and has built to a point where it needs to find an outlet. One of the nurses at the doomed Mid Staffs Hospital, a lady called Helene Donnelly, raised over a hundred concerns internally about the problems she could see unfolding on the hospital wards around her. Her observations were seen as criticism, she was labelled a troublemaker, her insights were ignored, in short, all conflict was avoided. If the NHS Trust had developed and maintained the capacity to manage and harness conflict and encourage diverse views, to welcome opinions and insights in a constructive way, then Helene would have been listened to and lives could have been saved.

Things get bad, awfully bad for patients when positive conflict is suppressed and avoided in hospitals. A report produced by Members of Parliament published in July 2021, suggested that a thousand babies die a preventable death in the UK each year, because a culture of shifting blame and remaining tight-lipped means that lessons are not learned after mistakes are made on NHS hospital maternity wards. That is twenty lives and the futures they had ahead of them, lost every week in one of the world's largest economies and most advanced healthcare systems. And it's not because the resources and equipment they need are not available, nor is it because the skills required are absent from the people present, it is simply because people are working in organisations in which they are unable to acknowledge their mistakes. And the problem is not restricted to maternity services. Research published by the British Medical Journal (BMJ) in 2019 suggested that one in twenty patients is exposed to preventable harm and of these twelve percent suffer from a permanent disability or die as a result. Considering the number of patient admissions to NHS hospitals in the UK was estimated to be around sixteen million each year, pre-Covid, the BMJ's estimate is alarming.

The report into the avoidable deaths occurring in Shropshire's Maternity Services released in 2022 claimed three hundred babies had been harmed or had died an avoidable death because of the unsafe practices that were tolerated in the hospitals maternity ward. The picture that emerged was one of people who knew what was going on but did everything possible to avoid conflict, they stayed quiet when they should have spoken up, leaders and managers focused on cheerleading, telling good stories when they should have been looking into the tragedies that were occurring all around them. They kept the peace at all costs, and what cost that turned out to be for hundreds of babies and their families. Needless permanent life-changing harm, avoidable deaths, emotional damage, and destruction of so many types and on so many levels occurs when we choose the path of least resistance and avoid conflict.

An open mind is a wonderful thing, an unquestioning mind is something else. The NHS needs to start to value uncertainty, and the desire for knowledge and understanding, over the charismatic and the wildly over-confident. We need people at all levels who are willing to lead beyond their authority. To maintain standards and improve, every organisation has not just to welcome feedback, but actively seek it, get out the office, talk to people, turn over stones and look for the problems, which are in truth as every good marketer knows, no more than opportunities to improve.

David Ogilvy, widely regarded as the father of modern advertising, used the example of a teaching hospital to describe the purpose of Ogilvy & Mather. He said, "Great hospitals do two things, they look after patients, and they teach young doctors". Ogilvy went on to explain that Ogilvy and Mather also did two things, it looked after clients and taught young advertising people. He understood that the key to continued success was in nurturing talent and developing people. He is famous for sending the newly appointed heads of each of office a set of

Russian Dolls. These were to be placed on their desk as a constant reminder they should always try to hire people smarter, better, and creatively and intellectually bigger than themselves. Upon opening the last of the dolls each newly appointed office manager would find a message reading, *"If each of us hires people who are smaller than we are, we shall become a company of dwarfs. But if each of us hires people who are bigger than we are, we shall become a company of giants."* His approach to looking for and hiring talent is the polar opposite of the approach taken by most managers in the public sector who, already having risen beyond the level of their incompetence have no desire to hire anyone that could challenge their status. Good managers in progressive private sector organisations are encouraged to hire people more talented than themselves. Their ability to recruit exceptionally able individuals often reflects well upon them. The less than mediocre managers that populate the ranks of the public sector are wary of those more driven, intelligent, and able than themselves. They fear such people, regarding them more often as threats rather than organisational assets. These managers hire down, they value compliancy over creativity and seek individuals who won't challenge their status or decision-making.

Perhaps there are exceptions:

A straight speaking Geordie, Jim Mackey, now Sir James Mackey following his knighthood in 2019, has been widely regarded as one of the most influential and forward-thinking figures in the NHS for many years. He has served as the Chief Executive of NHS Improvement and was more recently in the running to be the next Chief Executive of NHS England following the departure of Simon Stevens in 2021. Unfortunately, if perhaps unsurprisingly, he lost out to a more politically acceptable compliant applicant. Jim's previous robust and unphased appearances in front of parliamentary committees may have made him an unsuitably unmalleable candidate for the position of NHS England's Chief Executive in the eyes of the establishment.

The Northumbria Healthcare NHS Foundation Trust, the NHS Trust Jim has been Chief Executive of for over a decade, is one of the few NHS Trusts regularly held aloft by both patients and professional observers of the NHS as an exemplar of excellence in both the quality of the healthcare it provides and the management of its finances. Its staff engagement and morale are consistently rated as the highest of any NHS Trust in the country. Many GPs based in Cumbria refer their patients to Northumbria's hospitals for elective operations because they know their patients will receive the best available treatment in the shortest possible time. A sizable proportion of Cumbria's elderly population owes its mobility to the hip replacement surgeons of Hexham General Hospital. For many GPs, referring their patients into the care of Northumbria's NHS is a complete and utter no brainer. The alternative being to place them at the mercy of North Cumbria's NHS. Though these two NHS Trusts are separated by the shortest of distances, the only thing similar about them is the sound of their names. North Cumbria is widely regarded as the worst NHS Trust in the country, Northumbria the best. A choice between a long wait for a potentially botched operation performed by a locum surgeon with a lengthy recovery time and a free dose of MRSA thrown in, versus a swiftly and expertly performed procedure, is not really a choice. My uncle insisted on being referred to Hexham for his hip replacement. He said he wouldn't have gone to Carlisle Hospital for all the tea in China. After his operation and return home, he spoke about Hexham hospital in glowing terms. He and my aunt had been greeted and ushered into the hospital building and then directed to the right department by a trained volunteer working on behalf of the Trust. Customer service in an NHS hospital, whatever next; high quality locally sourced food, now there's a thought?

In September 2021, following Covid-19 and the subsequent and much-publicised build-up of the huge backlog in elective surgery it created, NHS England appointed Jim to advise on ways to address the issue and bring waiting times back down. Current estimates suggest between five and six million people are presently waiting for routine operations and procedures across the UK, around four hundred thousand of these have been waiting for more than a year. I've simultaneously envied the citizens of Northumbria and the staff of its NHS since working in Cumbria's NHS and finding out just how poor it was in comparison. I may be deluding myself, but I get the feeling that had I been employed in Northumbria's NHS, not only would I not have lost my job for Whistleblowing, but the need to even consider becoming a Whistleblower wouldn't have arisen. I've admired Jim's leadership of Northumbria's NHS hospitals for some time, and I arranged to speak with him early in 2023. He is refreshingly un-public sector and very un-NHS in his responsiveness and willingness to speak to people who do not operate in the same senior circles. His behaviour in this respect alone is the polar opposite of the hierarchically conscious self-promoting sycophancy that continues to dominate much of the NHS. I've known of meetings in the NHS that start with the customary round robin introductions in which attendees are expected to not only explain their role but also the salary band they are in. Many meetings in the NHS openly exclude staff from the lower banding scales. It's not that people in the NHS think that having good ideas or adding value to a discussion depends on your status, it's simply that they recognise that ideas won't be taken seriously unless they are seen to come from the right source. If Einstein had been employed as a Band Seven Manager in the NHS, he would still be asking for permission to go to the toilet, and his famous proclamation that imagination is more important than knowledge would have had him escorted out of the building. During the course of drafting this book I've emailed and tried calling a great many less significant figures than Jim from within the NHS and the wider healthcare system, many of whom haven't even replied, so I'm genuinely surprised and incredibly pleased that he's made time to talk to me. And it's clear after a few minutes of speaking with him that he is not a product of privileged entitlement or assumed greatness.

I start our conversation by asking if he feels it is realistic for people to think that we in Britain can have a top-notch health and care system in an increasingly fragmented society and a widening inequitable economy. As with all senior public sector officials, Jim does not feel able to criticise the government's economic policies and its record in office overtly. But as a dyed in the wool northerner born on the south side of the Tyne within a spit of the starting point of the famous Jarrow March of 1936, he cannot help but acknowledge that the wider public's health and wellbeing are wedded to their prevailing social and economic conditions.

I then ask about his views on the much-maligned concept of Foundation Trusts. Northumbria NHS Foundation Trust is one of the very few that seems to have thrived and I'm curious as to how an NHS Trust operating from over a dozen locations in a mix of rural and urban settings has managed to succeed when so many have failed, often spectacularly. Jim disagrees with my assertion that the idea of Foundation Trusts was fundamentally flawed. In his view, the overarching strategy was sound, but it was poorly implemented. I challenge this view as I think that a strategy can and only ever should be judged on what it achieved as opposed to its aspirations, however noble these may have been. There is no denying that through a mix of historical good fortune and competent leadership, Foundation Trust status seems to have worked well for Northumbria. Yet there is also no denying that chasing and achieving Foundation Trust status was a complete and utter disaster in other areas. While Northumbria NHS Foundation Trust was providing high quality clinical services to its patients and sitting on reserves of almost two hundred million pounds, its NHS counterparts in neighbouring Cumbria were providing some of the least safe services in the UK and were many tens of millions in deficit. In my view the obvious and many harms the pursuit and maintaining of Foundation Trust status caused to patients across the country and the significant damage it has done to morale and capacity throughout the entire NHS workforce, means it can only ever be deemed an abject failure in the wider sense. We agree to disagree.

We go on to discuss the wider health and care system and I ask how Northumbria NHS is coping with the problems of reduced capacity in Adult Social Care. I ask if he thinks social care should be brought under the banner and the control of the NHS at which point Jim reveals to me that Northumbria are currently trialing a pilot scheme in which social care settings would be run by the Trust and their care staff would be employed on NHS terms and conditions. This is a politically sensitive arena for an NHS Trust to enter because the intrusion of the public sector into the largely private sector-controlled world of social care could easily cause ructions at a national level. To many, including myself, the separation of social care from the NHS has always been and remains entirely illogical. The two areas are so inextricably interlinked and interdependent that to manage them successfully in separation from one another is neither possible nor pragmatic. One cannot succeed if the other is failing. Some call this worldview of interdependence, systems thinking, others common sense. There is a fine line between them. But as we all know by now, systems thinking or common sense, whichever you prefer to call it, is largely uncommon and especially so in the southern centric ivory towers of the public sector. For me, this proactive move by an NHS Trust, albeit an entirely logical and in many respects obvious move into the world of social care, is undoubtedly one of the most exciting and positive developments in healthcare I have come across. It enables better coordination of safer patient care, and it addresses the need for social care workers, many of whom do an incredible and undervalued job, to enjoy the employment benefits they deserve and take advantage of the opportunities for progression and development that being part of a larger public service institution like the NHS can provide.

Finally, I ask about the failed implementation of the fit and proper persons test for NHS directors. I'm keen to know if Jim thought the concept was solid or just another ill thought through top-down initiative designed to appease observers and ministers in the wake of the Mid Staffs tragedy. Again, he suggests the idea was good and he feels it's entirely appropriate that senior public servants are subject to scrutiny. But as with a lot of initiatives launched with good intent in the NHS, its execution was poor and responsibility for overseeing its eventual implementation was shoved back and forth between organisations, before finally landing half-formed at the Care Quality Commissions door. In his view NHS Trusts were not given the direction and tools to either understand or address its requirements fully. Though I don't think he would ever say so, Jim is street savvy enough to know that not every director and senior manager in the NHS has the integrity required for their role.

In his time as Chief Executive at Northumbria NHS Foundation Trust, as well as attempting to align social care, Jim and his team have enabled and led the development of numerous ground-breaking initiatives including the direct employment of local GPs and the setting-up of a separate self-sustaining facilities management company. Established in 2012 and initially designed to serve Northumbria, it now offers facilities management services on a commercial basis to NHS Trusts in other areas. The GPs of Northumbria Primary Care, a wholly owned subsidiary of Northumbria NHS Foundation Trust formed in 2015, are salaried employees. They are freed from the non-value adding and resource hungry burdens of property management, recruitment, and duplicated administration that eat huge chunks of the time available to GPs in traditional partner led practices. Perhaps not surprisingly, the GPs working for Northumbria Primary Care report having a better work life balance and being able to see more patients and practice their craft more effectively. In the private sector such consolidation would be seen as an entirely logical way to ensure that the precious clinical ability contained within Primary Care could be maximized and made as effective and efficient as possible. But again, in the public sector and the NHS, such simple yet impactful innovations are still the exception.

Jim was confident enough in the team around him at Northumbria Foundation Trust that he was able to undertake a two-year secondment with NHS Improvement between 2015 and 2017, safe in the knowledge that things would not go to hell in a handcart in his absence. In my experience there are too many NHS Chief Executives who live with an illusion of indispensability, who look to claim credit for everything and believe the organisations they manage will somehow cease functioning if they are not present. The reality I imagine is that most would perform better. After our meeting I reflect that Jim had been focused and calm, distinctly unhurriedly and considered in his responses. I'm left with the sense he has succeeded in avoiding the trap of becoming a busy fool by hiring and encouraging others to hire and develop able people who are then enabled and trusted to do their jobs. This is heartening, it's the opposite end of the spectrum from the established way of managing people in the NHS, which is to hire the less able who are less of a threat and then micro-manage and dictate to them. I'm sure he has his critics, but I can't help feeling that more Jim Mackey's in the NHS would be a good thing. The problem is that people like Jim appear to be the exception.

Leading and leadership is now, more than ever, the hottest topic in the world of organisations we inhabit; public, private and third sector. A 2019 article in Forbes Business Magazine estimated the world market for leadership training and development to be worth approx. $366B. That's a lot of money in anyone's book. The global market for corporate leadership and training is estimated to reach $650B by 2028. But in a world where leadership training and development appears to be an expensively funded priority, how is it that we exist in what some have labelled a post truth post trust era in which our perceptions about the authenticity of leaders have plummeted to all-time lows? We seem to have reached a point where we almost expect duplicity and mendacity from those in positions of authority. We are no longer shocked by poor behaviours, we are now more surprised when we discover examples of genuine servant leadership, humility, honesty, and integrity.

The vast majority of the current cadre of executives and managers in the NHS are not bad people, whatever that might mean to each of us. They are merely adapters who have learned how to thrive in the environment they have found themselves in. They are astutely aware of both the paths to career destruction and career success. The key to career success in the NHS and the wider public sector is to roll out the red carpet for the regulator and not the customer, be they patient, pupil, or victim of crime. Would you risk a well-paid career and a good pension by challenging the hierarchy?

Chapter 22: Oil and water, technology and the NHS

"The problem Tom is fuckwittery and poor management, plain and simple."

NHS Consultant; Cumberland Infirmary

It's not the answer I had expected when I asked a consultant surgeon who had been in the NHS for over thirty years, why in his opinion the health service remained so far behind in its adoption of technology. In fairness he did then go on to explain in more depth and slightly more diplomatic language what he felt were the reasons behind the digital disjoin, that straddles and inhibits the NHS. He said he wanted to use technology, to help his patients and manage his own and his departments workload. But every technological innovation he suggested or asked for, however simple to implement, was ignored, or kicked into the long grass while directors and managers dealt with other more pressing matters. In his private life he was facetiming family in Australia on his iPad, yet in his professional capacity he was told he had to ensure that patients were seen on a face-to-face basis for even the most basic of follow-up appointments. Some of the patients had to undertake a four hour round trip on public transport across Cumbria, just to sit for less than ten minutes in front of him and be told that everything was fine. Five years previously the NHS Trust he worked for had published and launched a glossy strategy outlining its digital ambitions to great fanfare, not one of the planned initiatives had come to fruition or looked like it ever would and the director who had developed the strategy had since left the Trust.

Towards the end of the last century management gurus were estimating that between fifty and seventy percent of the manual work being undertaken across the world could be done more effectively and efficiently using technology. That proportion will doubtless have increased significantly since then. The current state of the technological capacity and capability in the NHS is a disgrace. It is frankly gobsmacking that many of the systems used to capture and store our healthcare records do not talk to each other and that in the year 2023 there are still hospitals that do not have a fully digitised patient record system. That there are still people employed in the NHS whose job is to file paper records and push trolleys of written medical notes around hospitals is incredulous. The NHS spends over two hundred million pounds each year storing paper records at locations across the UK. In Late in 2022 I spoke with one of the ambulance services being held up as an exemplar in the adoption of technology in the UK. The service creates an electronic summary of the patient and their condition, which it then has to print off on arrival at the hospital to be handed manually to the receiving staff. I asked why they don't exchange it electronically and was told that the hospital system won't interact with the ambulance services system. It blows my mind that anyone can think that the process of exchanging pieces of paper is an achievement to be proud of in the year 2023. It's like learning to tie your shoelaces or straighten your tie at the age of thirty.

Have you ever asked yourself, why it is you can have an app on the smart device that sits in your palm which enables you to see all the interactions you have ever had with a global online retailer since you first opened an account, yet the NHS that we rely on at the most pivotal moments in our life, is desperately trying to play catch-up with technology and in some cases still sending faxes? I've used Amazon, other online retailers are available, since 2001. I've had access to twenty years of information about my purchase history at my fingertips for years now. I was a victim of credit card fraud once after a visit to a dodgy Chinese restaurant in Menorca, but to the best of my knowledge not once has my Amazon account been hacked into or my personal details compromised. It continues to baffle and amaze me that a bloke called Jeff, now astronaut Bezos to his friends, who started a business that originally only sold printed books through what we would now view as a terrible website in the mid-nineties, had better, more user-friendly, integrated technology infrastructure in 2002, than the UK's National Health Service, an institution that has been around since 1948, has in 2023. One is merely tasked with making profit, the other with saving lives. In 2002 Amazon reported its first quarterly profit on sales of less than $1B (one billion dollars). The annual budget of the NHS in the 2002/03 was approx. £65B. Amazons revenue at the time of writing is around $500B. Why has a business selling widgets, gizmos, and online services got more functional and secure technological capacity than Britain's NHS? How did that happen?

Good data informs decision-making:

One of the first and many faux pas I made when I joined the NHS was to ask the director responsible for measuring performance if I could be given access to the organisations' performance dashboards. I imagined someone with the title of director of strategy and performance would have a handle on, well, performance, and I assumed he must have access to a real-time dashboard of activity. He looked at me strangely, as if I had just addressed him in Swahili. *"What do you mean he asked,"* I explained that it would help me understand the work the Trust did and where I should focus the team's effort if I was to get a handle on what we did and where we did it. I wanted to understand the type and frequency of demand upon services, where the referrals into services were coming from and what the trends were. When I had worked for Carlsberg over a decade earlier, I had been able to access all the relevant sales and profit data I needed to help me do my job. I knew almost in real-time how many bottles of pop an account had bought and paid for and which of the more than five thousand stock items Carlsberg supplied that it was ordering, and when they were doing so. This information was used to great effect to track sales volumes and profit and to help each individual trade account understand how they were doing and what their stock trends were. It also enabled Carlsberg to forecast and manage its operations effectively. If improvement begins with understanding, then knowing where you are at any point in time is critical. As W Edwards Deming used to say, in God we trust, all others bring data. Initially I thought the director of performance was hesitant in his response because he didn't want to share the information that he must have access to, perhaps on the grounds of privileged information or commercial sensitivity. But no, he explained that he had no access to any such performance or activity related data and that the data itself probably wasn't being recorded accurately if it was being recorded at all. He told me that most of the data and information within the Trust was kept on paper, in various formats and in numerous separate locations. I was astonished.

What the director of strategy and performance was effectively acknowledging, was that he didn't have the first clue how the organisation he was a director of was performing, what it was doing, who it was doing it to, or how often and where it was doing it. His explanation for the absence of access to data was that classic public sector cop out of, that's just the way it is. It is the stock response of the disempowered, the disinterested, and the unaccountable. I left his office wondering how it could be that a commercial organisation selling sugary alcoholic liquid and sundries to the masses with global revenues of around one tenth the annual turnover of the NHS knew more about its day-to-day activities than one of the largest employers in the world, a publicly funded organisation responsible for the provision of healthcare to an entire nation. It was 2012 when I first posed this question, and though some NHS Trusts and bodies have moved forward slightly in terms of their ability to harness technology to capture and interrogate data, that progress has been tortuously slow and fragmented. The reality for many NHS Trusts is that little has changed. NHS mental health trusts are still recording activity on paper, which as a BBC Panorama documentary aired in 2022 into the state of mental health services in one NHS Trust revealed, is inaccurate and sometimes deliberately misleading. It amazes and perplexes me, that in 2023, twenty-five years after I first studied online with the Open University, there are still people employed in the NHS whose job it is to push creaking metal trolleys of paper records, newly created and old medical notes, around the premises of various hospital sites, up and down corridors, and across carparks in all weathers, all over the UK.

Haunted by the spectre of failure:

In 2011, as the world was beginning to truly feel and grasp the implications of the global financial unravelling of 2008, as rioters took to the streets of Europe's cities and buses and buildings in London blazed in front our very eyes, and as dictatorships that had prevailed for decades toppled around the world. The government and NHS seized the opportunity to capitalise on the doom-laden headlines dominating our screens and our minds and sneakily slipped out an announcement designed to slide under all our radars. It nearly worked. The announcement related to something called the NHS National Programme for IT, or NPFIT as it is referred to in hushed tones in NHS technology circles. The National Programme for IT was the NHSs attempt to implement systemwide technology across the entire institution. The programme was launched in 2002 amidst great fanfare. It promised cutting-edge technological innovations which would revolutionise patient care and make the entire NHS more effective and efficient in almost every respect. Patients would have access to their medical records online, web-based consultations with healthcare professionals would become commonplace, and GP Practices would be able to share vital patient data seamlessly with hospitals and ambulance services. NPFIT would save lives and make staff and clinicians more productive. What could possibly go wrong?

The NPFIT was initially allocated a budget of just over £2.3B to be spent over three years. Then with an inevitable, predictably depressing, and almost traditional familiarity, the length of time needed and the money the programme required started to grow exponentially and in 2006 the National Audit Office estimated the eventual costs would be almost £12.5B over ten years. Faced with a continuing and frustrating lack of visible progress, growing bills to the public purse, and having been effectively stonewalled by the programmes leaders who refused to share information with interested MPs, in April 2007 the Public Accounts Committee of the House of Commons comprehensively lambasted the project. The Chair of the Public Accounts Committee suggested that the biggest technology project in the world was turning into the biggest technology disaster. The report concluded that the programme could eventually end up costing more than £20B and suggested that no significant clinical benefit was likely to emerge from it. As quickly as the amounts involved increased, they just as quickly ended up in the hands of a handful of large consultancy and technology providers. As the turmoil within the programme grew and controversy started to openly manifest, some companies quietly removed themselves from the process before the shit could hit the fan and some were removed. The latter, perhaps with some justification, felt they had been scapegoated to cover over the cracks in a fundamentally flawed programme and then spent years disputing their expulsion from the money train. The Japanese IT giant Fujitsu entered a ten-year legal battle with the Department for Health and Social Care which continued until 2018. Fujitsu eventually received settlement for its troubles said to be in the region of £465M. Accenture, one of the largest technology and professional services consultancy companies in the world were one of the former. They left the programme apparently voluntarily in 2006 having pocketed a cool £2B for their efforts.

Under the terms of the contract, companies who left the NPFIT programme were potentially liable for up to half the revenues they had received. Contractors had apparently been very publicly warned by the programme director Richard Granger in March 2006 that if any of them walked away from the programme they would pay dearly for any disruption caused. Granger had also previously claimed that contractors would only be paid upon successful completion of their contracts and that the NPFIT contracts were eye-wateringly tight. In the case of Accenture's departure, they somehow deftly extricated themselves from the doomed programme having reportedly given back just £63M in compensation, less than four percent of what they had taken from the public purse and certainly not enough to make their shareholders eyes water. Four percent is a level of discount most retailers would happily give away in exchange for a large order. Granger left his very well-paid role leading the NPFIT programme in 2007, he had previously worked for Accenture. Why am I not surprised, I hear you sighing deeply to yourself.

The Department of Health and Social Cares official excuse for pulling the plug on the NPFIT programme was that they and the NHS had some sort of epiphany in which they realised that implementing a top-down centrally driven technology programme was not the right thing to do. This was total bullshit! To compound the madness, they then tasked each part of the NHS, each Trust and related body, to sort its own technology solutions out. If there was ever a recipe for a complete and utter technological clusterfuck, this was it. Can you imagine Jeff Bezos telling the various regions, divisions, and departments within Amazon, that they were free to choose the technology infrastructure they wanted because efforts to coordinate something centrally were not working? Or perhaps you visit a different branch of Tesco's only to be told they won't recognise your loyalty card and will only accept cash because that's how the local management team have decided to do things in this store? It simply wouldn't happen because any large organisation that allowed these inconsistencies to thrive within itself would not have made it past the first post of opening more than one store. Consistent functioning technology infrastructure is a prerequisite of operating successfully in competitive marketplaces. Come to Pizza Hut, you never know what you might get or if the tills are even working! It's not going to catch on, is it? The failure of the NHS National Programme has cast a long shadow over the NHS and left a legacy of indecision in its wake which prevails to this day. Everyone can see the potential for using technology to make health and care services more effective and efficient, to supply more equitable access to services and improve the working lives of NHS employees. But nobody wants to grasp the nettle.

Even the basics are bad:

In Summer 2017 I began work for the University of Central Lancashire UCLan in the new created role of Rural Health Innovation Manager. I was to be located at their recently rebranded campus the Rural Health Innovation Centre situated on the West Lakes Science Park in West Cumbria. With its views of the Cumbrian Fells to one side and the Sellafield Nuclear Plant on the other, it was as close to a real-life version of Springfield as one could get. Not being one to wait for permission I decided to approach NHS Digital, now part of NHS England, with a proposal seeking a small amount of funding and some executive support. I wanted to continue some research I had begun three years previously into the rich and varied landscape of GP Practice websites. I wanted to know how their respective patient populations interacted with them and what GP Practices were attempting to use them for. What had struck me when I joined the NHS, and something that still strikes me to this day, is that it has an incredible and unparalleled ability to ignore the blindingly obvious and an endless appetite for inconsistency. The upper echelons of the NHS and the academics who inhabit the hierarchies of Higher Education are a match made in heaven, or hell, depending on your perspective and the University was full of academics who felt the keys to making healthcare services sustainable would lie in their ability to harness technology, deploy artificial intelligence, no shortage of that I found, or use virtual reality, driverless ambulances, robot carers in homes and hospitals, or drones delivering prescriptions. Doubtless these were all the sexy areas in which funding was available for research, and though robots will assuredly become part of our healthcare system at some point in the future, the constant search for eye-catching solutions that may or not be on the digital horizon is doing little for patients and staff who need to see tangible improvements in healthcare services, in the here and now.

Having been around Primary Care for the preceding five years and having seen just how differently each practice ran and how incredibly inconsistent their websites were, the former small business advisor in me could see an obvious opportunity to pick some low hanging fruit by getting what I considered to be the basics right. I figured that if all GP Practice websites were designed around the information and service needs of their patients, it could make a useful and practical difference to patients and could help the GP Practices to deal with the constant rises in demand facing them. I know from experience what a huge asset for a small business and what a useful resource for its customers and stakeholders a good website can be. This I thought, was a no-brainer, a logical win-win if ever there was one to be had.

The history of most GP Practice websites is that they were not designed or created to meet the needs of their patients, carers, or families. They came into existence to meet the inspection requirements of the Care Quality Commission, who some years ago decided that each GP Practice must have its own website. In classically short-sighted box-ticking nonsensical regulatory fashion, neither the Care Quality Commission or NHS England then provided or offered any consistent guidelines or templates as to what these websites should look like. Nor any advice or guidance on how an effective website could be used to help GP Practices address the information and support needs of their patients and thus reduce demand on overworked GPs. Just as each GP Practice was later instructed by the regulator to set up a patient participation group, I have the mental scars, but not instructed as to what these would achieve or why they should have them, each GP Practice was told they must have a website. The why, the how, and the what of it, were never considered. What followed was an entirely predictable rush for every GP Practice to obtain a website simultaneously accompanied by a flood of private sector companies offering to supply websites to GP Practices at prices to suit every pocket. The result has been an entirely predictable incredibly expensive online car crash of gargantuan proportions.

After a year of pushing, persuading, and pestering the administrative gatekeepers and purse protectors within NHS Digital, they eventually if begrudgingly acknowledged that my proposal might have legs and agreed to give the University half the twenty thousand pounds I had requested to fund the research. I and some of the technology boffins from the University's IT faculty then started our research and documented our findings. We looked at a randomly chosen selection of several hundred GP Practice websites and noted what we found against a basic checklist of website functionality. We also spoke and met with dozens of GP practice managers to gain an understanding of how they perceived their own websites and what if anything they would do differently if resources, time, money, and expertise, allowed. The responses from some of the focus groups were fascinatingly candid. Many practice managers and staff acknowledged that their own GP Practice websites were so poor that if they were thinking of buying a product or service from a small local business who had such a poor website, they would have second thoughts about dealing with them. It's an incredible state of affairs that Britain's publicly funded Primary Care services provide a less user-friendly online experience than most local independent financial services companies.

The first thing to become abundantly clear was that very few GP Practices were able to update or control and adjust the content on their own website or had the capacity and capability to manage it in-house. The vast majority of GP Practices did not know how much their website was being used or what it was being used for, if at all. Most were locked into contracts in which they were paying hosting and design companies to maintain their online presence and had little or no control over any simple layout or text changes they might need to upload. We established that the website market for Primary Care across the UK was being served by hundreds of different providers, ranging in size from well-established corporates and relatively large organisations to one-man bands who ran their local GP practice website as a favour or a project on the side. One or two of the more tech savvy GPs had even designed and set up their own websites to save money. If the basic criterion for a useful website is that it is up-to-date, relevant, accessible, accurate, and half-reasonably designed and easily navigable, then these I have to say were particularly bad. But after all, the Care Quality Commissions requirement was only for each GP Practice to have a website, they hadn't specified it should be useful or used. As of July 2023, the Care Quality Commission still has no consistent criterion or measures relating to the quality of each GP Practice website, each practice's wider online presence, or its use of technology to meet the needs of its patients. Remind me again, how long has the internet been around?

The team at UCLan and I found that the layouts and designs of each GP Practice website differed from provider to provider. They ranged from the truly horrendously garish and terrible to the not too bad but still a long way from excellent. There was no consistency of approach or content. Many of the websites held out-of-date, inaccurate and incorrect information, and a worryingly large number of them did not meet accessibility requirements or cater for those with sight issues. Though the project was limited in its capacity to gather accurate financial information about the amount each individual GP Practice was spending on their website, the figures and estimates we did obtain would suggest the collective amount being spent by the public purse on this digital smorgasbord of user-unfriendly inconsistency at anywhere above four million pounds a year. It would not surprise me if the figure were five times that. The clinical opportunity cost of this patient facing inconsistency will never be known.

The ultimate impotent output of the project was the production by NHS England of some guidelines for web design aimed at GP Practices. There was no attempt to ensure that the guidelines would be adopted, or even acknowledgement that perhaps more direction from the centre might be required. Can there be a good reason on the face of the planet why every GP Practice website should not conform to a basic standard and be designed around the needs of its patients?

The NHS should be the most technologically enabled and digitally advanced healthcare service in the world. It has not had to negotiate the barriers of competitive rivalry that prevent the adoption of technologies which can readily interact with each other, a perennial problem that plagues the various healthcare systems and services in the United States and other countries. Nor has it, despite what you might hear, been starved of the funds needed to implement the technology it so desperately needs. The money has been available, it has simply not been spent well.

Chapter 23: **Proactive innovators unwelcome**

"The reasonable man adapts himself to the world, the unreasonable man persists in adapting the world to himself, therefore all progress depends on the unreasonable man."

George Bernard Shaw

Farhan Amin has been a GP Partner at the Burnett Edgar Medical Centre on Walney Island in Barrow-in-Furness for almost fifteen years. Walney Island and the surrounding area the practice serves contains some of the most deprived communities in Britain. Barrows changed fortunes are an amplified version of an all too familiar British story. At their zenith the towns shipyard, engineering, and munitions factories employed thirty-five thousand people. Retail parks and drive-through restaurants now fill the industrious landscape that once covered the town like a thick warm comforting blanket. Skilled well-paid work, opportunities for progression, and long-term employment, replaced by jobs requiring subsidies from the public purse to enable the people doing them to make ends meet while enabling their employers to profit from the retail sectors ambition to cut costs to the bone in its value destructive race the bottom. And though plans for submarine production are envisaged to create work in the next few years, it is unlikely Barrow will ever regain the former economic glories its grandiose town hall stands as a lasting monument to. Long term unemployment and the mental health issues that accompany it are rife, patients with multiple morbidities are common, and in recent years the social dissonance that has brewed in the air over Barrow for decades has made it an attractive campaigning ground for far-right groups. It is not a place for the feint hearted to practice medicine, especially for a local GP without a white face.

I've known Farhan for over ten years now. A slight, smiling affable man, he has a rare talent for combining humility and gentleness with incisive, intelligently informed, and unabridged candour. His energy levels and enthusiasm seem to know no bounds. A meeting with Farhan is how I imagine a drained battery feels after being recharged. First the shock of connection and sudden current, then the reassuring realisation of feeling reenergised, ready for whatever comes next and sensing what might be possible. I first met Farhan after being introduced by a colleague when I was working for the NHS in Cumbria. Using his own finances and time he had been developing an online resource for the community that he was designing in collaboration with his patients, and which they had chosen to call Patient Memoirs. The thinking behind the initiative was that people who lived with health conditions knew more about the non-clinical aspects of managing their conditions than any GP ever could. Farhan saw their knowledge and continually evolving experience as an untapped medical asset. To harness and share this asset the Patient Memoirs website would host a bank of structured clinically approved videos recorded by patients, their carer's, families, and loved ones. In these videos people shared self-care tips and talked about their experience of managing a range of conditions in a wide range of circumstances; anxiety, obesity, diabetes, incontinence, irritable bowel syndrome, post-natal depression, COPD, asthma, skin conditions, allergies, and Alzheimer's to name a few. Farhan believed that having access to this information could empower patients and help them understand and manage their own conditions by benefiting and learn from each other's lived experience.

The idea for Patient Memoirs developed following a chance meeting Farhan had with an elderly gentleman in Dubai Airport who shared his experiences of managing Parkinson's disease. Farhan recalls the practical insights being shared with him were not common knowledge to patients or many health professionals and he realised they could be incredibly useful to others with the same condition as well as those tasked with their care. He figured that if he could provide an open online platform for people with a health condition of any type to share their experiences, their coping mechanisms, self-management techniques, medication tips, and lived insights, it would not only be a useful resource for a range of audiences, but it could also help address the ever-increasing pressure on the practice and the local healthcare system. I thought the idea was one of simple brilliance and I promptly set about helping Farhan share what he was doing with a wider audience and seek further funding to support its development. I quickly found out that if an idea doesn't come from the *right place* in the NHS, then it doesn't matter how good, effective, or helpful to patients it might be, it will not get off the ground. In October that year Farhan's work as a clinical innovator trying to make a difference at the coalface of healthcare was recognised by the Health Service Journal, who named him as number one in their 2014 list of top fifty innovators in the NHS. The judges said the work he was doing was interesting, ground-breaking, and out there on the edge. But even with this accolade behind him, none of the local, regional, or national NHS bodies would entertain the idea of helping him develop and spread the Patient Memoirs website as an asset for patients and healthcare professionals alike.

What Farhan was trying to do could easily and relatively cheaply have been turned into a nationally recognised online resource which might have helped countless patients, alleviated pressure on Primary Care, and reduced demand on the entire health and care system. He was offering the NHS an oven-ready solution, but because he was a humble GP and in the grand scheme of things fairly low down the hierarchical pecking order, his idea was left to wither on the vine. Without the resources needed to support the websites evolution, Patient Memoirs was taken offline after a couple of years. In May 2023, in the face of public pressure and no small amount of anger about the declining state of Primary Care, the UK's Conservative government announced a package of measures with the stated aim of making it easier and quicker for patients to get the help they need from their local GP Practice. The heading in bold letters at the very top of this latest and snappily titled, *Delivery Plan for Recovering Access to Primary Care*, is to Empower Patients, a task in which NHS England says it will invest six hundred and forty-five million pounds over the next two years. The detail is classically vague, but people like Farhan, who it has to be said there are not enough of in the NHS, have been trying to get the simple message of patient empowerment to the upper echelons of NHS England and the Department of Health and Social Care, for years now.

Unfortunately, if past results are an indicator of future performance, what NHS England will most likely go and do in their attempts to satisfy the minister that they are deadly serious about achieving their newly accepted mission to empower patients, is create an executive programme board consisting of carefully selected and expensively headhunted and handpicked failed directors. The newly formed, *Empowering the Hell Out of Patient's* programme board, chaired ably and jointly by Lords Prattle and Bluster, will be housed on the upper floors of NHS Ivory Towers. The board will then initiate a recruitment drive for the many well-paid senior project managers and team leaders required to oversee and manage each of the many workstreams such an ambitious venture will need. The only mandatory requirement needed to secure employment in this doomed endeavour will be a copy of the latest Prince2

Project Management Handbook, generous lashings of wild over-confidence, and a CV containing a litany of expensive harmful failures thinly disguised as resounding successes. Cedric has led a series of high profile impactful organisational transformation programmes resulting in the realising of significant financial efficiencies, sounds so much better than, Cedric's attempts at creating culture change have been derided in the national press and led to an exodus of staff and a reduction of payroll costs at every one of the NHS Trusts he has worked in. These high-performance project teams will be housed in the closely guarded department of We Know Best and will have their elite feet kept firmly on the ground through a carefully planned programme of regular engagement with people called patients and service users. This engagement will take the form of being visited once a quarter by a carefully selected volunteer from the outside world, sometimes called the real world, whose job will be to share their lived experience with the elite. The opinions and insights they share, which are based on nothing more than experience and actually using NHS services, will of course be ignored. But they will be hailed as vital stakeholders and integral parts of the cleverly coordinated all-encompassing engagement campaign which was designed to ensure that patients and their needs were always at the centre of and were the ultimate focus of the programme boards attention. That should never be in doubt! The goal and final measure of success for the *Empowering the Hell Out of Patients* programme board, will be the development of a matrix laden graphic rich plan containing a series of vague nebulous recommendations, that ultimately and depressingly predictably, will culminate in the pissing up of a few hundred million pounds of public money against the seemingly inexhaustibly financially absorbent technology toilet wall of the NHS. At which point the next new government, or minister, will have another whizz bang idea and redirect the nations precious finite financial resources and the efforts of its finest leaders and project managers in yet another direction. You heard it here first.

I'll take the high road:

Early one morning in 2016, a few weeks after the clocks had gone back, the northern nights had lengthened and a Cumbrian winter was taking hold, I stepped from the frosty platform of Penrith station onto a warm inviting train bound for Edinburgh, perhaps my favourite British city.

Today was going to be a good day. Today would be a day spent away from the programme management office in which I was being carefully micro-managed out my career in the NHS. By this stage in my employment with the Cumbria Partnership NHS Foundation Trust I had been pushed passed the point of no return. I had been instructed to leave my employment in the NHS at the end of the following March having been relieved from my role on the grounds of poor mental health. Whistleblowers don't get sacked for whistleblowing. To keep me quiet and away from head office for the final nine months of my employment, I had been given the title of Telehealth Lead and relocated to a soulless uninspiring non-descript fabricated grey two-storey building situated on the main drag of an industrial estate on the edge of Carlisle.

Maglona House was a factory of public sector waste and inefficiency in which generally intelligent and mostly well-meaning people were employed in the busy, expensive, and unrelenting bureaucratic service of taxpayer funded value-destruction. The nine months I spent working there convinced me beyond doubt that there are managers working in the NHS who see Ricky Gervais's David Brent as a role model for good management behaviour and who think The Office was a public service highlighting workplace best-practice. The Programme Management Office at Maglona House was headed up by a young manager who still humbly describes himself on LinkedIn as *a gifted leader*. Most people thought he was a monumentally incompetent moron, and they were the polite ones, but accuracy and reality don't always make for appealing social media profiles. He never stopped going on about his MBA and constantly used the phrase, SMART Objectives (specific, measurable, achievable, realistic, and time bound) in every meeting he attended. He recently moved on to bigger and better things within another NHS Trust.

The building housed hundreds of employees and epitomised many of the ills that plague the NHS and public services in general. It was where most of the vague nebulous value-negating taxpayer funded functions specialising in unproductivity, insouciant insensitivity, and regulatory compliance that each NHS Trust is obliged to possess were based; Legal Services, or the dept. of *"it wasn't our fault"*; IT and the Technology Support Desk, the *"no you can't use that software"* team; Governor Support Services, the *"let's arrange a pre-planned and carefully orchestrated visit to one of the local hospitals"* crew; the Patient Advice and Liaison Service, the *"lets nip that complaint in the bud before the regulator hears about it"* team; the Data, Information, and Performance dept., the *"if we reclassify and recode these incidents then they won't show up as being an issue"* brigade; the loathed Information Governance dept., the only group of people openly despised even by their own colleagues; and of course a full troop of project and programme managers, the *"let's obsess about the process and not get too hung up on adding any value"* dept. Most of the employees were situated in a large open plan office flanked by senior managers and a director who watched proceedings closely through generously paid, suspiciously people wary, institutionally paranoid, and it must be said, inept self-serving and rather beady eyes.

The cost of running the Programme Management Office, the PMO as it was more widely known, ran into many, many millions of pounds each year. And in all the years it had been running it had achieved little if anything of any significance. One of its former senior managers, whose title was Deputy Director of Information, nobody I met knew what he did and even after meeting him myself I had no idea, had produced a lovely glossy and expensively produced document in 2013 entitled Enabling Excellence - A Strategy for Digital Health. In fairness to him, he had also ordered a hundred huge digital information display screens at a technology exhibition. These cost around £1k each and were to be situated in the GP Practices across the county. Unfortunately, he hadn't asked the GPs if they wanted them, they didn't and the screens, at least some of them if you catch my drift, were still sat in a cupboard when I left the Trust years after they had been bought. He also sent every GP in the county a copy of his Enabling Excellence Strategy for Digital Health he had so proudly created, well he and a firm of consultants, and a design agency, and a printing house, to be precise. He was then surprised when GPs responded to the landing of his glossy brochure in their in-trays by telling him they would rather the Trust got on with getting the basic qualities of its existing services in order, than sending them strategies full of fluff and waffling bullshit; their words not mine. Before leaving the NHS in Cumbria for another well-paid post elsewhere in the NHS, presumably in the time-honoured public sector tradition of moving on before one's ineptitude is uncovered, his final purchasing decision was to order a large number of Windows Smartphones, you may remember there was such a thing. These were to be issued to all senior staff to replace the more fully functioning and user-friendly smartphones they already had. Surprisingly, he had been challenged on this particular decision and advised to concentrate his efforts on upgrading the Trusts ageing versions of Microsoft Windows which were by this time becoming vulnerable to cyber-attack. Needless to say, he disregarded this advice. Few people used the phones he had purchased, and the Trust then became one of the many NHS Trusts across the UK that was hacked and disabled by computer ransomware known as WannaCry early in 2017. When I left the Trust in March 2017, staff in some services were being issued with basic Nokia phones and at the time of my publishing this book most of the aspirations laid out in the strategy created by the Trusts Programme Management Office have still not been realised.

Anyway, back to the story I was telling of how I had been invited to attend a conference in Edinburgh at which Scotland's digital healthcare strategy was to be launched by the Scottish Minister for Health. It was a grand and well attended occasion. I don't recall the name of the venue I just remember feeling like one of those very obvious and mildly annoying visitors to a city who is glued to the screen of their phone as it guides them to their destination, and then my surprise as I entered the main auditorium and saw how expansive and packed the venue was. I was genuinely looking forward to hearing about Scotland's plans for introducing digital healthcare services to its citizens. As well as reacquainting myself with the folks from the Scottish Centre for Telehealth with whom I had developed good relations, I had long been interested in the use of technology to enable greater access to services in remote and rural areas and I knew that Scotland was years ahead of its southern cousins in the application of technology in healthcare. I think this is in part due to its more consistent cleanly structured centrally managed operating model, and perhaps also simple necessity. Providing easy access to specific healthcare expertise for communities on the Outer Hebrides is a task that positively lends itself to technology. Necessity is the mother of invention. Unlike many of the public sector bodies I have attempted to work with over the years, I had found the Scottish Centre for Telehealth to be genuinely supportive. They were led by a very affable and accessible professor called George Crooks.

My main motivation for travelling to Edinburgh that day was to ask for and obtain something in exchange for nothing. Having been a salesman for some years after leaving school, I was fully aware my negotiating position wasn't attractive, but as we say here in Cumbria, shy babies get nowt and one of the many good things you do learn in the commercial world of sales is that if you don't ask the question, the answer is always no. Part of the proceedings in Edinburgh that day was an announcement about the release of a new secure video meeting service called Attend Anywhere. It was originally developed to support the provision of healthcare services in the Australian Outback where the term remote and rural really means, remote and rural. Attend Anywhere was to be initially deployed by NHS Scotland in a small selection of services that lent themselves more naturally to video consultation. The service would allow patients, GPs, and other health and care professionals in more isolated locations to access clinical expertise and consultations without having to travel lengthy distances, sometimes even by aircraft in the case of the more remote Scottish Isles.

In my increasingly frustrated majesty, I had arbitrarily decided I would ask NHS Scotland and the Scottish Centre for Telehealth if they would give the NHS in Cumbria, free access to their shiny newly purchased online tool. I was determined to leave the NHS on a personally positive note and do something to add value to the county I live in and love. I hadn't asked my bosses permission for this task; they had proved themselves utterly incapable of making decisions. However, I had spoken with some of the more forward-thinking clinical heads and managers from a selection of the NHS services in Cumbria. They were keen to see if using virtual consultations could save them and their patients time and money. Cumbria is England's most rural county, the collective mileage driven by NHS staff working on the patch at that time was more than five million miles each year. The direct costs in terms of expenses and staff time alone were staggering. And the opportunity cost this wasted time and money represented was huge. Using technology in places like Cumbria is an absolute no brainer.

During the lunchtime break I sought out the people I needed to speak with and at the first opportunity I got, I asked for six-months of unrestricted access to the Attend Anywhere videoconferencing system. I candidly and objectively outlined the challenges facing Cumbria's healthcare system and explained we were a long way up shit creek, with no paddle. The NHS in Cumbria needed help and new ways of working if it

229

was going to meet the rising demand for services in a large rural county with an ageing population. I told them the NHS in Cumbria could not afford to pay them even a token amount. The only reward I could offer was the opportunity for shared learning. To their great credit and without hesitation NHS Scotland said yes. There was no fuss, no conditions, pretence, or waffle. Perhaps they enjoyed the schadenfreude of being asked for help by a Sassenach, an irresistibly delicious opportunity to show their bombastic strategy loving implementation failing neighbours how to get things done. Who could blame them for that. But whatever their reasons, they agreed then and there to give the NHS in Cumbria complete access for a full six-month period to all the features of the technology service they had just spent over a year researching, evaluating, and buying. They also offered the support of a project manager to help with any implementation issues. I recall that meeting in Edinburgh as being one of the very few times during my employment in the NHS that I truly felt senior people in the service were cooperating, not playing power games and politics, but behaving collaboratively in the interest of the public, as I had always imagined such people should. If I had asked a neighbouring NHS Trust on the southern side of Hadrian's Wall to give the NHS in Cumbria access to software that they had just spent hundreds of thousands of pounds on, for nothing, they would have laughed me out the building and kicked me up the arse on the way to the carpark. I left the conference elated. There was just enough time and daylight to bag a couple of photos of the Castle and the monuments on Princess Street before catching the train back home.

The next day I took immense pleasure in telling the director in charge of the Programme Management Office what I had arranged with the Scottish Centre for Telehealth on the Trusts behalf. I explained I had already done the groundwork and consulted with the heads of half a dozen relevant services who had expressed a desire to be part of the Attend Anywhere trial. He nearly shat himself. He and his acolytes had been spouting hot air and pissing around with Gannt charts for years, achieving nothing but raised expectation and dashed hope. Here I was within six months of being placed in a holding role created to keep me out of mind and out of mischief prior to my departure, telling him I had just secured access to a comprehensive telehealth system that was ready to be deployed. Middle managers in the NHS are not supposed to do such things, to go to high profile conferences or speak with senior leaders, and they are certainly not supposed to just crack on and make useful things happen. Not without a strategy, a project plan with milestones, permission from the Information Governance dept., an oversight committee containing representation from all the value destroying depts., chaired by a disinterested director who will distance themselves from any failings but will beat their way to the front of the queue to take the credit if the initiative is deemed a success. God forbid that such initiative-taking behaviour and a can-do attitude should ever be tolerated in middle management ranks of the NHS. That would be incredibly embarrassing for all the risk averse panjandrums and jobsworths who have made their careers by attending meetings and ensuring nothing happens.

But yet again I had overestimated the character of my seniors and underestimated their capacity for duplicity. Sheer stupidity and ineptitude can only explain so much. And as the clock ticked towards the end of March and of my employment in the NHS, my attempts to introduce telehealth to service users and patients in the remote and rural communities of Cumbria were subtly and surely sabotaged. The first barrier to be put in my way came from the Head of Information Governance. She told me she wouldn't allow the system to be used by any services before the Trust had conducted its own assessment of the security of the software. Though I refer to it as software it was in truth an online platform hosted in the cloud which needed no installation in the way traditional software does. I explained to the Head of Information Governance that the software had already been deemed fit for purpose in every respect by NHS Scotland and suggested that if the software had been assessed and approved for use across the entirety of Scotland's National Health Service, then she could rest assured that whatever processes she was going to apply to the system wouldn't add any value to the party. NHS Scotland had also offered to share any information we might need in relation to their assessment of the products fitness for purpose. She was unmoved by my logic and kept repeating that if we experienced a data breach due to using the Attend Anywhere software, the Trust could be exposed to a multi-million pound fine from the Information Commissioners Office. When someone in the public sector invokes the name of the ICO, its designed to instil fear, as if the Spanish Inquisition are about to appear in the lens of your Alexa doorbell app. I suggested she ring the ICO and see what they said. Surely, I figured that would be better than guessing what they might or might not do, and who knows, they might ask why the Trust was going to conduct its own severely limited information governance assessment when NHS Scotland had effectively already done it on our behalf. She refused, saying it wasn't normal practice to make direct contact with the ICO, she hadn't done it before, and didn't feel they would welcome a direct approach. She was clutching at straws, and it was all becoming a bit embarrassing, almost obvious to both of us that her remit was to throw spanners in the works. I decided to ring the Information Commissioners Office myself. I found them very pleasant. They went to great lengths to explain that they wished more NHS Trusts would seek prior advice and guidance. The last thing the Information Commissioner wants to be seen doing is stripping money out the healthcare system by fining NHS Trusts for preventable data breaches. It makes them an easy target for the press and as appealing to the public as a cobra at a kid's party. The ICO agreed with my assessment of the situation and duly confirmed their rationale in an email which I then forwarded to the Head of Information Governance. She never replied. Then the Information Technology dept. stepped up to the plate and told the services who wanted to use the Attend Anywhere service that because it used the Google Chrome browser, it fell outside their accepted software policies and represented a security risk. Services were told they were free to use the Attend Anywhere videoconferencing software, but they should be mindful of the potential risks it posed. This seemingly well-intentioned innocuous intervention effectively killed the trial by putting the fear of God into any clinician or manager who had previously wanted to use the service. Nobody in the NHS will use a product or service if they have been told it poses a risk, even if it doesn't. They could read between the lines, and they all knew they would be vilified and hung out to dry should the slightest thing go wrong.

I left the NHS as planned at the end of March 2017. By then three months of the Attend Anywhere videoconferencing trial given to the NHS in Cumbria by NHS Scotland had elapsed and the product was still being assessed for its fitness for use by the panjandrums in the PMO. At the end of June and the end of the six-month trial, the service had not been used once in a patient facing situation and the Trusts access to the online platform was withdrawn by NHS Scotland. The ailing and visibly struggling NHS services of Cumbria had been gifted the chance to trial a technology solution that could have shown them where savings could be made, where precious resources could be freed-up, and how patients could be given easier access to clinical expertise. They had been given an unconditional leg up by another part of the NHS and they had spurned it for the sake of petty politics and personal vendettas. The director and senior managers of the Programme Management Office had never wanted me treading on their turf. They had no intention of allowing me to achieve anything, even if it meant NHS patients in rural Cumbria would suffer as a result. There are many reasons why the NHS is still rooted in the swampy foothills of the digital revolution that has shaped every other aspect of our lives. The availability of suitable technology is not one of them.

PART V:

Why isn't Healthcare Learning from its Mistakes?

Chapter 24: **Predictable avoidable tragedies**

"...when you rush toward something good, you need provisions preparations and precautions. Without them the intentions may be good, but the consequences can be disastrous."

Edmund Burke

Mid Staffordshire NHS Hospitals Trust achieved Foundation Trust status in 2008. On 06th February 2013, the final report into failings at the Mid Staffordshire NHS Hospitals Trust was published. I was working in the NHS when the report appeared into the public domain and details of what had occurred started to surface in the national press. The public inquiry itself had begun almost three years earlier in July 2010, and if its findings were being eagerly anticipated by patient groups, the press, and the wider NHS itself, they were even more eagerly anticipated by government ministers, and MPs from all parties. How tarnished was the nations totem and who was to blame? What emerged was extraordinary.

The picture the final report painted of how a hospital had palpably failed the very people it was supposed to be caring for and how its board had lost touch with its primary purpose, its sacred duty to keep patients safe, was truly shocking. For a period, it dominated the headlines; it was splashed across the front pages of all the main papers, it was everywhere on TV and radio. The web was awash with commentary and opinion. What came to light was a story of how a group of senior and experienced individuals in a public sector organisation had succumbed to a leadership phenomenon commonly referred to as summit fever. This had made them wilfully blind to any information, knowledge, data, views, or adverse insights, which had not supported their chosen direction of travel and their goal.

Summit fever is a mountaineering term used to describe the compulsion of climbers to reach the summit of the mountain, no matter the cost. The term became widely known following the 1996 Mount Everest Disaster in which a group of experienced climbers became fixated on reaching the summit. Despite losing daylight, and in the face of uncertain weather conditions, they insisted on pursuing their objective, and as they descended from the summit, they ran short of oxygen and were caught in a blizzard. Eight people lost their lives. I think what's important to take from the tragedy is the realisation that there was no shortage of experience in that group. Amongst the climbers on Everest that day were some of the most respected able mountaineers of their generation, but the prospect of conquering the worlds' highest mountain had made each climber wilfully blind to the incredible risks they were individually and collectively exposing themselves and each other to.

Directors at Mid Staffs Hospitals had become similarly obsessed with achieving Foundation Trust status. There was a great degree of kudos for the boards and directors of NHS Trusts that acquired Foundation status. The board of directors at Mid Staffs had set about achieving their financial goals by cutting overheads with incredible zeal. In one year, they reduced costs by almost ten percent. That may not sound a lot, but in a public service where staff costs are the largest proportion of overheads, it's like pruning your apple trees with an axe. Within a very short space of time the Trust had shed approx. one hundred and fifty members of staff including significant numbers of nurses. It was already known by the board and its chief executive Martin Yeates that the hospital was under-staffed in comparison with the national average. At this point a less than intelligent partially sighted man on a flying horse can see that reducing the nursing capacity in an already understaffed hospital is not going to end well. But early in 2008, Mid Staffs NHS Hospitals were duly awarded Foundation Trust status and the Chair issued a celebratory statement to all staff saying the Trust would be a genuinely excellent institution for the people it served. The detachment from reality in these words is worrying.

Almost at once, an inevitable and entirely predictable series of events began to unfold as the consequences of the decisions the board had taken came home to roost. Within months of being granted Foundation Trust status, the UK's health and care regulator, at that time an organisation called the healthcare commission, was forced to launch an investigation into the quality of the Trusts services including a review of the high mortality rates, the patient deaths occurring in the hospitals care. Numerous concerns had come to light including data from the annual NHS staff survey which alarmingly showed that despite the board's assurances, only one in four of the hospitals own staff would want their relatives cared for at the hospital they worked in. What the healthcare commission discovered in the course of its investigation was beyond tragic. They found a hospital where the wards were under-staffed, and on which neglected patients were dying avoidable, undignified and sometimes painful and lonely deaths. There were not enough doctors or nurses on the hospital wards and thirsty patients, some lying in soiled sheets, had been forced to drink water from the flower vases next to their beds to stay hydrated.

In the drive to reach their chosen summit the board had become wilfully blind to the reality of what was happening under its nose. And just like the climbers on Everest, there was no shortage of experience amongst them. The Chief Executive had nearly thirty years of NHS experience, the non-executive members of the board included a former deputy fire chief, a justice of the peace, a former head of probation services, two qualified clinicians, two chartered accountants, and a former director of public health. On paper, this was a knowledgeable intelligent group of senior leaders whose track record to this point suggested they had all the expertise and knowledge needed for the task at hand.

The initial report the Healthcare Commission compiled in March 2009 following its investigation contains the following candid and damning observation. *"The board claimed its top priority was the safety of patients. However, even though clinical problems were well known, and the trust declared a financial surplus in 2006/2007, it did not seek to redress the staffing problem it had exacerbated by reducing the number of nurses. The evidence suggests that the top priority for the trust was the achievement of foundation trust status. The failure of the trust to resolve the problems in the accident and emergency dept, or to invest in staff is not consistent with the trust doing its reasonable best to provide a safe and effective service for patients. It lost sight of its responsibilities to deliver acceptable standards of care."*

The actual number of people who died avoidable deaths in the care of the Mid Staffordshire Hospitals NHS Foundation Trust has never been officially agreed but informed estimates range from between four hundred on the low side to more than a thousand. All the brains in the boardroom, a group of people with more than one hundred and fifty years combined senior experience between them, had become so focused on achieving Foundation Trust status, they had lost their connection to one of the most fundamental purposes a hospital serves, the very why of its existence, as a place of safety and security for the sick. They had effectively insulated themselves from any knowledge or information that might counter their chosen perception or prick a hole in the illusion they were holding onto.

In each of the three years leading to the gaining of Foundation Trust status, the board had produced an annual report. Each year it talked about the improvements that had been made. Of patients being at the centre of everything, of critical views and patient feedback being welcomed, and of an NHS Trust with a vision to provide excellent, accessible, and sustainable services. As well as losing touch with their purpose, the board had chosen to forget the most basic principles of running a people-based service business, that you cannot reduce the number of people who have the skills required without affecting the capacity and quality of what you provide. Blindly reducing the nursing capacity in a hospital is like reducing the size of your fuel tank and wondering why you can't drive as far. I don't think the board was unable to see the links between the decisions they made to cut costs and the obviously predictable and tragic consequences, it seems to me they were just so focused on achieving Foundation Trust status that I don't think they even considered it. The 2007-2008 annual trust report for the Mid Staffs Hospitals Trust shows that the most attended meeting by all the directors was the finance committee meeting. Patient centric is as patient centric does. It seems the management of money was at the forefront of the board's mind, not its patients.

Shrewsbury and Telford Hospitals:

On 30th March 2022, the final report into the tragedy of avoidable deaths in maternity services that occurred at Shrewsbury and Telford NHS Hospitals in the period between 2000 and 2019 was published. The report contains the following observations under the heading, failures in governance and leadership. *Throughout the various stages of care the review team has identified a failure to follow national clinical guidelines whether it be for the monitoring of fetal heart rate, maternal blood pressure, management of gestational diabetes or resuscitation. This, combined with delays in escalation and failure to work collaboratively across disciplines, resulted in the many poor outcomes experienced by mothers or their babies, such as sepsis, hypoxic ischaemic encephalopathy and unfortunately death.*

The report goes on to say, *some of the causes of the delays were due to the culture amongst the Trust's workforce. The review team has seen evidence within the cases reviewed that there was a lack of action from senior clinicians following escalation. The review team has also heard directly from staff that there was a culture of "them and us" between the midwifery and obstetric staff, which engendered fear amongst midwives to escalate concerns to consultants. This demonstrates a lack of psychological safety in the workplace and limited the ability of the service to make positive changes.*

The damning report and the inquiry that preceded its publication, led by Donna Ockendon, contained input from members of staff who were discouraged from raising concerns. One of the many illuminating and disconcerting comments reads as follows; *I was told that everything was okay, that I shouldn't be raising concerns, and you know, that I didn't understand the system and that everything was fine, and you know, again just not to raise concerns. I was in tears because I was basically a rotten person and I shouldn't be upsetting the apple cart and, you know, it was irresponsible to raise these concerns. Afterwards I was completely shocked, I actually couldn't face going in for a few days.*

The report also observed that the leadership team up to board level had been in a constant state of churn and change for many years. That it had failed to foster a positive environment to support and encourage service improvement at all levels. And the board did not have oversight or a full understanding of issues and concerns within the maternity service. The report into the tragic maternity related deaths that had been unfolding for over a decade at Shrewsbury and Telford NHS Trust Hospitals was just another in a long line of shocking and necessary exposes of NHS services that only arose following patient and victim pressure.

But for many Donna Ockendon's report fails to acknowledge the systemwide problems the prevailing leadership and management style of the NHS creates. The annual report of the Shrewsbury and Telford Hospitals in 2015/16 was called Putting Patients First, it was the fifth annual report from the Trust to use that title. The foreword of the report was written by a then newly appointed chief executive Simon Wright in which he described in glowing terms how he had been walking the hospital sites, meeting the staff, attending department meetings, and hearing great stories about all the high-quality safe healthcare the Trust was providing. Simon was, in my view, an accident waiting to happen. By the time he had secured the role at Shrewsbury and Telford Hospitals, the newly appointed chief executive of the Trust had spent 20yrs in the senior management circles of the NHS. He had one previous employer, a large corporation, and no clinical experience. He was a product of NHS management culture. He had learned to survive, thrive, and climb the ladder. These are observations not criticisms. The truth remains that you do not progress in public services by challenging the hierarchy. His post at SATH NHS Trust was the fourth NHS location he had worked in. This is not untypical for senior figures in health and care services. But many who have worked all their lives in one location in a health and care service would argue, with some credibility, that if context is important, then a lack of knowledge of the organisation and its operating area, coupled with the absence of clinical experience might not be the best basis for anyone taking charge of a large hospital trust that provided services from multiple sites across a diverse rural area, and employed over six thousand staff. Our scene is starting to be set.

We can't know the exact questions the newly appointed chief executive was asking the staff he met at the various sites he said he visited. But we can guess if he had learned how to climb the NHS career ladder that he would not be risking the wrath of his new Chairperson by asking staff where things were going wrong and what could be improved. He was more likely looking to ingratiate himself into the fold, cementing their choice of appointment amongst his peers. I would suggest the reason Simon said what he did in the annual report is that he had read the room. The trust had been telling itself it was putting patients first for years and he wasn't going to come in and rock the boat. The staff he met who shared good news had told him what they felt he wanted to hear, and the board had neither capacity nor inclination to turn over stones under which they might find anything untoward. Incuriosity is a feature of most NHS boards.

After five years of publishing annual reports that told themselves they were putting patients first, the mantra would have become an unquestioned and accepted truth in the boardroom of the Trust. And it would almost undoubtedly have also become a mantra that staff had become familiar with. You can almost visualize the conversations in the teams across the Trust can't you, *"When you meet the new chief executive, give them an example of where we put the patient first, that's what they want to hear, they love it when you tell them that stuff, and telling them what they want to hear will also keep them off our backs"*. I've been in those conversations and worked in healthcare settings where people were tasked with finding good news stories for the board and the press. I imagine you may have as well. And which member of staff wants to be the one to tell the newly appointed chief executive that they even have a low-level concern, never mind tell them things are going to hell on a handcart in maternity services? Would you be the person that spoke up on your first meeting with the new CE and said you were concerned about maternity services, or any service for that matter?

As well as seeking confirmation bias that reinforced their perceptions, another significant factor that enabled what happened at SATH lies firmly with the board and how it functioned. At the September 2016 meeting of the Trust board, the board papers, agenda, and associated items amounted to just over fifteen hundred pages. If we ask our friend Google how long it takes to read this many pages, Google will tell you it takes the average person over forty hours. The September board meeting was scheduled to start at 1pm and finish by 6pm and there were ten people present at the meeting. This means members of the board had to be aware of, digest, understand, discuss, and then deliberate meaningfully on forty hours of reading matter in the space of five hours. This form of information overload is a recipe for wilful blindness. Interestingly, none of the twenty-five agenda items had the word patient in their title. The closest an agenda item came to talking about patients was the quarterly report from the hospital's own patient advice and liaison service, PALS, which crept onto the packed meeting agenda as item twenty-one. Patients were not important enough to be a monthly item. Patient centric is as patient centric does.

Amongst the fifteen hundred pages of board papers are references to the Trust preparing to apply for Foundation Trust status. It's not hard to guess which agenda items would command the focus of the board at the expense of other matters. At this point I think it would only be right to observe that the wilfully blind culture at SATH NHS Trust has strong echoes of Mid Staffs where the boards focus on achieving Foundation Trust status at the expense of everything else lay at the heart of the tragedy that emerged. Fifteen hundred pages of board papers, twenty-five agenda items, how can anyone, no matter how experienced, intelligent, or qualified, have had the time and headspace to absorb and interpret this much material and then provide meaningful input to the meeting in relation to all the items listed on the agenda.

People in such situations look to their peers for behavioural cues. When we are literally drowning in information, we look to others in authority or that we perceive as being more knowledgeable or informed than us, and we go in the direction we see the wind blowing. We look to see if the chief executive and the Chair think everything is hunky-dory, and we nod and agree. This is after all a hierarchy, and they are the folks currently sitting at the top of it. It is a form of bystander effect, or bystander apathy in which the members of the board had neither the time, capacity, capability, nor inclination to ask any searching questions about the situation that was clearly unravelling around them. Whether by accident or design, the over-crowded structure of the meeting had effectively reduced a group of otherwise intelligent people to the role of busy fools. Unfortunately, the agenda for that meeting within the SATH Hospital NHS Trust was not untypical. Many public services and health and care organisations issue board papers and meeting agendas at short notice that comprise of hundreds and hundreds of pages. The desire for reams of information is a recipe for disaster that doesn't serve the system, its employees, or its service users well. In her report published on 30th March 2022 into maternity services at SATH NHS Trust, Donna Ockenden suggested the Trust's board wasn't functioning. I would suggest it had become so wilfully blind, and overloaded with competing priorities, that it simply couldn't function.

Public relations and an organisation in denial:

In February 2016, just as the issues leading to the many avoidable and utterly tragic baby deaths that were soon to emerge at Shrewsbury and Telford Hospitals NHS Trust were steadily boiling to a head behind the scenes, the Shropshire Star was singing the local hospitals praises under the headline, *Oh baby! UNICEF award for Shropshire Hospitals Trust*. The article contained a quote from a representative of the hospital saying they had decided to join forces with Unicef UK's Baby Friendly Initiative as part of efforts to ensure all women using their maternity services were receiving the best care and advice possible. When I last viewed this story on the Shropshire Star online, the site was carrying an advert encouraging people to dump the NHS and avoid treatment waiting lists by purchasing private medical insurance from as little as £28/month. A struggling press will pander to whoever pays the bills and time poor journalists will print whatever oven-ready stories are sent to their desks by public relations and communications practitioners keen to gain a pat on the back from their chief executive.

The Baby Friendly Initiative was launched in 1992 by UNICEF with support and endorsement from the World Health Organisation, WHO. The initiative was originally set up to address maternity related issues in India and was adopted by the UK in 1994. Its purpose as described on the UNICEF UK website is to transform healthcare for babies, their mothers, and families in the UK as part of a wider global partnership. The awarding of Baby Friendly stage three accreditation is given following a rigorous assessment by the UNICEF team who must establish that recognised best practice standards are in place. The gaining of this apparently difficult to attain and highly prestigious award was featured heavily in the April edition of Putting Patients First, Shrewsbury and Telford Hospitals own internal propaganda bulletin, sorry I mean unbiased objective and insightful internal communications newsletter. The achievement of the award relating to the quality of the Trusts maternity services was unfortunately featured in the same edition as an article on end of life and bereavement care. Can there be a more poignant, tragic, and darkly ironic example of juxtaposing two normally unrelated areas of healthcare that turned out to have more in common at Shrewsbury and Telford Hospitals than anyone could imagine, or than they ever should have.

As well as saying the Trust was achieving an exciting step change in the pace of its transforming care programme, the Trust's Putting Patients First internal newsletter also highlighted the positive steps being taken to identify and reduce instances of sepsis. It's as if the entire communications strategy within Shrewsbury and Telford Hospitals was to take reality and turn it on its head. The gap that subsequently appeared between the rhetoric and the reality would suggest that the seeking of the UNICEF Baby Friendly Initiative was nothing more than self-serving back patting and a deliberate attempt to manufacture a false perception of quality while at the same time ignoring legitimate concerns being raised within the organisation. While researching this book I approached Shrewsbury and Telford Hospitals NHS Trust to obtain a copy of the application they submitted to UNICEF; they told me they had lost all copies of it and all records relating to it. I then approached UNICEF, who I had expected to play with a slightly straighter bat, but they also said they had lost all documentation relating to the application given by Shrewsbury and Telford Hospitals NHS Trust. The WHO have not yet replied to my query of October 2022 asking if they have a copy. Anyway, I can't imagine the parties involved would deliberately mislay information relating to a misleading application because to acknowledge the gaps that existed between the rhetoric and reality might be an incredibly embarrassing experience for all involved, can you? You cynic!

Excellence and tragedy are the next five minutes:

When management guru Tom Peters famously said that excellence is the next five minutes, I think he was making three important points. Firstly, that the achievement of excellence is a journey without a defined end, the path of continuous improvement is infinite. Secondly, he was acknowledging that excellence is the largely predictable aggregated result of lots of small incremental acts. Continue to focus on getting things right in the here and now and excellence will emerge. And thirdly, he was dispelling the notion that excellence is a thing that will suddenly manifest at some point in the future. If we can just get that strategy or that plan right, success will all of a sudden appear like the cavalry coming over the horizon. All we have to do is develop and execute the right initiative, and somehow excellence will be ours.

The best physical performances from the athletes, sports people, and performers we love to watch, the greatest breakthroughs, innovations and advances of our era have all been built on many tiny incremental steps that ultimately led to a point, often the point at which we first became aware of them. The iPod, the iPhone and the incredible success of Apple and the development of smartphones, tablets, and fitness trackers, are not the result of overnight innovations that emerged from an isolated planning process. They arose from the combining of a vast number of technological advances, some of which had been in the making for over fifty years. Anyone who has read one of the many stories of how teams or organisations succeed will know there is seldom if ever a single factor that changes everything. What are often held aloft as the great breakthrough innovations of our age are in reality the result of a gradual accumulation and combining of small incremental breakthroughs. And these in turn have their roots in earlier breakthroughs often made in unrelated fields. The seeds of what happens in an organisation or an industry sector in one, two, or ten-years' time are in the ground now. You can see them if you are prepared to look for them.

How many times have we witnessed the launch of a local or national strategy or plan that promises to take us all to the promised land, only to find ourselves attending the launch of another strategy or plan in a few years' time. Each time we are told that this time it will be different. But excellence is always a moving feast and achieving it is always work in progress. That new patient safety strategy, that vision and values statement directors are formulating, they will change little if anything. The answer doesn't lie in grand strategies, or what we might get around to doing in six months, or a year, it's about what we do in the next immediate period of time available to us and how we deal with what is directly in front of us that needs addressing in the here and now. And how well we do it will dictate our performance in the long run. Only in politics and the public sector is the creation of strategy celebrated over the achieving of results.

If we acknowledge Tom Peters was right, that the provision or production of an excellent service or product is the collective result of many small acts, then the reverse is also true. Tragedy and harm are also the sum total of what we do in the next five minutes. There are very few real curved balls, and patient safety is directly related to the sum total of collective incremental actions and inactions. Tomorrow's tragedies and future adverse incidents are the result of not doing things well in the here and now. Of walking past a standard, we would not want for ourselves, today. They are an accumulation of the small things we let slide, the irregularities, the inappropriate behaviours, the minor incidents of poor practice we tolerate. These set the tone and create the culture in our organisations. Events are therefore largely predictable and are merely points on a continuum that were arrived at because we were on a journey that led us to them. The logical outcome and a natural product of all the things preceding them.

What happened to my sister Alison, my childhood best-friend Johnny, and what has unfolded at Alder Hey Children's Hospital, Brithdir Nursing Home, Bristol Royal Infirmary, Gosport Hospitals, Greater Manchester Mental Health Trust, Mid Staffs, Morecambe Bay, Optima Care Homes, Shrewsbury and Telford Hospitals, Southern Health, The Hesley Group children's facilities in Doncaster, Whorlton Hall, Winterbourne, and what is presently still unfolding at Blackpool, Cumbria Tyne and Wear NHS, Essex Mental Health Services, Nottingham Maternity Services, the Infected Blood Inquiry, and the findings of the Cumberlege review into the use of medicines and medical devices, and what will inevitably be unearthed somewhere else soon, are the result of small incremental issues that were not addressed or challenged. And let's not kid ourselves, though these are the names of the tragedies we are aware of, they are not exceptions. They are merely outliers at the end of a continuum upon which all health and care organisations exist. There but by the grace of the Universe go many.

The good news is that if issues arise incrementally, and their cumulative impact is largely predictable, then they are also avoidable, preventable. Most things can be seen coming if you have the courage to look for, acknowledge and address them. While this is a good thing it is also a challenging thing for some to hear. That each tragedy in our health and care system is the logical outcome of the combining factors that led to it is something that report writers and the heads of inquiries shy away from highlighting.

Chapter 25: Asking the wrong questions

"If men could learn from history, what lessons it might teach us. But passion and party blind our eyes and the light which experience gives us is a lantern on the stern which shines only on the waves behind us."

Samuel Taylor Coleridge

These past few years, I've been invited to speak at the annual patient safety congress in Manchester. The event is a high-profile two-day affair that culminates in a glitzy awards ceremony celebrating those who have managed to introduce positive innovations into practice, despite the best efforts of the NHS. Its stated purpose is to promote and showcase the best patient safety initiatives occurring in the world of healthcare. It is, in reality, a dazzling if unwitting tribute to the inconsistency that plagues the NHS and the lack of direction and leadership that epitomizes and hampers publicly funded health and care provision in the UK. The event is sponsored by a plethora of mainly private sector companies who are interested in building networks to help them gain contracts to supply their various solutions and services to health and care providers. The congress is organised by Wilmington Healthcare, part of Wilmington plc. Wilmington is a globally active publishing, consulting, training, and data analytics company which provides a range of services to the healthcare sector. The company publishes the Health Service Journal, or HSJ as it is widely known in healthcare circles, a weekly print and online publication whose roots date back to the latter part of the nineteenth century.

The congress is a gathering of the great and the good, academics, commentators, and the well-intentioned from across the world of health and care. Drawn together each year to discuss the various safety issues facing the sector and share their shock and pontificate about the most recent significant incident of preventable harm or emerging scandal appearing on the horizon. There tends to be at least one every year so there is sadly always something of consequence to talk about. Naturally, a substantial proportion of the attendees are from NHS Trusts and related bodies. There is also good representation from the private sector, the social care sector and the third sector, particularly hospices, patient groups, and individuals with lived experience like me, who are keen to get involved and make a difference. There are bits of the event that I enjoy, and a lot that drives me nuts.

After taking part in two well received sessions in 2021, I was invited the following year to participate in the opening session of the congress. A prestigious panel discussion in which I would be sat next to various big hitters, esteemed and respected individuals from within the world of patient safety and healthcare regulation. I think they must have gotten me mixed up with someone else, but I bit their hand off and accepted the opportunity to join the opening session before they realised their mistake and changed their minds. I was to share the stage with three other far more well-known figures from the world of health and care. Sir Robert Francis QC, widely recognised as the NHS's troubleshooting equivalent of Sir John Harvey Jones and then the current Chair of Healthwatch England. A look at Sir Roberts bio reveals a man who has clearly forgotten the way back to his own front door. He sits on almost as many committees as there are days in the month. Professor Mary-Dixon Woods, listed as director and professor of healthcare improvement studies at the University of Cambridge, and Ted Baker, not the fashion label entrepreneur, but the former chief inspector of hospitals and head honcho of the Care Quality Commission. We were also joined that morning by the Director of Patient Safety for NHS England, Dr Aidan Fowler. And then there was me.

Ok, in all honesty I wasn't initially invited to be on the panel for the opening discussion of the congress. In truth I'm a relative no-mark in the mildly incestuous world of high-profile health and care gurus and the fact is I blagged my way onto the opening session after seeing its title and looking at the people who were on the panel. The discussion was entitled; *Why aren't we learning from past mistakes? Breaking the cycle of repeat errors to advance the safety agenda.* The irony I thought. Surely one look at the topic and the members of the panel would reveal conclusively why the NHS and the wider healthcare system isn't learning from its mistakes. The panel was essentially a collection of the established wisdom who have all been present for the past few decades as the NHS has been steadily sailing to hell on its handcart on their watch. Einstein was bang on the money when he observed that problems cannot be solved by the same minds that created them. Yet here was another well-meaning panel of experts, from within the system, and they were going to be asked why the

NHS wasn't learning from its mistakes. It was as if someone had said, let's gather a group made up of experts, academics, uncontentious individuals, people who are high up the hierarchical food chain, lost in theory and process on the upper floors of their ivory towers, and out of touch with the day-to-day reality, to discuss how the woes of the NHS can be addressed, because that's worked so well in the past hasn't it! Such discussions amongst overtly polite and ambitious people, who in my experience have never been scarred by the same sword they are trying to sheathe, end up in nothing more than navel gazing, nodding agreement, and ultimately inaction. I thought the panel could benefit from some diversity of thought and experience, so I put myself forward for inclusion, and to their credit, Wilmington agreed to my request.

Before asking the question, why isn't the NHS learning from its mistakes, it's worth pointing out that the NHS is most definitely not the only healthcare service in the world in which serious errors occur with depressingly predictable frequency. Healthcare systems and services by the very nature of their complexity make mistakes, lots of them. According to Nick Black, a professor at the London School of Hygiene and Tropical Medicine, the number of preventable deaths occurring in Britain's health and care services as a proportion of those treated is on a par with most other countries. If you factor in the inherent complexity of health and care services, couple it with human fallibility, the divisive divided hierarchical and reputationally sensitive cultures that prevail in many parts of the health and care sector in all parts of the world, then toss an increasingly and some might say aggressively litigious climate into the mix, and finally add hurting and often angry people whose need for answers in the wake of tragedy is simultaneously stymied by the organisations they want to engage with and stoked by a plethora of ambulance chasing legal services, you will have created the perfect adversarial climate for denial, defensiveness, and cover-up. The health and care sector is the legal professions dream.

Of course, there are numerous areas to explore in relation to why the health and care sector, especially the NHS, is not learning from its mistakes. But the first and most obvious thing to acknowledge is that an entity which exists only as a concept, as the NHS does, cannot possibly be expected to demonstrate that it is learning anything as a coherent unit. Though the question of why the NHS doesn't learn from its mistakes has been the title of many private and public discussion papers, inquiries, reports, and seminars, and the topic has been the subject of countless research thesis, the question is predicated on the assumption that the NHS is or can be looked at as a discrete identifiable and inspectable thing. A single object that can be analyzed and understood. This is fundamentally the wrong question to ask. The answer to the question, why isn't the NHS learning from past mistakes, a question many intelligent well-intentioned people inside and outside the health service ask themselves and each other on a frustratingly regular basis, is that you can't expect an entity that doesn't exist to learn anything. We need to stop talking about the NHS as if it were a joined-up coordinated service capable of harnessing its organizational memory and instilling the learning from disparate incidents into the many disjointed parts of itself. It's like asking why people in a town of ten thousand aren't learning from the mistakes of one. *We* aren't learning because there isn't a *"we"*.

According to researchers at The London School of Hygiene and Tropical Medicine, the number of preventable adult deaths occurring in UK hospitals is thought to be around twelve thousand every year. Due to the absence of reliable data from Primary Care, NHS services provided in the community, and mental health services, this number is thought to be a significant underestimate. In his recently published book, Zero, the former health secretary Jeremy Hunt recalls a conversation he had with the then Chief Executive of NHS England, David Nicholson, in which Nicholson explained to Hunt that the NHS harmed ten percent of its patients. In fairness we can discount the precision of this revelation. Nicholson was viewed by many as a complete dickhead who should never have been given the job as Chief Executive of NHS England after his involvement, or lack of, in the horrific events that occurred at Mid Staffs Hospitals when he was chief executive of the West Midlands strategic health authority. And the nice round figure of ten percent he is said to have quoted sounds worryingly like one of those, *lets pull an easily memorable guesstimate out the air for David when he meets the Minister*. In this book I am guilty of using the terms *avoidable death* and *preventable death* interchangeably so it's probably worth clarifying that what I mean by preventable deaths in health and care are those deaths that can reasonably be attributed to variations in the quality of the care provided. Academics apply a probability of 50% to their calculations, i.e., a death in a healthcare setting is classed as preventable if there is a 50% chance or more of the death being attributable to poor care.

In 2019 the World Health Organisation (WHO) estimated that the number of adverse events due to unsafe care was likely to be one of the top ten leading causes of death and disability in the world. The WHO report goes on to estimate that one in every ten patients is harmed while receiving care in hospital in high income countries and it suggests that nearly half of these are preventable. The WHO shows the three areas most prone to errors relate to diagnosis, prescriptions, and the use of medicines. The report also says that 15% of total hospital activity and expenditure is incurred as a direct result of adverse events, failure demand to give its proper label. The WHO launched the first ever patient safety day on 17th September 2019. I imagine that was a really good day to fall ill or have an accident. In 2023 it will be on Sunday 17th September so if you can possibly plan your illness and hospital admission in advance, and if the nurses, doctors, and ambulance drivers aren't on strike, then you should be safe. I mean, who would want to be a patient on the other 364 unsafe patient days. On balance I think it is a positive step on the part of the WHO to highlight what is an extremely important issue. The critical overarching component that appears to be missing from the WHOs analysis of the issues that lead to better patient safety, are any in-depth acknowledgement or informed understanding of the enormous and very real impact that poor leadership, inadequate management, inconsistent standards, and disjoined technology have in this area.

In the United States, a country that many might look to as a leading light in providing technologically advanced and innovative healthcare services, the numbers of people dying avoidable deaths in healthcare is estimated by a patient safety improvement organisation called the Leapfrog Group to be over one hundred and fifty thousand each year. That is three thousand people each week, one person every three minutes, and three times the number of people thought to die from gun related incidents in the USA. The Leapfrog Group was founded in 2000 by a group of large employers and other purchasers of health and care services in the United States. Their creation and launch coincided with and was fuelled by the release of what many regard as a seminal publication on the quality of healthcare in America. *To Err Is Human - Building a Safer Health System,* was published by the American Institute of Medicine in

2000. It's claim that almost one hundred thousand people were dying preventable deaths each year in America due to medical error and variations in the quality of health services, captured the attention of policy makers, the public, and of course the healthcare industry and healthcare insurers. The essence of the publication is that the intentions of good and able people are undermined by the cultures and processes within the systems they work in. If management schools ever needed a statistic to underline the difference that good leadership can make, then this is surely it. Worryingly, there are many within America's healthcare system who regard these figures as a significant underestimate.

Though the level of preventable deaths that occur in the NHS are comparable with the healthcare services of most other developed countries, before you pop open the champagne and dance around the room singing "*at least we're not as bad as them*", this being the standard response by most of the senior staff in the NHS when they find out they are not actually the worst at something, I would ask whether constantly comparing performance with the worst of the bunch is really the path to improvement? Our healthcare system kills less people than theirs, is hardly an inspiring strapline. Would you buy a car from a manufacturer who used the advertising slogan, the brakes on our cars fail slightly less than others.

But even if we err on the side of optimism and caution and use the informed estimate of twelve thousand avoidable deaths as our baseline, this still represents the equivalent of two Hillsborough Stadium tragedies occurring across the totality of our healthcare service each and every single week. An unseen, often undetected, and largely unacknowledged epidemic, relentlessly, but no less harmfully or tragically stealing the lives and destroying the futures and dreams of people and their families in countless communities, villages, towns, and cities across the UK. It is double the number of recorded suicides that occurred in the UK in 2019 and many times the number of people seriously injured or killed in road traffic accidents each year in the UK. It is thousands upon thousands of families and individuals needlessly suffering in numbed, isolated, confused, and hopeless silence because the service they entrusted to help their nearest and dearest, let them down catastrophically. The real tragedy for some is that they will never even know that the death of the person they loved and cared about was preventable. We trust the NHS and the people working within it, in an almost blind and too often unquestioning fashion.

It's said you should not attribute to malice what can be explained by incompetence, and I believe the truth behind much of what ends up in the press about collusion and cover-up, actually starts its life as nothing more than human error and then simply, often inevitably, and generally uncontrollably, within the hothouse of wilfully blind reputationally over-sensitive organisational hierarchical cultures, escalates; beyond anything anyone involved could have envisaged. Situations morph from being about very human mistakes made by an individual, the sort of horrendous yet regular error of judgement all normal fallible people are capable of making, into collusion and ultimately cover-up. The student nurse who had sex with my sister on hospital premises was not the first to do so and hasn't been the last. But what started out as a woefully poor yet entirely human decision on his part, precipitated a tragedy and led to a cover-up involving dozens of people and multiple organisations. Once the snowball starts rolling down the hill it reaches a point where it becomes too big to stop.

The other reason I believe the question, *why isn't the NHS learning from its mistakes,* to be the wrong question, is that in the climate we are in, it's disingenuous. To stand in the middle of the rubble of neoliberalism and ask, without a hint of irony, how can we make the NHS as welcoming, safe, effective and efficient and large as it needs to be to meet the needs of all those who now need its help safely and effectively, is an impossible ask. It's a pipe dream to visualize a brilliant health and care system standing proudly in the ruins of an increasingly dysfunctional society that creates so many of the physical and mental health challenges facing us. The NHS in its current state simply doesn't have the capacity, capability, or means to do anything other than firefight. The NHS can't learn and become safer in the present climate.

Chapter 26: Why don't more people simply speak up?

"All we have is a voice and the time it takes to learn how to use it."

Unknown

Some years ago, Debbie and I had the opportunity to visit Olduvai Gorge in Tanzania. Sometimes referred to as the cradle of civilization because of the incredible evolutionarily significant discoveries made there. Archaeologists and anthropologists exploring the gorge have suggested the presence of hominid fossils and stone axes it reveals are evidence of our ancestors living together and suggests the abilities we began to acquire there, to work as a unit and collaborate was *the* defining factor that differentiated us and has driven our evolution as a species ever since. Collaborating became the norm when we began to develop tools and began hunting in groups, a practice that was not only far less risky, but hugely more successful. In this world of groups, being ostracized was to be sentenced to a marginal existence at best and death by predation or starvation at worst. The existence of the group became so important to our survival that we became hardwired to place our security and safety over any desire we may have felt to challenge, to stand out, and risk exclusion.

The need to fit in remains such a strong force that it drives a great deal of our behaviour in all areas of our lives. For many of us in the modern world this force it is at its peak in the workplace, where success, status, and our financial survival can depend on maintaining relationships in the organisations we work in. Fitting in is often a subconscious act and in its most basic form is a highly effective psychological survival mechanism, one that protects our minds and helps us maintain a sense of self, and in some cases can protect us physically from harm. The Los Angeles Police Department suggest that the main reason young people join gangs is to establish an identity for themselves and achieve the acceptance and in turn protection of their peers. Gang members often see gang membership as an extension of, and in some cases a substitute for family. Our need to belong is incredibly strong.

Over the last few years, I've run seminars, developed an accredited online course in speaking up safely, and spoken with people working in the healthcare sector and the NHS at numerous virtual and in-person events, often unpaid. The thrust of my approach is that meaningful lasting improvement begins with understanding which starts at the individual level. I try to educate people about wilful blindness and help them understand its role in creating compliance, which can become unhealthy, in individuals, teams, and organisations. I explain that dropping our bananas, often bystanding passively while others have theirs stolen, perhaps on occasion encouraging and aiding such acts, and even sometimes stealing them for ourselves, is all perfectly normal human behaviour. We are the descendants of the hominids of Olduvai Gorge. Understanding what drives our behaviour and revealing the underlying causes that get in the way of people speaking up safely is a useful first step in starting to address the issue and create the conditions in which speaking up becomes a safe, normal, even welcome act. I explain to people that choosing not to speak up or in many cases even acknowledge an issue, doesn't make them inherently bad.

I can be mouthier than anyone about what I sometimes interpret as the spineless and cowardly choices to condone and conceal wrongdoing that senior employees in our health and care services frequently make. I have experienced more than my fair share of rage, and upset, and there have been times where I haven't been able to see beyond the red mist, but though I will always view anger as a useful emotion, a motivating sometimes tireless and exhausting companion, and a powerful catalyst for change, anger is not a place from which informed insight and improvement generally come.

When I first found out that other people had known what was happening to my sister Alison in the mental health hospital and had not acted decisively to stop it, I was incandescent, filled with fury. I was boiling over with a rage I couldn't control. I couldn't believe what I was hearing and what had been allowed to go on. I thought how could anyone with a shred of decency in their body, stand by and do nothing in such a situation? But as the years have passed and I have found myself in different work settings, including standing in the shoes of former colleagues in the National Health Service, I started to see and recognise first-hand the conditions that cause wilful blindness and ethical fading, and that ultimately lead to these sub-optimal seemingly inhumane but entirely natural coping behaviours.

As rationalising beings with a strong need to belong, who straddle many social settings, we have evolved to become experts in self-deception. We are the unconsciously selective guardians of our own preferred self-image. We view ourselves as more honest, more trustworthy, morally upright, skilled, courageous, or more able than the majority of other people. But the uncomfortable truth I remind myself of, is that I don't know what I would have done if I had been in their situation and had lived their lives up to that point. There could be so many reasons why nothing was said to the regulators or the police at the time by any of the people who knew what was going on. The culture of an organisation, particularly a closed culture like that of a mental health institution can be an immensely powerful but invisible silencing force. Was everyone assuming someone else would act? Was whistleblowing frowned-on and whistleblowers despised? Or maybe saying nothing was seen as a neutral act and not a choice to be silent. Or perhaps the established culture was simply one in which inappropriate and unlawful practices were tolerated.

I don't believe the mental health hospital my sister Alison was groomed and abused in was full of inherently bad people. Yes, some did display terrible judgement. And there were those who looked the other way and denied they knew anything. But we also know from the historical reports we have located that there were some who expressed concern. One female nurse stands out in particular; she observed what was happening with Alison and outlined her concerns in writing to the hospitals management. Every organisation, regardless of the quality of its people, has the ability to both help and harm. All the publicly funded organisations I have dealt with over many years, the NHS, Police, Crown Prosecution Service, Local Authorities, Coroners, and various regulatory bodies, have shown me there are no exceptions. The overwhelming majority of people working in these organisations are just ordinary people, doing what they are told to do, in the course of doing their jobs do. Jobs they depend on for income and status. It's easy to be critical of people who make mistakes and don't admit them and even more critical of those who are aware and whose silence condones them, and you will often hear people say that someone or something is either part of the problem or part of the solution, but I think in a complex world that's wildly over simplistic. The fact is that we all have the capacity to be simultaneously both part of the problem and the solution. We are all engaged in a constant interplay in which each of us, at any one time, are both actor and director in the same play. It's the degree to which we are aware of our roles that I think is important. I believe we need to acknowledge our own blind spots and biases before we are even able to recognise and importantly understand what goes on around us. Evolution has equipped us with traits, tools, and techniques that shape our behaviours, actions, responses, and thoughts, of which we are often unaware we are deploying or even possess. These include what could be called a necessary degree of wilful blindness, which enables the preservation of our desired self-image and facilitates our mental wellbeing. The duty I think we have to ourselves and each other is to develop our understanding and awareness of the eternal conundrum we are all to some degree embroiled in and retain our compassion toward one another. I'm not for a second suggesting that compassion equates to unchallenging acceptance and tolerance of the unacceptable and intolerable. People in publicly funded posts should be accountable and where appropriate held responsible for their choices and actions. But having a lens through which to see and interpret your own actions and those of the people around you and understand why people do the things they do and why others let them, is an important part of answering the question of why people don't speak up when they see something untoward and at times obviously harmful occurring in healthcare settings.

Though I would argue evolution and the learned behaviours it has given us are the primary reason people in health and care services choose not to speak up or at times even acknowledge what is going on around them, fear and futility remain the most commonly cited. The combination of fear that there will be repercussions coupled with a sense of futility that nothing will change anyway, creates a sort of learned helplessness in which the logical decision is to say nothing. Why risk the possibility of career terminal blowback if you don't think anything good will come from putting your head above the parapet. It's not the inability to speak that prevents people speaking up, or the absence of mechanisms by which they can do so. It's a host of more complex factors that have created conditions in which they often don't feel able to. How safe people feel about escalating issues and speaking up and how they choose to do it reflects the organisation they work in and their understanding of its culture. In my own case, the sense of safety I felt when I raised my concerns in the NHS did not reflect the reality of my situation. The assurance I held onto that I would ultimately be vindicated and respected by my peers was an illusion made possible in part by my own wilful blindness and selective perceptions of the events unfolding around me. I made assumptions about the culture of the organisation I was working in and failed to acknowledge the real drivers of behaviour. I made myself vulnerable without even knowing I had.

People who cause harm with intent, the deluded and the disturbed who commit deliberate acts of atrocity such as Lucy Letby, Harold Shipman, and Beverley Allitt are thankfully few and far between, but incredibly poor systems are everywhere. I can tell you from experience that when you are in a work situation, surrounded by people who are sometimes inadvertently unconsciously reinforcing each other's behaviours and opinions, it can be incredibly difficult to preserve emotional distance and remain impartial and objective. Group think kicks in, and the path of least resistance is always the one that has been trodden in front for you. Good capable people can find themselves trapped in toxic organisational cultures that force them to turn a blind eye to some really lousy things. Often subconsciously as a coping mechanism, and with no understanding of the potentially harmful impact being caused. In their efforts to manage their reputations, health and care organisations often discourage employees from talking openly and candidly about what they can see and know is not working well. Truth-Tellers may be labelled as troublemakers and whistleblowers ostracised. Many a career has been sacrificed on the altar of public relations and reputation management.

The underlying culture of fear that still prevails in many NHS and health and care settings, rewards those who want a friction free existence. Who don't rock the boat, raise problems to their colleagues or are perceived as risking damage to the organisation's reputation. The vast majority of the current cadre of NHS directors didn't become directors by demonstrating courage, stepping-up to the plate, speaking up, standing out, and challenging the hierarchy. That's not how you get on in the NHS. Most became directors by demonstrating unquestioning compliance to the hierarchy. Crucially, they were also seen by their colleagues and peers to rise through the ranks by behaving in this way, and that's how the cultures of blame, defensiveness, and wilful blindness persist and why more people don't speak up. Culture change in public services should be a priority for governments globally. It will also be one of the thorniest challenges to address.

Chapter 27: **The incurious culture at the Countess**

"We're just two lost souls, swimming in a fish bowl, year after year. Running over the same old ground, what have we found, the same old fears."

Pink Floyd, Wish You Were Here

The proverb *Fish discover water last*, is thought to be of African origin. Picture the scene. Two young fish are swimming side-by-side in clear warm tropical waters chatting, as they are prone to do. An older fish coming in the opposite direction looks over at them and asks, *How's the water today folks?*. The young fish respectfully acknowledge their peer and after it has passed, one looks curiously at the other and says, *What the hell is water?* When you have been immersed in something for a long time or have never known what any other environment might feel or look like, you become dulled to the possibility of other realities. Many who have spent their working lives and built careers in the NHS and whose entire existence is inextricably linked with their roles have become dulled to the possibilities and realities of the worlds that exist beyond planet NHS and the norms and expectancies they contain. They have swum in the waters of the same culture for so long that they tolerate and excuse actions, behaviours, and decisions that would not be deemed appropriate or in some cases even legal in any other setting. The culture has not made them bad people, whatever that phrase may mean, they have simply become wilfully often necessarily blind in the unconscious effort most humans make to fit in. A great deal of what occurs in some healthcare settings would not be tolerated in the middle of a city on a busy Saturday evening.

Late one night some years ago Debbie and I were woken by aggressive shouting, screaming, and loud angry banging sounds. We live on a terrace of four former railway houses and the entire row felt like it was shaking. My neighbour two doors down, the polite term for him is a bit of a geezer, was being violently attacked in his home. Two assailants had sledgehammered their way through the back door and were assaulting him and his wife. He was thrown onto the roof of an outside shed through a closed window before rolling onto the ground and limping off. Seeing what was happening I did what I think most people that I know would do. I picked up the phone and rang the police. The assailants left as quickly as they had arrived. As events unfolded over the coming weeks and suspects were identified and apprehended, I was asked to attend the upcoming court case as a witness. Something I readily agreed to. At no point during the course of events did I doubt that calling the police had been the right thing to do. I didn't wait two years before sending them an anonymous letter in which I shared my concerns and pointed out my suspicions. I didn't ask for permission from anyone to report what I suspected was happening. I felt lives were in danger and I acted.

But the action I took isn't the result of innate character traits. It was almost a reflex, a reflection of the norms I accept based on my upbringing and experiences. Had I been living in a rundown inner-city neighbourhood where crime was rife and violence was the norm, I would more than likely have done what the people I identified with in that setting might have done, bolted the doors and avoided looking outside. My actions were driven by what I have become accustomed to perceiving as normal. Two years ago, after a visit to a small business, I reported my concerns to the police that they were employing illegal cheap and possibly even slave labour. I wasn't sure, but that's not the point. The very thought of vulnerable people being exploited on my doorstep was enough to make me act. As it happens I was right, and they were convicted. It turned out I hadn't been the only one to share my concerns.

Dr Ravi Jayaram is a Consultant Paediatrician at the Countess of Chester Hospital NHS Foundation Trust. A place now wedded gruesomely and eternally to Nurse Lucy Letby and the new lives she so cruelly and senselessly ended and the newborns she harmed, some of whom were left with permanent brain damage. As details of the Letby case have emerged Dr Ravi and his colleague Dr Stephen Brearey have been widely hailed as the whistleblowers who helped put an end to the acts beyond description Letby was committing. Hurray for them I hear you say, and in some respects I echo your praise. The *but* you can I am sure by now feel coming, is that they both waited for an inordinately and inappropriately long time before finally sharing their suspicions and insights. Cheshire police reportedly first received notification something might be wrong in Spring 2017, almost two years after Letby is believed to have commenced her murderous spree. At Letby's trial concluded in August 2023, she was found guilty of murdering seven babies and attempting to kill a further six between June 2015 and June 2016. Cheshire police fear more will come to light as they look further into events.

Dr Brearey has subsequently, and I think in some respects courageously, acknowledged he should have gone to the police sooner with his suspicions. I applaud his candour. Dr Jayaram appears to be maintaining a position of blaming the hospital management for not being his conscience and going to the police on his behalf. In an interview he gave to ITV he said that when he and his colleague Dr Brearey finally met with the police in April 2017, it became clear within minutes to the officers there was something to be investigated. In short, Dr Jayaram is making the point that it was not difficult for him as an expert in his field to explain and communicate his concerns in a way that could be easily understood in a few hundred seconds. In doing so he is acknowledging that his suspicions could have been explained simply and quickly at an earlier point in time. Which again begs the question, why did he and his colleagues wait for permission to talk to the police if the grave suspicions they harbored were so easy to verbalize? I remain unsure as to whether this is something anyone should be proud of.

Though I understand the culturally toxic goldfish bowl Dr Jayaram was swimming in which distorted his view of what the right thing to do at the time was, I find his insistence on blaming others for what I would unambiguously label as his lack of action difficult to reconcile with my notions of responsibility and personal accountability. He and his colleagues should have taken their incredibly serious concerns to the police at the earliest opportunity. Dr Jayaram justifies the lack of action he and his peers took saying that as clinicians they put their faith in the system and in senior management. The truth I think is they had all become so culturally acclimatized they lost sight of the behaviours and expectations that prevailed in the wider society outside the organisation. A society which they were still very much a part of but from whose norms they appear to have become detached.

A group of highly intelligent skilled knowledgeable clinicians had become a shoal of fish swimming together in a shared culture of accepted norms and practices in which it became easy to reinforce each other's choices and behaviours. Intellect is no defence against culture. They were so immersed in the norms of the culture they existed in, that at points in time where they suspected defenceless newborn babies were being deliberately killed and harmed in their place of work, they appear not to have even thought to pick up the phone or go in person and talk to the police. Surely it is only on planet NHS that it could it ever be seen as satisfactory for people who suspect such heinous wrongdoing is occurring to think it is enough to merely share their concerns with management, then sit on their hands thinking they had done all they could. If there is a better case-study in the phenomenon and consequences of learned helplessness, I am yet to be made aware of it.

I recently met with a director from a large company that provides health services and operates care homes across the UK. We got talking about an incident that occurred in one of their locations where a resident had accused a male member of staff of sexually assaulting her. The manager at the care home had acted swiftly and rung the police before even reporting the alleged incident to their own regional manager. Apparently that's the standard procedure they use. The care home manager didn't need the consent of someone up the chain of hierarchy to permit them to do the right thing or to do it on their behalf. A serious offence had been reported and the law became involved at the earliest opportunity. The employee in question was immediately suspended on full pay pending the results of the police investigation. The accusations proved false, but the company had taken the individual out of the equation until the facts had been established in law. The gravity of the alleged offences had been acknowledged, an appropriately serious response was initiated, and caution and prevention had then prevailed. The safety of the patients in their care had triumphed over hierarchy and the misplaced concerns about reputation management that seem to dominate the minds of so many NHS directors and aspiring senior managers. Durable organisational reputations are not built by ignoring issues, they are built and reinforced by acknowledging and dealing with them.

Contrast the actions of the care home manager with the lack of response and action at the Countess of Chester NHS Hospital. The Senior Nurse Karen Rees reportedly ignored calls for Nurse Letby to be taken off the neonatal ward because she said there was not enough evidence to support the accusations being made. We may never know the exact details of the conversations that occurred between Nurse Rees and Dr Stephen Brearey, the consultant who is said to have rung her and raised his concerns. But I think the correct and organizationally appropriate response to the coherent raising of such serious matters from an experienced clinician would have been to act immediately and then seek to establish the facts. After all, the concerns Dr Brearey was raising related to the safety of babies. The data revealed a visible pattern of death and harms, and Nurse Letby was the common denominator. Dr Brearey was not a disgruntled fellow employee trying to get someone he didn't like sacked for stealing post it notes from the stationery cupboard or stealing his milk from the staff fridge.

In a recent interview with the press, Dr John Gibbs another Senior Paediatric Consultant working at the Countess of Chester Hospital at the time, reportedly said he also *tried* to blow the whistle on Lucy Letby. Dr Gibbs was one of seven consultant paediatricians summoned to a meeting with the then Chief Executive Tony Chambers. At the meeting, they were told Letby had done nothing wrong and that to draw a line under the matter they should write a collective apology to her for any upset and stress they had caused. Worryingly, Gibbs, Jayaram, Brearley and their colleagues all agreed to write this letter of apology. They said they had felt intimidated by Tony Chambers into writing it as they were told there would be consequences for failing to do so. Quite what was going on in their heads I have no idea, and I'm still unsure what *trying to blow the whistle* is versus actually blowing the whistle? For seven senior clinical experts in their field to be whipped into moral submission by a former nurse turned bureaucrat who had not a fraction of their combined years of medical experience or expertise, speaks volumes about the absence of courage as well as the prevailing culture.

By this stage Letby had been moved from the neonatal ward to an office-based role in the hospital's patient safety and risk department. Yes, real life really is so much more outlandish than fiction. This tactic of moving people out of patient-facing roles when serious concerns about them have surfaced has been employed in the NHS for many decades. Following concerns raised by staff about the behaviour of the student nurse who groomed and abused my sister Alison, who knows what else he got up to, he was given an administrative role in the patient records department of the same hospital. He was reportedly still in that post when Alison's medical records mysteriously vanished during the first investigation into her death. A coincidence I'm sure! Again, only on planet

NHS would it be seen as appropriate to deal with grave concerns about people committing serious crimes on hospital premises, by giving the suspected perpetrators a cushy office job with access to sensitive patient records. I've said it before, but it feels a lot like choosing to punish the crimes of the Yorkshire Ripper by taking his driving licence off him. I can see it now, Chief Constable Tony Chambers addressing his fellow senior police officers after finally apprehending Peter Sutcliffe. *Aye, that'll teach him. He'll not be able to rape and murder anyone without access to a vehicle. Anyway, as you all know we've got an inspection to prepare for so let's put a line under this business and all get on with our work.*

The hapless impotent, insular, cowed, and incurious culture at the Countess of Chester Hospital, a culture not untypical of NHS Trusts and public service organisations in general, enabled the ignoring and precluding of possibilities before they had even emerged. In 1988 a nurse called Joan had written to managers at the hospital where my sister was being treated, expressing concerns about the behaviour of a 35-year-old trainee nurse called Robert Scott-Buccleuch, who she felt was abusing his position to take advantage of Alison. Joan's letter was, surprise, surprise, ignored. Though I feel some gratitude that someone at least noticed what was happening and tried to intervene, and I also understand the cultural forces swirling around her at the time and shaping her actions, I will always remain vexed that Joan didn't see a need to call the police. When laws to protect the vulnerable are being openly disregarded and patients may be suffering harm, abuse and being placed in danger, is it really enough for anyone to write memos to management and appease their consciences by saying, I did my bit?

The horrors that unfolded at the Countess of Chester Hospital and the many tragedies and incidents of patient harm and neglect that have occurred in numerous NHS Trusts over the years are stories from which no heroes emerge. There are only victims. And it must be said, ingloriously incurious wilfully blind leaders who unwittingly enable and create the conditions in which these events happen. The directors and managers at the Countess of Chester NHS Hospital, who ignored the concerns consultants who worked in the neonatal unit were sharing with them, most certainly have many questions to answer. Cheshire police have now launched a corporate manslaughter inquiry to establish if senior staff from the Countess of Chester Hospital are culpable. And as harsh as it may seem, I also think the clinicians who relied on managers to do the right thing in the absence of applying their own initiative and exercising the courage of their convictions, also have questions to answer. I'm not suggesting Dr Ravi and his colleagues are in any way accountable for Lucy Letby's actions. But they and the rest of the NHS urgently need to recognise the serious and harmful impact the insular and unhealthily compliant cultures they are part of are having. Such cultures, cultures present in large parts of our health and care system, are the greatest risk to patient safety there is.

Now for a moment if you will, dwell on the following unedifying thought. If the culture of an organisation had become so opaquely unhealthy that its leaders, at least in name, felt it appropriate to ignore the concerns of experienced professionals about the safety of the most vulnerable people in their care. And if that same culture had so permeated the entire organisation that it neutered the internal compasses of its brightest most skilled employees, then what other poor practices, questionable behaviours, and patient safety incidents that could be viewed as less significant were already occurring on the wards and in the offices of the Countess of Chester NHS Hospital Foundation Trust. Thriving under the radar in a climate of abjectly disempowered wilful blindness.

Drowning in the shallows of the minutiae:

Just as the board of directors at Shrewsbury and Telford Hospitals were wilfully blind to the preventable deaths and patient harms occurring on their watch and their attentions were focused on less significant matters, so were the board of directors at the Countess of Chester Hospital NHS Foundation Trust. Interestingly, the records of the board meetings at the Countess of Chester relating to 2015 were only recently put back onto the Trusts' website after being mysteriously removed some months ago. Their absence from the website went unnoticed until someone spotted the links to them weren't working and sent a Freedom of Information request seeking access. Yes, that would be me.

A quick scan through the Countess of Chester board papers from the second half of 2015 and the entirety of 2016 reveals its leaders were suffering from all the usual behavioural biases and forms of wilful blindness present in many large institutions. The limited time and frequency of their meetings, they only met six times each year, and packed meeting agendas, ensured there was no room to be curious, only time to focus on the familiar. This kept them insulated from the horrific reality of what was unfolding on their watch. The then chief executive at the Countess Tony Chambers, had been appointed by the chair Duncan Nichol in 2013. Their terms of tenure ran almost concurrently. In my opinion the board papers show a chief executive and his Chair who worked closely together to present a united front, perhaps too closely to remain objective. I think they were also highly practiced in the art of managing and controlling a board. It is yet another regrettable inconsistency of the NHS that each Trust board of directors has its own ideas about what the role of its chairperson is. And every chair has their own perceptions of the scope of their role. Just a few years ago, Leeds and York Partnership NHS Foundation Trust created a nine-page memorandum of understanding to establish how their chief executive and chairperson should work together. Who says the NHS is spending too much on admin and bureaucracy? The word culture is mentioned once. There is no mention in the memorandum of patients or safety.

At each of the board meetings held at the Countess of Chester, attendees would be welcomed by the Chair Sir Duncan Nichol. A product of the NHS graduate trainee scheme Sir Duncan is a former Chief Executive of the NHS. He has over fifty years of experience working in Britain's most beloved institution. Or possibly one year's experience repeated fifty times, you can be the judge. After the introductory pleasantries, various apologies for non-attendance would be received and acknowledged, and the mind-numbing process of agreeing the minutes of the previous meeting would take its exciting course. After this the board would graciously receive a patient story from a service user or carer. How magnanimous of them I hear you say. These uncontentious stories, the patients they could really learn from were presumably only talking to them through solicitors, were collected and edited by the Trusts' in-house Patient Advice and Liaison Service. PALS as it is more widely known is regarded by many as the in-house department tasked with nipping patient complaints in the bud before they get out of hand. Once received the patient story would generate some shallow discussion and often a large helping of self-congratulatory smugness, before the board then thanked the patient or carer for sharing such a powerful story before moving on to the next agenda item. As with all such senior meetings in the public sector, the proceedings are littered with a great deal of talk about all the improvements the board planned to make.

Ironically, the Countess board meeting minutes contain a plethora of references to valuing the kind of organisational culture in which speaking up is encouraged and welcomed, which clearly went well, didn't it? And there are endless mentions of the good work being done across all parts of the Trust. Of course, it's useful for any organisation to know what it's doing well, but in healthcare it's more vital to look for where you need to improve.

At the Countess of Chester board meetings, the attentions of the Trust directors, its chief executive Tony Chambers and medical director Ian Harvey, appear to have been focused on a series of dashboards presented under the heading of board assurance metrics. Harvey is alleged to have told the consultant paediatricians who tried to share their concerns about Letby with him, to cease emailing him about the matter. He retired a month after Lucy Letby was arrested and promptly moved to the South of France. With a large pension pot donated to him by UK taxpayers. As well as reams of text, the papers for each board meeting contain a dozen pages of coloured dashboards full of graphs and indicators. These are followed by a series of exception reports. Then around ten pages of risks would feature, the crammed text in these only being readable with a magnifying glass. The structure of the meetings and the content of the board papers are the very definition of staring at the dashboard while crashing the vehicle.

The papers of the board meeting dated 07th July 2015 contain no reference to the three unexplained baby deaths and other harms that had occurred on the neonatal ward in June. The neonatal ward is not mentioned once in the one hundred and fifteen pages of the meeting papers. Preparations for a possible inspection by the Care Quality Commission are discussed and the board has given itself a green tick in relation to all the directors being fit and proper, my arse! There is also an agenda item relating to lessons learned, which asks, *When things go wrong, are thorough and robust reviews or investigations carried out?* The irony, if only they were.

The papers for the next board meeting in September of the same year, at just one hundred and sixty-seven pages long are pretty much a lengthier carbon copy of their July predecessor. The October agenda and board papers are a mere sixty-four pages and Decembers, an almost palatable eighty-one. At the December meeting, one of the governors, Mr Cross, thanked the fundraising team for their successful Walk for Wards event which has raised a substantial amount of money for a Babygrow appeal. All the board papers are laden with the usual feelgood paradigm reinforcing narratives, tempered in polite superficial language that never dares to truly express itself or even hint at what it might not be revealing. The board meetings appear void of any information relating to the significant issues unfolding around them. Members of the board appear ignorant of the unexplained baby deaths and harm occurring in the hospital they are at the helm of. They seem content to remain busily preoccupied with their pages and pages of dashboards and numbers and percentages. Presented in text that is difficult to read and overlaid with red, amber, or green to indicate whether whatever the text, figure or percentage in question is, should be interpreted as good, indifferent, or bad. It's the equivalent of management by joining the dots. The absence of well-intentioned curiosity and constructive challenge in the board meetings is glaringly obvious, lamentable, and ultimately tragic.

A month after Nurse Letby's conviction in August 2023, I attended a Northwest area gathering of the NHS Leadership Academy. The event held in Manchester contained a mix of the already senior as well as aspiring NHS middle managers hoping to scale the giddy heights of the hierarchy. A representative from the Countess of Chester Hospital was present. The morning session contained a panel discussion during which an NHS Trust Chair, a long-serving chief executive, a commissioning GP, and an NHS England regional director shared views on the current state of the NHS. The discussion was rounded off with a question-and-answer session. I put my hand in the air and asked the following, *The NHS is by many measures failing and the culture is widely recognised as dysfunctional. The panel have been at the helm as this has occurred and have never challenged what most can see as the nonsensical diktats and policies emerging from the centre. Do the panel think they are the right people to lead the NHS forward and do they feel they have the respect of the future leaders in the audience?* The session was quickly drawn to a close and the room full of people were encouraged to head off and seek refreshments. Over the course of the day half a dozen people I had never met before either congratulated or thanked me for asking that question. I quizzed them as to why they had never asked it themselves. Their answers differed slightly, but the kernel in them all was the fear of repercussions and the impact it could have on their careers.

A mere matter of weeks after the conviction of the most prolific child serial killer in modern British history, by an NHS nurse whose actions could well have been halted if raised voices had been acknowledged and courage exercised, yet here was fear, as large as life and still sitting squarely and visibly in the middle of the room, dominating interaction amongst NHS leaders and managers. And the board at the Countess of Chester Hospital NHS Foundation Trust still only meets once every two months. I wonder what lessons have really been learned,?

Chapter 28: The treatment of whistleblowers

"Opposition is true friendship."

William Blake

I think the descriptor, whistleblower, is becoming weaponized as an increasingly heavily loaded headline grabbing label. One I'm finding myself less and less comfortable wearing. As well as deep scars, the experience of whistleblowing I described in chapter 19 has given me a label. It's both a buoyancy aid and a hampering anchor that shuts as many doors as it opens. I'm frequently introduced to the groups and audiences I speak with as an NHS Whistleblower. I often use the W word in the opening slides I present as part of the introduction to me. It serves the purpose of grabbing an audiences' attention and it's factually accurate. But I'm starting to wonder if aligning myself with the description reinforces an, us and them, David and Goliath, Rebel Alliance versus the Dark Side dualist mindset that fosters antagonism and fuels misunderstanding and division. I was approached by an NHS manager who after hearing my story empathetically said she now understood why I hated the NHS. Nothing could be further from the truth. But whistleblowers in the NHS are seen as problematic agenda driven and vengeful troublemakers with an axe to grind.

In relation to myself the term applies retrospectively. Though I wasn't consciously aware I was whistleblowing, what I did, raising my concerns internally with the NHS Trust I worked for before then sharing them with the regulator, the Care Quality Commission, only after I was ignored by my own employer, is whistleblowing by any definition. Yet I didn't see it as such at the time. I was just engaging the appropriate parts of what I still wanted to think was an inherently honourable system with what I thought was genuinely useful feedback. Decisions were being made that I believed would make services less safe and I did what I thought was the right thing to do. I assumed the directors who were at that time making what I interpreted as poor decisions would be prepared to reverse these decisions when faced with relevant insights. I also assumed the regulators of the system would value my insights as they related directly to patient safety and would intervene according. Once reason inevitably prevailed, as I felt sure it must, all would then be well in Tom Bell's world.

Though I knew I might not be flavour of the month for a wee while, I would at least be seen as a man of principle and respected by my peers and directors for sticking to my guns. Suffice to say I was blissfully unaware of the strong cultural forces at work and woefully naïve about the incredibly harmful impact that raising my concerns, trying to have an adult-to-adult conversation as I like to think of it, would have on my career and my wellbeing.

Earlier this year I was once again invited to talk to an audience of healthcare staff at the annual Patient Safety Congress in Manchester. I and my session, entitled *Speaking Up Safely and Listening*, had been relegated to an afternoon slot on the second day following my display of candour when sitting on the opening panel the previous year. The theme of 2023's Patient Safety Congress, the 16th, was *Facing reality – honest conversations about safety"*. I expect next years' to be entitled, *Facing reality part two – having honest conversations about the need to have honest conversations*. Anyhow, one of the two key points I tried to get across in my presentation is that listening in a dysfunctional setting is as problematic as speaking up. If people sharing insights and feedback are under the impression those who know then have a de facto duty to act, for the people in supposed positions of influence and authority who listen and are made aware things aren't as they should be, this can put them in an incredibly invidious position. The second point I tried to explain and get across as subtly as I could, is that I have begun to think it may not be possible to speak up safely in the NHS.

Like many I am sometimes guilty of excess optimism. Tali Sharot's excellent book The Optimism Bias explains how we have become hardwired to look on the bright side. It's part of the human condition. But the more I see of how people who share what I would deem legitimate concerns in the NHS are so shabbily treated, the more I witness the very real presence of fear that dominates so much of NHS culture, and the more I see how the protection of reputation trumps openness and transparency, even I have reached a point where I think blindly encouraging people to boldly find their voice and speak up, is irresponsible. There is a real possibility their lives may be ruined by doing so. The message I now try to communicate to people working in healthcare who may have concerns they want to share, is one of warning, of the need for extreme caution, and the intelligent use of questions to air concerns without challenge. And if all else fails, anonymity and an audit trail large enough to cover their arse! The sad reality is that as things presently stand, the act of speaking up in the NHS can seldom be done safely without inviting unwelcome consequences.

The treatment of whistleblowers in the NHS hasn't improved since the abysmal and shameful way it tried to deal with Graham Pink, in fact the climate for whistleblowers is probably more toxic now than then. Nurse Pink is British nursing's first perhaps most famous whistleblower. He voiced concerns about the treatment of patients at Stepping Hill Hospital in Stockport in the late 1980's. He notified hospital management about the poor care of patients due to a lack of staff on duty in the elderly ward, where many were seriously ill or dying. Ignored by the hospital he then wrote to civil servants and MPs. Some of his letters were even published in the Guardian in 1990. The hospital management sacked him in 1991 for allegedly breaching patient confidentiality. As well as being an incredibly amoral and ethically shitty thing to do, it was entirely unjustified. Nurse Pink had never shared details about the patients on the ward in any of his correspondence. The climate for whistleblowers in the NHS, truth tellers as Nurse Pink preferred to be called, is less conducive to speaking out than I think it may ever have been. The NHS has become more politicised and reputationally sensitive than at any point in its history.

NHS England, NHS Trusts and the various assorted commissioning and oversight bodies that make up the NHS now employ the equivalent of a small army of people in communications and public relations roles whose remit is to stop what they immaturely deem bad news, reaching the world beyond the castle walls. This world beyond the walls is not merely the press, the public, patients and staff, it includes the regulator, NHS England, the local MP, and often even NHS directors sitting on the boards of the same Trust. Directors of the Cumbria Partnership NHS Foundation Trust where I worked, often held information back from each other in efforts to bolster their own standing. I don't imagine they were unique in the NHS in displaying these behaviours.

The creation of the role of a National Guardian for the NHS around six years ago, and the setting up of NHS Freedom to Speak Up Guardians, who are in theory supposed to be present in every NHS Trust across England, has not made NHS employees feel markedly safer in speaking up. In the view of many their presence has not made the NHS any safer for patients. The latest results of the NHS annual staff survey showed a decline in the proportion of NHS employees who say they feel able to speak up. As with anything context is key. I have met and spoken with Freedom to Speak Up Guardians who feel enabled and unhindered to do their job and who are regarded as genuine advocates for patient safety by their colleagues. Some go out of their way to build bridges with staff that are capable of carrying the weight of negative feedback. I have also met some who are frustrated and who have been given the role of a Freedom to Speak Up Guardian on top of an existing often demanding full-time job. Some NHS Trusts that are subject to staffing pressures are ticking the box to say they have created the post of a Freedom to Speak Up Guardian, but they do not have the will, the culture, or the capacity to take the roles seriously. In the initial stages of writing this book I sent an email to what I was told was an up-to-date list of all the Freedom to Speak Up Guardians currently working in the NHS. The return rate for people no longer in the role who had moved to other NHS Trusts or left the NHS altogether was around a third. In fairness the list has been maintained much more accurately in the last few months. The creation of the Freedom to Speak Up Guardians role was another legalistic well-intentioned whizz bang idea from the mind of Sir Robert Francis. When will he learn that you can't change culture with legislation.

Of course, whistleblowers no longer get sacked explicitly for whistleblowing in the NHS as Nurse Pink was, or in any other organisation for that matter. Times have changed and organisations and their generally servile HR departments apply more subtle pressures on those they consider unwelcome in the ranks. Whistleblowers are dealt with surreptitiously and indirectly. In my case I was gaslighted, undermined, bullied, belittled, ostracized, and ultimately reduced to tears in front my peers. I still recall that day as one of the worst in my life. My bosses then increased my workload so that at one point I was covering the work of five people. My mental health inevitably suffered, and I was then cleverly manipulated out the NHS on health grounds. Before I was forced out the National Health Service, I had been blissfully naïve about whistleblowing, truth-telling, and how quickly it would lead to being ostracised and the consequences it would have. At the meetings that were held to hear my appeals, there were people I had known and who I had sat down with over lunch many times in the preceding years, and who in private shared my concerns, but now they wouldn't speak to me. It's tempting to say they should have spoken up on my behalf, but would you? How many people in well-paid jobs with financial responsibilities would?

Sue Allison is a former NHS Whistleblower who became a Public Governor at University Hospitals Morecambe Bay NHS Foundation Trust in 2021. The role of a good governor is as a critical friend and Sue who also describes herself as an optimist by nature became a governor believing she would be able to use her lived and professional experience to help the Trust repair its culture. A dysfunctional and harmful culture that had been highlighted in the eponymously titled Morecambe Bay Investigation Report published by Dr Bill Kirkup in March 2015. In the wake of a number of avoidable baby deaths and a cluster of serious incidents, Dr Kirkup had been commissioned by the Secretary of State for Health to conduct an independent investigation into the state of neonatal and maternity services at the Morecambe Bay NHS Trust. His final report was scathing and his observations unambiguous. He criticised both the institution and its regulators in the opening comments of a detailed two-hundred-page document and stated that the findings it contained were stark and catalogued a series of failures at almost every level. He went on to describe the nature of the problems his investigation had unearthed as serious and shocking before stressing the importance of learning from the events in question.

In June 2023 Sue resigned from her role as a Public Governor. She believes Morecambe Bay University Hospitals NHS Foundation Trust has not only failed to learn the lessons of the past but is still using all the same old tried and trusted techniques to silence conscientious staff who raise legitimate concerns. The most common of these techniques is to threaten to refer prospective whistleblowers to the respective professional bodies they are members of, such as the General Medical Council, GMC, and National Nursing and Midwifery Council, NMC. This type of reprisal, often enabled and supported by tamed compliant fellow employees or colleagues who may have a grudge to bear or something to gain, is the most feared by healthcare professionals. The threat of being struck off by the professional body on whom their continued ability to practice depends, is often enough to dissuade concerned clinical staff from raising their concerns. In the post Sue placed on social media outlining the reasons for her resignation, she talked of a toxic culture that she believes exists in a core group of senior managers who perpetuate a climate of fear and reprisal, presumably in their efforts to protect themselves and the organisations reputation. She cited how people who had raised concerns were unfairly dismissed, had lost career opportunities, and were ostracised from their colleagues and social groups. Sue referred to one individual who had been bullied and harassed to the point where they now suffered from chronic PTSD. How sad, that in the wake of a report that screamed out for culture change if more young lives were not to be avoidably lost and families harmed forever, that the lessons of the recent past remain unheeded.

Looking back, I see now that a large part of the reason I became persona non gratis in the NHS was that I extended too much trust in openly sharing what I thought. I assumed I was in a psychologically safe place, an adult space in which all conversations, thoughts, and observations were not only permitted, but welcomed. I hadn't even considered the idea that my free speaking would be perceived as talking truth to power. I was so at odds with the culture, and I didn't even know it. I was in a fight I didn't know I had entered. By inadvertently raising my head above the parapet I had shown my hand and was labelled as a reputational risk to the organisation. I still prefer to give trust freely, old habits die hard, but I have come to realise that in some scenarios, extending trust blindly, isn't such a smart thing to do.

I can say to you now with absolute conviction that if I was put in that situation again, I would speak up and stand out again. And I'd probably do so in much the same way I did, because by the time I came to the point of whistleblowing, I had exhausted the more subtle and less challenging options available to me. I had been so proud to join the NHS, I was a reluctant whistleblower. Not because I had any insight into what would follow, I don't think I had a clue what was coming or of the impact it would have on my mental health, my career, or income. No, the reason I was reluctant is because I had always been known as that super enthusiastic can-do guy. Tom Bell was that tall confident bloke in designer glasses, a clean shirt and a smart suit who took things in his stride, who made things happen, who always sought the positives. I took great pride in having been pulled up by the bootstraps, by many others as well as myself, from being a homeless teenage rebel with a dodgy haircut and a lengthy juvenile criminal record, to becoming an experienced, knowledgeable, respected, highly qualified, shiny shoed tie wearing MBA graduate and a knowledgeable business advisor. The first member of the Chartered Institute of marketing in Cumbria to achieve Chartered status, vice-chair of the school governors, Chairperson of a local charity, and a former member on the steering group of the Northern Leadership Academy. I didn't want to become a whistleblower. I didn't want to be known as a whistleblower. I had preconceptions, ill-informed as it turned out, about the type of person a whistleblower is, and I didn't think that I was that type of person. I thought whistleblowers were the sort of people who sensationalised things, who had only become whistleblowers because they were dissatisfied, angry, unhappy, unable to communicate their thoughts & concerns effectively.

Becoming a whistleblower with all its connotations of being awkward, of breaking confidences, of not being reasonable, not being a team player, not someone to be trusted, being a troublemaker, a telltale, a rat, was not in my career plan. I completely understand why the very term makes some people uncomfortable. It's not a word I ever liked, but I got used to it. I even wore the label like a badge of honour for a while. I've learned most whistleblowers are just ordinary if passionate people, who care. Until I became a whistleblower I had suffered with something called *just world hypothesis*. If someone had lost their job and become an outcast because they had chosen to whistleblow, then they must have done something to deserve it. I now know that *just world hypothesis* is lazy thinking, a form of wilful blindness, and something we as individuals and collectively as wider society often find ourselves subconsciously buying into. Essentially it equates to believing the world is a just place, good things happen to good people, so bad things must happen to bad people who deserve it. I'm reminded how inappropriate my view of whistleblowers was considering what happened to my sister. Our conditioning runs deep.

Having unwittingly sacrificed my career in public service to blow the whistle, I consider myself a career failure but a successful human being. I would rather have the latter on my headstone. It's not just organisations that fall into the trap of chasing the target and missing the point. Whistleblower, whistleblowing, what loaded words they are. I could convince myself that my whistleblowing was a noble deed, a positive indicator of my character. But I'm no different to any-one else. I just had a strong motivation for truth-telling and a context I couldn't ignore which I can't take credit for. And in practical financial terms I had less to lose than most. But I did find that being true to my own internal compass, displaying integrity, and a touch of courage, had consequences. What I sacrificed is a sobering reminder that speaking-up, standing-out, can come at great personal cost, emotional and financial. The good gals and guys don't always win, and how I was treated after I was forced to whistleblow had an enormous impact on me. The consequences of my choices took me to the point of contemplating my own existence. Strangely, looking back, I can see now that I also gained a lot. More than I lost. Much more.

When someone reaches the point where they feel whistleblowing, making a protected disclosure, is the only option left open to them, they are in essence acknowledging that the culture of the organisation is not a healthy one. It logically flows from this that it should not be a surprise when they are vilified by these very same culturally collusive organisations. The opposite of courage is said to be conformity not cowardice. After all, even a dead fish can go with the flow. But the status conscious and economically driven environment we exist in puts huge pressure on people to continue to pull in a salary regardless of whether they agree with what they are being asked to do and how they may be being asked to do it, explicitly or implicitly. And the longer people are in post and the higher salary they are on, the more they have to lose by speaking up or standing out, or by aligning themselves with those who do.

If disagreement has been demonstrated by the organisation as the fastest path to redundancy, then can we really expect people with significant financial commitments and social standing to show dissent if they are asked to do something they might not agree with or think appropriate? Our innate need to belong, to maintain our place in the chimp troop we are in and our need to sustain our lifestyles and status are the basis for many of our actions, responses, and decisions. Whether we like it or not we are constrained in our deeds if not our thoughts by dependence on our employers and reliance on the rewards our continued employment provides.

"I'm so sorry honey, but we will have to cancel our holiday, sell the cars and the cat, and take the children out of higher education because I

quit my well-paid job today. I can no longer tolerate the unethical practices of my employer". That would be a brave or foolhardy homecoming speech for someone with a mortgage, children to bring up, and bills to pay. We are much more likely to deal with any angst we might feel about a toxic work culture, or what we perceive as our employers lack of ethics or questionable practices by listening to some loud music on the way home, grumbling to our family, our friends, and maybe some of our colleagues, before we finally console ourselves by rationalising; *"I will start to look harder for another job, I won't be there forever, perhaps we will win the lottery this week, then I will tell them where to shove it"*. Many people working in the NHS have become dependently compliant. Where else could a relatively unskilled administrator earn so very much for achieving so very little?

If you've ever worked at the sharp end of sales, selling commission only products as I used to, you quickly realise that if what you are selling does not meet the needs of the people you need to buy it, you are effectively screwed. I remain grateful that during this period of my life, the link between satisfied paying customers and the health of my bank balance became quickly and blindingly obvious to me. I have never forgotten the customer who politely but firmly reminded me that it was not my bosses' money, but ultimately their money that paid my wages. What this exposure to real life, as I described my time in the private sector to public sector colleagues who had never worked in any other setting, does for a person, is it teaches them to value feedback and welcome constructive criticism. To listen to what the customers are saying and to treat their insights like the precious gold dust they are. It also makes a person understand just how hard it is for some people to earn a half-decent wage and to not take a pay packet for granted. Good marketing is looking under the stones to find what customers don't like with a view to fixing it. This means good marketers who enter the public sector are naturally predisposed, almost hopelessly destined to become questioning employees who seek and identify areas where things can be improved or may be underperforming. Unfortunately, the term the public sector uses for such people, is whistleblower.

I am conscious that for many the term still has a derogatory almost secretive furtive feel to it. It's as if a whistleblower is a naturally nefarious untrustworthy person who has somehow done something wrong and should therefore expect retribution and estrangement from their employer and their colleagues. Nobody would deny that we need people in all our public services who want to identify areas for improvement and make changes. Perhaps we need to rethink the term whistleblower and use the words truth-teller Nurse Pink suggested back in the 1980's.

Legislating for integrity:

The All-Party Parliamentary Group (APPG) on Whistleblowing was established in 2018. A group of people I would describe as a collection of the politically motivated, personally self-interested, and conceptually ill-informed. They have come together with the *stated intent* of leading a campaign for root and branch reform of whistleblowing legislation and the introduction of an Office of the Whistleblower, presumably with soundproof walls. For the record, *stated intent* is not something All Party Parliamentary Groups, APPGs, opaque, fluid, elusive and unaccountable bodies that are often established and used as vehicles for private commercial interests, and of which there are many, have a reputation for living up to. The bill the All-Party Parliamentary Group on Whistleblowing have created to establish an Office of the Whistleblower and introduce new ways of working is currently navigating its tortuous passage through the stages of parliamentary approval.

The setting-up of yet another new body to address the absence of upright behaviour and personal integrity in organisational life is in my opinion a misguided effort to apply a feel-good legislative sticking plaster across the growing gaping increasingly visible oozing wound of behavioural amorality that blights the torso of public services. Yes, the private and voluntary sectors have significant issues, but it does seem a little ironic that the profit motive driving commercial organisations has made some large corporations more culturally receptive to bad news and more open and transparent in their reporting than the public institutions we pay to maintain. On its recent performance the Met Police would give the directors and traders of Enron a good run for their money in an Olympics for unethical behaviour. Perhaps the political imperative has now surpassed the profit motive as a reason for suppressing bad news, or maybe the two are so inextricably linked as to be indistinguishable?

According to some sources, the proposal the APPG on Whistleblowing is seeking to make law, could include the introduction of US style financial incentives for people who whistleblow. If so this will merely up the ante for all involved and encourage the NHS and other public service providers to reinforce the already thick defensive concrete walls of bureaucratic denial they live behind. It will also create perverse motivations for people to raise concerns for personal gain rather than principle driven reasoning or genuine public interest. And if evidence from North America is anything to go by, it will create greater defensiveness and litigiously nervous climates in every sector; public, private, and voluntary. Figures cited from the US Securities and Exchange Commission show instances of whistleblowing have risen by around forty-fold since financial incentives were introduced. They also reveal that the bulk of the financial resources expended in the entire system following the introduction of whistleblowing incentives, were spent on legal fees. The legal services industry will always profit from increased legislation no matter who wins the cases in question. The All-Party Parliamentary Group on Whistleblowing is thought to contain significant representation aligned with the legal industry.

Were it to be established, an Office of the Whistleblower would more than likely signal the end of the current Public Interest Disclosure Act, often referred to as PIDA. PIDA was introduced in 1998 and is widely regarded now as hopelessly ineffective. But the truth of the matter is that the Public Interest Disclosure Act hasn't become ineffective recently, it was always thus. It is only now as scandal after scandal after scandal has emerged, that the fact of its ineffectiveness can no longer be concealed, and it has had to be openly acknowledged as unfit for purpose. Based on the past ability of new and improved legislation to improve things, Duties of Candour, the Nolan Principles of Public Life, and Robert Francis's ill-fated Fit and Proper Persons Requirement, there is no reason for anyone to be convinced that a new Office of the Whistleblower will make the slightest difference to anyone other than the legal services sector and their useful advocates in parliament. As for the rest of us it might give some the false and dangerous assurance that it's safe to whistleblow. Scotland and the home countries already appear to have more workable robust arrangements in place and greater protections for whistleblowers and truth-tellers.

Were we still part of the EU, let's not go here Tom I hear you say, all companies in the UK over a certain size, public, private, or third sector, would by law now have to provide their employees and contractors with access to an anonymous electronic means of reporting concerns, whistleblowing, to their respective sector regulators and appropriate industry oversight bodies. The EU whistleblowing directive came into force in November 2019, and though some countries have not yet fully implemented its requirements, its implementation is an accepted and legally binding inevitability in all EU member states. The introduction of a similar system in the UK would I think be preferable to the creation of another office that will doubtless end up being yet another political point-scoring exercise that ends up chasing arbitrary targets while dashing hopes and missing the point of its existence.

Can decency, ethical awareness, honesty, humanity, integrity, humility, and morality be legislated for, taught and learned, or just be shown to be being taught. I don't know. I think I have part but not all of the answers, the issues are of course significantly bigger than me and my limited brain. But that's no excuse for not trying to start the conversation. I know real change is difficult. I also know we cannot collectively continue to stick our heads in the sand. The subverting of our humanity, the substituting of our internal compasses and decency in exchange for policies and procedures, and the surrendering of our obligations and responsibilities to each other to legislation and bureaucratic diktat is costing lives. Room must be made for candid conversations about the need for humanity, integrity, humility, and morality in public services, and about how we reached this point and how we can avoid revisiting it.

Chapter 29: **Why regulation doesn't work...**

"When mores are sufficient, laws are unnecessary; when mores are insufficient, laws are unenforceable."

Emile Durkheim

Rob Behrens is the UKs Ombudsman for non-devolved government business and English Ombudsman for the NHS. The organisation he oversees is tasked with what many would regard as an increasingly impossible perhaps even invidious task. The Parliamentary and Health Service Ombudsman service, commonly referred to as the PHSO, is the public body with the unenviable job of making final decisions on complaints that have been referred via MPs and those not resolved by the NHS, UK government departments, and other selected public services. In the present post-pandemic, politically toxic, increasingly litigious and financially challenged climate, it must be like being the fire safety officer in a fireworks factory in which everyone is a chain smoker.

There is, unsurprisingly, no shortage of demand for the PHSOs services. The Parliamentary and Health Service Ombudsman officially came into being in 1993 when the former Parliamentary Ombudsman Service was expanded to include the monitoring of health services. A culturally and structurally strange marriage in many respects and one in which divorce proceedings seem long overdue. The number of queries the PHSO receives and the complaints they are asked to consider has fluctuated over the years, but the trend has risen steadily for as long as they have existed. In 2003 the number of enquiries to the PHSO service was less than 15,000. By 2023 this had climbed to almost 130,000. Unsurprisingly, well over two thirds of these queries relate to health services. The Parliamentary and Health Service Ombudsman is now primarily a health service complaint handling service. The need for a dedicated Health Service Ombudsman has become operationally irresistible yet appears politically undesirable.

The PHSO is one of many ombudsman services operating across Britain. The Ombudsman Association website contains details of fifty-two different ombudsman bodies in the UK. These serve the public and private sectors and include financial services, higher education, housing, pensions, motors, rail, and even waterways. Many of the home countries have their own ombudsman responsible for statutory public services like policing and health. Ombudsman services are supposed to be impartial and objective, operating without fear or favour. They are normally funded through contributions from the industry they oversee or the public purse. The need for ultimate impartial sources of arbitration dates back as far as the history of humankind's existence in groups and tribes and the emergence of disputes requiring independent and objective perspectives to be resolved. The existence of modern ombudsman services relies almost entirely on the failure demand created in other parts of the public and private sectors and their workload is therefore a useful indicator of the levels of failure demand being generated. In a perfect world, there would be no ombudsman services. Their existence is just the visible tip of an exceptionally large iceberg made of self-interest, cultural insularity, mistrust, reputation management, and the inability of people and organisations in every sector to engage in meaningful honest conversations with their stakeholders.

I first met Rob Behrens, albeit briefly, when he spoke at the annual Patient Safety Congress in Manchester in 2021. I'd previously been in touch with the PHSO in relation to the abuse of my sister Alison many years ago. They'd been as much use as a chocolate fireguard. And having worked closely in and around healthcare for a decade I'd remained aware of their existence, and I remained a critic. But I had been heartened by the candour Rob expressed during his presentation at the Congress in which he was, for a Crown servant, unusually open about the limitations in which the service operated. He seemed willing to acknowledge what they would like to do differently and highlight publicly their limitations.

I had pressed for a meeting with Rob ever since hearing him speak and finally got to meet him as winter began to release its grip early in 2023. I wanted to discuss his role as PHSO, the challenges facing the organisation he leads, and the forces at work in the wider system it operates within that were driving demand. We met on a damp grey day at a stylish Italian Café in central Manchester, the city their head office was relocated to following significant cuts to its budget around five years ago. A tall unassuming man who manages to combine the gravitas his role requires with a half-decent sense of humour, Rob is under no illusions about the challenges facing the ombudsman service in such interesting times. He had recently returned from a visit to Ukraine, and though it's not within my understanding to say he had experienced an epiphany, I got the distinct impression that whatever he had witnessed had genuinely affected him. He spoke with humility and great admiration about the efforts of his counterparts in the Ukrainian Ombudsman Service who were somehow continuing to function and manage a burgeoning workload in the midst of horrific conflict.

We discussed the confusing landscape from the perspective of a patient or service user wanting to raise a genuine concern or make a complaint. Estimates suggest there are well over a hundred different organisations who can be contacted in the event someone believes something may have gone wrong in the provision of a healthcare service for them or their loved ones. Duplication would be a massive understatement. The confusion caused to people who are often already in a state of unprecedented distress adds to their grief and frustration and fuels their anger which is then understandably vented on every organisation they are signposted to or eventually and sometimes serendipitously find their way to. This mix of publicly and voluntarily funded local, regional, and national organisations, including patient associations, advocacy bodies, interest groups, local branches of Healthwatch (sigh), Citizens Advice, and the Care Quality Commission, are over and above the existing mechanisms operated by NHS Trusts themselves, such as Patient Safety Liaison Services, or PALS as they are widely referred to and the newly formed Integrated Care Boards who replaced the former Clinical Commissioning Groups. To put the icing on this bitter tasting cake of inconsistency and complexity, local government and social care services have their own ombudsman. If you know the system, then you know where to go and many of the organisations that exist do complement each other's activity. But few NHS Trusts have a handle on who does what and none offers a ready reference route-map to people who want and need to know where to go for help. It may be unfortunate but it's little wonder the PHSO staff who answer the telephones are frequently shouted at by those who eventually make it through the labyrinth of options.

As a Crown servant, and for better or worse, Rob is bound by the terms of his employment in relation to what he can say and about whom he can say it. But he spoke as openly as I think he deemed possible about his frustrations with the current complexity of the landscape, the way the Ombudsman service in England is structured, and the limitations to its remit. We talked of how the Scottish Public Services Ombudsman is structured and I sensed he was envious of how services in the home countries work, seemingly with a clearer remit, a more refined focus, and greater powers to intervene. I asked him if following the significant budget cuts, the PHSO had been subjected to in the previous decade, whether he felt the organisation had the resources needed for the growing task at hand. Rather than saying yes or no, he diplomatically pointed me to the number of staff employed by the Financial Services Ombudsman which at over two and a half thousand is around five times the number of staff employed by the PHSO. Data can be incredibly useful when painting pictures of our priorities.

Rob is no stranger to conflicting opinions, the PHSO operates in a highly emotive and politically charged environment and has faced a great deal of criticism from many angles, often justifiably. I recall my own frustration at the lack of responsiveness shown to the concerns I raised about my sister Alison. More recently a PHSO employee had somehow managed to send me a letter relating to a concern I had raised which referenced an organisation I had not even engaged with never mind complained about. This experience followed hot on the heels of an email I received from the Crown Prosecution Service which contained references to a certain Mr Assange. So much for the bright young modern graduate educated workforce. I like many others have developed low expectations when it comes to public services. Administrative employees in every area of the public sector are hampered by restrictive cultures and inherently less responsive and efficient than their profit-driven counterparts in the private sector.

In recent years, an organisation called the Patient's Association has been openly critical of the PHSO, accusing it of not only being ineffective but exacerbating the angst felt by people who approach it seeking help. Though the Patient's Association have altered their stance slightly, they are still far from fully fledged fans. One former complainant to the PHSO, a determined and highly informed lady called Della Reynolds, became so frustrated by her experience of the PHSO that she published an unambiguously titled book called, *What's the point of the Ombudsman.*

The book contains a selection of detailed case studies and observations which lead readers to conclude the PHSO is inept at best, corrupt at worst. I spoke with Della when I was publishing my first book in 2020. She is an intelligent articulate lady who continues to research and observe the PHSO extensively. Della along with similarly interested peers runs a group called *PHSO the Facts* (phsothetruestory.com) and posts regularly on the group website. PHSO The Facts point out that even though the number of enquiries to the Ombudsman has risen, the quantity of complaints that are investigated has fallen significantly from a peak of over four thousand to just over six hundred, meaning less than two percent of all initial enquiries are fully investigated. The Ombudsman's response to this observation is that the way enquiries are dealt with and classified has changed and many cases are now handled as something called a primary investigation and not a detailed investigation. The PHSO also points out that they are resolving a small but growing number of complaints by mediation. A practice they are committed to doing more of.

For form to follow function I would agree wholeheartedly with Della that the PHSO in its present form isn't fully effective and cannot meet the expectations placed upon it. Where we may differ is in our assessments of why this is, and of what needs to change to make it what it needs to become to meet the needs of healthcare service users and lead to lasting improvements in publicly funded health services. Someone once told me there is a fine perceptual fine line between ineptitude and tyranny, that at its worst and even with the best of intentions to begin with, our experience of a really bad bureaucracy can be no different from tyranny. In my view an ombudsman service with responsibility for publicly funded health services should be overseen by and accountable to the public it serves.

Rob strongly disagrees with the opinions of Della and *PHSO the Facts*. He tells me he has been upfront in admitting past failings, but he believes the group's opinions to be outdated and not based on the organisation as it is now. The PHSO are, by their own acknowledgement, far from perfect, and the evidence would suggest the organisation is overstretched and significantly under-resourced to tackle the challenges it faces. Which publicly funded institution isn't? But Rob is at least prepared to put his head above the parapet and regularly and publicly writes to senior ministers and those in power expressing his concerns and reminding them of the opportunities that exist to learn from the past while encouraging them not to repeat previous mistakes. The concerns he has about public service organisations are not only conveyed to ministers but are published widely. He has consistently and openly criticized the fobbing off of complainants and the tendency for NHS Trusts to put their own reputations above patient safety. The Ombudsman service through both its chief executive Amanda Amroliwala, and Rob himself, have chastised the NHS very publicly at the local and national levels for its defensive and siloed approach to dealing with its own dirty laundry. The criticisms the PHSO voiced in 2023 in relation to the corrosive culture unearthed at University Hospitals Birmingham NHS Foundation Trust, were stark and frank.

Rob seems genuinely concerned about the need for public service organisations in the UK to demonstrate strategic leadership at the national level. He bemoans what he sees as the decline of integrity in the civil service, which he suggests followed the findings of the Leveson Inquiry of 2012 that exposed inappropriate links between the press and many arms of the establishment. He is also critical of what he sees as a cultural hegemony of class and professionalism that dominate and perpetuate the many outdated public service structures and mechanisms that presently exist. He offers an example of the close ties between many of the senior regulators tasked with overseeing the activity of public bodies they were once employed by and questions how independent any individual in such a position can be. In his role as Ombudsman, he has aired his concerns about proposed legislation that would allow employees in healthcare settings to share information about incidents and mistakes in so called safe spaces. His concern is that the proposal in its current form would allow people to admit and acknowledge errors outside established internal channels and away from public scrutiny. The subsequent knowledge of which would then remain hidden from other interested parties, including patients and their families as well as the PHSO itself. Since we met the proposal has become enshrined in law, even though it contravenes internationally accepted best-practice and guidance. It feels like a backward step, and I can see it causing no end of issues and even more angst for people in pain who simply want answers.

There is no doubt in my mind that Rob would welcome significant reforms and consolidation across the ombudsman and patient support landscape. Where we might disagree is about who should lead the redesign of the service and who should oversee and measure its performance and hold it accountable. The board of the PHSO currently reads like the usual public service roll call of the great and good with the obligatory smattering of CBEs, Professors, former high flying civil servants, and senior executives, none of whom appear to have any lived experience of the issues the organisation they oversee is tasked with addressing. But regardless of the detail, the sooner England has a standalone appropriately resourced healthcare ombudsman whose remit encompasses the entire health and care arena, the better. Those who know me will understand that I don't offer professional respect to anyone in any part of what might loosely be referred to as an arm of the establishment, lightly. But Rob is one of a small, very small, number of people I have met who occupies a senior position in public service, to whom I would.

The Care Quality Commission:

There is an old joke about a guy who loses his house keys. He has been out on the town and comes back home a bit worse for wear. He is fumbling around on the floor under a streetlight when a passer-by stops and offers to help him look for them. After a few fruitless minutes, the passer-by turns to the drunk guy, and says, are you sure you lost them here? To which the drunk guy replies, I don't know, but I thought I would look under the streetlight because I couldn't see anything in the shadows. The drunk guy is the anecdotal embodiment of the Care Quality Commission. The CQC are the UKs statutorily appointed and publicly funded regulator of health and care services and they have a pretty horrendous track record of not knowing when things are about to go horribly wrong. In many cases they have had the wool deliberately pulled over their eyes and then issued ill-informed assurances that have enabled problems to grow in scale and added to the time it took to deal with them. They look in the places they can see for the things they expect to find. They seldom if ever, step outside their remit to explore or look for the things they don't know that they don't know. I recall that at the same time their predecessor the Commission for Health Improvement was berating the Garlands Mental Health Hospital in Carlisle for its cruel and degrading treatment of patients in the late 1990's, there were reports of patients on the wards being raped. The regulator hadn't even considered the possibility that a culture in which the cruel and degrading treatment of patients was condoned, might also be harboring some even darker behaviours. It only looked where it thought it should look to find what it expected.

The CQC are routinely misled and misdirected, at times unwittingly and at times deliberately by the NHS Trusts and related bodies they are tasked with inspecting and regulating. The NHS Trust I worked for launched an extensive and expensive organisation wide internal communications campaign in preparation for its upcoming CQC inspection. Staff were briefed and instructed on what they should and shouldn't say to the CQC inspectors. Leaflets and internal bulletins were dispensed to every employee and staff were left in no doubt that the expressing of a critical view to any member of the CQC team would be viewed negatively. At the same time this was occurring community nurses were being told there was no money available for patient information leaflets. The Trust played the inspectors like a cheap fiddle and after avoiding what many people had predicted would be, and should have been, a poor rating from the regulator, directors openly expressed their relief that the CQC had been sufficiently managed and hadn't been able to look too closely under the bonnet. As the director of quality and nursing said to me at the time, *"It could have been a lot worse Tom"*.

Of the various scandals that have been surfaced in the UK's health and care system, few if any have been surfaced by the very regulatory body we fund to unearth them. The tragedies that have been exposed have been brought to our attention by the efforts of persistent individuals, the parents, siblings, children and relatives of the harmed, patients and collectives of patients, their families, friends and sometimes the wider community, and at times the local press. The CQC's simplistic Ofsted style headline rating system is acknowledged by many observers as woefully inadequate and a complete and utter waste of time. Many of the tragedies that have emerged in Britain's health and care sector occurred within organisations that the CQC had recently rated as Good, and in some cases even Outstanding.

In September 2022, an orthopaedic surgeon called Shyam Kumar was found to have been unfairly dismissed. Dr Kumar had raised numerous concerns to his employer, including observations about health staff being bullied, clinical staff who wanted to air concerns being silenced, and situations that could lead to serious patient harm. His story and subsequent entry into the growing club of NHS Whistleblowers, would not be untypical, shocking, or even newsworthy, if Shyam had been working for an NHS Trust. But the role that Dr Kumar was unfairly dismissed from was not with an NHS Hospital, or NHS Community Services, or an NHS Mental Health Trust, it was with the Care Quality Commission. Dr Kumar was an orthopaedic surgeon who held a part-time role as a special adviser on hospital inspections for the CQC. He was unfairly dismissed because he made the mistake of thinking the regulator would be keen to walk the talk it was telling others they should live by.

And what fine talk it was. The stated mission of the CQC is *to make sure health and social care services provide people with safe, effective, compassionate, high-quality care*. The cut and paste corporate guff on their website, doubtless stripped from another organisations *who we are* webpage by the lickspittles who tend to thrive in the dark seedy cellars of communications and public relations departments, goes on in reassuring tones to tell us that, *the Care Quality Commission exists to encourage services to improve and take action to protect the people who use health and care services.* The words, **take action to protect people** are emphasised in bold font, standing defiantly out from their meeker fellows in the sentence like the silhouette of Clint Eastwood in a scene from Pale Rider. Unfortunately, it would seem the font used for these words is one of the few bold things in the entire organisation.

And then there are their values. Who doesn't like a good set of corporate values? Random words with positive associations, hunted down and plucked from the air above a secret fairy garden during management awaydays and leadership retreats by deluded soulless corporate automatons, grasping at words and phrases like children chasing butterflies with pink nylon nets. These sets of organisational values; can an organisation even have values? are generally a direct contra-indication of how an organisation will behave in reality. They have become nothing more than a vapid shapeless shield behind which duplicitous acts, negligence, mendacity, and a general lack of integrity and transparency thrive. Who can forget that global bastion of corporate values Enron, and its publicly stated values of Respect, Integrity, Communication, and

Excellence? The Care Quality Commissions stated values are Excellence, Caring, Integrity, and Teamwork. No cause for concern there then!

Between 2015 to the time of his eventual dismissal in 2019, Dr Kumar had written to his senior colleagues in the Care Quality Commission raising a number of concerns. Shyam Kumar's case and the findings of the tribunal which exonerated him and chastised his former employer, were accepted by the CQC. We are reaching new low points in relation to the existence of integrity in our public services when the UK's publicly funded regulator of health and care services is prepared to turn on its own to maintain the status quo and avoid rocking boats. But hey, don't worry, its only matters of life and death we're talking about.

Regulation isn't working:

It is obvious to anyone with an eager eye to see and even to those with a passing interest that the regulation of health and care services as it stands now is not working. The increased levels of legislation and mushrooming layers of bureaucracy are not changing the culture or curbing the harmful behaviours that are present in our public services. They are in fact making them worse. When management cultures are so dysfunctional, and widely noted for being so, simply creating more boxes to tick and asking for more and more reports from organisations and individuals who are already predisposed to playing the game, is a fool's errand. The bumbling failed introduction of the fit and proper persons test for NHS directors offers ironic proof of this.

Regulation doesn't stop people doing terrible things. More often than not it simply gets in the way of people who are trying to do good things. But when something goes wrong in the public sector, there are always calls for more regulation, which leads to more bureaucracy, which strips more resources out the system, which shifts focus and further alters behaviour, and ultimately leads to more problems, and so the cycle goes on. Regulation is a surrogate for real trust that multiplies in its absence. Without real trust, hard-earned and evidenced in the daily acts of individuals at all levels, the introduction of more and more measures simply becomes a never-ending bizarre game of cat and mouse, a constant circle of evasion and misdirection. A weird arms race of superficially benign conniving duplicity in which those deemed suitably regulated are rewarded for demonstrating compliance and the displacing of their efforts and precious resources from doing to deceiving. Regulation is a dance of mirroring and anticipation, an elaborate façade that has become the preoccupation of chief executives, directors, and senior managers in healthcare. It is also extensively used as a stick to be waved over staff who are routinely berated over the numbers and generally demoralised as they watch peers with a preoccupation with arbitrary targets and measures climb the organizational ladder while those with a focus on patients have their voices muted. And of course, the people who suffer are patients and staff. Precisely those the regulations are supposed to protect. Health and care systems, the organisations, teams, and individuals within them, have through necessity become increasingly focused on keeping the regulator at bay. Many people working in health and care services, including the voluntary sector, feel increasingly detached from what they originally thought was the true purpose of their work.

The circus of regulating, monitoring and whistleblowing has become an absurdity. Without morality at the level of the individual, and trust that is earned and shown by honest deeds rather than empty promises and strategies, it won't matter how many recommendations ministers and regulators make, they will all count for nothing. Government are raising our hopes to be inevitably dashed and tossing our money to the wind if they think they can legislate for morality whilst continuing to recognise and reward the dishonest behaviours that chasing meaningless targets encourages. Our public services have become awash with people who would rather roll out the red carpet for the regulator than their patients.

Chapter 30: **Advisors & thinktanks**

It was six men of Indostan, to learning much inclined, who went to see the elephant, though each of them were blind, that each by observation, might satisfy his mind.

The first approached the elephant, and, happening to fall, against its broad and sturdy side, at once began to bawl: "God bless me! but the elephant, is very like a wall!"

The second feeling of the tusk, cried: "Ho! what have we here, so very round and smooth and sharp? To me tis mighty clear, this wonder of an elephant, is very like a spear!"

The third approached the animal, and, happening to take, a squirming trunk within his hand, thus boldly up and spake: "I see," said he, the elephant is very like a snake!"

The fourth reached out an eager hand and feeling about the knee said: "What this wondrous beast is like is mighty plain to me," it is clear that the elephant is very like a tree."

The fifth, who chanced to touch the ear, said: "Even the blindest man can tell what this beast resembles most; deny the fact who can, this marvel of an elephant, is very like a fan!"

The sixth no sooner had begun, about the beast to grope, than seizing on a swinging tail, that fell within his scope: "I see," said he, "the elephant is very like a rope!"

And so, these men of Indostan, disputed loud and long, each of his own opinion, exceeding stiff and strong, though each was partly in the right, and all were in the wrong!

Then a passing consultant entered the debate and said: "I can tell you exactly how an elephant looks, I may have never seen one, but I've read lots of books. The elephant in size is somewhere between a rhino and a giraffe and can best be represented using a matrix or a graph."

So, often in theologic wars, the disputants I'll ween, rail on in utter ignorance, of what each other means, and prattle about an elephant, that none of them has seen!

J G Saxe (mainly); The Blind Men and the Elephant

Every strategy document I have read about the state of health or social care, how to fix the NHS, Primary Care, healthcare, how to improve social services, be it children's or adults, seems to focus on doing more. How can services be more effective and efficient. How can we help the people working in social care to make better use of their time and resources. How can processes be streamlined. Or to use that classic private sector phrase, how can the assets be sweated more. I've found during my time in and around public sector services, that a strategy or a grand plan, is often a surrogate for real action or activity. When a minister, or a new chief executive, or a new head of service wants to make their mark, they create a new strategy. When a tragedy occurs that piques the national interest and makes the headlines and front pages, then the creation of a new strategy is boldly announced as the remedy. If the things that were broken, the issues we face could have been fixed by a new strategy, as we have been told they would be, then we would be living in Nirvana by now. Creating strategies has become an industry. The health and care sector has published enough strategies over the last two decades to pave the M6, more than once!

The NHS and its constant seemingly incurable neurosis, is a godsend for providers of professional services eager to sell their wares, and a lucrative and reliable income stream for the numerous think tanks and advisory bodies keen to tell it why it is struggling and what it could and should be doing differently. Stating their platitudes and opinions like back seat drivers on an old bus competing in a road race, they are like the counsellors of the book of Job, offering their words without knowledge, staffed, and led by the out of touch and intellectually aloof cold and timid souls Roosevelt criticized in the now much-quoted *Man in the Arena* speech he addressed to the people of Paris in 1910. These bodies and their leaders have a vested interest in securing their own perpetuation, they are not in contact with the realities of life as many experience them. Importantly, because they adopt a narrow unchallenging approach that interprets issues and works to address them within the confines of the system as it presently exists, rather than as it might be, and focus on issues in isolation that preclude the wider systemic drivers of demand, they are also in my view, a large part of the reason why the health and care sector is failing to learn from its mistakes. Their remit appears to be one of telling the stakeholders they work with in the health and care arena how to continue to do the wrong things rightly. Their business model depends on the avoidance of conflict, upward challenge, or upsetting anyone in a position of influence, thus ensuring they are invited back to the table the next time a profitable consultancy contract is up for grabs.

Widely respected and long-established, The King's Fund are one such organisation. An independent public health think tank originally founded in 1897 as the Prince of Wales Hospital Fund for London, their name was changed to The King's Fund after Prince Edward, their original benefactor ascended to the throne. Their main source of funding comes from a significant endowment gifted to them in the early part of the twentieth century by Lord Mount Stephen, a Scottish Entrepreneur who rose from humble beginnings to reportedly become the richest man in Canada. The King's Fund is currently sitting on assets and reserves of over two hundred million pounds. The Fund does produce some useful research, some of which I drew on while writing this book. But if you were to look at its track record and ask the simple question, would anyone have noticed if you hadn't been here, the answer from most quarters, and certainly those who represent the interests of patients, would be a resounding no. It's a strange situation that the one thing many so called think tanks appear to do least of, is think, critically or systemically. The King's Fund would argue that it has worked with many influential stakeholders from within the healthcare system to understand the problems they are facing and has conducted and published a great deal of useful widely cited research. But organisations like The King's Fund are inherently nepotistic. They have become an entrenched part of the system they are seeking to observe and understand, an echo chamber that engages with the usual suspects who in turn collectively reinforce each other's perceptions and biases. Asking a group of senior executives from a selection of NHS hospitals to talk about the challenges facing them, is not a recipe for producing innovation or systemic challenge on any level. The turkeys aren't about to start voting for Christmas by challenging the status quo any time soon.

The Health Foundation is another incredibly well-funded body whose stated mission as an independent charity is to improve the quality of health and health care in the UK. Its bold aim is nothing less ambitious than to create a healthier population. I'd revisit that one and quit while I was so disastrously behind if I were them. The Foundation scrapes admirably by on the proceeds of a small endowment of over five hundred million pounds it received in 1998. It now has assets defined as long-term investments of just over 1.2 billion pounds. From these and other grants it acquires, as well as the thirteen million pounds it spends on its own salaries including remuneration packages of over a hundred thousand for ten of its senior staff and a mere quarter of a million for its chief executive, it also spends tens of millions of pounds each year on a range of activities including the giving of grants, events, funding and publishing research, leadership training, and supporting a large nationwide network called the Q Community. Aimed at people working in the health and care sector and designed to facilitate and increase collaboration and drive innovation, the Q Community, which is jointly funded by the NHS and of which I have been a member for some years, has by any yardstick of visible meaningful achievement other than purely activity, been a spectacularly ineffective and expensive failure. A further lesson, if one were needed, in the futility of expecting innovation and radical new thinking to come from within the existing echo chambers of a culturally moribund system.

In its selfless attempts to improve the health of the nation, in 2017 the Health Foundation provided significant funding to a new body called The Health Improvement Studies Institute situated in the University of Cambridge, confusingly referred to as THIS. The stated vision of the THIS Institute is to place itself at the forefront of a movement that recognises that improvement activity in healthcare should be based on evidence and should generate evidence; sounds logical, albeit blisteringly obvious. Its mission, it claims, is to enable better healthcare through better evidence about how to improve through the creation of a highly credible and actionable evidence base. There's more, but I'm sure you're getting the picture by now that everyone appears to be on the same mission to collaborate, co-create, innovate, run events in partnership with each other and generally engage with the same old people and organisations who have always been engaged with, in the shared hope that the health of the nation can somehow be improved through their efforts.

The King's Fund, the Nuffield Trust, the Health Foundation, the THIS Institute, and the Q Community, when combined with the myriad local, regional, and national initiatives, University Health Innovation Campuses, specialist networks, patient safety bodies, and arms-length agencies, all offering think tank style workshops, collaborative forums, networking events, improvement services and support for innovation, is a recipe for the dilution of allegedly scarce resources. The duplication of knowledge and effort within this merry go round of politically pusillanimous well-intentioned navel gazing is immense. More importantly, the opportunity cost of continuing to look in the same places for acceptable answers to the wrong questions is an unproductive distraction. Such think tanks offer thought and narrative over impact, dealers in hope, they are largely a surrogate for real improvement that culls curiosity and diverts scarce attention and resources from looking outside the silos and echo chambers. It was after all a global pandemic that drove the adoption of technology in parts of the NHS that had resisted it for years, not the endless stream of strategies and papers that talked about the potential of technology being produced by the King's Fund or any other of the UK's self-appointed healthcare think tanks. As one healthcare worker put it, *"Coronavirus has been a system laxative. We've made changes in two weeks that would have taken up to five years before Covid"*. And it is a young teenager called Greta Thunberg who has done more for our collective awareness of climate change and had more impact than the many think tanks and institutions endlessly agonizing over its potential impacts while waffling about what to do next. Meaningful change rarely comes from within existing structures, institutions, and systems. But the inherent challenge within Einstein's overtly accepted truism that the solutions we need will not and cannot emerge from the same thinking that created them, has never been truly welcomed by the people, organisations, and institutions it is most applicable to.

In their defence, The King's Fund annual wage bill is less extravagant than its counterpart the Health Foundation, standing at a mere ten million pounds of which only one million was paid in total to its eight key management personnel in 2021. Its website boldly proclaims their ideas are changing health and care. If they are then it doesn't look good for them, but they've doubtless been saying something similar for the entire one hundred and twenty plus years of their expensively entitled existence. And yet there remains little evidence of their impact. Britain's physical and mental health continues to decline as the nation's health and care services accelerate merrily to hell on their speeding handcart. The Health Foundations annual report for 2021 says they are *looking forward to making progress in 2022 and beyond, for the benefit of the UK population and, in particular, the most vulnerable in society.* I'm not sure that the swelling and disenfranchised ranks of Britain's growing, and increasingly impoverished foodbank using citizens, many of whom work in health and care, will ever see any meaningful benefit arising from the detached polite challenge free pontificating of the insulated compliant self-serving middle classes who populate the upper echelons of such out of touch institutions. One can only presume these institutions and the people in them need to keep telling themselves the story of their virtue and value to justify and validate the futility of their ongoing existence.

Pirates ahoy!

In February 2023, the headline feature on the Open Democracy website was, *NHS becoming cash cow for consulting firms as contracts quadruple in value.* The article said that NHS England had allocated £83m to outsourced consultants in the previous financial year. It went on to say that several of the consultancy firms that had been awarded work in the previous year had also been involved in the now infamous, ineffective, and eye-wateringly expensive NHS test and trace debacle. Observers estimate the total cost of the test and trace fiasco to be around thirty billion pounds, the majority of which appears to have been spent without scrutiny. The exact figure may yet be revealed by the recently launched Covid-19 Inquiry into the UK government's handling of the coronavirus pandemic. To those who have worked in and around the world of health and care, the names of the main consultancy services outlined in the Open Democracy article, read like a list of the taxpayers most wanted public service vampires. All the usual suspects were there: Deloitte, KPMG, PwC, McKinsey, Boston Consulting Group, and PA Consulting. What also emerged was that some senior executives in the consultancy firms hired by the NHS, were reportedly paid daily rates of almost seven thousand pounds. An annual salary equivalent of one and a half million pounds. I had a conversation with a consultant who worked on the doomed National Programme for IT who told me of people charging £1500 for half a day's work with no tangible results for their activity.

But we shouldn't be surprised. The NHS is thought to have spaffed at least ten billion pounds of our money, much of it up the private sector consultancy wall, on its doomed now much dissected National Programme for Information Technology that ran between 2002 and 2011. In fact, £83m is relatively little compared to the vast irrecoverable sums the NHS has spent on private sector business consultants in recent history. In 2010 as austerity was costing many of us our jobs, the NHS reportedly spent £313m on private business consultants, this amount increased year on year and by 2014 the figure had almost doubled to £640m. In 2014 it dropped to £419m and in 2018 just before the onset of Covid, it was estimated at just over £300m. These significant amounts do not include the money spent on private sector business consultants by social care services or the Department of Health and Social Care. Before Thatcher was elected to power in 1979, annual UK government spending on consultants was estimated to be around £6m. Under her conservative government it rose swiftly to almost a quarter of a billion. Public service spending on private sector consultancy services in the UK in 2022, was £2.8 billion.

The consensus of many within the NHS is that the intervention of consultants does more harm than good, and the evidence would suggest they are right. Research undertaken by staff from the Universities of Bristol, Warwick, and Seville, highlighted by the not-for-profit media channel The Conversation in 2018, concluded that spending on management consultants in the NHS was associated with greater inefficiency and worse patient outcomes. The research looked at the impact of external consultants by studying the performance of a hundred and twenty NHS Trusts over a four-year period. Interestingly, the researchers found that this correlation wasn't due to the hiring of consultants by persistently poorly performing NHS Trusts, many of the Trusts only found their performance deteriorating after the intervention. Of course, it would be disingenuous to suggest that using consultants leads directly to inferior performance. The performance of any part of such a complex interconnected system such as healthcare is subject to many systemic factors and wider forces beyond any single organisations control or influence. What I think it would be safe to say, is that the use of consultants whose revenue depends on repeat business, and whose scope and remit is limited, compounds and stores insidious problems by ducking the real issues. Issues that those who work within the system are often if not always much more aware of and informed about than the shiny shoed

MBA sporting people in suits being paid a small fortune to dispense their academic wisdom without sticking around to see the results.

In June 2022, gross global revenue for the consultancy firm PwC, exceeded fifty billion dollars in a twelve-month period for the first time in its history. Rising profits as well as revenue enabled the company to pay around a million pounds in bonuses to each of its almost eight hundred UK partners. If it's true that by their fruits ye shall know them, then it would seem overseeing the demise of Britain's greatest achievement, failing to acknowledge and surface the issues that are creating demand, and generally making things worse for the people who work in the NHS and the patients it serves, is highly profitable business.

Exceptions to the rule:

The Centre for Health and the Public Interest, CHPI, is a small and lean healthcare focused think tank. It describes itself an independent non-party think tank promoting a vision of health and social care based on accountability and the public interest. Its markedly less waffling description differentiates it from its long-established rivals. The CHPI's very use of the dreaded A word, accountability, is probably enough to send most public service panjandrums seeking a think tank behind which to hide their creative paucity, scurrying in the opposite direction. The public sector doesn't do accountability. The Centre was founded in 2012 in the wake of what it says was a growing democratic deficit in the way decisions about health and social care policy were being made. The CHPI is a registered charity that runs with minimal overheads and has around a hundred thousand pounds in assets. With limited resources, volunteer board members, and the help of an unpaid network of expert contributors, its Director David Rowland, who is not paid a prince's ransom, has overseen the publication and promotion of numerous reports that have been featured and then discussed in the national media. The post, briefing documents, and reports placed on the CHPI website are a refreshingly direct and challenging alternative to the dry, overly polite, and generally uninspiring documents churned out by other think tanks. David's observations on the emergence of a two-tier healthcare system in Britain, are insightful and thought-provoking.

I've spoken with David in the past and I corresponded with him as I was gathering ideas for this book. I asked him about the present challenges facing the NHS and whether he saw the need for a different and far more systemic approach to dealing with them. Though I found his answers to be candid, informed, and less politically sensitive than his counterparts, I still sensed some reticence to fully acknowledge the systemic scale of the challenges facing health and care in this country and the political ideologies that have precipitated them. David, like many others, is against the idea of radically reforming or restructuring health services, arguing instead that the NHS has endured since 1948 because it provides the fairest, most effective efficient way of providing healthcare to the population. But this I think is a largely UK-centric if laudably patriotic view and is the argument typically wheeled out by people who mistakenly still believe that all Britain's good old NHS needs is a bit more funding.

Our planet, Britain, our cities, towns, communities, families, you and I, our lives, expectations, aspirations, and concerns, look quite different now than in 1948. The landscape has shifted irrevocably. The last seventy-five years have surely been the most transformative in human history. The planets population has tripled, life expectancy globally and in the UK has risen significantly, our climate is changing and large parts of our ecosystem are collapsing, the internet is embedded in our world and in our lives, the wall fell, and while advances in science and medicine have been immense and though the world is now largely free of many of the diseases that plagued our ancestors, HIV is still a threat, a global virus has once again shone a spotlight on our inherent fragility, and the prevalence of many relatively newly discovered conditions has increased massively; there are an estimated seven hundred thousand autistic adults and children in the UK alone, and our increased life expectancy means more of us than ever are likely to experience conditions such as Cancer and Alzheimer's at some stage in our lives. And many of the seismic changes in society, our workplaces and work patterns, and the shifts in attitude, and the events and megatrends foreseen by futurists such as Alvin Tofler, have come to pass.

The NHS has not endured because it is the best health and care system possible, many would argue, with some credit, that it is not enduring; just ask the one in five GPs under 30 who reportedly quit the profession in 2022 and the healthcare assistants and nurses who are leaving their jobs to work in the private sector or stack shelves in Sainsbury's. The NHS is surviving, and only just! because the gaps that have emerged in its provision as it has struggled to cope with the increasing and unreasonable politically driven demands to deal with everything that lands on its doorstep, have been filled by the efforts of a growing number of social enterprises and the goodwill of many of its long-suffering staff. To keep repeating the mantra that all the NHS needs is more money, feels like yesterday's answer to a challenge that has already escalated beyond the point at which such a simplistic remedy might have once been applicable.

I find myself asking why even a new and slightly edgy healthcare think tank like the CHPI would shy away from highlighting the big issues of our time, of shining a questioning torch on the political choices and ideologies that drive demand, and I wonder if they, just like many of us, and in fairness just like I used to be, are afraid of being labelled as socialist? I wonder if a think tank that operates in the health and care arena, can influence and be effective if it is not political? The French philosopher Foucault suggested that the real task of a society was to criticize the working of institutions which appear to be both neutral and independent, and to do so in such a manner that the political violence which has always exercised itself obscurely through them can be unmasked, so that in turn they can be made visible and fought. Foucault believed people are engaged in political struggle all the time, whether they know it or not.

Another pleasantly responsive, disarmingly modest, hierarchically blind, and refreshingly action-oriented exception to the institutional impotent ineffectiveness that appears to permeate the world of healthcare think tanks and consultancies, is Bev Fitzsimons. Bev was until recently Chief Executive of The Point of Care Foundation whose stated mission is to humanize health and care. A former Fellow in Health Policy from the King's Fund, she left to become more hands-on and get directly involved in improving healthcare services on the ground by making a positive difference in the here and now. The Point of Care Foundation became an independent social enterprise in 2012 after splitting from the King's Fund where it had been run as an in-house programme since 2007. Bev is not an extravagantly paid chief executive by any stretch and Point of Care runs on modest resources with a small staff of around a dozen who provide training and consultancy to a range of health and care-related organisations. Bev is keen to point out to me that the Kings Fund have been incredibly supportive of their efforts. Okay yes, at this point I am forced to admit that the King's Fund may have done something useful.

The Point of Care Foundation originally relied on grants for its survival, but Bev and her colleagues' ambition to make the organisation self-sustaining has brought the foundation to a point where it runs as a viable social enterprise, generating over ninety percent of its revenue from selling its services and expertise. One of their specialisms is in providing training in something called Schwartz Rounds, named after an attorney from the USA called Ken Schwartz who was diagnosed with terminal cancer in 1994. During his treatment he noted that what had mattered to him most on his palliative journey, were the simple acts of kindness from his caregivers, which he said made the unbearable bearable. Upon his death he left a legacy for the establishment of the Schwarz Centre in Boston whose aim is to foster compassion in care. Schwartz Rounds are now globally recognised in health and care circles. They are a structured facilitated forum in which all staff, clinical and non-clinical, can come together and talk about the emotional and social aspects of working in healthcare. They are conducted in a psychologically safe space which encourages open and candid sharing. Their broad aim is to explicitly recognise, acknowledge, and validate the experiences and emotions of staff and to help reconnect people working in health and care with their patients and in turn with their own purpose and personal passion for providing care. Healthcare at its sharp end is an incredibly demanding vocation, one which is often hampered by the demands placed on staff by those micro-managing and monitoring them. Schwartz Rounds are a way of reminding everyone involved in patient care that compassion for their patients and each other are vital components in creating the conditions in which safe and humane care can be provided.

Humanizing healthcare feels like a noble, pragmatic, and necessary aspiration. The Point of Care Foundation from where I am standing would appear to be achieving a great deal more for the NHS and its patients with limited resources, than its cash-hungry private sector counterparts have ever achieved, as they fleece the public purse before merrily pissing their taxpayer bonus funded vintage champagne up or down the nearest Italian marbled convenience. Bev disagrees strongly with my views about the lack of value that I believe the majority of think tanks and traditional consultancy firms add to the NHS and the public it serves, but after speaking with her I am left with the distinct impression that the NHS at every level needs a whole lot less value destructive PwC, BCG, and KPMG, and a great more POC compassion and humanity if it is to stand a chance of surviving in the long run. I wish whoever follows in Bev's footsteps the very best.

PART VI:

The Role of Charity

Chapter 31: Taken for granted

"Being taken for granted is an unpleasant but sincere form of praise. Ironically, the more reliable you are, and the less you complain, the more likely you are to be taken for granted."

Gretchen Rubin

A couple of years before the outbreak of Covid-19, I was online following a live speech being given by Simon Stevens, who was then the head honcho of NHS England. He was addressing a gathering of highly paid senior minions. I think he may have been presenting at the annual NHS Expo jamboree. Anyway, a day on which all these people are in one room is probably a good day for everyone else in the NHS including its patients. Perhaps not the total waste of public money it appears. Then, as if on demand, like trained circus animals the assembled great and good applauded Simon, when he announced with obvious pride that the UK spends less money per head on healthcare than Germany.

I swore and sighed, deeply. Did he really say that out loud as if it was something to be proud of, I thought? Have I really just watched the chief executive of the nation's most treasured asset crassly announce that the country that led the industrial revolution spends less on the health and care of its citizens than its neighbours? Is this man proud to hold our NHS aloft as a leading competitor in a self-destructive race to the bottom of the which government can get away with healthcare for its citizens on the cheap league? I wondered, who will he compare us to next year? Mexico, Estonia, Lithuania; perhaps in ten years, Zambia, Sierra Leone, or possibly Armenia? Pundits place your bets now. I watched in amazement as the besuited primates not only greeted this depressing revelation like compliant chimps, but then, just as caged apes in a zoo hurl their own waste at the unsuspecting curious who are unfortunate enough to be within range, they started tweeting this deeply saddening fact into cyberspace, presumably to be shared even more widely by the layer of monkeys beneath them who are as unquestioningly sycophantic.

Why weren't they booing, chanting for his resignation while making obscene gestures in the air? Had the audience consisted of frontline staff, over-worked nurses, unpaid carers, cash-strapped charity volunteers, poorly paid homecare visitors or patients on hospital waiting lists, they would be throwing their chairs at Simon like punks at a Bay City Rollers gig. Before placing him unceremoniously atop piles of expensive unread values and mission statements and auctioning the opportunity to light the glossy pyre to an eager baying crowd. But no, the upper echelons of our NHS applauded as they nodded their unthinking admiration.

Of course, Simon, now Baron Stevens after being knighted for services to healthcare, neglected to tell his adoring audience that Germany has around a third more doctors and many more hospital beds per head than the UK. A statistic meaning it will naturally spend more per person on healthcare and one I imagine the Germans take considerable pride in. Nor did he mention Austria, Belgium, Canada, France, Iceland, Ireland, Norway, and Sweden, who along with dozens of other countries, spend more per head on healthcare than the UK. Citizens of these countries live longer.

He also, incredibly importantly and many would argue very ungraciously, forgot to remind his overpaid audience that the hospitals and services they are paid substantial amounts of public money to manage, are more and more reliant on a growing army of unpaid volunteers and the largest voluntary sector in Europe. That we have reached the stage where a cadre of self-serving public sector profligates are dependent on the efforts of the millions of selfless individuals who give their time and effort for nothing, and the thousands and thousands of social enterprises that coordinate their efforts should alarm us all. Britain's NHS and Social Care services would collapse on their arse tomorrow if the third sector, the charitably funded carers services, cancer nurses, and air ambulance services, all packed up and went home.

Estimates prior to the pandemic suggested that along with some of if not the highest levels of volunteering in Europe, the UK had between three and five million unpaid carers, a number that has since risen significantly. The country and its healthcare system runs, in no small degree, on the goodwill of unpaid labour. *"Your NHS needs you"*, said the Daily Mail as it promoted a campaign to recruit unpaid volunteers into the NHS. The last time I looked, its owner Viscount Rothermere, was a non-domicile who pays no UK income tax. The heroic fundraising efforts of Captain Tom are filling a revenue gap many have knowingly created.

When did reliance on charity to enable a government to spend less on the health of its own people become something to be proud of? When did our national dependence on lotteries, bucket rattling for donations and endless campaigns to fund overstretched voluntary services become a good thing? Spending less than other civilized countries on the health of your own citizens would never be something to shout about, other than inside the safe cosy sycophantic and thoughtless echo chambers that NHS management circles have become. What is the opposite of brightest and best?

I wondered if anyone in the room with Simon, perhaps an intelligent quick-thinking journalist from one of the specialist health publications or possibly the national press would have the courage to challenge. To raise their voice above the crowd and ask; Simon, should we be proud of spending less on healthcare and being increasingly reliant on charities, volunteering and private sector services to fill the gaps our under-funded, under-resourced, mismanaged under-led NHS is leaving? Of course, nobody did. The conventional wisdom always triumphs in rooms filled with those eager to please and everything to lose.

Desperate to show support for their leader the acolytes continued filling Twitter with the ignoble content of his speech. Yay, let's hear it for our NHS, clearly dying on its arse and more reliant on charity than other countries, woo, woo, #but-just-keep-saying-the-right-thing-to-secure-your-significant-salary. Simon says put your hands in the air and your posts on social media. I picture the conference goers after a few publicly funded drinks in the hotel bar that evening. *"Oh god, I thought Simon was brilliant when he stuck it up those overly caring compassionate and sickeningly efficient Germans today, don't you think?"*

I was ashamed, saddened but not surprised by the lack of courage, thought and challenge. As a former NHS employee, I have seen the unbearable pressures under-funding and mismanagement place on staff and witnessed the harm, sometimes fatal, done to patients. As Chair and Trustee of a local charity at the time I know how stretched resources have become. And as a patient myself I have first-hand experience of the impact. In the last few years alone, due to the lack of capacity in the system, I and many of my friends and family have spent money on private health services including mental health counselling, surgery and physiotherapy.

Once again, the Germans can observe the ineptitude of their ass-like English counterparts. I could almost guess the content of the German Health Minister's next speech, and it would not have been how proud they are of spending less on the health of their population than the Brits. German patients get such speedy access to hospital services that data on waiting times is not even collected at the national level. Proof if it were needed that chasing meaningless targets is nothing but a harmful distraction, a wasteful misdirection of scarce resources that should be deployed in adding value to patients. Germany also publicly funds much of the activity that we in the UK rely on charitable donations to provide. The German healthcare systems capacity and swift response in dealing with the initial outbreak of the Covid-19 pandemic, was acknowledged globally as exemplary. Simon forgot to mention the minimal waiting times German patients enjoy to his audience.

Chapter 32: Picking up the pieces

"The aim of giving is to put the recipient in a state where they no longer need our gifts."

C.S. Lewis

If societies are built with bricks of ambition, ingenuity, and enterprise, on foundations of equity and justice, supported to grow by the pillars of public infrastructure, and glued together with the mortar of human interdependency and mutual respect, then once the all-important foundations of equity and justice on which they all stand, fracture, they can only be held in place by the scaffolding of goodwill and charity. If Britain's health and social care services were a tourist attraction like York Minster, they would have been invisible for decades now. Hidden as if undergoing an extensive programme of refurbishment behind layer upon layer of plastic sheeting stretched expansively over an extensive, creaking, and surprisingly expensive network of charitable scaffolding. Were this scaffolding to ever be removed, the artefact behind it would crumble to the floor in a matter of moments. Not only are health and social care services in the UK overly and unsustainably dependent on the voluntary sector, but the voluntary sector is also incredibly reliant on their continued incapacity. They are locked together in a strange symbiotic self-perpetuating relationship with fluid boundaries that is mutually beneficial for them, but not necessarily positive for those they say they exist to serve.

We have a long-standing love affair with charities here in the UK. In 2019, the Queen's Nursing Institute was recognised by the Guinness Book of Records as the World's oldest charity. The global charity Oxfam was founded in Oxford in 1942. Save the Children was established in London in 1919. The children's charity Barnardo's was set-up in 1866 with Thomas Barnardo opening its first so called Ragged School for destitute children in 1867. And the Salvation Army which began life on the streets of East London in 1865, now boasts a presence in over one hundred countries with a reported 1.7M members involved in everything from dealing with the needs of the homeless to running food banks.

There are a great many who say the presence of so many charities in the UK is a good thing, including their many chief executives and well-paid directors. And in the main, we are encouraged to view them as a positive indicator of Britain's can-do attitude and a healthy barometer on the state of our individual humanity and community cohesion. This is the view of the glass half-full types, often pragmatic and well-meaning if at times misguided and self-serving. To them the growing yawning cracks appearing in the foundation of our societies are the result of things occurring that are beyond anyone's control. To try and address the root causes of the shaking building would be too difficult. The ongoing era of austerity that followed the financial collapse of 2008, the cost-of-living crisis many are facing right now, which is the result of greed and failed policy, these are not things mere mortals can influence. The best thing we can all do is just keep calm and carry on, bend over and take it, and while we are at it hand out any loose change we may have in our pockets. Charities cheerily shake their buckets and increasingly apply modern media techniques and tele-marketing companies to tug on our heartstrings as they co-opt us into scraping up the shitty externalities that they tell us a universe beyond our understanding is throwing at us. Come on everyone, let's all wear a red nose to show that we accept the presence of hungry children in the UK in the 21st Century as inevitable. Charities unavoidably legitimize the presence of the issues they say they are on a mission to resolve. Can there be anything more perverse than pictures of smiling Tory MPs announcing the opening of food banks in their constituencies? What next, President Putin opening leisure centres for Ukrainian refugees?

Shaking buckets for dignified deaths:

There are over two hundred hospices in England alone, most of which rely heavily on funds raised by voluntary donations and legacies. Between them they provide care and support for more than three hundred thousand dying people and their families every year. I had the pleasure of meeting the manager of a hospice in the Midlands recently, a lovely lady from Birmingham with a warm black country accent that reminded me of the television puppet Hartley Hare from the children's show Pipkins. She told me that the hospice she runs needs to fundraise almost ten million pounds each year just to keep the lights on and pay all its overheads. That's around two hundred thousand pounds that needs finding each and every week. Hospices provide critical end of life care on their premises and increasingly in the community.

Would it surprise you if I told you that a sizeable proportion of the most emotionally demanding, physically complex, and clinically specialised palliative and end-of-life care provided in the UK is charitably funded. This care is made freely available through the network of hospices. Aside from The Sue Ryder Foundation and Marie Curie, who operate from multiple locations, the majority of the UK's hospices are run as independent charities. These rely on charitable donations from a range of sources including bucket shaking and grocery bagging in local communities, national fundraising initiatives, legacies, lotteries, corporate sponsors and supporters, and retail activity. Though the proportions of public funding available to hospices vary between the home countries, charitable sources account for the bulk of all hospice revenues with hospices typically receiving the remaining third of their total annual funding requirements from the NHS and the public purse. Some hospices provide specialist care for young children and teenagers, some solely for adults and some provide hospice care for all age ranges. They are equipped to meet an increasingly wide range of patient needs and multimorbidity's, neurological diseases and terminal illnesses, lung, heart, kidney conditions, and cancer. In 2021 their combined annual turnovers exceeded £1.6B. Prior to the pandemic hospices were providing inpatient care for over fifty thousand people each year and hospice at home services were supporting over three times that number of patients in their communities. The valuable and vital work of hospices impacts upon the life's, deaths, and lives of hundreds of thousands of people each year. Many hospices also provide a range of bereavement and pastoral support services for the families and loved ones of those who are in and have been in their care.

There is no meaningful statutory right to a dignified compassionate death for citizens of the UK. Some readers might note that following the numerous recent reports into the quality of many NHS maternity units there is no right to a safe birth either. No matter its method of funding, the quality of palliative or end-of-life care we and our loved ones can expect to receive is, like much of the health and care available to people in Britain today, a postcode lottery. Its quality and availability are the combined random sum of the wealth, the propensity and capacity for charitable giving within a given community, and the attitudes and priorities of local health and care commissioners. Hospices that operate in more well-off areas are typically if unsurprisingly better funded and resourced than those in areas of lower wealth and higher deprivation. Perversely, health and care commissioners in more deprived areas are also less likely to have the discretionary funds available within their budgets to distribute to local hospices as their resources are more likely to be fully committed propping up whatever struggling statutory health and care services are on their patch. It is a constant tension in our health and care system that the deprived areas typically in need of more funding to support the voluntary services needed in their communities, are less likely to be able to access it from the overstretched budgets of local health and care commissioners. Access to good quality hospice care is patchy and inconsistent. Hospice UK, the body that represents the interests of the hospice sector in Britain, estimate that less than half the number of people and their families who could benefit from expert end of life care, will receive support from an appropriate hospice service.

Though the presence of a charitably funded network of hospices highlights a gaping hole in the UK's publicly funded healthcare, one of the sectors undeniable achievements is that it has well and truly busted the myth that locally focused charitable organisations are somehow less able to provide high quality, clinically complex professional services in a highly regulated operating environment. Hospices are subject to the same regulatory scrutiny as NHS Trusts and hospital settings and many hospices consistently receive higher quality ratings from the Care Quality Commission than their statutorily funded NHS Acute and Community Hospital counterparts. These third sector providers, many of whom rely on a cadre of committed volunteers and whose board members supply their services and ability without cost, have become an essential and significant part of the UK's health and care system. The dedicated and often highly skilled people, nurses, clinicians, and support staff who work in the hospice sector offer a wonderful example of the professionalism and good practice that is possible in a health and care service.

Much more importantly than the random sometimes arbitrary ratings of the Care Quality Commission, are the comments and feedback hospices receive from patients and their families. The incredible worth and enduring significance of knowing that those most precious to us were able to die a dignified death in as caring, compassionate, and comfortable a setting as possible, cannot be underestimated. For many of us the loss of a loved one becomes an increasingly significant and unforgettable moment of truth as we age. A poignant emotive point in time and a peg on which we hang myriad recollections. The rationalizations or regrets we might harbour regarding the actions and decisions we and those around us made at a pivotal point in our lives will stay with us in perpetuity. We hold onto these defining moments for the rest of our days. We are given them whether we ask for them or not. I have seen and felt the palpable release of stress a family has experienced, the tears of relief they cried when they were told a bed had become available for their dying mother at the Eden Valley Hospice in North Cumbria. The reputation of NHS acute services in North Cumbria is such that few would want their loved ones to die there. In fact, the local hospitals track record of providing poor care is so firmly established that many families will do everything they can to ensure their loved ones are not even referred for treatment there; many enter, not all return.

If it seems unfair of me to compare the quality of services provided by a hospice with those of an NHS hospital, that perhaps hospices can give better care because they are small and fleet of foot and that large systems gets in the way of providing compassionate person-centred care, then I would ask you to consider if it is genuinely unreasonable to expect a nations publicly funded health service to be as good as, if not better, than its charitably funded counterparts? I don't think it is.

A nation of beggars and givers:

The charity sector, often referred to as the voluntary or third sector is unsurprisingly in the wake of growing and obvious inequality, growing globally and exponentially. Increasing numbers of what are also called social enterprises are being set up in almost every nation. It is now one of the largest employment sectors in Britain and the United States. A report published in 2022 by the British Council in partnership with Social Enterprise UK, suggests there are approximately eleven-million social enterprises across the world. The third sector in America presently employs as many people as manufacturing, over twelve million and the UK has one of the most proactive charitable sectors in the world. The one hundred and fifty thousand voluntary organisations that make up Britain's third sector are thought to contribute nearly twenty billion pounds to the economy each year and between them employ almost a million people. Whatever you choose to call it, the voluntary, third, or social enterprise sector, it is a growing global presence. While many view the rude health of the third sector as a positive thing, I don't think it's a statistic any developed nation should be proud of. The presence of a thriving charity sector is an indicator of inequality and unmet need within society. It is in large part no more than a direct reflection of the serious levels of failure demand that exist all around us. Need is a fast-flowing flood of dirty untreated water we misguidedly think we can tame and cleanse just before it enters the sea rather than dealing with its sources upstream.

The UK's public services increasingly depend on charity. In some ways it feels as if we are heading back toward the Victorian era in which the shrinking state is retreating and gifting the needs of the less fortunate to our collective personal philanthropy. Our health and social care system, parts of the economy, and many of our communities and neighbourhoods, would quite literally crumble into varying states of dysfunctional chaos and terminal decay if each and every charity in the country were to close its doors at once. Ambulance operators would be run ragged if the many patient transport services provided by volunteers decided to shut shop. Cancer services would implode were it not for the work of charities like Macmillan Cancer Support and Marie Curie. The palliative wards of hospitals would be utterly unable to cope without the extensive network of charitably funded hospices that exist throughout the UK. And accident and emergency departments and mental health services would be overwhelmed, their wards crammed beyond comprehension if the charities that provide suicide prevention and mental health support services to the citizens of the UK were to cease operations. The Samaritans, Mind, Rethink Mental Illness, Young Minds, Student Minds, Place2Be, Together for Mental Wellbeing, and Calm, to name but a few. These are all charitable bodies that between them deal with millions of requests for help each year and support hundreds of thousands of people to stay afloat amidst the madness we call modern life, each and every month. And demand for their services is, unsurprisingly, growing. And if the charities providing help and support for those with physical needs decided to call it a day, the UK would be swept up shit creek faster than an MP chasing an outstanding expense claim.

In 2021 Macmillan Cancer Support engaged with nearly two and a half million people affected by cancer, supported over a hundred thousand people through a dedicated support line, and helped tens of thousands deal with the financial implications of their condition. Macmillan cancer support is now such an integral part of the health and care landscape here in the UK that it trains health and care professionals and many of its staff are embedded in NHS Trusts. Then add Action for Children, Age UK, Alzheimer's Society, Barnardo's, British Heart Foundation, Children in Need, Crisis, Fire Fighters Charity, Help for Heroes, Leonard Cheshire Disability, RNIB, RNID, Hearing Dogs for Deaf People, Shelter, Sue Ryder, The Stroke Association, Parkinson's UK, Children with Cancer UK, Teenage Cancer Trust, the various regional Air Ambulance Trusts, and the many, many thousands of other national, regional, local, and community-based charities into the mix and it quickly becomes clear that Britain has become a nation dependent on charity. And then of course there are the food banks situated across the country, apparently now twice as many of them exist than McDonald's outlets. Some are even situated in hospitals providing help directly to NHS employees.

Of the three legs sometimes regarded as necessary to prop up the seat of a functioning society, the private, public and third sectors, the UK's charitable third sector seems to be bearing a disproportionate amount of the weight right now. In fairness it has been doing so for some years, but its presence and the need for its services have been amplified by a pandemic, a cost-of-living crisis, and decades of inept government. According to the Charities Aid Foundation, Britons gave almost thirteen billion pounds to charities in 2022. That's almost as much as the UK's entire and seemingly omnipresently promoted fast-food sector. Charity is big business.

A nation of takers:

In such a cluttered fragmented and often overlapping organisational landscape, there is a great deal of inefficiency and as in every field of human endeavour, no shortage of self-interest. In 2022 I resigned from the unpaid role I had held with Eden Carers. I felt the organisation I was chairing and the behaviour of the voluntary sector itself, was becoming so self-serving and fecklessly frustratingly unchallenging, that it was unwittingly becoming a large part of the problem. In its efforts to please its funders and paymasters, the voluntary sector is replicating the self-perpetuating and largely pointless practices of the public sector, and I didn't want to be part of that. The carers charity I was involved with directly employed around a dozen people and coordinated the activity of a number of volunteers who gave their time and effort for nothing. I think charitable organisations operating in the health and social care sectors naturally attract a large cohort of people who want to do work that makes a difference. And the staff I met and chatted with from Eden Carers were no different to the staff of other voluntary organisations I had worked with during my time as a small business advisor. They displayed a strong sense of purpose, they wanted to as great a degree as possible, to add value to the world rather than be financially successful in the more traditional and in my view increasingly anachronistic if unfortunately, necessary economic sense. Such values centred people are becoming more and more ill-suited to working in charitable organisations that are increasingly being forced by their funders to adopt a public sector style tick-box approach to their work. This target chasing box ticking mentality had been pragmatically if uncourageously adopted by the management of my local carers charity in an effort to satisfy its main funder, the local authority. But the institutional and innovatively restrictive approach to working this created was visibly eroding the good will and camaraderie in the charity's small workforce. Competent staff were leaving. The problem with recruitment and retention became so bad that discussions about the constant turnover of employees was almost a standing agenda item at board meetings. To see this ongoing exodus of disillusioned staff in such a small business was thoroughly depressing.

The carers charity I was part of is just one of many thousands of small charities spread across the UK that are in theory at least, attempting to fill the gaps left by the orchestrated retreat of statutory publicly funded services from Britain's debt-laden, misery-stained battlefields of inequality and injustice. But the reality is that the charities and voluntary organisations who make up what is often collectively referred to as the third sector, third sector meaning neither purely private and commercial, nor statutorily publicly funded, are a patchwork quilt of inconsistency, waste, and unchallenging unhealthy acquiescence.

Their awkward presence in our world of plenty stands like a strange statue with two distinct sides and faces. One side looks earnestly, deeply, unnervingly, and challengingly, into all our souls, wagging a firm pointed finger at the inherent and obvious inability of capitalism to display humanity as globalism reneges yet again on its disingenuous cross-fingered promise to serve us all. The other hand of the same side of the statue reaches out, needy and open as it simultaneously offers us atonement and self-assurance. The opposite side and face of the statue looks on at the societal carnage unfolding all around it with a curious mix of uncertainty and coy opportunism. There is cash in chaos and the increasing lack of capacity and capability in public services to address the issues many are facing is a commercial opportunity for the savvier third sector operators. Few if any charities are run by unambitious unselfish saints. After all, as C.S Lewis noted, the logical goal of a truly selfless charity would be to see the end of the need it was created to address and thereby make itself redundant. How many charities do you know that have done that?

Eden Carers was one of five different carers support organisations that formed a wider network of carer support services across Cumbria. The duplication they embodied is a microcosm of a much larger national issue. These five different charities supplied services on behalf of one local authority within the terms of a single contract. They did this from five different locations, with five different chief executives and salaries, with five different office managers, five different pension schemes, five different sets of contact details, phone numbers and email addresses, five different ways of doing things, five separate annual risk-assessments and governance requirements, five accountants and auditors, five different and not insubstantial levels of cash reserves, and five different websites designed and updated by five different suppliers, you get the gist! This fragmentation and duplication effectively offers the worst of all worlds to everyone, the public purse, the employees, other than the senior executives, and the people they purport to serve. Their small size which is less a reflection of niche specialism and largely a product of a continued focus on self-perpetuation at almost any cost, not only stands in the way of achieving meaningful economies of scale and simultaneously confusing the hell out of service users, but it precludes each of the organisations in question from developing their people and providing consistent and consistently high-quality services. It also robs them of the strategic capacity and ambition to develop innovative ways to better meet the needs of their service users. The stock response by such organisations to the observations I have just made would be to say that one size won't fit all and that they are each individually structured to meet the unique and specific needs of the people in the communities they serve. This is, to get all technical on you for a moment, total and utter bollocks, and equates to nothing more than a plea to tolerate mediocrity, value inconsistency, and continue to pay for obviously duplicated resources.

The uncomfortable truth that finally swung my decision to resign as the charity's chairperson, was that most of the well-intentioned money that was finding its way into the buckets shaken by the shivering selfless volunteers who fundraise to support the charity, was merely perpetuating the unnecessary overheads needed to keep the organisation and its senior staff in the manner to which they had become accustomed and adding to a growing pile of already significant financial reserves. The combined salaries and pension contributions of the five chief executives of the carers support bodies in Cumbria was around three hundred thousand pounds per annum at the last count. And each individual charity was sitting on hundreds of thousands of pounds in reserves. Along with the ceaseless churn in staff, the agenda item discussed most frequently at meetings of the trustees was which bank the charity should open another account with to minimize the risk of losing its reserves by having all its financial eggs in one basket. Talk of how to squirrel funds away and fortify the empire took priority over talk of how to spend money on people in need who might really benefit from it.

Ground control to Major Tom:

You might remember the Tesco Christmas advert of 2020. The company drew on the ongoing challenges the nation was facing due to Covid-19 and adopted the appealing strapline, *Tesco says there is no naughty list this year*. The advert used humour to highlight and excuse all the things that people had done during the pandemic. It contained a collection of people drawn from selected demographics, with one admitting to buying far too much loo roll, a parent who admitted not teaching her kids at home, and a bearded man apologising for not washing his hands for long enough. The only bad behaviour that the advert made an exception of, was a young man who admitted in a quiet ashamed voice that he had not donated, to Captain Tom. He then redeemed himself by explaining that he had arranged a charity bake off and once again all was well in the world.

For anyone who doesn't know the strange tale of Captain Tom, those recovering from a coma or perhaps just landing from another planet, Captain, now Sir Thomas Moore, was an elderly gentleman who decided he would raise funds for the NHS during the pandemic by walking a hundred laps around his garden before his hundredth birthday on April 30th, 2020. The collective madness which subsequently unfolded was bizarre and disturbing, a classic case-study in media fuelled groupthink. Captain Tom's actions were firstly publicized to the local press and small-scale social media. Then in what seemed like the blink of an eye, they were seized upon by the mainstream media and politicians from all parties who were desperately seeking a good news story and a worthy hero to uphold. Tom, cuddly, ambling, unassuming, modest, Werther's chewing Tom, was turned into a totem, a shining sanctified beacon of hope and positively. To be seen with him or to talk positively about him became an indicator of worthiness. Here, in the midst of an unprecedented international crisis and a nations despair, was an inspirational good news story featuring a charming decorated ex-veteran who appeared to be displaying the kind of spirit, grit, and noble charitable intention that personify the bulldog with a heart spirit which many Brits believe is embedded deep within their DNA. Cor blimey guvnor, it's enough to bring a tear to yer eye innit, parss me vee ankies will ya.

A powerful spell had been cast upon the people. If someone had dared step forward to declare they were Captain Toms former lover or revealed an estranged love child, they would have been burned at the stake or stoned by the public live on GMTV. The nation watched, enthralled each day, as Captain Tom walked his ten daily laps of the garden moving slowly but steadily closer to his goal. And as he did so the fundraising tally skyrocketed faster than the total on a prepay gas meter. Spurred on by the press the publics donations exploded beyond anything that he or anyone could have imagined. At one point the JustGiving website, the online platform being used to collect donations was said to be struggling to handle the volume of traffic and financial transactions his fundraising page was generating. A kind of collective madness had gripped the country in which nobody was allowed to criticise what was unfolding in full view of everyone. Nobody asked what the NHS charities were, or why they were indeed even needed. Captain Tom spoke loosely and vaguely about his efforts being all about the nurses, how they were doing such a magnificent job and how they deserved every penny of whatever funds he could raise. The BBC talked of Captain Toms service record and spoke of his steely determination. Piers Morgan referred to him as a national hero in our darkest hour since WWII. Any vestiges of real or even curious journalism that were left in the UK died a very public and painfully sycophantic death as reporter after reporter dutifully lined-up to film and interview the UK's newest hero or talk with members of his close family.

On 16th April 2020, as Captain Tom entered the final ten laps of his journey, soldiers from the 1st Yorkshire Battalion were present to form a guard of honour. Shortly afterwards he then became the oldest person to top the UK singles chart as he and Michael Ball released a rendition of, You'll Never Walk Alone. And in July 2020 he received a knighthood from the Queen in the grounds of Windsor Castle. Sir Toms place in history is secure, he is a household name.

Captain Tom had apparently started his stroll around the garden with the aim of raising one thousand pounds for NHS charities. The final amount he raised is believed to be more than thirty-eight million pounds. It was so significant that a new organisation was formed to manage and distribute the funds. The Captain Tom Foundation was incorporated at Companies House on 05th May 2020. Most of the money raised was committed to an organisation called the Association of NHS Charities. More widely known as NHS Charities Together, they are a network of over two hundred charities that work with NHS services, and are sometimes based in hospitals, mental health, acute, community, and ambulance Trusts across the UK. They undertake a range of functions including refurbishing and enhancing hospital facilities, consultation suites, patient and family waiting areas, and staff rooms. They also fund the purchase of equipment and technology and pay for things like patient transport services. The NHS Charities Together website says they exist to help the NHS go further, which seems like a subtle way of saying they use charitable donations to plug the gaps in public funding and make up for the incredible levels of waste and overpaid managerial duplication that eats a sizeable proportion of NHS budgets. I recall how NHS directors and managers in Cumbria would beg for money from the various Hospital

League of Friends charities to improve facilities in the local hospitals, while at the same time the Trust was sat on tens of millions of pounds. Why spend your own organisations reserves when there is charity you can take the money from instead. The accounts of NHS Charities Together at the end of 2021 showed they had just over eighty-five million pounds in the bank. In the same year they spent almost a million pounds on advertising and marketing, over half a million on contractors, agency staff, legal and professional fees, and paid nearly half a million pounds a year in salaries to four key management personnel. Nice work if you can get it.

To put the enormous amount that Captain Tom raised in context, it's almost enough to pay the litigation and compensation costs for a decent sized NHS Trust for a year and half; North Cumbria University Hospital's Trust paid out over £28 million in damages in the financial year ending March 2019. In the same year, its chief executive Stephen Eames was awarded a CBE for services to the NHS. Stephen, who told the local press in 2018 that although he earned a quarter of a million pounds a year, he was a noble public-spirited soul as he had not taken a pay rise in three years, was clearly deserving of his award. Alternatively, Captain Tom's efforts could have funded around five percent of the money apparently wasted on procuring unfit PPE equipment from questionable companies linked to members of the Conservative party. Captain Tom would be delighted. So, while the politicians applauded Captain Toms efforts, some were shamelessly engaged in less than charitable activities of their own. I suppose charity does begin at home, it just seems that if you're a member of the Tory party, it ends there as well. But politicians will be politicians, and we really must stop expecting them to behave morally.

The UK's affection for Captain Tom has not dissipated, he was after all a likeable old codger who enjoyed a trundle around the lawn, and in fairness having seen how some members of his family have behaved following his death he probably wanted to spend as much time out the house during lockdown as he could. But while our affection may endure, our faith in what he achieved was seriously dented when in June 2022 the Charity Commission announced it was opening an inquiry into the affairs of the Captain Tom Foundation. Having started looking into the charity's dealings in March 2021, the UK charity regulator decided there were further grounds for attention. In its first year of operating the charity spent more on management costs than it gave away in grants. It then tried to appoint a family member as its Chief Executive on a salary of one hundred thousand pounds. Charity really does start at home doesn't it.

Charity is playing an increasing role in our society. And charities that are well run have a lot to teach our publicly funded health and care services. But though they may save our collective conscience by picking up the pieces and dealing with the messy human issues we have learned or been conditioned to walk past, our reliance on bucket shakers, local lotteries, and the fickle goodwill of those with income to spare, is not a sustainable solution to dealing with the systemic challenges facing society.

PART VIII:

Safe in Whose Hands?

Chapter 33: **If Carlsberg did healthcare**

"Everything in moderation, including moderation."

Oscar Wilde

At the start of the millennium, and on the off chance the human race has survived, and this book has stood the test of time I should make it clear I mean the third millennium, the global beer brewing giant Carlsberg decided it needed to reinvigorate its much maligned and infamous Special Brew brand of beer. Over the years Carlsberg Special Brew had taken on legendary status as the preferred choice of closet alcoholics, a source of central heating for tramps, and the ingredient in many a stand-up comedians routine. Its acquired acrid taste and strange texture, somewhere between fizzy marmite and liquidised charcoal, and its high alcoholic strength of 9%, not dissimilar to a decent German pudding wine, had made the brand synonymous with alcoholic excess and brown paper bag style drinking. However, the brand was an incredibly stable and profitable seller and while Carlsberg were conscious of its impact on their lower strength less liver damaging brands, they quite understandably did not want to distance themselves from the significant profits the product was generating. So, the marketing gurus decided to do some research to help them understand the profile of Special Brew consumers.

To their great delight, they discovered that the very same product which was the source of so much derision and mirth was actually the chosen tipple for a good number of the nation's General Practitioners. It seemed that the UK's lovable local doctor liked nothing more than to relax at the end of a busy day with a glass of Special Brew. Armed with this newly acquired behavioural insight the advertising and research agency excitedly called the marketing bods at Carlsberg and a new promotional campaign for Special Brew was born. The brand would henceforth be promoted under the humble claim of being nothing less than, The Beer of the Gods. A series of campaign posters were created with images of frolicking Greek Gods brandishing cans of Special Brew and presumably well on their way to being shit-faced above the strapline, The Beer of the Gods - Probably the Most Special Brew in this World or Any Other. The message was clear, Special Brew was no longer a dirty secret to be drunk from brown paper bags or sipped furtively behind closed doors, it was the unashamed beer of choice for the intelligent, the erudite, the enlightened, and the respected.

Unfortunately, what Carlsberg had not researched or perhaps chosen not to think too much about, was that rates of breakdown, self-harm, and suicide amongst General Practitioners were at that time some of the highest in the UK. Rising workloads, changes in the structure of healthcare, and increased complexity in their caseloads had created intolerable conditions for many GPs working in small or single-handed practices, some of whom were tragically choosing to end their own lives. The Beer of the Gods was in reality a mental crutch for all those overworked GPs who simply could not face yet another visit from one of the worried well, who having watched Gillian McKeith extol the virtues of colonic irrigation on television the previous night would ring the practice at 8am in the morning insisting on an unnecessary rectal examination to allay their unfounded fears of imminent death. Special Brew was the tipple of choice for the desperate and the depressed. Not such a great advertising strapline I'll grant you.

Aside from its questionable marketing research methods and its well-pricked place on the World Health Organisations dartboard of organisations it would like to destroy, there is much that the world of health and care as well as the wider public sector could learn from Carlsberg and many other large corporations like it.

I was thirty years old when I joined Carlsberg at the end of summer 1998, I was inducted as part of a group of new employees. There were around a dozen of us who had been hired into various different roles and we came from a diverse mix of industries. I got the sense Carlsberg wanted to hire people who would bring something new to the table. The company made no secret of its view that the future of brewing in the UK would be hugely different to the past. The era of the organisational dinosaurs, the job for life regardless of performance, the boozy lunches, and the inflated expense accounts that had typified the British brewing industry up to that point, was ending. The induction process and the content was quite simply superb, I still draw on some of the learning I acquired during my induction. Sadly, it was the polar opposite of my induction experience into the NHS ten years later. I had never worked for a high-profile global blue-chip corporation before and the attention

Carlsberg paid to me and my fellow newbies was designed to allay our concerns, to make us feel like valued members of a team and a part of something larger than ourselves.

Between 1998 and 2003, the UK and the wider world's brewing industry was going through an unprecedented and turbulent period of restructuring. The process of global consolidation was gathering pace and the size and financial scale of the acquisitions each of the big players in the market was prepared to make were eye-watering. In 2001 Coors Brewing of America bought Bass Brewery in a deal worth $2Billion. The distinctive red triangle of Bass was an iconic UK brand. Dating back to 1777, it is thought to be the world's oldest trademark of any product type. The formerly stable world of brewing was being rocked to its core, and Carlsberg, like its competitors, realised it needed to both develop and execute a first-rate strategy if it was going to survive and thrive in an increasingly competitive globalised marketplace. One of the key areas the organisation realised it needed to focus on was its IT infrastructure. It had acquired numerous regional and international brewers who had their own IT systems and Carlsberg wanted to standardise its technology to enable it to manage its global supply chains more efficiently and enable its customer facing operations to be more effective and responsive.

To achieve its goals the company decided to implement an IT solution from a company called SAP, a German firm and one of the world's leading providers of such solutions. I remember the launch of the internal communications campaign at which all employees were being informed about the decision. The local briefing that I attended was held at a Carlsberg distribution depot situated on a small industrial estate on the edge of the picturesque town of Kendal. The briefing had been well researched and was I think brilliantly executed. A very personable middle-aged man called David who had driven up from Northampton the previous evening set the scene. His audience included the draymen who delivered the products, the installation and cellar maintenance teams, the depot managers, and my colleagues and I from the sales and investment team. David explained the rationale for the new IT infrastructure that was coming and which everyone would eventually have to work with. He seemed to hold no knowledge back, talking openly, explaining the global picture, and describing the perfect storm of increasing financial pressures on the business and changing consumption habits that were coming. He shared the organisations thinking about what the future landscape of the sector might look like. His presentation raised a lot of questions and he proactively invited and encouraged queries, concerns, and thoughts from everyone present.

Though he wasn't in the least bit domineering, David left everyone in that room that day in no doubt the future was coming towards us all at a rapid pace, and change was needed. Our world was in flux and new systems and ways of working had to be introduced to address the fresh challenges facing us and capitalise on the emerging opportunities that would arise. Leaders had chosen a strategy. The direction of travel had been set. The company would now sink or swim on the basis of this and other decisions made by people in positions of responsibility. Intelligent people, carefully selected, hired, paid, and expected to take such decisions. At no point during the decision-making process or the rollout and implementation phase did anyone senior within Carlsberg say, *"if you don't think this new system will work for you or meet your needs, then don't worry, just continue to do your own sweet thing, and everything will be fine."* The message was clear, you are welcome to stay on the bus and we will do everything possible to equip you for the journey, or you can hop off and find another bus without any hard feelings. The leaders of the organisation had chosen a path, they had made decisions, and for better or worse had set a course which everyone would be expected to follow. The decision-making process and the style of leadership in Carlsberg and across much of the wider private sector is the polar opposite to the public sector, especially the NHS.

The NHS's inability to make decisions and implement strategies is internationally recognised. About five years ago, I had the opportunity to speak with a Finnish health minister who had been involved in the adoption and use of technology across many of Finland's health and care services including its ambulance service. To ensure that patients even in remote and rural areas, of which Finland has many, could receive the best care possible, the ambulance fleet was being equipped with technology that would allow ambulance crews to view patient records, monitor a patients' condition, and access, enter, and share information onto a shared care record while in transit. They were light years ahead of the UK. I asked the minister what she thought was the key to choosing and implementing the right technology. She replied, *"Someone has to make a decision, and in your country, nobody seems willing to."* Sometimes others see us more clearly than we can see ourselves.

During the time I worked for Carlsberg I was able to plug my laptop computer into any suitable network and almost instantly it would be updated with the latest data. I and my colleagues could see which accounts had bought and paid for what, down to the smallest bottles of pop and cases of mixers to the largest barrels of lager and ale. The company had staked its global future on implementing the sort of technology infrastructure that would enable it to accurately monitor and understand its own business, to reveal trends and the type and frequency of demand for its products at any point in time. Businesses in the private sector, large and small, understand that the presence and availability of useful data is inextricably linked to the presence of functioning technology infrastructure. If you want data in the 21st century, you need functioning information technology infrastructure.

I left Carlsberg in Spring 2003, admittedly slightly heavier than when I had joined. I had spent an interesting and hugely enjoyable five years working as a New Business and Investment Manager in the Northwest of England. At its most engaging and best, my role entailed developing business investment plans and forecasts with experienced savvy operators who wanted to loan money from the brewery to create a new outlet or expand an existing licensed premises. At its worst, it was arguing with the half-pissed members of the John Street Catholic Social Club committee on a rainy Wednesday evening in Workington over the price of a barrel of mild. Carlsberg were good to me. I was encouraged to create and become involved in national initiatives, the company supported me financially with the final year of my MBA and placed me on their accelerated leadership programme. I chose to leave Carlsberg in the wake of a restructure which would have meant moving to the UK head office in Northampton if I was to progress my career. I have nothing against Northampton, but it's not the Eden Valley where the people I know, love, and want to be around are.

Chapter 34: Learning from the private sector

"Weighing benefits against costs is the way most people make decisions and the way most businesses make decisions if they want to stay in business. Only in government is any benefit, however small, considered to be worth any cost, however large."

Thomas Sowell

In its simplest stripped-down form, the NHS and the wider health and care sector is a business that supplies two products which create manifold benefits. These products are services and information. Because the benefits it provides are defined by the people, the patients and service users who access its services, the families, communities, and societies they are part of, the businesses they often work in and the organisations they may support, they are so vast and often as ethereal as they are vital that they are impossible to summarise. We may capture the data that tells us how many operations a hospital has undertaken, but how do we measure the joy each patient experiences on receiving extra years of life or assess the relief a person feels when they are told they are ok, or the depth of the despair that grips them when they are told they are not. Healthcare is at heart a services business and as such there is a great deal it could learn from the many private and third sector companies who successfully supply services to thousand, millions, and sometimes billions of customers locally, regionally, nationally and globally.

The intransigent arrogance and unwillingness of the NHS and publicly funded health and care services to look for and learn lessons from other sectors has allowed a succession of seemingly intelligent leaders and senior managers to effectively burn our public services in front of our eyes while warming their own hands over the flames. The rife and glaringly obvious incompetence, ineptitude and short-sightedness that typifies what has been allowed to pass for leadership and management in the NHS for the last thirty years and more, has brought the service to the point of crisis that it, and in turn we in the UK, are now so clearly facing. Just as many of us have become understandably wary of the career politicians that have come to dominate parliament, I believe we should all be wary of people who have made their careers in public service yet who have never strayed beyond its boundaries. A desk has always been a dangerous place from which to view the world. And a desk in a publicly funded ivory tower isolated from the realities of life and from which the wider view is only of someone else sitting at the same height in a neighbouring publicly funded ivory tower, is nothing less than a recipe for disaster.

Amongst the many things I learned from my time in the private sector, especially at the sharp end of sales, is that as far as the company you work for is concerned you are only as good as your results, the tangible quantifiable value you add to the organisation. The organisation you work for can and should treat you with dignity, but it doesn't owe you a living. And the customer is the one who ultimately pays your wage. No customers means no revenue and no revenue means no pay. Some of this may seem incredibly obvious as well as slightly mercenary, and as with every sweeping statement it should be interpreted according to context. But every organisation, whether it be a shareholder owned global behemoth, or an employee run cooperative, has a responsibility to its stakeholders to sustain itself. To hold onto ineffective and inefficient practices is irresponsible and to shield and accommodate unproductive or value destructive employees is not only unfair to those who are productive, it precludes those who are willing and able, from the opportunity of gainful employment.

I regularly hear Chief Executives and senior directors from NHS Trusts, local authorities and housing associations comparing themselves to the leaders of FTSE 500 listed companies. I have to resist the temptation to throw my phone through the television screen or slap the front of the car radio. They complain bitterly when they are harangued in the media for poor performance or when they are criticised for taking substantial salaries and benefits from the public purse, while adding little if any value. The stock response of most publicly funded healthcare leaders appears to be to tell their interviewer that someone of their experience and seniority could easily get a much better paid job in the private sector. They then compare the number of employees they oversee with similar sized organisations from the private sector who pay their senior leaders substantially more. The message these highly paid administrators are keen to convey is that they represent good value for money and are in fact, underpaid not overpaid. The logic being that if they were in charge of a similar sized organisation in the private sector, they would be earning millions each year and acquiring lucrative stock options rather than receiving the measly two hundred thousand pounds a year they are currently being paid.

We are supposed to believe that senior figures in publicly funded health and care services only do what they do because they have a calling, because they are passionate about the field they work in. The reality of course is that most of them have risen above the level of their incompetence, and in truth they know they are onto a good thing, they wouldn't get a job in charge of a commercial company operating in a competitive environment if they tried. In fact, if a high-profile private sector company hired a former NHS or public sector chief executive as its new leader, its shareholders would question the mental health of those on the recruiting panel before selling their shares and swiftly investing the proceeds in the competition.

I've worked at many levels in a mixture of businesses. As a teenager I worked for a brand-new manufacturing micro start-up that quickly went global, for a brief period I shared an open-plan office with the billionaire founder of Phones4U in my early twenties, then I joined a small dysfunctional yet strangely enjoyable family firm in the telecoms sector, before leaving to work for Carlsberg. After that I became a project manager and small business advisor for almost a decade, just to clarify, that's giving advice to small businesses, not being small and advising businesses, and I was a Chartered Marketer for twenty years. I've been fortunate to meet and work with hundreds of business people, innovators, entrepreneurs, thought leaders and diligent managers from a broad range of businesses in many different industries. Over the years I have begun to understand the depth of my ignorance and gleaned a decent grasping of the basic principles of business. And having spent over a decade working in publicly funded organisations including the NHS and chairing a charity for five years, I have seen the differences between the private, public, and third sectors, and importantly, I understand the drivers that create these differences. The two chasms separating the private sector from the public and third sectors, are the presence of competition, and the power of consumers.

In 1979, a Harvard Business School Professor called Michael E Porter introduced a theory of business to the world that he labelled the five forces of competition. Porter was no Deming, and like many distinguished academics he had merely analysed and distilled the experiences and implicit knowledge that many leaders and managers in successful corporations already understood and were familiar with. But to his credit he joined the dots of his theory together remarkably lucidly, and presented the concept in an appealing way that could be easily taught and understood if not quite as easily addressed. Like any good business management theory, the value of the five forces model of analysis is in the questions it raises rather than the quick conclusions people may want to draw from it. Porter had reached the conclusion, one which has been tested and remains intact, that the competitive nature of an industry and its capacity for innovation are linked to the presence and relative strength of five forces that are universally present to some degree in all competitive marketplaces. These five forces are the relative power of the suppliers to an industry, the power of the consumer base, the presence and availability of substitute products or services, the threat of new entrants to the market, and the inherent competitive nature of the sector itself.

     For example, if you are a wholesale business selling do-it-yourself and home improvement supplies to tradesmen and the public and you can access your supplies from a choice of manufacturing sources, then your suppliers will compete for your custom, and you will benefit from favourable pricing. In relation to the power and spread of your consumer base, if your custom comes from a plethora of small trade accounts and do-it-yourself enthusiasts then these customers are unlikely to challenge your prices as they don't have the negotiating power to drive them down by demanding reductions. Your chosen pricing and profitability are then further influenced by the presence and availability of substitute products and the threat of new entrants into your marketplace, a marketplace which may become attractive to other significant competitors if good profits are seen to be available within it. In relation to the final factor, the inherent competitive nature of your industry, this is dictated by how crowded with competition your chosen marketplace is, how similar your products and services are to others and the degree to which they can be differentiated to stand out from your competitors. Steel brackets and countersunk woodscrews are after all, much of a muchness. This last point highlights the importance that organisations in the private sector place on developing innovations within their businesses as a means of creating competitive advantage and of the effort companies put into building brands as a way to increase custom and create profit by differentiating between otherwise similar, sometimes even identical products. Can the tomatoes in one tin really differ from those in a different coloured tin sat next to it on the same supermarket shelf? Are the blades in your razor that are made in Germany any better than blades made using the same processes and machinery in another country? I'm sat here writing with a hot mug of Marmite, well it's actually Aldi's own version of Marmite, yeast extract is yeast extract isn't it? I can't taste the difference.

Looking at any industry, business sector, or area of commerce through the lens of Porters five forces is a useful way of starting to identify and understand the forces at work in a given marketplace. Those that shape the current behaviour of organisations and consumers and those which might be influenced or manipulated to change the existing dynamics in the organisations favour. The purpose of Porters model is to help organisations find a position in their industry that can be profitably defended. It helps with the process of strategy formulation and the creation of competitive advantage. It is an established truism that the more an organisation understands about the behaviours and needs of its customers, the better it can meet them by the most effective efficient and profitable means. When applied to public services, the view through Porter's lens is particularly revealing. Contrast the presence of Porters five forces in competitive private sector marketplaces with the complete absence of these same forces in the arena in which public sector services are provided and the first thing that should quickly become apparent is that the absence of consumer-focused innovation in public sector services is not the product of organisational ineptitude, it is the entirely logical consequence of these organisations operating in competition free environments. Why commit resources to innovating and improve the offer to your consumers if these same consumers have no alternative source or choice of supply. Why even focus on the needs of your services consumers when they have no power to influence what you supply or how and when you choose to make it available?

When well-paid public sector executives compare themselves to highly paid private sector executives, they are either deluded, disingenuous, or genuinely ignorant of the different dynamics that define and dictate the conditions of their respective operating environments. I don't want competition in public services or private ownership of them.

Watching the unravelling of Thames Water is all the evidence any of us should need that the privatisation agenda that Thatcher promoted is a road to nowhere. When public services are run for private interest the public is exposed to the worst of all worlds, the avarice of shareholders and the inertia of monopoly. What would be useful to acknowledge and have a conversation about is how the gap in the effectiveness and efficiency of public services created by the absence of Porter's five forces can be addressed. What are the foundations of the business model we need to build sustainable effective and efficient public services on.

Chapter 35: The vital role of the press

"In England, the Press is more centralized, and the public more easily deceived than elsewhere."

George Orwell: Homage to Catalonia

The need for high quality journalism and impartial media channels has never been greater. There are a great many well-meaning commentators, think tanks, and membership bodies who hold strong opinions and agenda driven points of view on the state of Britain's health and care services, and the taxpayer's role in providing them. But by and large they speak from within their silos and represent the interests of the actors in the system as it currently stands. They sidestep and ignore the bigger issues that need addressing. If improvement begins with understanding, then the debate about the present state and the future of publicly funded health and care in Britain, and the rest of the world, needs informed impassioned imaginative people, who will bring insight, realism, and aspiration to the table. People who are unafraid to highlight the links between the impact of unchecked political ideologies and the health and wellbeing of their fellow human beings. We need influencers engaging with and through the media at every level who are prepared to challenge the narrative that the health and care system can be fixed in isolation and who are able to expand the scope of the conversation. The present state of journalism in the UK, especially the apologist passive style the BBC has adopted, is a long way off the pace. Good investigative journalism is a scarce resource. A media landscape of George Monbiot's, perhaps with a touch of Roy Lilley's court jester humour, would be a good start.

In my earlier work I referred to a superb book written by an author called Nick Davies. First published in 2008, Flat Earth News remains an excellent, contemporary, and highly readable expose on the declining state of the British media. I also suggested that we are living in what many call a post-truth era by which I think they mean a post-honesty era. An age in which we seem drawn to people who lie politely over those who swear honestly. Fake news and finely polished bullshit are now the norm. And it is still my view that ably resourced good quality investigative journalists who set out to get under the skin of the issues that really matter, have become an endangered species. The role of a well-resourced functioning press, able to speak truth to power, is an incredibly important element in a functioning democracy. Whoever owns and influences the media controls the collective mind of the people. In the decade since Flat Earth News was published, hundreds more local and regional newspapers have closed and what news media channels are left, whether press, TV, or radio, have been paired to the bone to survive. This is not good news for anyone wanting to live in a society built on trust where transparency is the norm. Though the internet provides opportunities for individuals to be heard and social media revelations will increasingly have their place, there is no substitute for a well-resourced press willing and able to stand toe-to-toe with vested interests, and that has the will and ability to identify and highlight the issues of our time we should all be aware of, and hold the public institutions we pay for, to account.

Because the ability of the press to locate and investigate the important issues affecting us has been decimated. We now exist in a climate more conducive to flawed decision making, cover-ups, corruption, nepotism, poor and even dangerous practices in our public sector services, than at any other stage in our recent history. Yet conversely in times of increasing austerity when demands on people's finances are more than they have been in living memory, the temptation to cut corners, the hiding of mistakes to preserve personal status, and the committing of crime for personal gain become significantly greater. A country in which there is less and less capacity to scrutinise the unscrupulous, combined with a population subjected to extreme financial pressure is not a good combination. If you are the senior manager of a public sector service earning significantly more than your ability would earn you elsewhere, with a good size mortgage, university fees to pay, a status symbol car to maintain and a large safe pension pot to look forward to, will you be the one to blow the whistle on financial irregularities, unsafe practices, sexual abuse or unexplained deaths occurring on your watch?

We are effectively living on the edge, if not already in, a dystopian spin doctors' dream in which no one seems able to hold anyone to account for anything anymore, and few of us have the time or inclination to care. We quickly forget yesterday's lies as each new day brings forth more bullshit for us to wade through. Boris's Lockdown parties and now his WhatsApp messages, Matt Hancock's unevidenced spouting's that care homes were having a protective ring thrown around them, whatever that was supposed to mean, Herd Immunity, and a Brexit Bus that suggested leaving the EU would free up hundreds of millions of pounds that could be spent on the NHS, ringing any bells yet?

The substantial loss of effectively resourced press capacity in the UK means many local papers and radio stations, including the BBCs regional networks, are unable to supply anything other than basic levels of news coverage to increasingly time poor, distracted and apparently insouciant audiences more animated by online spats between footballer's wives than gaping and destructive social injustices. Worryingly, much of our local press is now so stretched for content to fill the pages of its increasingly thin editions, it has become entirely dependent on the asinine news releases that stream like cheap confetti from the public relations teams, the bullshit departments of our public sector services. Many of the public relations and communication departments of NHS Trusts are now staffed by former journalists, plucked from amongst the rubble of what is left of local media. These gamekeepers turned poacher who have experience of what news outlets look for in a story and with existing contacts inside the press are welcomed enthusiastically by publicly funded services desperate to manage their reputations. And most of the articles and press releases they submit often go unchecked by editors and are then reprinted and broadcast exactly as they were submitted; unscrutinised and unquestioned. This means that where it suits them, the spin doctors in our public services can exploit an incapacitated press to spread rose-tinted messages of success. Sometimes in deliberate efforts to divert public attention from something less savoury. This constant unchallenged stream of unicorn fluff has become the sandwich filling for much of our local media. Our local papers and TV channels are effectively held together by unedited public sector propaganda and fatuous feel-good stories.

Perversely, the press and media's growing reliance on large swathes of content from the very organisations they should be holding to account, means these same channels are not only unable to challenge, but they are also increasingly unwilling. In Cumbria in recent years, the local press has been more absorbed in tales about the difficulties of car-parking outside the hospitals than the unnecessary deaths occurring in them, and the astronomical levels of compensation being paid out as a result. The uncovering of the most significant healthcare tragedies and scandals of the 21st Century throughout the UK has so far been largely down to the efforts and tenacity of harmed patients and the loved ones of those killed. It has had little to do with an increasingly impotent and cowed press.

The dark art of propaganda:

In the presently accelerating era of austerity, we entered almost fifteen years ago and the resulting relentless and undeniable demise of public services, many of which needed significant improvement before the economy crashed, has been eased and enabled by the rise of the role of public relations. Spin over substance has become a surrogate for performance and impact. The importance the practitioners of the dark art of spin have to their paymasters is huge. For any group of senior executives wishing to hold onto their well-paid publicly funded jobs, while pleasing their political overlords and feeding them the messages and soundbites they crave, and simultaneously running their organisations within shrinking inadequate budgets, keeping those pesky regulators off their back, and managing their reputations in the eyes of the public they are paid to serve, they must become better and better at reporting on the less and less they are able to do. The answer to the problem of how to continue to provide good quality public services when the odds are so clearly stacked against you is not to challenge or point out the obvious to your overlords, it is to become brilliant at documenting the sweet nothing you are doing. Public relations is *the* tool of choice that enables poorly functioning organisations and the executive tasked with leading them to create the illusion they are successfully holding all their plates in the air.

A well-resourced communication department and savvy public relations practitioner have been must-have accessories for street-smart executives in public sector organisations for some years now. When it comes to celebrating success without being honest about the all too often avoidable mistakes they make, the NHS has read and memorised the illusionists' guide to life. It is this contrast between what public sector bodies want to be seen as, versus the reality of how they behave behind closed doors that causes much of the mistrust and anger between them and the families of service-users they have failed.

Public organisations talk of compassion and values in their press releases and in their annual reports, yet they are anything but in their day-to-day dealings. They talk of being listening organisations who value the opinions of their staff and service users but seem happiest running round with their fingers in their ears ignoring the people who work for them and fund them. Despite years and years of us all being constantly reassured that the insular defensive cultures in our NHS are being addressed and that lessons have been learned. A release in June 2023 from Dr Jayne Chidgey-Clark, National Speak Up Guardian for the NHS, suggests fewer NHS employees now feel comfortable speaking up and that staff increasingly feel that raising issues in their workplace is a futile and personally risky exercise. NHS Trusts tell us they are patient centred as they scrap budgets for patient information. Our press is filled with a carefully selected narrative fed to them by public bodies, who behind the scenes, continue to display the same old familiarly destructive and harmful behaviours. Little has changed. Talk is cheap in the public sector, and all too often a distraction from reality.

The language of public relations professionals is itself the very essence of insincerity, of feigning authenticity in pursuit of self-interest. Public relations thrives in the absence of positive personal and organisational character traits, and courage. Practitioners of the vile art fully understand demand for their services is highest where principled leadership is absent, underhand, amoral, and detached. The bigger the problems under the hood, the greater the need for a shiny bonnet. The development and widespread use of the seemingly benign term, public relations, is itself an exercise in rose-tinted positivism and rebranding. Public relations was acknowledged by its founder Edward Bernays as simply a more politically acceptable way of describing propaganda. Bernays was a relative of Sigmund Freud and is often referred to as the father of PR. The word propaganda understandably acquired negative connotations after its widespread use by Hitler's Nazi party.

The online Cambridge Dictionary defines propaganda as information, ideas, opinions, or images, often only giving one part of an argument, that are broadcast, published, or in some other way spread with the intention of influencing people's opinions. Google currently defines it more straightforwardly as information, especially of a biased or misleading nature, used to promote a political cause or point of view. Considering such sinister albeit entirely correct associations, it's easy to see why Bernays and co decided the word propaganda itself, urgently needed a remake. I guess Edward couldn't be accused of not practising what he preached, and I imagine he has an amazing inscription on his headstone. I'm almost sure it won't say, here lies Edward, master manipulator of public opinion whose ideas inspired the work of the tobacco industry lobbyists, the manufacturers of harmful pesticides, and the climate change denial movement.

One needs no better example of the public relations driven style of management that has come to dominate public services and the NHS than the tragedy that unfolded at Mid-Staffs Hospitals. At precisely the same time as the hospital was shedding registered nurses and reducing its ability to care for patients, so that its compliant directors could meet ill-informed foolish and unrealistic arbitrary financial targets, it was describing itself as having a can-do attitude. The use of public relations was not only being used to delude the regulators and the local community, but its shallow messaging was being eagerly consumed by the Trusts own leadership team. They had in effect started to believe their own hype.

When I joined the Cumbria Partnership NHS Foundation Trust in January 2012 it had a well-staffed and well-resourced communication and public relations department. The combined budget for the team's salaries and their associated activity was around four hundred thousand pounds a year. At the time they were one of about two hundred and fifty NHS Trusts. I've spoken with many other Trusts during my time in and around the NHS, a lot of whom have even larger communication and public relations departments. Simple arithmetic suggests that if the average annual budget for communication and public relations in each NHS Trust is half a million pounds, then collectively they spend about one hundred and twenty-five million pounds on these activities each year, call it a billion each decade. This figure does not include the public relations and communication budgets of all the other NHS bodies and associated agencies in the healthcare system. When I left the NHS five years later, there were fewer nurses working in the Trust but more people in the communication department than when I had joined, and still no budget for patient information leaflets.

The well-resourced public relations departments of our public sector, whose sole purpose in life is to jealously protect and maintain the reputation of their organisations and the senior executives who lead them, are presently running unchallenged rings around the shrinking skeleton of our media.

    We are living through an era that requires more scrutiny than ever. There are some excellent examples of fledgling and semi-established news sources that are doing their utmost to highlight the issues the mainstream media shies away from. News outlets such as The Canary and Double Down News are trying to break the deadlock of news inertia and apathy, but their reach is presently a fraction of their less conscientious and less contentious risk averse and sometimes commercially subservient counterparts. In my previous book I asked if it would be too much to expect of the BBC, the nation's publicly funded broadcasting service, to support the creation of a dedicated public sector scrutiny team. One that employed good quality investigative journalists across the regions of the UK and gave them the resources needed to scrutinise and hold local, regional, and national public sector service institutions to account, including health and care, police, councils, and social services, without fear or favour. I justify the paying of my BBC licence fee in my head by telling myself that as long as they continue to commission David Attenborough and Chris Packham, then I'll keep on paying it, but the quality of their journalism leaves a great deal to be desired.

    Though the reasons may have changed, the observation Orwell made in 1938 about the public being more easily deceived seems more accurate than ever. Our collective awareness is now deep in the territory of not knowing what we don't know and more and more at the mercy of misdirection and spin. If this remains the case it will be difficult to shift the debate and the publics focus from the siloed debates about a crisis in the NHS and healthcare services, to the wider crisis in society that has been brought about by the pursuit of a chosen political and economic ideology and its accompanying narrative that a successful well lived life, must be a materially laden one. The question is not, *is the NHS fit for the future* as the BBC asked in its special and despairingly dull documentary marking seventy-five years of the NHS recently, the question is, will the future be fit for us. Any future that isn't fit for the majority will be a future in which publicly funded health and care services can never cope.

Chapter 36: **Healthcare is a political football**

"Socialism is a scare word hurled at every advance people have made in the last 20 years. Socialism is what they called public power. Socialism is what they called social security. Socialism is what they called farm price supports. Socialism is what they called bank deposit insurance. Socialism is what they called the growth of free and independent labour organisations. Socialism is their name for almost anything that helps all the people."

Harry S Truman

The NHS has been used as a political football since its creation seventy-five years ago. In the early eighties, before The Iron Lady became seemingly invincible, Mrs T was losing the affection of the nation. Her privatising policies had led to fears about the future of the nation's beloved NHS which were causing great concern amongst Tory ranks. To alleviate these concerns, she was famously forced to pledge to her party and the public at the annual conservative conference in 1982, that *"the NHS is safe in our hands"*.

In 1997 the incoming Labour Party included no less than nineteen references to the NHS in its election manifesto. Tony Blairs New Labour pledged to introduce tough quality targets for hospitals, to safeguard the basic principles of the NHS and remove the top-down style of management that had grown under the Conservative Party. Labour also promised to begin the process of abolishing mixed wards, and said it would treat more patients, root out unnecessary administrative costs, and spend the significant amounts of money it predicted would be saved on more frontline care. Words are cheap. Patients of the NHS are still being treated in mixed wards twenty-six years later.

In their 2010 election manifesto, the Liberal Democrat Party referred to the NHS a mere seventeen times. They stressed their commitment to its maintenance and promised to cut the amount of bureaucracy and the costs associated with it. To limit the pay of top NHS managers, some of whom were (and many of whom still are) being paid significantly more than the Prime Minister as well as vastly more than they are worth.

In 2019, the Tory Party manifesto went shit or bust and included forty-five references to the NHS. They promised amongst many things to recruit an extra fifty thousand nurses, six thousand more doctors, provide patients with fifty million more GP surgery appointments a year, improve staff morale, and build forty new hospitals. Much of what they promised has not and will never materialise. But they talked the right talk to get them past the electoral post.

And who can forget the infamous Brexit leave campaign bus that toured the UK and graced the screens of our smartphones, televisions, and pages of the national media in 2016. The shiny red mobile poster chugged across the country like a Hammer House remake of a Cliff Richard film, conveying its implied misleading promise that if we left the European Union, we would be able to redirect £350M each week to the NHS. What better reason could any red-blooded blue passport holding Brit need to secure their vote to leave, than the future of our very own beloved NHS.

We may at times, nearly all the time I think, feel with just and increasing cause that we are governed by imbeciles, but they all know how to appeal to enough of us to secure their share of the vote. And while Thatcher knew she would never get re-elected if she didn't stand up publicly for the NHS, when asked during an election campaign in 1987, whether she trusted the NHS enough to use it, she openly admitted that she herself had private healthcare insurance. She said that she did not wish to add to NHS queues, how noble I hear you say, and wanted to be able to access healthcare services at times and dates to suit her. Wouldn't we all Margaret. But dress her motives up as we wish, to me her comment is just a typically political and evasive response to a simple question. And a polite way of saying she didn't think the NHS was fit for purpose.

Importantly, it also remains true that the greatest single threat to any individual MPs chances of re-election to parliament are the closure or reduction of NHS services in their constituency. The former leader of the Liberal Democrats and current MP for Westmorland and Lonsdale, Tim Farron, has built a long and successful political career on weaponizing the issue of the NHS to galvanise the local electorate. Tim has been the local MP since 2005 after wrestling the area from a significant Conservative majority which they have never regained. He has increased his majority by constantly speaking out in support of local NHS services and fiercely resisting any changes to them that his constituency may view unfavourably. He has organised frequent protests and numerous high-profile campaigns, such as the *Hands off our Hospital* campaign to protect and increase the quantity of NHS services provided locally at The Westmorland General Hospital. A relatively small district hospital run by a historically dysfunctional NHS Trust situated on the southern outskirts of picturesque Kendal.

Tim supplies a vote-winning combination of topical content for the local press while appealing to the health concerns of an elderly and ageing constituency. In 2017 Farron was forced to resign his position as leader of the Liberal Democrats after it became clear that his views on same sex relationships were less Freddie Mercury and more Fred Flintstone. For most MPs, stating publicly that you thought gay sex was a sin in the eyes of a fictional entity, would be the end of their political careers. But not for Tim. He may think some members of the local community deserve to burn for eternity in hell, but he wants their medical needs dealt with locally before they go. The smiley faced locally revered MP for Westmorland can survive even the possession of such misguided, deeply offensive beliefs, and anachronistic bigotry, as long as the local NHS is seen as being safe on his watch. No MP survives the closure of their local hospital.

Soundbites and quick fixes:

A report by the House of Commons Health and Social Care Committee into the future of general practice, published in October 2022, opens by painting a grim and depressing picture of a service and a profession in decline. The first paragraph of the summary contains the following statement, "*...the profession is demoralised, GPs are leaving almost as fast as they can be recruited, and patients are increasingly dissatisfied with the level of access they receive.*" Then in typically arrogant ivory towered parliamentary fashion, the report summary goes on to state, "*...the root cause of this is straightforward: there are not enough GPs to meet the ever-increasing demands on the service...*" This crass and simplistic assertion, on which the proposals that emerge from the committee's report are then built, is an incredibly reductionist and ill-informed statement for a group of allegedly intelligent people to make. Any meaningful reference to the root causes of the pressures on Primary

Care in the UK should include the many things that are creating the rising levels of demand and also acknowledge the changes occurring across the wider system.

There are no single parts of Britain's publicly funded health and care services, including Primary Care, that should or can rationally be looked at in isolation and then *fixed* by simply recruiting more people. Just train and hire more GPs, throw more resources at the problem, just throw more bodies onto the battlefield to fight the ever rising and relentless waves of demand being thrown at the NHS, is precisely the kind of sticking plaster solution focused thinking that has brought Primary Care and the entire apparatus of publicly funded health and care in the UK to its knees. For any group of MPs, or anyone for that matter, to look at Primary Care in isolation without explicitly acknowledging the need to adopt a holistic and systemic approach to improving the overall health and wellbeing of the entire population and the structure of the system it works within, is woefully simplistic at best and a recipe for disaster at worst. I recall suffering with it when I was younger but premature evaluation it would seem, is no longer the preserve of the male species.

The full report produced by the committee contains a number of recommendations, areas in which it suggests changes could be made to improve the position of Primary Care. These include committing more funding to train an additional one thousand GPs each year; minimising the administrative burden on general practice; retaining older GPs for longer by reducing their pension tax liabilities; promising to lower the average number of registered patients per GP to help general practitioners manage their workloads; improving the IT systems to make them more GP user-friendly; and increasing the continuity of care that patients experience from their local GP Practice, which roughly translates into patients being able to see the same GP on an ongoing basis. The report suggests improving the continuity of care will lead to fewer unplanned hospital admissions for conditions that can be effectively treated in the community. Though there is evidence to support this assertion in relation to treating patients with dementia, the field of behavioural sciences might suggest that continuity of care creates the potentially unobjective conditions in which a GP could fail to diagnose a serious condition correctly. When it comes to my health and wellbeing, I'll take access to objective informed up-to-date expertise over the comfort of visiting a familiar GP on the edge of retirement. It's often noted by healthcare professionals that just because patients might like a particular GP, does not mean they are the most effective in dealing with their condition. My sister-in-law liked the clinician that told her she could fool the tests run by the local smoking cessation team by simply avoiding tobacco in the 24hrs prior to being tested. Likeable, yes, effective, no.

Lacking insight, ambition, and urgency, the House of Commons report comes across as just another attempt at rearranging the deck chairs while the ship of Primary Care along with the entire NHS fleet spins and heaves in the eye of a perfect ideologically driven storm. The report is incredibly insular and contains no references to the Primary Care or healthcare systems in other countries, countries such as Sweden who appear to be leading the way. The report ducks the blindingly obvious need to restructure Primary Care, failing to acknowledge the significant efficiencies that could be achieved by combining GP Practices. It makes no mention of the increasingly large amounts of GP capacity and capability being lost to the growing list of private healthcare providers who are offering them better terms and conditions. Nor of the glaring need for a more central and influential role for public health in reducing demand. Or of the pressing need to identify and address the estimated one in five visits to GPs that are thought to be unnecessary. A significant figure that various research groups and interested bodies in the UK including NHS England have consistently highlighted during the last few years. If a mere quarter of these unnecessary visits alone could be addressed, it would reduce the number of patient visits to Primary Care by around fifty thousand every single day. Nor is there any mention of the use of video or virtual appointments, and there is only one explicit almost passing reference to the potential for exploiting technology alongside a mildly dismissive story about the use of artificial intelligence to handle routine diagnostic work. The conventional wisdoms embodied in this report and the many others like it that are produced by politicians and think tanks, are not the kind of radical thinking needed to achieve meaningful change in any part of the UK's health and care system. The committee that created the report had been chaired by Jeremy Hunt.

Chapter 37: Has the NHS been set up to fail?

"Politics is too serious a matter to be left to the politicians."

Charles de Gaulle

As winter 2018 approached, the UK government did not extend a warm welcome to the arrival of a United Nations Envoy to Britain's shores. Professor Philip Alston, at the time the UN Special Rapporteur on Extreme Poverty and Human Rights, came to our shores to undertake an extensive eleven-day research visit between 05th & 16th November. This extraordinary decision by the United Nations, to send an envoy to one of the world's wealthiest economies, an established First World country, was unprecedented. For the UN to even feel the need to contemplate such an endeavour is an utterly damning indictment of the structural injustices and inequalities within our nation that have become clearly and undeniably visible to the rest of the developed world. Professor Alston's findings, presented to the General Assembly of the United Nations the following year, were stark. The opening paragraph of the document reads as follows:

Although the United Kingdom is the world's fifth largest economy, one fifth of its population (14 million people) live in poverty, and 1.5 million of them experienced destitution in 2017. Policies of austerity introduced in 2010 continue largely unabated, despite the tragic social consequences. Close to 40 percent of children are predicted to be living in poverty in 2021. Food banks have proliferated; homelessness and rough sleeping have increased greatly; tens of thousands of poor families must live in accommodation far from their schools, jobs, and community networks; life expectancy is falling for certain groups; and the legal aid system has been decimated.

Professor Alston's summary reads like a rallying cry for the UN to declare war on the neoliberal despots who run Britain and liberate its downtrodden people. The report goes on to state that much of what it refers to as the glue that has held British Society together since the Second World War has been deliberately removed and replaced with a harsh and uncaring ethos and as the direct result of a chosen ideology rather than the prevailing economic conditions of the period.

If Professor Alston's report were the United Kingdom having its homework marked in front the entire UN class, then it had not only had the blackboard rubber thrown squarely and accurately at its head, but its pants were down, and its bare arse was being openly and stingingly spanked on the teachers table at the front of the classroom. The visit of the UN envoy and the subsequent and widely circulated report that emerged as its outcome, were hailed by many at the time as the wake-up call the UK Government needed and one that could not be ignored. Here was a report from arguably the most impartial authoritative source available, a report that illuminated many of the inhumanity's afflicting one of the world's leading economies, a founding member of the United Nations itself. Yet nobody in government blinked, nobody admitted they had failed, and certainly no one hung their head in abject shame at the tragic and avoidable human misery they had overseen and inflicted. The creation of the post of a Minister for Suicide in October 2018 was designed to show concerned parties that the UK government was taking the issue of rising suicide levels and in particular the growing crisis of male suicide and mental health, seriously. But the appointment has in my opinion been a point-scoring and up-to-press valueless political gesture by a government whose time in office and thinly veiled neoliberal ideology has driven many people to desperation and beyond. Regardless of the colour of my politics I can count the number of politicians I have sensed the presence of true empathy within, on one hand, two fingers to be precise. But Caring Conservatism, really? that has to be one of the most misleading and cruel oxymorons ever. It's like the BNP trying to secure votes based on their diversity and inclusion policies. What's next, Friendly Fascism?

The National Health Service is quite possibly the world's greatest and most visible edifice to socialism. Its existence is a towering flaming beacon of fairness that stands for so much more than the sum of its often, dysfunctional parts. The Latin root of the word socialism is thought to be sociare, which means to combine or to share. Collaboration is the means by which the human race evolved. Our ancestors became unwitting socialists to ensure their survival. Socialism is merely acknowledging our collective responsibility for one another. Socialism is humanity and collective compassion. Since the fall of the Berlin Wall in 1989, and the unchecked promotion of consumerism and relentlessly stoked rise of greed, the "*S*" word has become maligned and misused, deliberately, and mainly by those with little interest in fairness unless it is on their terms. It was self-interested uncontrolled capitalism that dragged the world to the edge of a financial cliff in 2007. It was a huge collective act of taxpayer funded collaboration that was needed to stop us going over the edge. Capitalism fucked up and was saved by the application of socialist principles. It's beyond ironic that many neoliberals owe their continued financial health and wellbeing to the ongoing collecting of tax contributions from the masses.

The existence of a publicly funded health and care service is an anathema to neoliberalism and its Ayn Rand loving dark hearted acolytes. And like it or not, they are firmly in charge right now. If you think that a change of government in Britain from red to blue will reverse this state of affairs, you are an optimist. It will undoubtedly help, but Labour Party supporters in the Blair Tradition should never forget that Thatcher herself proclaimed her greatest victory to be the emergence of *New Labour*.

In 2005 a newly elected still youngish MP and future Health Secretary called Jeremy Hunt was one of a number of Tory MPs and public figures who co-authored a political pamphlet called *Direct Democracy: An Agenda for a New Model Party.* Earlier that same year the Labour Party under Tony Blair had secured a historic third consecutive election victory and short of a global financial meltdown, as if that could happen, many Conservative MPs were convinced they needed a new radical approach if they were to ever regain power. The hundred-page rallying cry to neoliberal arms they created, a galvanising trumpet call to the Thatcherite faithful to reclaim the true principles of Toryism, these being fuck you I'm alright, sorry I mean, we're all in this together, is thought to have been the brainchild of Conservative MP Douglas Carswell. Carswell later defected from the Conservative party and stood for UKIP in the 2015 general election, in the process becoming its first elected member of parliament. The paper was later rebranded as *Direct Democracy: Empowering People to Make their Lives Better,* presumably to make its intent appear more cuddly and less self-serving.

The fundamental assumption underlying the document is the capitalist credo that people's lives will only be made better through the acquisition of things and the increased availability of stuff. There are no references to humanity or compassion in the hundred pages of blurb. Other contributing authors to the social Darwinists woolly manifesto for unrestrained capitalism, include the recent chancellor of the exchequer and failed maths student Kwasi Kwarteng, and a rubber faced Eton shaped Bullingdon Club brat and insatiably hungry black hole of human compassion and authenticity, called Michael Gove. A political wrong un if ever there was one. My mum used to tell me I'd be judged on the company I kept. My friends and I stole cigarettes, robbed the school tuckshop, ate magic mushrooms in history lessons, and engaged in acts of minor criminal damage. The crimes of my teenage peers and I pale in comparison to the socially destructive sins of the Conservative Party. And a group of young teenage boys wandering the streets of a northern market town dressed like dickheads in brass buttoned jackets from Ede & Ravenscroft Tailors of London, would have been subjected to regular sessions of physical and verbal correction. As one of the first people to sport a pair of tartan bondage pants in Penrith, I speak from experience.

Not satisfied with their first plan to secure world domination, Carswell and one of the fellow co-authors of the Direct Democracy document, Daniel Hannan, who with Carswell was co-founder of the Vote Leave organisation that successfully if misleadingly campaigned for the UK to leave the European Union in 2016, which as we all know is going really well isn't it, went on to publish another book in 2006 called, *The Plan: Twelve Months to Renew Britain*. The book, yes, I have read it, and yes, I resented, really resented paying for it, is a revealing, at times semi-interesting mix of half-truths, political populism, and broad sweeping statements, smattered with the odd selectively chosen fact in an attempt to give it some credibility. The book, which if I had bought as a paperback would have joined Jeremy Hunt's book "Zero" next to the toilet, always handy in the event of a toilet tissue shortage, is an initially appealing attack on the credibility and legacy of politicians and parliament which then confusingly culminates in a cry for parliament to be given greater levels of unchallenged supremacy. This would enable parliament and the increasingly wacky and self-interested corporate-serving MPs who wangle their way into it, to implement even more unevidenced experimental policies a la Truss and Kwarteng, which would doubtless lead to significant and of course potentially profitable social problems and upheaval. Cleverly and somewhat disingenuously, the book then argues that local councils and public services should be held to account for how well they pick up the pieces of whatever social issues emerge. The gist of the book seems to be a call to make government the servant of capitalism which is then allowed to run a mock and cause problems, for which an underfunded public sector will then be held accountable for solving. If government policies are leading to more suicides, then don't worry, just shout at the NHS for not addressing the issue. If crime becomes rampant, not a problem, just blame the police for not doing their job. And if providing housing to rising numbers of the homeless becomes an issue for local authorities, just point a wagging finger at their abject failure and tell them they must try harder. When a political party says it wants light touch government, it generally means it wants the power to implement policy without the responsibility for dealing with its consequences. Let the market prevail and to hell with those it leaves behind.

Carswell has the unfortunate appearance of the love child of Sam Eagle, the pedantic bird character from the Muppet Show, and Statler or Waldorf, the two old characters from the same show who entertained a generation shouting insults from the safety of their private balcony. Rather like politicians and GB News presenters. Carswell is no longer an MP after deciding not to stand for re-election as a UKIP candidate in the 2019 general election. The truth is that he'd likely shot his self-serving bolt and didn't stand a chance of re-election. Douglas has since floated like a toxic turd that refuses to sink, across the Atlantic and is now the President and CEO of the Mississippi Center for Public Policy in the USA, which he calls the greatest republic on earth. The center is a right wing (not arsed about other people) think tank (repository of entrenched opinion) whose stated purpose is to educate the public about the benefits of individual liberty (we want to be able to do what we want), low taxes (every person for themselves), and light regulation (we want to be able to do even more of what we want with impunity).

The centres website contains a fascinating slightly frightening series of motivational video talks for neoliberals, such as; *How to Beat the Left*, an informative session in discussion with the marmite caricature that is Laurence Fox, in which guidance is offered on how to stop the spread of ideas from that pesky group of people who believe in fairness. Fox reportedly told The Times in 2019, he had been totally radicalised against woke culture and political correctness by watching videos on YouTube.

The internet has a lot to answer for doesn't it. Then there is a presentation entitled *Fossil Future*, a talk by an interesting, perhaps I mean dangerous, chap called Alex Epstein. Alex tells us that if plants could vote they would vote for more carbon and coal, and then encourages us all to use more fossil fuels if we are really serious about climate change. If plants could vote Alex, they would probably vote for the ceasing of deforestation and the abolition of the human race. And suggesting we should use more fossil fuels is like telling someone with lung cancer to inhale more cigarette smoke if they really want to get better. Go figure? Epstein runs a separate think tank, an oxymoron if ever there was one, and is closely aligned to the climate denial brigade. He is also a former fellow of the Ayn Rand Institute. For those who haven't read Rands work, she was a 20th century writer of fantasies who expressed political views that were somewhere right of Thatcher and Reagan. Satan is probably still debating whether or not to grant her entry into Hell. Rand should never have been allowed out the house unaccompanied; hindsight is wonderful isn't it. And then there is Riley Gaines, a blond-haired blue-eyed Trump supporter who is vowing to take on and confront woke extremists and ideologues. Riley says she wants to defend and protect America's daughters against the woke left. It's not clear if she wants to defend the original daughters of America who were robbed of their lands and livelihood and who would I imagine be quite open to the idea of acknowledgement and restitution, or just people like her. Riley's father Brad played football for Vanderbilt University, named after its founding donor a wealthy transport magnate named Cornelius Vanderbilt. Vanderbilt funded the setting up of the University in 1873 to help heal the divisions of the civil war and build social cohesion; good effort but you can't win them all Cornelius!

Carswell is one of those glaringly, gloriously obviously, and eccentrically out of touch products of the upper one percent of the population. If he had been born into a poor former mining family on the Mirehouse estate in Whitehaven, he would be that unemployable bloke who never gets out of his pyjama bottoms, leans on the garden fence shouting random phrases at passers-by, before occasionally defecating in the middle of the street. We would simultaneously pity and be wary of him. *"Don't worry children, it's just Douglas, you know how excited he can get when he sees a dog"*. Carswell is the son of a highly respected Physician Wilson Carswell, who graduated in medicine and surgery from Kings College in 1961 before becoming a Fellow of the Royal College of

Surgeons in 1967. Wilson practiced medicine in numerous countries in Africa, and Douglas spent his formative years in Uganda and Kenya before going on to gain a master's degree in British Imperial History. I bet his dad was as proud of Douglas on graduation day as mine was upon finding out I was appearing in Juvenile Criminal Court. Carswell's voting record while an MP in the UK shows a man who voted for the privatisation (some call it theft) of public assets, voted against the public ownership of railways, against further gambling regulation, for restricting legal aid, and against a central register of lobbyists, that cadre of corporately interested people who exist to subvert democracy. While voting against any reductions in student fees, he was simultaneously happy to plunder the public purse for tens of thousands of pounds in expenses to support the setting-up of a second home in London. This use of public funds confused many people as the property he was said to be spending taxpayer's money on turned out to be further from parliament than the existing flat he already owned in the city itself. Superior quality soft furnishings are so much more important than equitable legal systems or affordable education.

Dug has now clearly found his tribe in Mississippi. He has swapped his previously starched shirts and strained stuffed tie appearance for a more casual open collared and homespun look. His face now sports a modicum of trendy stubble, presumably on the advice of an image consultant keen to keep his muppet lineage under wraps. But Carswell and his ilk are not to be mocked because they look and often sound like the less intelligent cast of a Jim Henson spin off show. They are to be feared. The worrying thing about people like Carswell, and the other entitled arrogant IYIs (intelligent yet idiot) that infest the muddy waters of the worlds political cesspits, is that they don't have to achieve mainstream political success to exert significant influence over public opinion and in turn mainstream political policy. By stirring up the edges of the pond such populists seek to influence what happens, often very successfully, at its centre.

Consider the UK's decision to leave the EU. The referendum that led to it came about as the result of opinions expressed by a few fringe politicians and campaigning led by some now defunct political parties, movements, and of course think tanks. But these relatively small parties and limited interests, succeeded in scaring the mainstream political parties just enough to make them alter their policies to ensure they could continue to appeal to the majority needed to keep their hold on political power. David Cameron would not have promised the electorate a vote on the UK's membership of the European Union had he not felt backed into a corner by the threat of losing some marginal seats to UKIP, the United Kingdom Independence Party. The UK would not have entertained devoting time and attention to a referendum on its membership of the EU, had it not been forced into it by the opportunist and populist campaigning of UKIP. UKIP knew its candidates didn't stand a chance of being elected in the numbers required to exercise strong political influence in the traditional sense. But taking a model of political influence that has been applied in many other countries, UKIP engaged large sections of the population who felt excluded, fed them a narrative that fuelled and amplified their woes, and then offered a simple solution to them.

It should concern anyone interested in the future of the NHS and Britain itself that politically ambitious neoliberal leaning products of privilege like Jeremy Hunt are given positions of incredible influence overseeing arguably the most vital function of a civilized society. If leadership is creating the conditions in which things can happen, then the current climate in which capacity and capability in the NHS and Social Care has been decimated, is the result of a particular type of leadership that has allowed this to happen. I think that because we in Britain take the existence of the NHS so much for granted, many of us are unable to grasp the notion that it may be being deliberately and systematically undermined to the point where we are forced to accept radical changes to the way healthcare is structured, funded, and made available to us, because these changes will be sold to us as the only way out of the crisis that publicly funded healthcare is in. There will of course be little if any reference to how the crisis came about.

Hunts tenure as Health Secretary was the longest in recent times, serving, or serving up the NHS on a plate to the privateers, as Health Secretary from September 2012 to July 2018. During his time in office, there were no meaningful developments in the adoption or implementation of technology. The NHS stands as a largely analogue island in a rising digital ocean. The implementation of usable patient facing technology and internally enabling digital infrastructure has been one of the most pressing issues facing the NHS for over two decades. The adoption of technology is one of the most obvious routes by which any organisation in the modern age can become more effective and efficient. Hunts well-rehearsed answer to how the NHSs woes would be solved was always, by using technology, yet during his six years as Health Secretary, extraordinarily little progress was made and there was almost no central direction or coordination of effort. NHS Trusts were effectively free, if finance and resources allowed, to do their own sweet technological thing without thought for how it might interact with other parts of the NHS and the wider health and care system around them. A sixteen-year-old business studies student could recognise that this would be a recipe for disaster in a national service that depends on the cohesive coordinated actions of its many parts, Primary Care, Acute Hospital, Community Services, and Ambulance services, to provide joined-up safe care to its patients. Yet somehow this basic logic escaped the allegedly erudite technology savvy Health Secretary. I sometimes wonder how these people get out the house without their mums tying their shoelaces.

Nor was there any attempt to even identify never mind remove the many obvious resource consuming administrative and bureaucratic barriers that get in the way of good care. Or to address the toxic cultures that have created the litany of tragedies plaguing the NHS and which drive many good and skilled people from the workforce. And Hunt oversaw, in full view, the significant declines in retention and recruitment that were occurring and accelerating across the NHS workforce. The current much publicised crisis in healthcare recruitment and retention did not appear unexpectedly from behind a bush. It is an entirely foreseeable problem which Hunt knew about yet did nothing meaningful to deal with. In 2018, he was accused by the Royal College of Nursing of worsening the workforce issue by his decision to support the quiet withdrawing of NHS bursaries which had covered the cost of postgraduate nursing degrees. Like most of the challenges facing our health and care services, the workforce challenge has been coming clearly, loudly, and in full view of those prepared to look in its direction, for years.

As for the present state of NHS mental health services, children's, adults, and older peoples, Hunt's record is appalling. It could be argued he made significant steps toward achieving the promised parity of esteem between NHS physical and mental health services by reducing the ability of each so that they would be equally terrible. A novel and innovative approach many hadn't considered, and few would have supported. As of

2023, NHS mental health services remain seriously and often dangerously underfunded and short-staffed. Around a quarter of some NHS mental health services are now provided by private companies offering mental health care, who make and take significant profits from the public purse. The NHS, we, are paying around £2B a year to private providers of mental health services because the NHS does not have the beds or capacity to deal with them.

Hunt, very visibly, spent a great deal of time on the wards in NHS hospitals, and spoke persistently and reasonably eloquently about his passion for and his belief in the NHS and its founding principles. But by their fruits shall ye know them and like all politicians his actions and inactions were speaking louder than his words. The legacy he has left us is only a good one if you happen to have shares in a private healthcare provider. That Britain's greatest public asset was in the hands of a man who co-authored a document advocating private health insurance and the management of public services by companies whose sole reason for existence is the production of profit for them and their shareholders, is staggering. Hunt's time in office as Health Secretary, almost mirrors my period of employment in the NHS. Few of those I worked with regard it as a golden period. It was not a good time for the NHS. It was a period of blindingly obvious strategic impotence and inaction in which many people within and around the healthcare system were justifiably asking, where is this all leading and just who is in charge of the nation's health service?

My point is not that the NHS is more or less safe in the hands of any one particular political party or ideology, red, blue, yellow, or green. My point is that the political landscape has changed immeasurably since 1948. And if the NHS stays under the control of the current political classes, subject to the increasing ideological influences of fringe interests, viewed as a totem to be torn down, or an asset to be weaponized by the politically ambitious, then it will be in the wrong hands. Our health and care services are not safe in the hands of the soundbite superheroes whose ill-thought-out canned catchphrases are designed to capture votes and whose promises and pledges are ultimately never kept.

We can no longer leave the management of and decision-making about our nation's healthcare services in the hands of political parties who now more than ever are influenced by commercially driven lobbying, and steered by rogues, the self-interested, and the indifferent. The NHS may have been created with noble intent by political will, perhaps it will stand as the greatest political achievement of all time. But both the physical and political worlds in which the NHS was imagined and born are very different to the ones we live in now. We expect, with good reason and with a growing awareness and sense of the possible, to have many years in our lives, and a great deal of life in our years. Our health is simply far too important to be entrusted and left in the hands of the mainstream political parties, the politicians, and panjandrums we are presently saddled with. I often wonder how desperate or mentally lazy we must have become to even entertain our politicians appeals to identify with us. We're all in this together; my arse we are! Politicians are great us telling how much politics matters and then when things don't go as expected we are told that things were beyond their control and there's nobody to be held accountable.

Events, not soundbites, are the voice we should hear screaming at us to recognise that we live in a world in which the previously unthinkable seems to look increasingly and worryingly possible. The NHS has been identified by many on the right as an unwelcome totem of socialism as well as a potentially incredibly lucrative source of profit. They feel health and care should be a business just like any other. A commercial arena in which access to clinical expertise and compassion is exchanged like a commodity between those who can afford to pay for it and whoever wishes to profit from its sale. Those of us who are comfortable being called socialists, or woke, a word I don't really understand or wish to, should not, cannot, take the continued existence of collectively funded healthcare in the UK for granted. We should be worried and aware that the roots of a good deal of current Tory policy can be tracked directly back to published ideologies such as *Direct Democracy: An Agenda for a New Model Party* and *The Plan: Twelve Months to Renew Britain*. These are inherently selfish political manifestos created by the entitled products of Charterhouse and Eton. The privileged children of empire who were brought up in countries where need is everywhere and there is little capacity for caring for the less fortunate. These are not the right people to be placed in positions of power in which they can implement outdated ideologies and policies upon the health and wellbeing of an entire nation.

Carswell, Hunt, Kwarteng, Gove, Patel, Braverman, Cameron, Johnson, Sunak, pick a name, any name, and almost any political party.

None of these are people who inhabit the same world the majority of us occupy, or who have the best interests of everyday people at heart. Despite their well-rehearsed protestations to the contrary. The important thing to remember is that we, you, I, we would probably be just like them if we had lived their lives and inherited their biases. It was Aristotle who purportedly said, give me the person until they are seven, and I will give you the adult. A mantra repeated and used to profound effect by the Catholic Church and many other institutions requiring unquestioning adherence and loyalty. So as much as I and many others might like to mock the political elite and their wannabee acolytes, they are the natural products of the environments they have been raised in. Nobody is born a neoliberal or a socialist. Our politicians were not born selfish, blinkered, ignorant of, or wilfully blind to the plight of others. They are not inherently bad people, whatever that might mean to each of us. Their definitions of success are naturally limited, and they are merely doing what they have been told and have learned they need to do, in order to get them where they have been told they need to be or rightfully should be. Feigning empathy, playing with vague semantics, and promising the impossible are all legitimate acts if you have been brought up to apply behaviours and words as merely tools to craft your way to success. Such people do not adopt their positions and make decisions as choices, their acts are the default product of design. Expecting them to behave in any other way is flawed and wishful thinking on our part.

Chapter 38: The rise and role of private healthcare

"Health care is a human right, not a privilege...ultimately universal health coverage is a political choice. Its takes vision, courage, and long-term thinking. But the payoff is a safer, fairer, and healthier world, for everyone."

Tedros Adhanom; Director-General World Health Organisation

The debate about what does and doesn't and what should and shouldn't fall within the scope of a universal publicly funded healthcare system, may never be a simple one, and proclamations such as the one made by the Director-General of the WHO above are steeped in context. Tedros is an Ethiopian born in Eritrea which separated itself from Ethiopia following a bitter and bloody war in 1993. Conflict and political instability have meant Ethiopia and its neighbour Eritrea remain among the world's poorest countries. Nations plagued by rural and urban poverty and on the frontline of climate change, they are places of frequent drought in which malaria and malnourishment are leading causes of death. It was the poet philosopher and teacher Rumi, who observed that the wound is the place where the light enters. Tedros lost his younger brother to malaria at an early age. The aspiration and drive that comes through lived social experience and personal loss is clearly at work in his thinking.

It must be strange to be the Director-General of a global organisation with a unique helicopter view of the challenges facing each part of the planet and its citizens. At times I imagine Tedros finds himself pondering how people in one part of the world are dying because they have nothing to eat while others are dying because they are eating too much. Ethiopia has twice the population of Britain but less than one tenth the number of hospital beds; the UK itself has one of the lowest number of hospital beds per capita in Europe with just under two and a half beds per thousand people. France has just under six hospital beds per thousand, and Germany has almost eight beds per thousand of its population. Ethiopians can only dream of such things, the country currently has around one hospital bed for every three thousand five hundred of its citizens, and one tenth of a doctor for every thousand people. Set against this context I'm guessing Tedros's aspirations for universal healthcare coverage are very different to many in the western world and I would understand entirely if cosmetic ear correction surgery, smoking cessation services, or the provision of diabetes clinics for the avoidably obese don't feature highly in his priorities for public funding.

Of course, the fortunate wealthy few of Ethiopia, like the fortunate wealthy of any country, can access and pay for private healthcare services in the specialisms and locations of their choosing, should they want or need to. It has long been the case that if you've got the cash, you can access the care. The global market for private healthcare services is estimated to be growing at almost ten percent a year and is forecast to rise from a mere five and a half trillion dollars in 2022, to over eleven trillion dollars by 2030. The self-pay healthcare market in the UK, which until now was widely regarded as a politically sensitive small niche market, doubled in value between 2010 and 2021. The impact of this global growth on recruitment and retention cannot be underestimated. Clinicians, experienced nurses, physiotherapists, podiatrists, radiographers, neurologists, and speech language therapists to name a few, can often earn more working three days a week in the private sector than they can in a week with the NHS. With less hassle and micro managerial interference to boot.

As enthusiastically as I've embraced the internet, for as long as I can remember, opening my personal email inbox has been like playing a game of administrative whack-a-mole. After two decades I've finally stopped receiving emails offering me Viagra. I am no longer inundated with requests to help Nigerian businesspeople transfer vast sums to UK bank accounts in exchange for generous risk-free handling fees. I've stopped being blackmailed with the threatened release of an embarrassing personal sex video. On average I only get one or two emails a week offering to make me rich with cryptocurrency. And no more emails entitled, Sexy Russian Lady Seeking Nice English Man are making it through my spam filter. But now, as quickly as I can unsubscribe from one email marketing promotion with headers like, *Paying too much for your health cover? Save up to 66%!* or offering to help me, *Jump NHS Waiting Lists*, or *Avoid NHS Queues*, I somehow find myself on the receiving end of another, then another, and another offering me private health insurance. I'm not sure unsubscribing from email lists really works or maybe it's my mid-fifties demographic that invites every private healthcare related service on the planet to invade my inbox. Deleting these emails, along with

Googles incessant attempts to sell me its latest must-have device, that is until next year's comes out, has become a weekly task. In the wake of a global pandemic and its impact on an ailing mismanaged public health and care system that was already squeezed beyond sustainability, private healthcare and private health insurance in the UK is understandably booming.

Bupa, Nuffield Health, Spire Healthcare, are just some of the many private health providers who have significantly upped their social media presence and launched slick emotionally engaging television and media advertising campaigns to increase public awareness and uptake of the services they offer. The combined advertising budgets of the private health providers competing for business in the UK now runs into many tens of millions of pounds. There are marketing agencies specialising in promoting private health and care services. This morning as I was writing and looking at an article on the Sky News website, one of those cheesy semi-personalised location sensitive adverts popped up. Beneath a picture of a carefree young man and two children running merrily laughing through a field, the text read, *Penrith residents are skipping the NHS queues with private health insurance.* The advert was from a company promoting private health insurance called UsayCompare. Their website says *Private health insurance gives you the opportunity to skip never-ending queues and get faster access to GP appointments, referrals, treatment, and surgery.* And according to the promotional blurb, this peace of mind can be yours for no more than the price of your daily Latte. The website then tries to soothe any qualms of conscience that left-leaning potential customers may be having by saying that their services do not compete with the NHS but complement it by offering to reduce waiting times; my arse I said to myself. More on that shortly.

Private health providers and the healthcare insurance industry are ramping up their marketing to capitalise on and fill the widening and profitable gap that circumstance, managed decline, insouciance, ineptitude, and our collective wilful blindness have created. Capitalism is a shiver of sharks that must keep moving forward and eating to survive, and clouds of blood and the scent of rich pickings have spread quickly throughout the newly profitable post-pandemic oceans of health and care. A December 2022 report by the Office of National Statistics revealed one in eight adults in the UK had paid for private medical care in the previous year. Just under half of these had used healthcare insurance, sometimes referred to as PMI (private medical insurance), with the remaining majority paying for private care themselves. Money Supermarket, Which Health Insurer, Go-Compare, UsayCompare, and even the cuddly Meerkats from Compare the Market, all are offering increased access to a broader range of healthcare insurances. The first benefit they all highlight is the chance to avoid NHS waiting lists and gain quicker access to treatment. The private sector knows which buttons to press to gain the attention of its intended audience. In its annual state of the sector report for 2022, the Independent Health Providers Network (IHPN), the body representing the interests of private healthcare providers in the UK, stated that the prospects for independent providers were positive; an understatement of gloriously epic proportions. A poll undertaken by the IHPN shows almost 90% of its members expect the most significant growth in their markets to come from self-paying patients. A recent poll reveals that one in five adults in the UK expects to pay for clinical treatment in the coming year and almost half of Britons would consider using private healthcare if they needed treatment. I have two friends just a couple of years older than me who have each paid for their own hip replacements within the last 12 months. I imagine every board meeting of the IHPN now starts and finishes with a series of rousing hurrahs and celebratory Mexican waves.

On Saturday 18th February 2023, the extremely conservative, normally parochially jingoistic, and editorially Alan Partridge style newspaper that is my local rag, the Cumberland and Westmorland Herald, carried two separate stories of serious challenges facing the local NHS. This was unusual. Most local papers are now a conduit for the unfiltered stream of diversionary public relations fluff the communication departments of local NHS Trusts spew out on demand to keep their respective chief executives happy. The first story in the Herald related to a two thousand five hundred percent rise in 12-hour waits for Accident and Emergency admissions at North Cumbria's NHS hospitals. The solution to which, according to an elected local councillor was to work more closely with voluntary services. Where do they find these people? The second story related to increased waiting times for patients experiencing a mental health crisis in Cumbria. This article highlighted the large amounts being spent each month on hiring agency staff by the NHS Trust tasked with providing, or not it would seem, mental health services to patients in the area. The snappily titled, Cumbria, Northumberland, Tyne and Wear NHS

Foundation Trust, was set to spend almost twenty million pounds in a single year hiring agency nurses due to challenges recruiting and retaining its own staff. The vacancy rates in some of its health services and mental health units were said to be more than one in four. The Trust responded to the press saying it was trying to encourage mental health professionals to come and work in the area by offering incentive payments for new starters and funds for them to relocate. In essence doing what every other challenged NHS Trust in the country is doing and issuing an open invite to the inexperienced and the less than mediocre to come and ply their trade on the unsuspecting citizens of Northern England. The Trust went on to say that things had improved in recent months due to a successful programme of international nurse recruitment. The article about the increase in mental health waiting times finished with the pragmatic if somewhat depressing request that anyone suffering a mental health crisis in the area should contact the Samaritans. A phone number and email address were provided. It's like Sainsbury's offering an apology for not delivering the products you've paid for in advance before advising you to go to your nearest foodbank if you really need something to eat. If the choice for a parent whose child may be experiencing a mental health crisis is either a year on a waiting list or to suggest that they have a chat with a charitably funded albeit generally brilliant volunteer, then it's no wonder people are increasingly turning to private healthcare services for themselves and their loved ones.

Choice and opportunity are everywhere!

In summer 2021, Boots the omnipresent high-street pharmacy chain bought by the US company Walgreens in 2012, launched its own online doctor website. A range of online treatment, testing kits and assessment services are offered by Boots in partnership with a San Francisco based company called Lemonaid Health. The option to video call a GP is provided by a company called Livi, headquartered in Sweden. Livi presently operates in numerous European countries under the trading name Kry, which means healthy and well in Swedish. A self-funded GP appointment with Livi costs £39 and a mental health therapy session, costs £65 for fifty minutes. Livi also works with some NHS GP practices whose patients can access its GP appointment service at no charge. The strapline in large letters at the top of the Boots online doctor homepage offers, *Convenient Care Without the Hassle*. It's as if private sector healthcare providers implicitly know that the public's present perception of the NHS and publicly funded healthcare in the UK, is that it isn't convenient, it isn't hassle free, and it isn't responsive. To a large degree they are right. Superdrug, the UK's second largest retail pharmacy, launched its online doctor service a decade ago in 2013. It offers online appointments with a GP for £38.99 as well as access to prescription services and a range of online healthcare and wellbeing treatments. These include online photographic skin diagnostics for £20, diabetes assessment and management kits, morning after pills from £9.99, and a seemingly endless range of STI services presumably popular with students and a potentially worrying indicator in the rise of sexually transmitted diseases attributed to the increase in individuals engaging in casual sex attributed to apps such as Grindr and Tinder. A promotion on the Lloyds Pharmacy website offers access to an online appointment with a GP for the discounted price of £20; was £49.99. The site says appointments can be obtained in as little as 30 minutes and are available between 8am and 8pm seven days a week. A monthly subscription complete with its own App is also available from Lloyds Pharmacy. Their strapline is *a more convenient way to see a doctor*. The Livi service used by Boots states that the doctors accessible through its portal are also part-time GPs whose work in physical GP surgeries in England makes them well-equipped to assess patient's symptoms. There is also a well-produced short video on the website extolling the benefits of working for Livi and encouraging doctors to apply for work. The benefits look extremely attractive, and I think if I was a GP I would be tempted. Lloyds Pharmacy similarly promote their online doctors as having years of experience who also work in NHS hospitals, and GP surgeries. To which the question must be asked, are these doctors managing their work life balance, or just clinical guns for hire who are being offered the opportunity to have their cake and more?

In the late nineteen nineties Britons were spending approx. fifteen billion pounds each year on out-of-pocket healthcare costs and voluntary health insurance schemes. This amount has since risen steadily year on year and in 2019, just before the onset of Covid-19, it exceeded forty billion pounds. If the pandemic was the god of private healthcare capitalisms gift to neoliberals, the cost-of-living crisis may be the only brake on its growth; time will tell. In April 2022, the Mail Online ran what it called a private health care special feature entitled, *should you shell out to beat the NHS waiting list crisis...the answer might surprise you.* In the feature the editors suggested, perhaps unsurprisingly and probably with Viscount Rothermere's beady eye on future advertising revenues, that private healthcare might not be as out of reach as readers thought. And for anyone considering taking the plunge into the expanding world of private health and care, the Mail Online had thoughtfully and helpfully spoken to the UK's top private healthcare experts who were of course, more than happy to point out where people considering using private healthcare services should start their journey.

The Mail Online article included some carefully selected case studies. Debbie, a 61yr old artist from Norfolk had been told she would have to wait two years for a knee replacement if she wanted it on the NHS. Debbie's doctor helpfully advised her it would be better to go private. To cover the £12,000 cost of the operation, Debbie had paid an initial deposit on her credit card and took advantage of a handy interest-free repayment scheme offered by the private healthcare provider. Paul, 81, an otherwise fit and healthy former soldier from Dorset was said to have spent just under £9,000 of his savings to have speedy surgery on a slipped disc which enabled him to get back on the golf course in a matter of weeks. Then there was the highly emotive and carefully choreographed story of Ed Jones, a former IT manager who was diagnosed with an inoperable brain tumour at the age of 50. His private health insurance provided access to a relatively expensive life prolonging drug that was not available through the NHS. The drug called Avastin, is used to alleviate certain cancer conditions and is on the World Health Organisations list of essential medicines in relation to its use in the treatment of eye disease. Though Avastin is approved and used in many countries including the UK, it remains unavailable on the NHS. The UK's National Institute for Health and Care Excellence (NICE), the body tasked with assessing and approving all treatments available through the NHS, have cited the high cost of Avastin as not being compatible with the best use of scarce resources. These are presumably the same scarce resources used to pay the six figure salaries and pensions of the thousands of hapless executives, programme managers, and private consultancy firms who have drained funds from the NHS like Piranhas stripping the bones from an unlucky Spectre Agent in a Bond movie. If only the NHS had the same disdain for executive level failure and ineptitude as Ernst Blofeld. It would certainly liven up the annual appraisal process for NHS directors wouldn't it.

Ed's widow Sue claimed the access to Avastin that his private healthcare insurance covered, thought to cost around £21,000 a year, gave her and their two daughters a precious further four years of life with Ed. There is surely no better definition of priceless than time spent with loved ones. The article went on say that because of this experience, Sue had chosen to pay for private healthcare insurance for her and her family at a cost of around £3,000 a year. Who would blame her? But how many families have that money spare? Rather than encouraging its readers to buy private healthcare insurance it might have been useful if the Mail Online had undertaken some investigative journalism and asked why NICE feels it is acceptable to withhold expensive drugs from UK citizens while saying nothing about the blatant waste of resources that anyone who has spent more than five minutes around the NHS can readily name. At a February 2023 meeting of the All-Party Parliamentary Group on Healthcare Infrastructure, it was highlighted that despite the tens of billions of pounds spent and wasted on trying to drag the National Health Service into the digital 21st Century, NHS Trusts were still collectively spending £230m a year maintaining moulding dated paper records and leasing buildings to store them in. This amount alone would cover the annual cost of Avastin and a host of other expensive treatments for thousands of NHS patients each year.

Though the levels of personal and household debt arising directly from healthcare costs in the UK are presently much lower than in the United States, they look set to grow significantly in the coming years. A July 2022 article in the Mirror entitled, *Brits go into debt due to staggering cost of private healthcare amid NHS long waits*, handily juxtaposed with adverts for equity release, cited a 40% increase in the number of people paying for private healthcare operations. But as every good marketer knows the minor detail of money and its absence shouldn't be allowed to get in the way of commerce. One person's healthcare funding need is a lenders opportunity. Spire Healthcare, who offer a wide range of treatments, surgeries, tests, and scans, has an online finance calculator on its website and offers a range of payment plans to potential patients through a third-party finance provider. Nuffield Health similarly offers loans through a third-party finance company and a company trading as Norton Finance offers unsecured and secured borrowing specifically for medical loans. Love it or loathe it the modern marketplace is an incredible mechanism, and the private sector is adept at interpreting what the rest of us only sense unfolding on the horizon.

And if one person's healthcare funding need is a lenders opportunity, then one person's unpaid medical debt, is a debt-collectors bread and butter. LRC is a UK company based in Nottingham. They supply specialist healthcare debt-recovery services including, credit control, pre-legal collections, litigation, and enforcement solutions to a range of public and private healthcare organisations throughout the UK. LRC claims that when it comes to healthcare debt recovery, they can not only chase the unchaseable, presumably on their way to infinity and beyond, but will do so in a manner that protects their clients' reputations. The content of their website makes it clear that though they may not have grasped the basics of physics, they understand the politically sensitive climate in which they are working as well as the direction the economic wind is blowing. At the foot of their webpage are numerous endorsements from some of the organisations they supply services to, including BUPA, and James Paget University Hospitals NHS Foundation Trust. It's a sobering realisation that the lending of funds and the chasing of consumer debt accrued by UK citizens who may have borrowed money to pay for essential operations and procedures, often performed in NHS hospitals by NHS trained consultants, will become an industry in 21st Century Britain. Sure, if you decided to pay ten grand for some new gnashers because your ambition is to be a contestant on Love Island and you default on the payments, then don't expect sympathy. But the idea that the bailiffs might knock on your door because you've defaulted on a loan for a knee replacement you needed after being knocked off your pushbike, is positively Victorian.

The article in the Mail Online stated that many people had simply given up hope of getting help on the NHS and went on to say the pandemic had sparked a mass exodus from NHS services with two million Britons now biting the bullet and choosing to self-finance the vital medical procedures they needed. It may be true that some have given up hope of getting the treatment they need on the NHS. But if there has been a mass exodus from publicly funded healthcare services, it was only reinforced by the pandemic, it's been in the making for decades. In its article the Mail Online was keen to highlight without any sense of irony or journalistic curiosity that many of the best private healthcare consultants also practise their craft in the NHS. Read into that what you will.

In January 2023, the Guardian reported over seven million people were waiting for NHS treatment in England alone. Needless to say, the Guardian adopted a different angle. Its article revealed how numerous NHS Trusts were promoting the private healthcare services available from within their own hospitals, provided by consultants on those same hospital payrolls, to patients on the hospitals own waiting lists. In essence these NHS hospitals were encouraging patients that they knew were waiting for treatment, to cough up a few quid and jump the queue. The investigation undertaken by the Guardians sister newspaper The Observer, revealed numerous NHS hospitals offering fast track access to private medical services for those prepared or able to pay while simultaneously warning other patients that hospital services were extremely busy. It's similar to the practice some airlines have adopted at airport check-in desks. Airlines would understaff their check-in desks and deliberately build up big queues, they would then wheel out other members of staff to sit behind an empty check-in desk next to the big queue with a sign offering it as an express check-in facility. In exchange for a mere £20 the weary baggage laden passengers waiting in the queues the airline had deliberately built up by understaffing its non-express check-in desks could be ushered through to their departure gates like VIPs. One such NHS hospital said to be engaging in this dodgy practice was the James Paget University Hospitals NHS Foundation Trust. The hospitals website boasts of having ten operating theatres that can cater for elective and emergency surgery and is situated in Great Yarmouth just a few miles east of Norwich. Perhaps best not tell Debbie from Norfolk.

This approach to managing the waiting lists of patients needing access to NHS services is alarming, some might say amoral. Of the many peculiarities within Britain's NHS, surely one of the least understandable is that someone who chooses to pay can jump the queue and be treated more quickly and effectively in the same publicly funded hospital and by the same consultant, as a taxpaying taxpayer funded patient. You could be or have been a high-rate taxpayer who contributed generously to the public purse and the NHS throughout your life. You might even have sat on the committee of the local hospitals League of Friends and raised money from coffee mornings to pay for the nurses dining room to be refurbished. Yet your treatment could be delayed because someone who might not have paid a penny in taxes has been gifted or borrowed the money needed to gain instant access to the very medical expertise you consistently funded and supported voluntarily for years. And in doing so, has nudged you down the queue. That's beyond bonkers and clearly unfair.

Regardless of their differing ideologies and audiences, both the Mail Online and the Guardian were tapping into the palpable collective anxiety about the capacity and capability of the NHS that is gripping Britain. It's an anxiety that is permeating every part of British society concerned about not only the future of the British National Health Service, but the future of Britain itself. There is a genuine sense amongst many within healthcare circles, clinical, managerial, providers, observers, regulators, and charities, that the NHS and wider healthcare system of the UK is now at a point of crisis never experienced before. In the midst of this, for directors and senior managers in the NHS to play into the amoral hands of the marketplace and willingly facilitate the creation of a two-tier healthcare system in which the NHS itself is providing and subsidising the infrastructure needed for the upper tier to operate, is a spectacular and incredibly short-sighted own goal.

I'm a former Chartered Marketer and a firm believer in the transformative power of enterprise and the ability of competitive marketplaces to drive innovation. I was not helped to progress from driftless teenage inactivity petty crime and social detachment by the efforts of the state, but by an entrepreneur. I'm not against the existence or availability of private healthcare. There will always be those willing and able to pay for it and as many if not more who want to profit from it. And it's no secret the NHS and the public sector could learn a great deal from private enterprise in whatever field it operates. What concerns me and I believe should concern us all, is the gradual introduction and accepted use of the private sector to fill the gaps and paper over the cracks that decades of conflicting policy goals, spineless leadership, greed, and self-serving neoliberal thinking have created. There seems to be no coherent plan to develop a brilliant national health service for Britain and no vision of what that might look like. Instead, there seems to be a growing tacit acceptance that the NHS can never be and that we should never expect it to be, brilliant. That we Britons should accept that the very thing we are most proud of is entering a period of almost terminal decline during which it will be propped-up by a constant stream of make do and mend solutions provided from outside. Eventually we will reach a point at which the transition to a largely privatised healthcare service will become perceived as the only practical option. We have been heading in this direction for quite some time and are much closer to the point of no return than many might believe.

Nuffield Health, as well as its well-publicised fitness and wellbeing centres, runs a wide national network of hospitals, clinics, and medical diagnostic centres across the UK. Spire Healthcare has almost forty hospitals located across the UK, a dozen clinics and two specialist cancer centres. Spire are reportedly the largest private provider of healthcare by revenue in Britain. Though smaller than Spire in revenue terms, Circle Health Group boasts of having the UK's largest national network of private hospitals. It provides neurological and musculoskeletal rehabilitation services and is investing heavily in technology, including robotics and AI. Since its inception in 1947 BUPA, the British United Provident Association has become a household name, one of the largest private health and care providers in Europe and an increasingly global company employing over eighty thousand staff. Well-resourced global operators like HCA Healthcare, the world's largest private hospital group have been providing specialist services and urgent care from various locations in London and Manchester for some years now. The private sector actors are already in play, providing an extensive range of generalist services and specialisms and understandably building their capacity and capability to capitalise on a globally growing sector that will be here for the long-haul. A recent estimate by the GMB suggested there are approximately six hundred private hospitals in the UK operating around ten thousand hospital beds between them, almost as many as the entire population of Ethiopia has access to. Circle, Spire, Nuffield Health, and Ramsay Health Care UK are waiting like angelic commercial mercenaries for their cue to step further onto a field of battle that offers rich rewards to the victors.

Chapter 39: Lessons from history

"What we learn from history is that people don't learn from history."

Warren Buffett

If you think the NHS will be here forever and you feel I am verging on melodramatic fear mongering, then I would ask you to dwell on the following. In 1950 the UK produced over half the worlds exported cars and employed over a quarter of a million people. Britain's production of cars was only exceeded in terms of quantity by the enormous industrial post-war might of the United States. The UK lost its status as an industrial and manufacturing epicentre some decades ago and while many mourn these changes, we all by and large accept that our economy is now utterly reliant on the service sector. Even though manufacturing was once hallowed and revered as an enduring source of future prosperity and a firm foundation on which to build the nation's economy, we have, if uncomfortably at times, become resigned to living without it. Other than the self-serving complacency of the entrenched, hierarchical, and insular management which typified the British car industry and contributed to its decline, the forces driving its demise were different to those presently strangling our health and care system. But where there is a strong anecdotal similarity is that the demise of the British car industry was allowed to unfold spectacularly and in full view, in no small part because just like the NHS, its existence and its place in the future was so resolutely taken for granted. The belief of those in the ivory towers and amongst large swathes of the public was that Britain's manufacturing prowess was unsurpassable. Attitudes towards newer so called inferior foreign products were entrenched and it was unthinkable by many that people in the UK or elsewhere would even contemplate driving a German or Japanese car, never mind buy one. But things change, and when the direction of travel isn't clear we find ourselves at the mercy of the change others want to impose upon us rather than the changes we might want or need. What a tragedy it would be if in fifty-year's time, historians, business authors, and academics are trawling over the narrative bones of speculation that describe how predictable and obvious the decline and collapse of the British National Health Service was, in much the same way the demise of the UK's car industry has been posthumously analysed. In the 1990's less than one in ten dentists were private. Now more than seventy percent of dentistry in the UK is provided by the private sector. We should not take the future existence of the NHS for granted.

If we, you, and I, continue to passively observe the undeniable decline of our NHS and watch the ongoing integration of a plethora of private healthcare providers gradually becoming accepted essential parts of our nation's health service, we will ultimately end up with an even more uncontrollable and incredibly expensive monster than the one we have now. It will of course be sold to us by right leaning politicians, their cheerleaders in the press, and the unprincipled who will benefit, as the best option possible. In reality it will offer the worst of all worlds to its patients, its staff, and the taxpaying public.

What we will end up with is a healthcare system that mirrors the well-documented dysfunctional structure and failings of our privatised utilities and rail services. Britain's rail network is a mess. And our health services are hot on its heels if not already ahead in many respects. The so-called privatisation of UK rail services that began in the early nineties has been nothing short of a complete and utter disaster for everyone except the shareholders and well-paid executives of the train operating companies who've benefitted from huge public subsidies for the last three decades. The long-suffering taxpayers of the UK are now shelling out more than they ever have, even prior to privatisation, in subsidies to the rail network and its train operating companies. An article in the Spectator of November 2022 reported that the annual subsidies paid towards running Britain's railways had amounted to £13.3 Billion in the year to March 2022. A figure equal to around £500 for every household in the UK, whether they use the railways or not. In exchange, and I like many of you can speak from experience in this regard, citizens who choose to travel by train in the UK, and most don't, can expect lower punctuality and a poorer quality of service than the majority of their better run European counterparts, or Tier 1 national services as they are officially classified by the Railway Performance Index. And yes, there is such a thing. Britain's railways are currently classed as Tier 2 on the index, hovering precariously above such global icons of public infrastructure as Latvia, Romania, and Slovakia. I have travelled on many a Northern Rail train that wouldn't have looked out of place in Madhya Pradesh, and on which I also felt less safe to boot. If any more salt should need pouring on the weeping railway shaped wound already inflicted on UK taxpayers, then consider that the annual cost of subsidising the railways does not include the ceaselessly spiralling budget for HS2, the divisive much derided plan to create high-speed rail links from Manchester and Leeds through Birmingham to London.

Thatcher's promise that the private sector would liberate the public purse from obligation, deliver unparalleled effectiveness and efficiency for rail passengers and the taxpayer, while simultaneously attracting freight shippers away from Britain's congested road networks, now looks rather misguided at best or the result of a psychotic episode brought on by sleep deprivation at worst. Perhaps my social circles are limited but I have yet to find anyone who thinks that the building of HS2 should be prioritised over funding the NHS and paying its doctors and nurses their rightful due.

What was supposed to provide more for less, is in fact giving British taxpaying citizens less for more. Though the socio-economic opportunity cost of such ideologically driven flawed policy decisions as the privatisation of the UK's railways and utilities is massive, their impact is seldom if ever felt by those who make them. As Thomas Sowell, author, economist, and political commentator has said, it is hard to imagine a more stupid or dangerous way of making decisions than by putting those decisions in the hands of people who pay no price for being wrong. I would add to his observation that it is even stupider to put decisions in the hands of people who will ultimately profit when they do go wrong. After all, my perception that the UK railway system is a shambles due to its poor performance and continued need for subsidies would probably be very different if I held shares in one of the various train operating companies. But public funds are of course finite unless you are an irresponsible bank in need of a bailout, and the very same precious and finite public funds being greedily swallowed by the corporations with insatiable appetites now running Britain's rail services and utilities, could have been put to infinitely better use supporting the UK's health and social care systems. In May 2023 Macquarie, an Australian banking group that owns various infrastructure assets in the UK and controls Southern Water, posted record profits of almost three billion pounds the previous year. Macquarie's top commodities trader earned tens of millions in profit related bonuses. Southern Water has been heavily criticised for discharging sewage into the sea around the UK. The private sector is in it for the private sector.

I ask myself if it can it be right on any level that my ninety-year-old mum has to spend what little life savings she has paying for the care she needs after a lifetime of working as a nurse and bringing up three children on her own, while public funds are given by the wheelbarrow load to private sector executives and shareholders? Many of the train operating companies profiting from the UK's rail network are now owned in part or in full by international conglomerates, some of which are state-owned in their countries of origin. This means UK households are not only subsidising the carnage that passes for a public transport system in this country, but they are also propping up the value and profits of corporations and state-owned institutions based in Germany, Hong Kong, Italy, Japan, and the Netherlands. What was once a treasured if at times mismanaged national asset, bought and paid for by the people of Britain, is no longer owned and run for their benefit. Successive governments have, just as with the NHS, failed through ineptitude and error to grasp the necessary nettles, or refused through mendacity to even acknowledge their existence. There is now a great deal of talk about renationalising Britain's railways.

The debate around the existence and role of private healthcare in the UK is not a simple one. And it should certainly not be an ideologically driven debate of, yes Britain should, or no Britain shouldn't. There has always been and in a global economy will undoubtedly always be, a multi-tiered health and care offer based and available in the UK. There should be room in a developed economy such as ours for a vibrant enterprising and innovative private health and care sector that markets its services to and caters for those who want and choose to use it from this country and abroad. The excellence and innovation that competition is capable of creating can be a source of learning, knowledge and ultimately progress for all the stakeholders in the health and care sector. The idea that Britain should have nothing other than a Soviet style national health and care service is, I believe, a misguided recipe for less than mediocrity. Where I believe clarity and change are needed is in the role private health and care is encouraged to play and how it fits around and not within publicly funded healthcare services. There is a massive difference in choosing to use a private healthcare service because you want and can afford an instant access or premium service, a luxurious room with a widescreen television and restaurant quality food and having to use a private healthcare service because the nations publicly funded healthcare system, is not up-to-scratch. That's not citizen or consumer choice, that's Hobson's choice.

It strikes me that the first step to establishing a clearer role for private health and care services in the UK will mean establishing a clearer remit and role for publicly funded health and care services. We have to have a meaningful citizen-led and informed user-focused conversation about what type of publicly funded health and care services we need and want and importantly can sustain. We need to dispense with the notion that the NHS is somehow immune to the principles that have traditionally underpinned the business model of every effective, efficient, and successful organisation on the planet. There are few if any business models in the world that would encourage the doing of everything as a sustainable strategy. Yet we continue to think the NHS can and should survive as an effective efficient entity that will provide every kind of health, care, prevention, and wellbeing related service under the sun while simultaneously dealing with everything society and the whims of the universe throw at it. This is a wholly unrealistic expectation on our part that we have bought into out of convenience and lazy thinking, and one which is fed by a politically disingenuous narrative that tells us we really can have it all. The American economist, author, and conservative commentator Thomas Sowell's presciently noted that in a world made up of flawed human beings there are no solutions, only trade-offs. We can't all have it all without compromise, without some give and take which will inevitably leave some feeling aggrieved.

While there is no reason Britain cannot have a brilliant publicly funded health and care system, it cannot continue to be a health and care system that tries to do everything. Brilliance in any field requires focus of attention and depth of resources. The jack of all trades is recognised as the master of none. It is a pointless and wasteful exercise for politicians to continue to rabble rouse their constituents into pushing for the NHS to supply every imaginable specialist treatment and protect every existing service within their local hospitals when these services are often clearly unsustainable and in some cases unsafe.

The false and unrealistic expectation which has been fostered in us, that it is our right to have access to every available publicly funded healthcare service on our doorstep, has led to billions and billions of pounds being wasted on building, equipping and refurbishing NHS healthcare facilities and specialist units that are often under-utilised and unused. In April 2018, the Health Service Journal carried the story of how numerous NHS hospitals had mothballed scores of wards and closed them to patients because the appropriately qualified staff needed to work in them were unavailable. One hospital in the Northeast of England had nine wards containing a total of 270 beds lying empty. The health fronts on which the NHS should fight must be chosen, managed, and protected carefully.

Chapter 40: Too important to fail, too big to fix

"People in an organization commonly or typically give disproportionate weight to trivial issues."

C. Northcote Parkinson

Roy Lilley is a well-known figure in health care circles. A self-styled and widely respected health writer and commentator, sometimes referred to as a health policy analyst he has written frequently for the Guardian Newspaper and appeared on Sky and GB News. Roy is often called on by the media to share his opinions, of which he has many, on the parlous state of Britain's health care system. A talented artist, he has held numerous senior positions in NHS Trusts and has chaired and facilitated various strategically significant panels tasked with understanding how parts of the healthcare system are performing and how people's health and care needs are being met by the NHS, their expectations, and their experiences. A former conservative councillor and NHS Trust Chairman who has tweeted his thoughts and ideas to the many thousands who follow him on Twitter for as long as I can recall, Roy's weekly e-letter is said to reach around three hundred thousand email in-boxes each week. His cutting, and incisively informed blogposts on the *NHS Managers* website he runs, are read, and shared enthusiastically, if sometimes surreptitiously, by tens of thousands of NHS employees.

Roy says and then shares in his own unique style, what most people in the NHS already know but are too afraid to say out loud themselves. Drawing largely on his private sector experience he highlights the blindingly obvious with a mix of disbelief, passion, and humour. I think for many managers in the NHS, his observations provide a welcome release valve for the frustrations they experience on a day-to-day basis. Selected colleagues and I used to look forward to receiving and discussing his latest rants when I worked in the NHS. His role in the health and care system is akin to that of the court jesters of old who were permitted and often expected to use humour to highlight the absurd and ridicule the establishment and its office holders from a safe, relatively safe, space. Comedy was tolerated as a surrogate for change and in many respects, this is still the case. Comedians offer a means by which we can laugh at the manifold ridiculousness of life, while simultaneously accepting it.

Roy was instrumental in setting up *The Academy of Fabulous Stuff*. An online platform created in 2015 with the intent of encouraging and enabling people working in the worlds of the NHS and Social care, to share their ideas. The homepage currently features a video of Dr Phil Hammond, the much-loved, unless you're a Tory, and well-known GP, author, comedian, and regular contributor to Private Eye. The site boasts of having over half a million page views since its launch and of hosting over three thousand allegedly fab ideas which can be accessed for free. Roy is also Chair of the Institute of Health & Social Care Management and has published numerous books over the years, including one on managing difficult people, which having spoken with him, or more accurately been spoken at by him, I would say was an exercise in self-help. He can be incredibly opinionated, verbose, often contentious, and on occasion a mildly annoying character, but most of the time his observations are on the money.

The frustrating thing about reading Roy's insightful and entertaining blog posts and emails over the years, and trawling the Fabulous Stuff website, is that little if anything meaningful appears to have ever happened because of it all. The mantra of the Fabulous Stuff website seems to be that lots and lots of slight changes can make the big difference we all know is needed. A frankly muddle-headed idea which is clearly total and utter bollocks, and for which its continued existence depends on ignoring the many sizeable and obviously destructive elephants in the room. Such approaches to fixing the healthcare system, an inherently assumptive statement but one few would argue with, including Roy himself, remind me of how my mum would tell my sisters and I as young children, that if we looked after the pence the pounds would look after themselves. This may have been a short-term feel-good solution to the financial problems my family were facing at that time, but we all knew the real reason we were impoverished was that my absent father wasn't coughing up the maintenance he should have been. The truth of the matter was that dad wasn't paying the pounds which meant we had nothing to look after but the pennies.

The notion of driving impactful sustainable change across an entire health and care system by focusing on the small things, however laudable and well intentioned, is a distractive form of wilful blindness. It is merely the flip side of not making time to identify, acknowledge, face up to and tackle the large things. I'm not critical of Roy and his colleagues for recognising the need for change and then setting up the Fabulous Stuff website as a means of achieving it. I imagine it was considered a pragmatic thing to do in a healthcare system epitomized by its inertia and inability to innovate, and I'm almost certain some good will have come of it. What I am critical of is the constant encouragement to focus on the small things in the hope that whatever benefits are realised will somehow combine and save the wider system. It's an utterly un-systemic fragmented approach which strikes me as offering sticking plasters to patients in need of major heart surgery. The notion that health and care services can rescue themselves by simply finding more effective and efficient ways of dealing with whatever is being thrown at them is like teaching self-defence techniques to people fighting an alien invasion with sticks. The NHS and Britain's wider health and care services are not struggling with their cultures, their finances, their quality of care, and their ability to recruit and retain staff because diabetic patients need a new healthcare app on their phones, or because staff need to adopt slightly better ways of doing what they already do, as useful as such things might be. Britain's publicly funded health and care services are under the cosh because we live in an increasingly market driven and personally demanding society, and an indifferent neoliberal dog-eat-dog commercial climate in which the participants are happy to externalize the human costs of their activity, and which is in turn creating unmanageable levels of need. We can't and will never achieve a world-leading health and care system and a physically and mentally healthy population by ignoring the conditions that create demand. A systemic approach is required, and the growing opportunity cost of looking in the wrong direction for the answers to our challenges, is huge and becoming more obvious every day.

I spoke with Roy in January and asked what he thought needed to happen if Britain was to build and maintain a health and care system fit for the future. I suggested radical change and systemic reform are needed if the NHS in any recognisable form is to be salvaged for the next generation. Roy dismissed the need for any radical restructuring instead suggesting that as long as the NHS is given the money it needs, which he estimated at a four percent annual increase in funding year on year, then it will continue to get by. I was surprised. It's an interesting stance to take for someone who has previously been in favour of scrapping a great deal of the non-value adding hierarchical apparatus sandwiched in the many layers of the NHS, of which there are no shortage. After our exchange, conversation would imply more interaction than engaging with Roy allows, I couldn't help wondering if he had become a bit battle weary. Perhaps succumbing to the scale blindness which affects so many of the well-intentioned people who want to make a difference to the NHS. Scale blindness is the sense that a problem is so big that it can never be resolved. Issues like climate change and global poverty fall into this mental space. One of the symptoms of scale blindness is that we replace it with something behavioural scientists call the law of triviality. We focus and fixate on the small things we feel may be within our power to alter, while ignoring the bigger issues.

The scale of our ambition – a fixation on the small things:

In early February 2023, some senior NHS figures from the Big Smoke tweeted their obvious delight about the creation of a set of standardised consent forms. The forms were be made available for use across a selection of NHS surgical services in London. The chirpy social media posts hailed the arrival of the new process, which was essentially nothing more than the release of a standardised document as, "*an amazing achievement*". The post went on to make it clear that adopting the new process, using the new form, wouldn't be made mandatory, or enforced in any way. The tweet was merely an awareness raising exercise to encourage people in the relevant departments of NHS Trusts across London to adopt the new recommended guidance and use the standardised documentation. The release behind the tweet went on to highlight the significant levels of hard work, stakeholder engagement and collaboration between service users and clinical specialities that had been undertaken to enable the amazing achievement in question to come to fruition.

An amazing achievement. I mean really, what the feck. You'd think they'd created a cure for cancer. Just how far off the pace has the NHS and the senior figures within it fallen when the standardising of a form is celebrated as an amazing achievement. An achievement is my wife Debbie walking the last 22 miles of Hadrian's Wall in 6hrs wearing sandals because I had lost one of her walking boots. An amazing achievement is the guy that jogged steadily if wearily past us both on his way to completing the entire length of the wall in under 24 hours. An amazing achievement is not creating a form. What is truly amazing is that after 75 years in existence this and many other basic aspects of running a business have been allowed to go unaddressed inside the nation's publicly funded health service. And the great administrative victory in question, should anyone actually choose to adopt it, will only apply to a limited number of services in less than one in ten of all the NHS Trusts across Britain. Amazing, my arse. The irony is that at the same time as these most basic principles of running a business are being celebrated by the NHS, presumably with Mexican Waves, much whooping, high fives, and belly bumps, we are also being constantly, if unsurprisingly told by NHS Trusts that the many, many, well-paid senior executives and managers employed within the NHS are adding a great deal of value to our healthcare services. They are not the wastes of space and drain on the public purse the Daily Mail and Daily Mirror would have us believe. No, they are in fact an essential part of the skilled administrative infrastructure needed to provide modern effective and efficient healthcare services.

    I tried to imagine how this latest in the line of the NHS's many utterly underwhelming self-declared amazing achievements might have played out in a private sector setting. Maybe in a business employing over a million people with a turnover of billions and whose sole task for the last seven decades had been to provide services to an entire population. Let's imagine the scene. An excited young manager screeches into the head office carpark as fast as their hybrid will allow. They don't bother parking in a designated space, on this red-letter day protocol doesn't apply. Abandoning their car outside the main entrance and not even turning to shut the driver's door, they run into the foyer before hurdling the security barrier and heading for the stairs. No lift for them, that would be too slow today. They bound up the stairs two steps at a time, breathlessly, excitedly, brushing past anyone in their path as they head for the top floor. Running along the executive corridor they burst into the board meeting unannounced. *"Stop, stop the meeting"*, they cry, *"You'll never guess what we've done!"* The room holds its breath as everyone around the grand boardroom table looks expectantly at each other and murmurs. Steadying themselves, holding their chest to catch their breath the bright young manager on whom everyone's eyes are now focused like lasers, speaks. *"The team and I have met and had conversations with some of the department heads and even some real customers from outside the organisation and we've done an incredible thing. You might not believe this, but we've only gone and created a really amazing new referral form."* Everyone gasps, you can cut the air in the boardroom with a knife. Yes, a new form, that's right. *"And no, of course we won't expect staff to get rid of their old forms or stop doing things the way they used to if they don't want to. But this form is so much better and neater and tidier and easier to understand, and we think if you just tell everyone that it would be super, super appreciated if they decided to use it, then it could be the gamechanger we've all been looking for."* Cue rapturous cheering as members of the board stand and applaud, hugging each other and forming a queue to shake the new proteges hand before they then carry them around the company carpark aloft in the chief executive's chair while their fellow employees shower them with rose petals and praise. Forgive my cynicism, but the amazing achievement I think most NHS employees and patients would like to see happen in the NHS is for it to gets its collective technological shit together and be nationally consistent with its processes and procedures. Is that really too much to ask in the year 2023?

If you listened to the networks of NHS directors and managers griping on LinkedIn, you would think the world of health and care would stop turning if they all downed tools and went home. I have a sneaking suspicion that the NHS and our health and care system would probably function far more effectively and efficiently from the patient and clinical perspective if every director and senior manager in the NHS took the year off. It may even be cost-effective to pay them just to stay out the way, which would have the added bonus of freeing up space in hospital carparks for patients and the people who actually add value. Let's face it, which of us knows of a patient turned away from an important operation because the Transformation Project Manager was ill that day! The question is, what are the managers in healthcare services and the NHS actually doing and what do they think their role is if it is not to ensure that the very basics of running a large organisation are in place? The explanation I think is that the NHS has become so stifling hierarchical and moribund that the small victories are celebrated because they have become the only ones available.

All the meaningless strategies directors and managers are busily and incessantly engrossed in writing, the roadmaps to nowhere they are tasked with developing, and the values, visions, and organisational mission statements they are enthusiastically creating, are nothing but a distraction from the real work. Writing plans and strategies with lovely matrixes and graphs might be exciting, but getting the basics in place is important, especially so in healthcare settings. Without the basics in place, grand plans are doomed not only to fail but will continue to dent and damage morale by constantly raising expectations before ultimately and inevitably disappointing.

PART IX:

Hope is Not a Plan

Chapter 41: So, what can be done?

"All problems exist in the absence of a good conversation."

Thomas Leonard

Of course, it's easy for me or anyone else with a mind to for that matter, to observe, share experiences, opinions and occasionally pass exasperated judgement. Often merely increasing the intensity of light being shone onto issues many people already knew or had an inkling about. I think we in Britain know our country and the wider world is in a state of parlous unparalleled unfolding flux. We may differ about the extent of it, it's hard to judge the scale of a storm until its passed, but we are all living it to some degree. We also know, though are not always prepared to acknowledge that our public healthcare system, the jewel in the crown of our national belief, the NHS, is in crisis. Like many of the UKs public services it has been systematically under-resourced and ineptly managed to a point where we are justifiably afraid for its future. Yet rather than try to steer our way clear of the neoliberally constructed concrete wall the bus we are all travelling in has been slung toward, we persist in covering our eyes or directing our attention out the side windows like distracted puppies looking for something novel and transient to capture our attention. Hoping against hope and all logic for a miracle to occur. Perhaps we think the problem is not ours to deal with, or maybe deep down we feel the challenge is simply too big to face. That saving the NHS and reimagining the future is a bridge too far, an enormous task beyond any perhaps even all of us. Our illusory unfounded hope is presently much greater than our genuine belief that the NHS can be sustained. We desperately want to believe it will be here forever, while simultaneously we are beginning to realise and being systematically bludgeoned into acknowledging it may not be.

But we should not and must not forget that the present we live in was once a distant and highly improbable future that didn't exist. Our recent and not so recent ancestors would look at the lives we live, the way we live them, the length we lead them for and the social structures we lead them within, in absolute astonishment and utter disbelief. While many of us in developed economies, whatever the present interpretation of that might mean, are seeking to optimise the quantity of our self-actualisation, the day-to-day attentions of most of our great grandparents were focused firmly on the lower tier of Maslow's hierarchy. The neoliberals may be trying to rewind history and move more and more of us back into poverty and increasing dependence, but the present we live in and the expectations we have are radically and irrevocably optimistically different from the past. There is therefore nothing to stop the near future being just as different from the present as our present is from its own recent past. I and many others would argue that the very survival of our species on earth and our collective health and wellbeing will depend on the future being radically different from the present. The prevailing science supports this view. The alternatives however possible, are as undesirable as they are unimaginable and unconscionable.

So, if there really is no wealth but life, this life, what can be done and where can we begin if we are to save the NHS and build the capacity and capability of publicly funded healthcare in Britain? We can start by talking. By having open courteous courageous informed and unflinching conversations with each other and then with our local councillors and elected MPs about the things that matter most to us. You can make a choice to get involved with one of the numerous pressure groups like 38Degrees, Every Doctor, Keep Our NHS Public, National Health Action Party, NHS Support Federation, SOS NHS, The 99%, We Own It, and other groups and organisations that are trying to save the NHS and influence government policy. And if you don't agree with every part of their chosen ideologies and plans, you can endeavour to try and shape their agendas or do your own thing.

Of course, this will not come easily to everyone. As well as being largely disengaged from the things that matter, large parts of society have either lost or perhaps never even recognised the value of good conversation. Genuine dialogue in which people seek to understand rather than merely seek to be understood, to get their point across and reinforce their own prejudices and entrenched views. But change, innovation, development, progress, all begin with thought and conversation. Let's dispense forever with the disempowering notion that we shouldn't talk about politics in polite company. Imagine if every single person in Britain wrote a letter to their MP explicitly explaining in simple humane language that what matters most to them is their health and the health and wellbeing of those they love and care for. Telling their MP that they want to live in a country with a publicly funded healthcare service fit for the future. Few of us will give two hoots about Brexit or the number of parking spaces on the high street when we are lying injured or become suddenly and seriously ill and there isn't an ambulance on the horizon or enough staff to deal with us at the nearest hospital.

We need to shake the Britishness that has stymied our ability to have meaningful conversations about important matters. We need to become more French, more Greek, more Scandinavian, less inward, less insular, and get comfortable talking about politics and public services in an informed and less superficial and less spoon-fed fashion. I'd rather listen to an ambulance service response time estimate for the coming week at the tail end of my local news bulletins than a weather forecast which is generally more accurate and available anytime from my smartphone. Unless each of us starts to use our voice we will be remembered as the nation that played Candy Crush while our healthcare system burned. If saving the NHS seems an impossible task, I am told the way to eat an elephant is one bite at a time. So, if the only question is, where to start, let's begin with conversations.

The following twelve suggestions are my conversation starters. Do feel free to let me know what you think of them and if you should decide to read them in isolation, then please do bear in mind that the context leading to them is contained in the preceding chapters.

Chapter 42: **Start with purpose**

"If you don't know where you are going, any road will take you there."

The Cheshire Cat (Alice in Wonderland)

The creation of a collectively funded healthcare service free to access at the point of need is truly the greatest possible embodiment of civilization. An implicit acknowledgement of the ties that bind us, of our undeniable interdependency and need for each other. It is an edifice of humanity at its very finest. However, its current manifestation in Britain is as a fragmented, dysfunctional, disjoined, cumbersome incoherent system. The NHS is quite possibly the least well managed under-led inconsistent disparate collection of entities purporting to be a coherent institution on the face of the planet. The worst managed franchise in the world.

Improvement of anything begins with understanding. Efforts designed to fix or improve something, a person, a process, a building, an organisation, a system or society, must start from a place of seeking to understand what the purpose of the entity in question is and establishing what it could, should, wants or needs to be. The *Can we fix it, yes we can*, simplistic Bob the Builder style politically popular approach to dealing with the NHS and healthcare needs to change to a more nuanced and thoughtful, *Before we try to fix it, let's firstly understand what it is and the forces that are impacting on it before we wade in and create a whole new set of largely predictable problems that will bite everyone on the arse.*

At this point it's worth introducing the thinking of Peter Drucker, probably one of the greatest best known and most revered business thinkers, social observers, and influential consultants of the modern era. Drucker's approach to understanding organisations starts by asking what the purpose of the organisation is and qualifying how it measures success. His thoughtful approach to intervention also powerfully reinforces the benefit of asking the right questions before jumping in with solutions. An idea the NHS and its very many leaders could learn a great deal from. In a short book he wrote in collaboration with numerous leading management and leadership gurus, called, *The Five Most Important Questions You Will*

Ever Ask About Your Organisation, Drucker suggests there are, you guessed it, five preeminent questions that can and should be asked of any organisation. If you are familiar with Simon Sinek's book, Start with Why, or have watched his Ted talk about the need to start with the *why* before moving to the *what* and the *how*, you might find Drucker's questions have a familiar ring to them.

The first and most fundamental question Drucker suggests any organisation must ask of itself is *why*. This question goes straight to the heart of things; what is the *why*, the purpose, the mission of the organisation? You would think that the answer to this question is blindingly obvious in the case of the NHS and Social Care services. But as I pointed out earlier, no two people seem to have the same idea of what its purpose is or should be. I also alluded to the fact that the health and care system of a nation can't be looked at meaningfully in isolation of the country it exists within. The question of purpose is probably the hardest question to answer in relation to our NHS and healthcare services. It is also not a question we can or should let the NHS itself, or Social Care, or any government department or minister answer on its behalf. NHS services belong to the citizens of the UK and are paid for by the taxpaying public, you and I. As such we should have the largest say in establishing the purpose of the services we fund that exist to serve us.

To this end the next UK government of whichever political persuasion should put on its grown-up pants and agree to a referendum about something genuinely worthwhile. A referendum that seeks the public view on three questions. Firstly, what do citizens feel the *primary long-term* purpose of government should be? For example, is it the creation of wealth and the growth of the economy as measured by GDP? Or is it the health and wellbeing of citizens and creating the conditions in which people can live fulfilling healthy lives? Is it living in harmony with our environment? Could it be the defence of the nation and the safety of the population? Or combinations of all these things to lessor or greater degrees. The questions asked and the answers to them will help clarify our expectations of government and the future role of public health as either a hapless bystander or a meaningful policy compass and a counterbalance to the manifold commercial forces that don't give a toss about our health and wellbeing. As has been discussed at length in this book, and in many other places by a great many other authors and orators, we are in desperate need of a better yardstick with which to measure the success of government than endless unsustainable economic growth and the ceaseless quest for more material possessions acquired at the expense of the planet, our precious finite time and effort, and our mental health.

Secondly, *do people feel the NHS and Social Care should be taken out of political control and placed in what might loosely be called a people's trust*? This could be an entity that would effectively stand alongside but outside of government. The world's largest social enterprise. The NHS may have emerged from the mind of socialism, but has it now outgrown its political heritage? If as a nation we decide that our health and wellbeing is the most important thing to each of us, then is it time to think differently about where the ownership and accountability for the institutions that support our health and wellbeing lie? Is healthcare too important to be entrusted to government, to politics, and the many agendas of politicians?

Thirdly, *are there things people feel that publicly funded health and care services should do more or less of and if so what are these things.* Can and should our publicly funded healthcare services continue to try and be all things to all people, to do everything and all too often do it badly, or are there areas they should focus on? Should patients needing certain services hold an insurance policy to cover the cost of using them? Should the NHS work in partnership to support international centres of niche medical expertise to achieve clinical economies of scale, just as we presently work in partnership with NATO allies to collectively achieve military economies of scale. Should levies and taxes be placed on certain activities that can then be redirected directly to healthcare? The number of people who end up in hospital and worse after falling off a mountain bike at the Whinlatter Forest Bike Park near Keswick in Cumbria is staggering. Is it fair or efficient that the finest trauma surgeons in the country spend disproportionate amounts of their time dealing with the largely avoidable, or that the precious money we donate to air ambulance services is consumed with insouciant entitled impunity?

As a society we may well need to accept that we can't have it all. And as science and research progress there will be more potentially expensive treatments available for an ever-expanding range of as yet unidentified illnesses. There will have to be choices made and compromise that will impact on all aspects of life. We can't continue to pursue a neoliberal low tax low wage economy that also provides a publicly funded universal healthcare service to the employees of rootless tax-avoiding corporations seeking low-cost locations for their businesses with *free* healthcare for their employees thrown in. The UK can't continue to compete in the global inward investment race to the bottom without creating more of the poverty and inequality which are the sources of a great deal of demand on our healthcare system.

Consider the issues emanating from the online gambling industry highlighted earlier in this book. If this sector isn't reined-in and some of its consumers inconvenienced, how many more people will take their own lives and how long will it be before there is a gambling addiction clinic in every major town sucking resources and clinical ability away from other areas of our healthcare system? Neoliberalism will continue to unashamedly unleash its havoc-wreaking cash hungry genies upon society at every opportunity, externalising the costs to us and our health and wellbeing so long as there is a profit to be made and public services and charities who will pick up the pieces. We should not accept this as a normal acceptable state of affairs, and we need to stop revering, rewarding and respecting those who make their fortunes from doing it. We should place the irresponsibly self-interested into health and wellbeing halls of shame, not shower honours upon them. The three quarters of a billion pounds currently sitting as assets in the Denise Coates bet365 Foundation should, along with the tax relief doubtless claimed on them, be taken and redistributed to debt advice charities, relationship guidance services, and mental health providers.

Chapter 43: A National Health and Care Service

"Learn how to see. Realise that everything connects to everything else."

Leonardo da Vinci

Let's take the care sector out of private profit driven hands and make it part of a National Health and Care Service. The NHS and its many well-paid executives persistently blame the social care sector for the pressures the NHS is facing because of the lack of capacity in social care to take new patients. The argument goes that the absence of beds in social care means NHS Trusts have to hold onto patients longer because they cannot discharge them safely into suitable care settings. This semi-disingenuous narrative often peddled by the very same people who agreed to the significant reductions in hospital beds that have occurred in the UK over the last three decades, has become the convenient go to rationale when explaining why the NHS is struggling with demand. The UK now has around half the average number of hospital beds per capita than other OECD (Organisation for Economic Cooperation and Development) EU member states and approx. a third the capacity of Germany. Some would say the mere presence of extra beds would achieve little for the NHS right now as there are not the staff to oversee them. They would be right. But no more so than those who observe that the outflow of well qualified experienced staff from the NHS has largely been due to the poor leadership and management they have been subjected to.

Why oh why, in a country whose hospital healthcare system has so little capacity that it has become utterly dependent upon and inextricably bound to a largely independent and profit driven care sector, do NHS and care services remain distinct and separate? How long are we going to put up with a fragmented second-class technologically disconnected social care system which diverts the surpluses it generates to the personal bank accounts of its owners and offshore tax havens serving the private sector. Why is care divided from the National Health Service? Private care services and their employees should be brought into the public sector on terms and conditions that reflect the vital work they do and the unsociable hours they often work. Employees working in the care sector should then be upskilled and trained to deal with the increasing levels of multiple morbidity and complex degenerative conditions they deal with on a day-to-day basis. The Alzheimer's Society estimates that over 70% of people in care homes are suffering with dementia or severe memory problems. Can it be right that we are asking people with minimal training often on minimum wages, to deal with some of the most vulnerable and clinically complex in our society?

David Rowland of the Centre for Health and the Public Interest suggests that running two separate healthcare systems in the UK, the NHS and Social Care, has nothing to do with delivering equity or improved health benefits to patients or people using services. He feels it has been set up in this way to limit the costs to the state of providing care for older people and younger adults with disabilities by transferring these costs back to individuals. In his view the current model of delivery of social care through the contracts between local authorities, individual users, and private companies, is highly detrimental to service users because it attaches a pound sign to each element of care and thus contributes to the commodification of a caring activity. I think he may be right.

It seems a touch bonkers to say the least that the sector that deals with the very citizens who consume the greatest proportion of NHS services is distinct from that same system. Wouldn't it make sense for the care sector and the NHS to be integrated, to ease the exchanging of patient information and enable patient records to be accessed?

On the 8th of June 2023, the Fabian Society published *Support Guaranteed: The roadmap to a National Care Service*. The report, instigated by Wes Streeting MP, then Shadow Secretary of State for Health and Social Care, and commissioned by UNISON, sets out to establish and develop a *National Care Service* over the course of a decade. The document includes 48 recommendations for an incoming government and suggestions for a timeline for reform. The work to join health and care services together that Jim Mackey, the former chief executive of Northumbria NHS Foundation Trust, initiated in Northumbria some years ago is already ahead of this curve. Moves to integrate health and social care could be further enhanced by the addition of the hospice sector. This would reduce the postcode lottery of palliative care and further increase the scope for record sharing. It would also provide more development opportunities for employees in each of these three presently distinct yet inextricably linked fields.

Chapter 44: Get a grip on Primary Care

"Quality is never an accident, it is always the result of intelligent effort."

John Ruskin

The disjoined and inherently fragmented nature of Primary Care in the UK is ineffective and incredibly inefficient at best. At its worst it is inconsistent and unsafe. It survives in its present format more as an accident of history than a product of user informed or needs led design. Its structure as a loose collection of small businesses of infinitely varying size, and culture is stifling the opportunities for greater coordination and innovation that undoubtedly exist. Its loose unstructured nature hampers the realisation of the many economies of scale that would be available to a truly national primary care service. Its structure also limits the service's collective ability to learn and thus restricts the inherent potential of itself and the people who work within it. Its absurd unique combination of ubiquitous disjoined smallness is an anachronism that offers the worst of all worlds to its patients, staff, the wider healthcare system, and the public purse. The current make-up of Primary Care as a flotilla of individual inconsistent independently steered ships means there is neither constancy of quality, of purpose, or consistency of control and oversight. Radical rethinking and restructuring of Primary Care in the UK is absolutely key to building an effective efficient healthcare system that works for all its stakeholders and is designed around the needs of those it is funded to serve.

Primary Care is the shop window of and the front door into the NHS. Well over ninety percent of Britons total interactions with the NHS occur in Primary Care. The overwhelming majority of patient referrals that end up in acute and secondary settings come through Primary Care. Just as few of us would ever want to arrange a meeting with a legal professional at a solicitors practice simply to say we have met with a solicitor, few of us want to attend a GP Practice just to see a GP. What we do want from our engagement with professional services of all kinds including Primary Care, is access to the expertise and experience we hope and trust these services possess. In the event we might need specialist professional legal help, none of us would arrange a visit to a solicitors practice that did not have this legal expertise. Property conveyancing is very different from family law and human rights – you get the point.

Nobody would visit a GP Practice if they did not believe it possessed or could facilitate access to appropriate clinical ability or medical expertise. The clinical experience and medical expertise Primary Care possesses, in business parlance, is its core competence, its USP. The unique selling proposition each GP Practice has that pulls us toward them when we think we need a solution or a service only they can provide or that can only be accessed through them. In the commercial world and certainly in the healthcare system of the USA, the clinical expertise and experience within each GP Practice would be viewed and managed as something referred to in management circles as a core competence. This is a term used to describe the key asset any business possesses that its own existence and its component parts depend upon, and which in theory they exist to optimise. An organisations core competence is the thing it does that it is known and valued for.

Yet the way Primary Care is presently structured in the UK means a great deal of its core competence, its most precious and valuable asset, the clinical capacity, capability, knowledge and expertise its people possess, the very kernel of the activity for which GPs and their colleagues in Primary Care spend years in training to be able to provide to their patients, is wasted. Infinite amounts of finite time are eaten by non-value adding tasks. Administration, management, and regulatory compliance minimise the availability of Primary Cares core resource, consuming its use and effectively reducing the value it is able to add. It's a bit like paying for an expensive top-class orchestra to perform at your child's wedding and then trying to save money by asking the members of the orchestra to do the catering and run the bar as well as perform. Reducing the time they have available to play their instruments and entertain guests would be foolish. The value of the orchestra is in the collective musical abilities its members possess. Serving food would be a poor use of the skills they have honed. Their performance will suffer, and no guest is likely to go home with a clean wedding outfit. There is no business other than NHS Primary Care that I can think of which so limits and restricts the use of the one key differentiating competence it possesses and for which it is so highly valued by its users.

In 2012, in the face of significant upcoming changes to the structure of healthcare services in the UK, a survey of its members by the Royal College of General Practitioners revealed that over eighty percent of GPs did not want anything to do with the business of planning and commissioning or organising services, this being a central focus of the planned change. GPs made it very clear to the various policy makers and panjandrums that they wanted to be GPs, not bureaucrats, administrators, or spreadsheet pilots. The vast majority of GPs I was working alongside at the time did not favour the introduction of the changes contained in Andrew Lansley's Health and Social Care Act. They viewed it as a divisive and short-sighted policy. This view proved to be correct. The act saw many experienced GPs being dragged unwillingly, unwittingly, and ill-equipped into the time-consuming, attention diverting, energy sapping and ultimately pointless exercise of trying to oversee the process of competitive commissioning for the many NHS services provided on their respective patches. The overwhelming majority of GPs did not commit ten years of their lives to train to become a GP so they could then give their time to the managing and monitoring of local healthcare services as well as the running of their own small businesses and the provision of care to their communities. Few had received any training in how to do so, and it showed. The result of Lansley's reforms was to place some of the most experienced GPs in the healthcare system under even more pressure as they tried to juggle the demands of being involved in overseeing the provision of healthcare services in their area, while still functioning as general practitioners dealing with the everyday health and care demands of their practice populations. They had neither the time to be efficient businesspeople who had a handle on the unfamiliar beast they had been tasked with controlling, or effective GPs.

To take the medically knowledgeable brains of some of the most well-intentioned and intelligent people in society and then use this precious finite resource as ineffectively and inefficiently as our publicly funded healthcare system has a continual habit of doing, is a recipe for waste and inconsistency. For publicly funded Primary Care to be sustainable it must be viewed as one part in a wider public health system and designed, structured, and managed to consistently meet the majority of predictable demand it deals with on a regular basis. The golden rule of running effective services is to design them to meet the majority of predictable demand in the most efficient ways possible, and to use the efficiencies this then releases to deal with the unusual and the niche. In short, if you master the basics of dealing with what is largely foreseeable, it allows you to commit resources to deal with the unpredictable and the unexpected, which in the world of healthcare is always just around the corner.

The clinical experience and medical expertise that GPs and the many other health and care professionals who form the front line of the NHS possess, must be treasured for the precious resource they are. They must be liberated from the many cumbersome tasks and activities that eat their time, attention, and effort, while doing nothing for patients and the healthcare system other than reducing its collective capacities and capabilities. This will free Primary Care to use its value-adding resources, its greatest asset, the precious medical knowledge its people possess, for the benefit of the patients it is there to serve.

If you listen to the one size won't fit all brigade, an argument that neglects the benefit of having a large-oversized coat available to lend to guests on a rainy evening, you might be tempted to think the local inconsistencies of Primary Care are one of its endearing features. Don't be fooled. The inconsistencies in Primary Care do not serve the needs of its patients, more worryingly they are potentially harmful. And if you listen to people who have worked in the NHS for too long, you may be convinced that change in Primary Care is impossible because each GP Practice is its own business so GPs can't and won't be told what to do or how to do it. What the naysayers from whichever camp they come from cannot deny, is that the current structure of Primary Care is unsustainable. Change is needed, necessary, and long overdue. To leave Primary Care as it is, would be the unsafe choice. In its present form it does not have the capacity or capability to lever its core competences and build the physical and technological infrastructure that would benefit both it and its patients. Nor is it able to offer its workforce the opportunities for personal development and professional specialism that would be available in a larger organisation.

The first thing I think that needs to happen to enable those working in Primary Care to focus on the needs of their patients rather than the piecemeal running and inconsistent administering of their own small businesses, is that GPs who are funded by the public purse, should be directly employed as GPs by the NHS. Many people already think their GP or the GPs working at their local practice are NHS employees. If the nurses, midwives, physiotherapists, consultant psychologists and psychiatrists, mental health practitioners, the neurologists, oncologists, radiographers, the cardio, colorectal, orthopaedic, maxillofacial, spinal, transplant, trauma, and urological surgeons, are all employed by the NHS in the NHS Trusts they work in, why can't and why shouldn't general practitioners also be directly employed under the umbrella of the NHS? Three quarters of a century after its creation, the NHS has never really gotten to grips with Primary Care. General Practitioners should work in the NHS, for the NHS, under contract to the NHS.

Chapter 45: Centralise processes to create consistency

"The problem with the NHS Tom, is that nobody seems in charge."

Finnish Health Official

In a world in which the need for individual self-expression and a perceived desire on the part of professionals for greater autonomy, centralisation may seem an anathema to many. But when it ensures consistency, which in health and care services translates into better safer care for patients, increased effectiveness for service users, and greater efficiencies for the public purse, its benefits should not be ignored. W Edwards Deming observed many years ago that quality relies on consistency. And it's a mantra every successful brand owning organisation on the planet knows to be true. Yet for some reason, as with many other well-known business truisms, those tasked with running the NHS don't feel central direction or the enforcing of consistent quality standards is important. The irony in this is that the unspoken desire of most NHS executives and senior managers in the regions and localities is for greater direction from the centre. They are crying out for it. Its absence is creating a costly and wasteful mix of inaction and uncoordinated action.

In 2014, Lord Rose, the former Executive Chairman of Marks & Spencer was commissioned by Jeremy Hunt, then Secretary of State for Health, to explore and report back on the state of leadership in the NHS. I was working in the NHS when the findings were published in June 2015 in what became known as *The Rose Report*. In his summarising, Lord Rose made some simple, practical, and in my view long overdue recommendations. Amongst them was the idea that every part of the NHS should share the same single high-level vision statement and that each employee, at whatever level they worked, should be given a single consistent handbook, a sort of, *this is how we do things guide.* Lord Rose suggested these should be issued to every member of staff throughout the NHS, at every level. For readers who have worked in a large corporation his suggestions smack of obvious and useful corporate motherhood and apple pie. Of course, all the employees who purportedly work within the same organisation should in so far as is possible share the same sense of purpose, they are in theory all pulling in the same direction and aiming for the same outcomes. Lord Roses recommendations, based on decades of experience gained in the private sector, were ignored. Kicked into the long grass by the senior bods in the NHS who felt that a corporate type such as Lord Rose could not possibly understand how the NHS worked. The reality is that I think he did, and importantly, he understood that for many people, its patients, and its staff, it quite simply was not working. He also understood that without a shared common purpose, any improvements made could only ever be piecemeal and would produce minimal benefit.

What the well-paid public servants who occupied the upper echelons of the NHS were really objecting to, was that they perceived Lord Roses suggestions to create consistency as being a first step toward greater centralisation. Centralisation is not a welcome concept to those who have spent their careers and much public money building and justifying the existence of disparate empires. It has also in our age of personal liberty and choice become an irrationally and unnecessarily dirty word, associated with authoritarianism and control. For the senior executives at the top of the myriad towers looking over the vast NHS landscape, the C word and the consistency that would follow it brings the possibility of comparability, increased visibility, and potentially accountability. It would also feed the appetites of other interested parties, patient bodies, interest groups and the media. Furthermore, in a decentralised under-led inconsistent variable system, when things go wrong as they inevitably will, with depressingly regular predictability, the centre can abdicate responsibility and distance itself from any harm done. Have you noticed how when tragedy strikes in a particular NHS Trust or hospital setting, it's never the responsibility of the centre, or the policy makers. It's always narrated as the fault of the local actors in the system and of how they decided to do things. Heaven forbid that a tragedy might occur due to a lack of direction or control from the centre.

The C word is also quickly and conveniently demonized by lazy thinkers and those with vested interests outside the centre. When faced with a discussion about greater levels of central direction or control, every wannabee local or regional empire builder, spouts out the phrase, *one size won't fit all*, before vocally drumming up local support to protect services, generally services they are employed on a good salary to run, from the controlling, unfeeling, and uninformed influences of those ill-intentioned fascist centrists. Of course, the very same people protesting in pursuit of their own parochial agendas are more than likely using online retail delivery and banking services located in other parts of the UK because purchasing products and managing finances online in your own space and time is infinitely more convenient and user-centric than having to waste time visiting the high-street shops and banks in their limited opening hours. They want a consistent service from the people and organisations they deal with, they just don't think the rest of should have a right to such things.

Those who insist on using public money to design their own bespoke version of services to meet what they perceive as a unique set of local needs, may be genuinely well intentioned if not misguided. But often they achieve nothing more than protecting the very communities and populations they serve from the expertise and help their service users and communities really need. For a service to be locally relevant and responsive, it doesn't always have to be situated on the doorstep. Just ask Jeff Bezos or the nice delivery driver that brought your latest online purchase, or anyone who has accessed an online learning experience.

The NHS is in dire need of greater central direction and control. At the time of writing this, there are a multitude of separate NHS Hospital and Community Trusts and numerous bodies with varying nationalised and regionally structured equivalents in each of the four home countries. There are then the many regional ambulance services and a separate entity responsible for managing blood donations called NHS Blood and Transplant. There are Fifteen Academic Health Science Networks whose stated remit is *to function as healthcare systems integrators responsible for linking the different parts of the health ecosystem to drive innovation and create wealth*; whatever the feck that means in practice, email me if you know! Then there are the thousands of GP Practices in varying states and with varying capacities and capabilities situated in communities across the UK. And let's not forget the many other functions, though again nobody is sure what these are, which are operated by or in partnership with NHS England. Add to this mix the hundreds of supporting, I use that term loosely, and overlapping local, regional, and national bodies and networks, the names of which change with alarming frequency, and we have a cast-iron recipe for confusion.

But here is the real problem. In amongst all these NHS related organisations, bodies, and functions, and do bear in mind that the list I have touched on is a long way from exhaustive, there is effectively nobody in charge. In fact, it could be argued the proliferation of this smorgasbord of disparate sometimes competing organisations, bodies, and functions, is the logical outcome of nobody being in charge, and of a longstanding vacuum where there should be leadership, direction, coordination, and control.

For those who worry that central direction means inflexibility, I should emphasize that by consistent, I don't mean rigid or inflexible. The best services have the ability and the capacity and capability to be consistently flexible. Public Services, especially health and care services, should be consistently flexible, responsive to the needs of the people they serve. If there truly is no wealth but life, then the purpose, vision and ethos of the NHS should be the subject of a continuous conversation with, and influenced as much as possible, by the public that use it. Our healthcare services should by definition always remain works in progress. If we want an effective and efficient NHS, now and for the future, it must be far better led and become much more consistent.

Chapter 46: Decentralise oversight and accountability

"It is hard to imagine a more stupid or more dangerous way of making decisions than by putting those decisions in the hands of people who pay no price for being wrong."

Thomas Sowell

Like all good soundbites, there is a significant degree of truth in Thomas Sowells observation. The idea of decentralising oversight may seem a little at odds with the previous suggestion to centralise processes and create consistency, to me it is entirely logical. Centrally agreed standards would make it much easier to implement consistent and transparent local oversight and accountability mechanisms. If all the stakeholders in a system know what's expected from it and what success looks like, it follows that measuring its performance and interpreting the actions of those leading it will be easier. I'm also conscious this recommendation may feel a touch ideological, perhaps even a bit *power to the people*. It is my strong view that public services ultimately belong to the public. I am of course aware that some publicly funded services might not benefit from being opened-up to community control and oversight. The armed forces and intelligence services spring to mind. But it should, if I have authored this book well enough, be obvious by now that the NHS and our health and care is far too precious to remain as a political football to be kicked around by every party in their endless and tedious spats of childish point-scoring.

Many public services could and perhaps should be explicitly classed as social enterprises, though most have slipped the chain of accountability that once linked them to their taxpaying stakeholders. Public services exist in theory at least, not to serve a commercial purpose, but to have a social impact, address market failure, or provide a service that should not be subject to commercial interests. For example, the provision of justice, health, education, and equitable access to essential services. If we accept that the twin levers of choice or control are the two most obvious ways of influencing the quality of any product or service, then it is fair to say that the users of public services including the NHS, currently have neither. Users of public services have little if any choice and minimal if any control or influence. And giving choice is not an efficient way of creating quality in public services. It simply leads to duplication and confusion. In relation to the public services we use, I don't think any of us want choice in the traditional sense. Our desire is for easy access to consistently good quality services that we have confidence in. So, the remaining lever left to drive improvement in public services is control, the question becomes, by whom and how.

The running of the UK's health and care services must become detached from excessive political influence. Britain is a country that has by almost every measure lost faith in its politicians and the process of politics itself. Various polls have been conducted over the course of the life of the NHS asking whether British citizens feel they can trust politicians. The so-called golden age of British politics in the mid-20th century during which almost two thirds of the country felt politicians were good honest people doing their best for the country, are now a distant barely believable memory. More recent surveys conducted since 2010 show that over two thirds of the UK population feel politicians are out of touch and almost two thirds of us think politicians are in it for themselves. In February 2019, the Independent published a story saying just nine percent of people in the UK felt politics wasn't broken. I am surprised the figure was that high.

If the idea of community control and oversight of health and care services sounds overly radical, there are two strands of thought I would ask you to consider. Firstly, think for a moment if you will about the role of a jury in a court. A random often diverse group of people are drawn from the local community, and they become the arbiters, the ultimate point of authority in the delivery of justice, perhaps the most important function any society can provide to its citizens. If the hallowed and pivotal role of the jury still holds, the idea that twelve people good and true can sit at the apex of a nations justice system, then there seems no logical reason why members of the community cannot become essential and valued parts in the oversight and monitoring of many public sector services, local authorities, prisons, education, and policing as well as health and social care. Some might suggest at this point that the role of councillors, school governors, hospital governors, and the like provide this control and local accountability already, and the only reason we think they are ineffective is that people do not engage with them enough. In my experience, this is not the case. People do not engage with them because they are ineffective. In parts of the UK the voter turnout for the 2018 local elections was less than one in three. Ten of my wider family were members of the local NHS Trust, but in a decade not one of them was ever asked for their views, yet the regulator of NHS Trusts was kept happy because the local NHS could show that it had signed-up large numbers of members and was therefore engaging with its local community. It, like many other NHS Trusts, chased its target for membership, but completely missed the point of doing so. It is no wonder people have simply stopped believing that they will be listened to, engaged with meaningfully, or that their views matter a jot to anyone in public office.

The second strand of thought is that not that long ago the provision of NHS services in each area and region was overseen, if not always effectively, by something called a Community Health Council. These were succeeded by Public and Patient Involvement Forums, which then became Local Involvement Networks known as LINKS, which in turn preceded the creation of the chocolate fireguard we now call Healthwatch. The home countries all have their own take on community oversight and involvement. Wales has retained a version of its community health councils. I think a conversation about reintroducing revised and strengthened versions of Community Health Councils would be a good starting point on the journey towards effective local oversight and genuine accountability.

In relation to the vast majority of public services we consume, we have little if any choice. The term customer suggests a degree of choice about how and where we access and consume publicly funded services and amenities. We can't choose which organisations provide our public services to us, which council, which police force, which adult or children's social care service. It took a meteor strike to remove the dinosaurs from the earth and create the conditions in which humanity would eventually thrive; hold that thought! But if you had consulted with the dinosaurs about the need for them to leave the earth in order to facilitate the dawn of humanity, they might have nodded politely and understood the concept at the intellectual level, but I don't think they would have volunteered to take part in a mass extinction event. The point I am making here is that the turkeys won't vote for Christmas. Change, and the recognition that it's even needed, seldom comes from within the established order. Discomfort drives change and the future belongs to those who are dissatisfied with the way things are. Perhaps our health and care services can become the shared commons of our era? We do already own them after all.

When I was young and arrogant, I might have looked strangely at someone who told me they were an expert by experience. Now I not only look to them with respect I also listen closely to what they have to say. There really is no substitute for experience and who better to oversee, monitor, and guide the role of healthcare services and oversee the people tasked in the service of leading them than citizens, patients, and service users, with first-hand experience of them? Perhaps a network of citizen oversight panels could exist at the local, regional, and national levels. We might introduce peer reviewed performance related pay for healthcare directors, chief executives, and chairs? Now there is a thought...

Chapter 47: Implement consistent systemwide technology

"Our future success will be directly proportional to our ability to understand, adopt and integrate new technology into our work."

Sukant Ratnakar

Some of the developments and advances in technology that have been widely adopted in the last few decades alone include the internet, analog and digital mobile telephony, DNA sequencing, GPS tracking, smart-tagging, digital photography, fibre optics, email, mobile phones, iPhones, laptops, tablets, home computers with Windows, PowerPoint, Outlook, X-Boxes, virtual and augmented reality, genome editing, microprocessors, nanotechnology, touchscreens, cloud storage, Bluetooth, Wi-Fi, IOT, social media, electric vehicles, photovoltaic solar power, domestic robotics, CRM systems, Google, engine management systems, smartwatches, lithium-ion batteries, voice recognition, biofuels, non-invasive laser surgery, and magnetic resonance imaging to name a few. We have come an immeasurably long way since the height of technology being offered as a prize to contestants on the Generation Game was a coffee percolator, a teasmade, or an electric bedside alarm clock.

So why in this era of terabytes, nanoseconds, and remote monitoring, when I was transported to Carlisle Hospital up the M6 by ambulance a couple of years ago were the paramedics unable to access my medical records while I as a passenger could have been looking at my Amazon purchase history or banking online? Why is it that the chatty ambulance driver is able to use facetime to keep in touch with his family in Poland, yet his colleague the nice lady sat in the back of the ambulance with me is taking physical notes in transit to be handed in person to the A&E Consultant on our arrival at the hospital? Why don't the component parts of the technology in our healthcare services talk to each other? Why is it that NHS employees are using distance reducing cost-effective time-saving life-affirming technology in their private lives, yet are drowning in paper and using arcane record storage systems while carrying clipboards and biros around at work? Why, amongst such a tsunami of easily available safety enhancing patient enabling resource maximizing electronic options and solutions is the NHS and our entire health and care system so woefully behind in its adoption and rollout of technology?

Almost every single local, regional, national and global business operating in the private sector has had to embrace and make technology work for them in order to survive. Highly skilled artisans running micro-businesses use technology in one form or another to promote themselves and manage transactions and finance online. Even the local food producers, traders and nick-nack stalls at Keswick market offer contactless payment. The mobile network operator that sent me a new sim-card in the post this morning knew it had been delivered before I did. And I don't buy the argument that we should expect less innovation within healthcare because it is somehow more complicated than any other type of business. Tesco is a business that turned over almost $61B in 2022/23. The supermarket stocks around seventy thousand products sourced from thousands of suppliers who in turn access hundreds of thousands of interconnected supply chains. Love it or loathe it, Tesco has adopted and uses technology expansively to make it more effective and efficient. The grocery giant fulfills around a million online orders every week and its stores collectively receive over thirty million visits each month. Toyotas global turnover is around six times that of Tesco. The company sells its products in 170 countries and manages some of the most complex supply chains and interdependent commercial relationships on the planet. The infrastructure Toyota has in place allows it to control and oversee the movement of over half a million parts and accessories every day. Bigness and complexity undoubtedly create challenges but in and of themselves are not barriers to introducing technology. More often than not they are the logical product of implementing it effectively. Functional technology isn't an organisational *nice to have*, it's a platform on which many businesses are built.

In November 2022, the former Secretary of State for Health Patricia Hewitt, was commissioned by the serving Health and Social Care Secretary Steven Barclay to lead an independent review of the forty-two newly established Integrated Care Systems (ICSs) across England. It's a tried and trusted technique amongst politicians who oversee public services that when they are in doubt about what to do, clueless, but want to be seen to be doing something, they get someone else to write a review or a report for them. That way if it works you can take the credit, and in the more likely event that it doesn't, you can distance yourself from the report quicker than an MP can claim their expenses. The report Hewitt produced, imaginatively titled, *An independent review of integrated care systems*, was published in April 2023. Amongst the large bland smatterings of conventionally accepted wisdoms and muddled motherhood and public sector flavoured apple pie that make up the bulk of such documents, the report called for the newly established Integrated Care Systems, of which there are forty-two, and of which none are actually integrated in anything other than name, to have greater autonomy and accountability for sharing data in their efforts to improve the health of the respective populations they serve.

Autonomy, of course Patricia, that's just what they need, why didn't we all think of that? The autonomy to carry on making their own disjoined messes in every region of the country. What a great idea! It seems Hewitt has learned nothing from the dysfunctional money sucking technology vortex the NHS has been sucked into since the spectacular failure of the National Programme for IT almost twenty years ago. The idea that we should let the forty-two Integrated Care Systems go and do their own thing in the absence of central direction and some much-needed decision making by NHS leaders, feels like a recipe in waiting for another expensive technology disaster. The only thing that may stop each Integrated Care System from spaffing copious amounts of taxpayers' money up the technology wall on pet projects, yet again, is the notion that they might be held accountable should everything go south. But don't bank on it.

What would have been more useful is for Ms Hewitt to have identified the one ICS region where the technology was in an obviously appalling state. The architectural equivalent of Coventry Cathedral after WWII. This could then have been designated as the ideal testbed, a pilot site, a sandpit, call it what you will, chosen to be the part of the healthcare system where the best way forward for the entire NHS and Social Care sector could be established in relation to adopting and implementing technology. To get it right in one place and then use this as the blueprint for the wider system would surely make more sense than letting multiple flowers, incredibly expensive flowers at that, bloom and then predictably wither in splendid, disconnected, and disappointing isolation.

If the NHS can get it right, the productivity gains would be huge. Just as they have been in other industries and sectors that have adopted and implemented technology effectively. And the data that appropriately interested parties could be drawing on from the application and use of a central technology platform would be immense. The potential exists for the NHS to become a world-leading source of insight, learning, and innovation. Importantly, our data needs to be securely held and maintained. Encouraging the creation of disparate IT systems across the nation seems counter intuitive to ensuring that whoever is tasked with the coordination and security of our data is not only clearly visible and accountable but has the economies of scale and expertise to do the job well.

The myth promulgated by the technicians that are interoperability standards obsessed, that open standards for interoperability will solve everything because we can just connect system A with system B and any other system, is madness and has proven to be false. The USA moved away from the notion of best of breed and plug and play ideologies over a decade ago. Clinicians and care givers need a single view of the patient record and a standard set of the functions they need to treat their patients; referring, documenting, ordering, prescribing, viewing, scheduling, communicating, all the things that healthcare providers commonly do for and with their patients. It's not presently favourable to speak against the open standards ideology, but it's not working for patients or clinicians as it stands.

Had basic joined-up technology been in place and its findings available to view on screen and in real time by clinicians, managers, and directors at the Countess of Chester Hospital, the pattern of deaths and harms that Lucy Letby was causing on the neonatal ward could have been made almost instantly visible to anyone with access to the system. The shift rota reveals at a glance that Letby's presence is the one consistent factor each time an unexplained death occurred, or an unexpected harm was inflicted. My forty quid doorbell can alert me when someone is approaching. My twenty quid remote camera in the garden can ping me an alert when a hedgehog, or a cat, walks across the line of sight. Yet apparently no one at the Countess of Chester Hospital received an alert to investigate when three babies died in quick succession on one of their hospital wards? There is no justifiable reason why in the second decade of the 21st century joined-up technology and anomaly raising alert systems are not in place across the entire NHS.

Chapter 48: Trash the targets

"Every measure that becomes a target becomes a bad measure."

Goodhart's law

What truly matters to each of us cannot be measured, easily quantified or at times even verbalised. We may tell those closest to us that we love them this much and more as we stretch out our arms as far apart as they will go, but we can't quantify our love as a percentage, nor I imagine would we want to. Perhaps what truly matters to each of us cannot be measured because it remains beyond the language of measurement. The feeling I get when the sun is on my face, or look up at the stars on their pitch-black canvas through a cloud free sky, or nurse a helpless hedgehog back to health, see the smile on one of my many nephews and nieces faces when I introduce them to the delights of using power tools, or when I hear the jauntily clanking bells on the necks of the sheep climbing out the valley below my favourite holiday spot in Kefalonia, or just sit quietly at the bottom of the garden with a glass of Glayva and a decent cigar after a day working outdoors. What I feel when I sit on the sofa with Debbie on a Friday evening with a cold beer and a hot curry, is contentment beyond description. How I feel when I have come off a video call or out of a meeting at which I have had my intellect fed with what my good friend Andra calls brain candy, is more than can be expressed on a happy sheet rating scale. How I felt when I was at rock bottom and contemplating suicide could not be quantified. And even when I tried, I could not be understood.

Yet the machine minded, the policy makers, the qualified yet unexperienced suburban occupant ants of the public sectors ivory towers, most of whom will never have slept rough, spent the night in a police cell, been the victims of injustice or even cleaned their own gutters, they think everything can and should be quantified. These ill-informed citizens of the black and white world of degree educated certainty whose faith in the structures of society has never truly been tested, they abide by the rules and feed the systems insatiable desire to measure whatever is capable of being measured, while all the time trying to make what they have measured matter. It is impossible to accurately establish, to quantify, the damage that targets have caused throughout public services across the world. The impact of the slavish adherence to them that permeates the entire health and care system has been nothing short of catastrophic. Planet NHS is littered with the debris filled bomb craters and traumatised employees still reeling from the impact of each short-sightedly launched target driven initiative that has been exploded onto the landscape of the NHS in recent years. Targets and the healthcare systems continued focus on meeting them have cost many lives, caused untold harm to far too many, and relentlessly stripped layers of spirit, passion, and commitment from a devoted workforce.

The notion that everything can and should be measured are the lazy thinker's and the politico's way of attempting to demonstrate the public purse is obtaining value for money. Their presence has become the means by which the lobotomised soulless political automatons who lead our political parties can blandly demonstrate to the electorate how their approach to running public services is working. Ministers, civil servants, and the press have become fixated on them, and in turn public sector executives and managers have had to become equally obsessed with them. Acknowledging the sacrosanct importance of targets, kneeling unquestioningly at the altar of meaningless arbitrary performance measures, is the key to ensuring a friction free career in public service and healthcare management.

Targets became increasingly prevalent in public services during the last three decades, largely as a result of a concept called New Public Management which began to emerge in the 1980s. New Public Management was a broad label used to describe the various ways its proponents felt public services could and should be made to run in a more businesslike fashion. The term itself is thought to be a product of neoliberal ideology which believes that only competitive marketplaces are capable of producing efficiencies in relation to the running of organisations and the provision of goods and services. Of course, in a truly neoliberal economy, the UK would not have an NHS. There would be no publicly funded healthcare. And had John Ruskin been a neoliberal, today he would be famous for his much less quoted observation that, *"There is no wealth but an ostentatious excess of cash at your disposal."*

When executives and managers focus on chasing multiple targets and ticking a constantly changing stream of seemingly endless regulatory boxes, rather than prioritising the needs of their service users and staff, it creates an organisational culture of inappropriate focus, bureaucratic overload, and organisational attention deficit disorder. It blinds people and prevents the organisations they are tasked with running from seeking to understand and address the issues that really matter and masks the sources of risk that inevitably lurk in the shady spots of every large organisation. This relentless pursuit of meaningless targets, numbers and percentages periodically plucked from the air and the minds of people far removed from the reality of life, is sneering at our very humanity, mocking compassion, and destroying the NHS. The world-renowned psychologist Carl Rogers astutely observed that what is most personal to each of us is also most universal. The things that really matter to you and I are generally the same things that matter most to all of us; belonging, loving and being loved, feeling safe, secure, and sane, being acknowledged, noticed, and heard. These are things that cannot be meaningfully measured. Nobody's headstone boasts a reference to being in the upper quartile of attentive partners or top ten percent of economically productive citizens. Yet.

We need to know the hospital consultant seeing us is competently interested in our situation, not driven to deal with us in the average allotted timeslot only to find we must revisit them next month when our condition has deteriorated because there was no time to get to the root of our illness during the first meeting. Some years ago, I had an appointment with a GP from my local practice which continued long after official practice opening hours. He had deliberately booked me the last slot of the day because he wanted to speak with me in depth about my depression. He understood we wouldn't be able to squeeze a meaningful encounter into the ten minutes usually allotted for a face-to-face patient appointment. He knew I needed to start taking anti-depressants if I was going to climb out of the deep hole I was in and avoid harming myself. He made time to hear my concerns and acknowledged and addressed all the previous macho foolish objections I had raised to taking medication for the mind. He realised that an investment of his time upfront would pay dividends in the longer term. We spent at least forty minutes talking, until finally I reached a point where I understood and agreed with his suggested course of action. Up until then I had been a semi regular visitor, not quite a frequent flyer as some GPs refer to their better-known visitors. But in the four years since that appointment, aside from being summoned for my

Covid-19 vaccinations, I have visited my local GP practice just twice. One of these was to attend a routine scheduled health check for men of my age. My point is that the GP I saw that evening acknowledged my humanity. He listened and I felt heard. He understood that my unique Tom shaped needs wouldn't fit into a ten-minute sized slot and by making time to recognise what mattered to me he was able to give me the treatment I needed. Perhaps more than I had been prepared to admit up to that point. He spoke to my anxieties, dealt with what had become the looming possibility of my suicide, and ultimately if less importantly saved a good deal of time and money. He provided value to the healthcare system and to me, its service user, by navigating around the very targets and measures he was supposed to comply with. The same targets and measures that the pedantic peddlers of New Public Management deem necessary if public services are to become more effective and efficient. Morons!

During the last few years, I have asked numerous NHS related organisations to share the list of targets they are held accountable for and to whom they are accountable. Very few have responded voluntarily. I have had to resort to using freedom of information requests, and many have failed to even respond to these. NHS England have been unable to provide a complete answer to my request. They have so many targets that they literally don't know where to start collating them into one place. The obsession with targets and ratings and the management of reputation at all costs has fuelled a plethora of terrible decisions and tragedies, and it continues to underpin the culture of blame and denial that allows the many thousands of avoidable deaths occurring in the NHS each year to occur, with depressing predictability, year, after year, after year. The theory proposed some years ago by Goodhart remains true. As soon as a measure becomes a target, it ceases to be a good thing. Targets pervert and alter personal and organisational behaviour. Period.

I think most of us want to feel that the public organisations we fund are there to meet our needs as users of their services. Whether expressly or not, we think we should be the focus of their efforts. But we are not seen by the people who sit atop these services as customers. It's not that these are terrible people who sit in oak panelled offices spinning on black leather chairs stroking white cats while thinking of world domination, they are merely mortals who have recognised that career success in the public sector is not built on committing your energies into creating excellent user experiences. Career success in the public sector is about pleasing the regulators and the government depts that provide your funding. This means becoming brilliant at reporting on what you are doing, not being brilliant at supplying what your service users think you provide. Cohn's Law astutely states that the more time people spend in reporting what they are doing, the less time they have to do anything. Organisational and system stability is ultimately achieved when you spend all your time reporting on the nothing you are doing; if you doubt the veracity of this statement, just spend a couple of hours watching parliamentary debates, if you can. The focus for leaders in the public sector, is not to delight the users of their services, it is to get better and slicker at reporting on the nothing that is happening.

This target focused approach to work is incredibly demoralising for the very many devoted, passionate, professional people, who work in the NHS and healthcare services. Many of whom chose their path into healthcare and the NHS as a vocation, an opportunity to do something that matters and makes a difference. These people want to be measured by the impact they have on the lives of the people they help, not constantly beaten with a stick for *under-performing* according to a set of meaningless arbitrary and constantly shifting metrics.

You will hear people say that the problem is not targets per se, it is just a case of getting the right ones. There aren't good targets; TOD, target obsession disorder, should be a recognised condition in the NHS and in the wider public sector. TOD has been destroying public services and eroding staff morale for decades now. Targets, what are they good for, absolutely nothing, say it again, targets, repeat to fade - you get the gist!

But if there are no targets, I hear you say, how will we know how the NHS and our public services are performing. How will we know if they are doing well or not? The straight answer is that we don't know now, we just think we do. What we are told *good performance* currently looks like, is a myth. The numbers paraded to the regulator, printed in annual reports, and then waved in front the press, mean little to anyone other than the regulator and don't matter a jot to most patients, service users, their families and loved ones. We and the media need to stop treating them as if they do. *Oh, you know, I'm ever so pleased my Frank was seen within the 4-hour A&E target, I know he was killed by an inexperienced surgeon, but at least he was admitted quickly.*

Targets give comfort and distract, but they are essentially an illusion of quality offered to us in the absence of meaningful information. And make no mistake, there is not a single public sector organisation that does not know how to game the numbers so they can give their regulators, overseers, and ministers, the perception of performance they all crave.

Trust, not targets, is what's needed. I say we equip and trust the people that are doing the jobs that add value, to do them. Targets exist in the absence of trust. If targets are a disease crippling the NHS, trust is the largest part of the cure. When we cannot trust organisations or the people in them to do the right thing, we create legislation, regulations, and laws to force compliance. But you can't build trust with regulation or create positive cultures with more legislation or percentages. If you recall how little trust the staff at Mid Staffs Hospital had in the ability of their own hospital to look after their loved ones, that for me was the most telling data available to indicate that something was about to go horribly wrong. Trust was essentially the only indicator that mattered, but trust cannot be quantified and so its validity was ignored by those in charge.

In 2021, the Harvard Business Review revisited a series of findings on the importance of trust in organisations. Compared with people at low-trust companies, their research showed people at high-trust companies reported 74% less stress, had 106% more energy at work, gave 50% higher productivity, had 13% fewer sick days, had 76% more engagement, 29% more satisfaction with their lives, and 40% less burnout. Quite how anyone manages to measure energy at work is beyond me, but can you imagine the impact on the morale and recruitment and retention of the NHS if its workforce were working within genuine cultures of trust? It would transform capacity and revolutionise the experience of service users.

Developing trust will entail freeing people from the tyranny of ticking boxes, filling-out spreadsheets, and compiling reports nobody reads. We need to let health and care professionals get back to practising their craft while encouraging and enabling them to continually improve what they do, not merely incentivising administrators and managers to become ever more brilliant at reporting it. Measuring the cow never made it fatter, but it did get in the way of it grazing. The resource sapping regime of targets needs dynamiting out of existence. TNT, trust, not targets, is the way forward. Let the health and care professionals do their jobs. It is time to trash the targets for the NHS. They have become a meaningless surrogate for performance that give comfort to people in ivory towers, removed from the day to day, who do not understand that instructing organisations to stare obsessively at the dashboard inevitably leads to them crashing the car.

Chapter 49: **Mandatory training for leaders & managers**

"It takes considerable knowledge to realise the extent of your own ignorance."

Anon

Here in the UK, it's not that long since you had to apply annually for a licence to own a dog, yet now you can rise high in the running of a vital public service without any specific assessment of your fitness. Consistent mandatory training and development and peer assessment should be a requirement of continued public sector employment for executives, directors, non-executive directors, chairs, and managers at all levels. With great authority comes great responsibility and with great responsibility should come great accountability. The traditional models of management are broken, they were designed in an era where the hierarchy went unchallenged and the capacities and capabilities of the vast majority of people were not even acknowledged, never mind untapped. The need for and the age of the hero leader, if it ever really existed, is gone. And certainty is a bad thing, in fact it is the only thing I'm certain of.

If good leadership is about creating the conditions in which the right things can happen, the task of leaders and managers in healthcare services must be to create the cultures and climates of trust in which all staff are able and want to give the best of themselves. They must be servant leaders who see their role as enablers, barrier dismantlers, policy and practice shapers who turn to the centre and inform it with information and data drawn from the practice of delivering services. It is unacceptable that we have created a healthcare system in which thousands of non-clinical administrators who are unable to effect meaningful change are able to collect six figure salaries at the taxpayers' expense. The boards of most NHS Trusts could be replaced with a basic form of Artificial Intelligence and most of us would never notice the difference.

Effective leadership and genuine positivity is about confronting things, not denying their existence. The public service leaders and managers of the future will need educating differently. We need the curious, the conflict harnessers, the coordinators, problem discoverers, policy challengers, who have courage, humility, and morality. People who will bring themselves, their vulnerability and their humanity to the table. People who are willing to have their own performance judged by the extent to which others believe they have created the conditions in which the right things can happen. Changes will not come about if we continue telling the same old dry stories of why we need culture change in the NHS, in the same old tired comfortable polite ways. The more we hide from our problems the more we run into them. Organisational and systemwide failure and thinly veiled internal fighting are the only things presently emerging from the continued insistence on avoiding productive conflict that typifies NHS leadership and management.

In my time in the NHS, I noticed many of the leaders I came across had an unswerving belief in their own abilities and they saw the presence of doubt as an issue, as corporate disloyalty and weakness of character. I don't and it's not. This unswerving belief in themselves has blinkered them, it has cost patients their lives and many, many employees their wellbeing. There is a phrase I heard some years ago which has stuck with me; *Decisive action in the hour of need denotes a hero but may not succeed*. There are numerous ways of interpreting this. What I take from it is that being decisive is not always successful. It's easy to appear decisive, launch a programme or respond to a situation, but if the goal within it is to secure your own reputation as a person of action, then the results will be sub-optimal at best and possibly disastrous at worst.

John was the best man at my wedding over thirty-five years ago. He took up teaching in later life and was gifted enough to gain entry to Durham University to study for his first degree. I remember him ringing me one evening, he'd had something akin to a revelation. After entering the library at Durham University, he had an overwhelming sense of his own ignorance. It was as if he had suddenly been made aware of the presence of such knowledge and insights that he said he had never felt so small and ignorant in all his life. Then his journey into education began. But it began from a place of humility, a real sense of him knowing just how little he knew. I have seldom if ever heard senior healthcare managers acknowledging their own ignorance or using the word humility, let alone acting with it. Hierarchy rules, there is no room for questioning or doubt and views from those lower down in the pecking order are not welcome or encouraged. There is a significant mismatch in the levels of perceived competence versus actual ability in all public sector management circles.

As a middle manager in the NHS, I recall being asked to let a young graduate shadow me for a few days as part of their progression through the NHS Graduate Trainee Scheme. My shadow was a smartly suited shiny shoed eager young man in his early twenties who quickly informed me he had chosen to join the ranks of NHS management over a more lucrative career in accountancy, be still my beating heart, because he said he was passionate about the NHS and wanted to give something back to society. I think I managed to keep a straight face. Giving something back is a stock phrase trotted out by people who feel the need to disguise their desire for a comfortable well-paid post in public service as something saintlier. Having him around was a bit like taking a life size cardboard cut-out to meetings. He had been well briefed in all the traditional practices of the corporate Jedi. He said yes in all the right places, he looked to the most senior people in the room for his behavioural cues, and he didn't ask any challenging questions. He seemed to me to have neither the life experience, knowledge, curiosity, or desire to look beyond the rigid measures he had been told he must care about if he was to make his mark. Nor did he display any real interest in people and the things that matter to them. I don't blame him, he was young, and someone had placed a terrific opportunity at his feet. I empathised with him and simultaneously pitied him; I had once also been keen to please. And in fairness to him, many of the qualities I believe are needed in NHS leaders and managers can only come with experience. But this bright young thing, convinced he was set to be one of the solutions to the challenges facing the NHS, was at that point in time, almost certainly destined to become just another one of its problems. The last time I checked on his career progress he had been promoted to the role of director of performance, chief target chaser to you and me, at a large NHS Trust in the Northwest of England. His future looks bright, the future of the NHS under people like him, does not.

From the northbound platform of Manchester's Piccadilly Rail Station, travelers may still be able to see an old building on the front of which is a large sign proclaiming *Everything is Connected*. We need people in positions of leadership and management in the NHS to be versed in systems thinking. Wider context is key, and nothing exists and therefore cannot be fixed in isolation. Implementing disconnected solutions creates problems elsewhere. Systemic challenges are like balloons, squeeze one part and the air simply moves. We need decision makers who want to understand the wider context. What organisations need, are leaders who recognise this issue and actively create the conditions in which people have the time and space to commit and focus on producing thoughtful and thought-through solutions. Leadership is about realizing others potential, not reducing normally intelligent people to the role of busy fools who juggle their workloads and find their attention diluted by focusing on so many summits that they are reduced to a state of inertia and ineffectiveness in which ill-informed decisions create further risks, which in turn require further management attention. It remains true that we are where we are because of decisions made previously, consciously, and otherwise.

If we are to create the conditions of continuous improvement, in which the need for improvement can firstly be recognised and openly acknowledged, then we need people who are comfortable looking into areas that cause concern. This means we also need people to be aware of their tendencies to label events and others as positive or negative and all things in between. It's ok not to be ok in both a personal and organisational context. What's not ok is to put your head in the sand and pretend otherwise, not to create the time and space for introspection, to talk about and air the personal and organisational issues and concerns that we all have. It is said there are no wrong thoughts, only the refusal to think. All things are works in progress and most things that go wrong are in truth only highlighting opportunities for improvement if we are open to seeing them that way.

The effective training and development of good leaders and managers will be essential if the NHS and the wider world of health and care is to deal with one of the thorniest and seemingly most intractable issues facing it. Attracting, recruiting, valuing and retaining the workforce it needs.

Chapter 50: **Attract, recruit, value and retain**

"In healthcare people aren't merely the organisations greatest asset, they are the organisation."

Tom Bell (standing on others' shoulders)

What is a GP Practice without GPs? What is a hospital without clinical staff? What is a hospice without nurses? What is a talking therapies service without therapists? What is a care home without carers? These statements are self-evident, yet our health and care system's track record in attracting, looking after, caring for and retaining staff, the very bedrock of each and every service provided, is woeful. The clinically qualified staff employed in health and care settings, whether they work in the public, private or voluntary sectors, are not merely their organisations most important asset, they are the foundations on which the organisation sits.

You'd think it would be easy to manage staff well, especially in the protected competition-free operating environment of the NHS. Attract, recruit, employ flexibly, train, develop, value, and retain. Many of the world's most successful private sector companies, some in the field of health and care, do this extremely well. And importantly in competitive labour markets they understand the need to also continually improve their ability to do it really well. The top spots in the annual rankings of the best companies to work for both globally and in the UK are prized and hotly fought for by companies keen to attract talent. The NHS, currently listed as one of the world's top ten employers by staff numbers, does not feature in these rankings. Britain's best loved brand is trumped by wholesalers, firms providing cyber-security products and companies selling Pizza and accountancy services. This needs to change. The NHS and Social Care sector needs to develop a reputation for being one of the best employment and career choices available for clinical employees and one of the most explicitly selective and exclusive for its management, administrative and support staff. I think most people want to work for an organisation, public, private, or voluntary, that they can be proud of and in turn feel valued by.

When I was inducted into Carlsberg some years ago, my fellow newbies and I, the fortunate few selected from the hundreds that applied for our jobs after a rigorous and demanding application process, were made to feel valued. We were taken to every department and part of the business. We were shown the brewing facilities and met some of the senior brewers. We were introduced to the finance teams, telesales and call handlers, the technical and support staff, the distribution managers, and the draymen. We each spent days with various parts of the business in our respective regions, shadowing other's roles, learning what people did, how they worked, and the challenges they faced. We were told about the history of the organisation, where it operated, what its plans were, and how it saw the future unfolding. I recall being effectively locked up in a hotel, a very nice one somewhere on the outskirts of Sheffield for two weeks, learning about the organisations pricing structures, its entire product range, and how to use the company's computer systems. Even though my role was customer facing, I wasn't allowed near a potential customer on my own for over a month after joining the company. Carlsberg was and remains incredibly precious about its reputation and the value of its brand. The company had no intention of letting an overly enthusiastic untrained new employee loose on its profitable free trade account base in the Northwest of England.

In contrast, my induction into the NHS was a one-day sheep dipping exercise. After which I was left to awkwardly bumble my own way around head office to find the other departments in the building and locate the emergency exits, fire extinguishers, and first-aid kits. I didn't even get paid for over three months, and my experience wasn't uncommon. Carlsberg encouraged all its employees to reply to non-urgent emails within two working days and respond to requests from colleagues for help and assistance at the earliest opportunity. In the NHS many of my emails to managers often went unanswered. If I had been made to feel like a valued part of something larger than myself by a company whose motive was profit and whose continued existence depended on the sale of sugary alcoholic liquid to the masses, I was made to feel awkward, ill-equipped, and unwelcome by an organisation tasked with providing publicly funded healthcare services to citizens of the UK. There is something strangely arse about face in this isn't there?

A study published in 2022 by the Health Foundation revealed that NHS nurses had endured over a decade of falling wages. Researchers found that the average earnings of nurses fell each year in real terms between 2010 and 2017, at twice the rate of those working in other industries. In May 2021, the Health Service Journal reported that even Tory MPs had observed that no other business treats its staff as badly as the NHS does. That is quite an admission from the party that opposed the national minimum wage and now wants to hinder worker's rights to strike peacefully. My mum blames the challenges facing the NHS and the demise in the appeal of nursing as a career on what she describes as the shift from caring to counting. As far as she is concerned the introduction of professional management into the NHS was one of the systems biggest, if not its greatest mistake. Mum worked in the NHS in the hallowed era when matrons ran and ruled the hospital wards. She still interrogates me as if I were a patient, *have you eaten today, you're looking peaky Tom, are you taking care of yourself, are you still smoking cigars,* and *are you sure you're drinking enough* to which I quickly reply yes before she can utter the word *water*. A conversation with mum is always part medical consultation.

In June 2023 NHS England published the *NHS Long Term Workforce Plan*. In an attempt to make it look like the writers of the plan knew what they were doing and were adopting a comprehensive approach to their work, seventeen of the plans hundred and fifty-one pages are the list of references. Most impressive I hear you say, and in its defence the plan does contain numerous references to the need for culture change and also implies, without specifically acknowledging, that the entire NHS needs a higher standard of leadership and management if it is to retain its employees. The workforce plan talks about creating a clear employee value proposition, and developing organisational cultures that are values-driven and consistently compassionate.

It's no secret the NHS could learn a great deal from companies in the private and third sectors as well as some of the public service institutions in other countries that have established a track record and reputation for attracting, recruiting, and retaining employees successfully. Yet in all of the NHS workforce plans seventeen pages containing the almost two hundred references to other documents, plans, research papers and sources of insight, I can find only two that relate to sources

426

from outside the NHS and its related world of thinktanks and closely affiliated like-minded organisations. This wilfully blind insular arrogance that continues to look only within its own siloed thinking for the solutions to its problems is deeply entrenched in the NHS. It is also a large part of the reason that nothing changes. Henry Stewart, originally the founder of Happy Computers is the author of *The Happy Manifesto – make your organisation a great workplace* and *Creating Joy at Work – 501 ideas for creating a happy, productive workplace*. These superb publications highlight examples of what a good employee culture looks like and of the behaviours good employers demonstrate. They contain distinctly different language and adopt a quite different approach to understanding what motivates and retains staff than the *NHS Long Term Workforce Plan*. The culture of the NHS will not develop or change if it only ever engages with its fellow birds of a feather and the established purveyors of the traditional wisdom. These being the same hapless ineffectual bodies and schools of thinking that have watched and pontificated as the entire health system has been pushed to the edge of existence.

The workforce plan is heralded by the chief executive of NHS England as one of the most seminal moments in the institutions 75-year history. But the government and NHS England have been publishing plans that recognise the need for and promise to recruit more staff into health and care services ever since anyone can recall. None of them have come to fruition in the way they were promised. Research suggests that over half the people who leave a job leave their boss rather than the organisation they work for. Though there is evidence to suggest this analysis is an oversimplification, the strong correlations between the quality of management employees are subjected to and their commitment and importantly performance, are indisputable. If the NHS hierarchy continues to underplay the impact the absence of genuine leadership and principled management is having and fails to acknowledge how this has created the conditions that have forced many people to leave the NHS, then plans that promise culture change without addressing the wider issues will not make the slightest difference. What the system measures and makes matter and who gets rewarded and for what, has the greatest influence on managerial behaviours and in turn a huge impact on how employees are treated and thus where they choose to direct their energies.

Chapter 51: Scrap the Care Quality Commission

"Inspection does not improve quality, nor guarantee quality. Build quality into the service in the first place."

W Edwards Deming

Of all the high-profile tragedies, scandals, and fiascos that have dogged the NHS and Social Care over past decades, not one was originally discovered or unearthed by the official government appointed regulator of health and care services in the UK, the Care Quality Commission. Or its predecessors, the Commission for Health Improvement, and the Healthcare Commission. The CQC currently costs taxpayers in excess of two hundred million pounds each year. But as it presently exists the CQC is not fit for purpose. It is staffed and led by people who have moved from one part of the healthcare system to another who consistently fail to look for the cultural indicators of unsafe care and seldom get under the bonnet of what is really happening in the settings they inspect. In many cases, the CQCs easily manipulated inspection processes have meant they were duped into approving the continued provision of poor care and even ill-treatment of patients by providing what ultimately proved to be a false quality rating. I worked under an NHS director who launched a comprehensive and expensive internal communications campaign with the explicit objective of influencing the outcome of a CQC inspection by making sure staff did not say anything negative about the Trust. No expense was spared.

Outstanding, Good, Requires Improvement, Inadequate, what do these Ofsted style arbitrary snapshots and wholly inadequate descriptors of complex interconnected organisations and the multiple services they provide mean to service users, patients, staff, and local communities? My GP Practice was rated *Outstanding* by the Care Quality Commission because it was perceived as having an active patient participation group. This motley and aged group of which I was once part consisted of half a dozen patients who liked to come together for a cup of tea and a chat but had never influenced anything the practice did. The practice website still looks like it was designed by a student in the early nineties and the phone call return system is variable. Sure, the doctors are great, but to label the practice overall as outstanding, that's quite a stretch. As for the local acute hospital, that has been in various measures over the decades. They are currently listed as *Requires Improvement*, a step up from the *Inadequate* they were previously labelled as. But what does that mean to me or any other local person? It's not like Trip Advisor where we can use ratings to help us choose where to take our custom. The ambulance crews in the area will still take you there if you need urgent attention, you won't be asked if you have a preference. Local GP Practices still refer patients to the hospitals many services and most of the staff remain constant. There are no other employment options available and no other NHS Trusts close at hand that clinical staff can go to work for.

When the Care Quality Commission comes to town and dishes out an undesirable rating, the only thing that generally happens is a promise of improvement is issued and a change at the top of the organisation is made; *hospital bosses promise improvements will be made in the wake of latest assessment*. The NHS in North Cumbria has had almost twenty changes of chief executive in the last quarter of a century. The CQC have never taken the blindingly obvious systemic factors that surround the provision of healthcare services in the area into account in their ratings. Nor do they take the time to talk meaningfully with patients or service users. This being the only audience whose views in the end really matter. As was noted earlier, we as the consumers of public services have neither the luxury of choice nor the lever of control.

Let's change the role of the regulator from feared, loathed, and ineffective enforcer, to adviser and monitor. The traditional role of the business adviser is to add value by sitting at the centre of a web of knowledge which grows with each interaction. They become a repository of best practice, and the sum of their accumulating knowledge becomes an increasingly informed and valuable resource. The Care Quality Commission should switch their focus from regulation and inspection, to advising, to ensuring and monitoring the consistent spread and application of accepted best-practice and know-how as part of a virtuous cycle of continuous organisational and system-wide improvement. A critical friend that holds the common vision of what good looks like and helps every organisation in the system move towards that point. A system advocate unafraid to identify and name the wider barriers and issues that may be hindering progress.

Chapter 52: Remove Public Relations from the NHS

"Few people have the wisdom to prefer the criticism that would do them good than to the praise that deceives them".

Francois De La Rochefoucauld

Earlier in the book I introduced you to the wonderful aphorism that feedback is the breakfast of champions. As vomit inducingly cheesy as it sounds, there is a wealth of truth in it. After all, if you don't know what you are doing wrong, you can't fix it. Every precious pearl, including the most perfectly formed, starts its life as an unwelcome piece of grit that found its way into the oyster.

Before we go any further let us briefly separate the role of communication, genuine communication, from Public Relations, PR as it is more widely referred to. The role of PR is not a virtuous one, in fact its very label is a deception. The evolution of PR has its roots in some fairly dark aspects of our history. The term, Public Relations, is its own greatest success story. Public Relations was formerly known as propaganda. And though it has existed in many guises for thousands of years, Roman Emperors used it effectively as a means of manipulating opinion as did the Catholic Church, its practice and modern methodologies were honed and refined by more recent use within Nazi Germany. Its negative post-war connotations meant the overtly manipulative term propaganda needed to be ditched in favour of something cuddlier and so public relations as we know it was born. This reinvention allowed the practice to continue while disconnecting it from the role it played in the rise of Hitler and Nazism. Public Relations tactics have subsequently been deployed in the denial of cancer linked to smoking, the rebranding of damaging chemicals as fertiliser, and more recently, and perhaps most harmfully and shamelessly, climate denial. Naturally, the world of politics is awash with it and its practitioners.

Propaganda, the original and accurate descriptor of PR is defined as information, especially of a biased or misleading nature, used to promote a political cause or point of view. Public Relations is not about relating to your public, as nice as that might sound. PR is about trying to shape people's views by telling them what you want them to hear and encouraging people to look in one direction while something untoward is happening elsewhere. Quite simply, PR is not about being objective, impartial, open, transparent, or informative; and as such it should have no valid role in the running of publicly funded services.

The PR function and the role of the trusted communications adviser have become increasingly indispensable to senior executives in all our public services and NHS Trusts. The practitioners of the dark art are seen as essential aides, confidantes who can successfully help chief executives, senior directors, and chairs navigate the seas of meaningless targets and regulatory measures by helping them master the art of the management of credit, not to be confused with the actual creation of value or the meeting of service user needs. The trick to maintaining your position in public services is to get good at taking the credit for what would have happened anyway, and presenting and reporting on what you intend to do, which is vastly different to doing what you could or will be doing. The balance between doing good and talking about it has been completely lost in all our public services, especially the NHS. You may recall we touched on Cohn's Law earlier, it suggests public sector organisations ensure their sustainability by getting better and better at reporting on the nothing they are doing. One of the primary drivers enabling this shift has been the unchallenged adoption of Public Relations within our public services. Public Relations has been the means by which increasingly stretched incapacitated public services have maintained the illusion of performance against a backdrop of rising demand and in real terms, significantly decreased resources. The use of Public Relations to proffer the appearance of success while services struggle to deliver amidst the dust and rubble of the neoliberal experiment, is akin to dressing the homeless in evening wear to disguise the emergence of grinding poverty.

The following passage is taken from a superb and very readable book called *It's not how good you are its how good you want to be*, written by Paul Arden, a former executive creative director of Saatchi & Saatchi.

> *"For six months we worked on a government scheme devised to help school leavers get jobs. The best people in the agency worked with passion to help solve a social problem. The resulting work was marvellous, and there was a lot of it. It was rejected. All of it.*

We had failed to understand, not the brief, but the politics that lay behind it. All the minister wanted was for the public to know he was spending X millions on advertising for the scheme. To let people know he was doing something about it. It was a PR exercise for him. It had nothing at all to do with humanity".

The final nail in PRs coffin if another is needed is social media. Can any senior manager in their right mind still believe that what goes on inside a large public service organisation, any organisation, stays inside that organisation? Does any leader worth their salt not realise that failing to act on, admit, or acknowledge that something has happened is more detrimental in the long-term. Social media enables information to seep unrestrained between disenchanted disillusioned staff, their families, friends, and wider communities. It provides previously powerless patients and service users a platform from which they can air their experiences widely. The hapless hired PR cheerleaders of the NHS can shake their coloured pom poms, dance as vigorously as they like, and implore us to sing along as loudly as they want, but we can all see the reality, the thinly disguised chaotic carnage unfolding around them.

I believe access to a single version of the truth, unfiltered objective information, empirical facts, and data in relation to our healthcare and wider public services for that matter, should be the right of every citizen. Where there is no threat to national security, then true openness and transparency should be the public sectors default position. Why shouldn't you or I, as taxpayers, citizens, patients, or carers, have easy access to the information we want about the services we pay for, services that exist in theory, to serve our needs? Its far more useful for any of us to know what the quality of our local hospital services are really like, than to hear that the Chief Executive has been awarded a CBE. Should public services that rely on our financial support be able to choose what we as their shareholders and stakeholders, their employees, service users, and the wider public, are entitled to know about their activities, the good, the bad and everything in between. Should they have the right to decide when certain facts and information are to be withheld, in order to protect their reputations behind the guise of maintaining public trust? I don't think so.

It is time to say adios to the PR function in healthcare services as they presently exist. The role of any communications function in a publicly funded service should be impartial and non-partisan, especially in a service that is as critical and important to us all as healthcare.

Chapter 53: Complete transparency and openness

"Sunlight is said to be the best of disinfectants."

Louis Brandeis; US Supreme Court Justice

Once the cancer of the dark art of public relations has been removed from the body of our publicly funded healthcare services, then we can have a conversation about the kind of information we would like made easily available. Complete transparency and openness will help facilitate the development of a wilfully aware health and care system. The availability of factual information that is consistent and accessible across every part of the health and care system and by any interested party should be the aim. Usable relevant information that can be easily accessed, interpreted, and understood, that serves the needs of all stakeholders, including employees, service users, carers, oversight and scrutiny committees, patient interest groups, and advisory bodies and consultants. In place of the puerile spin and immature cheerleading that presently passes for communication in our NHS, lets create a national information and data department, coordinated centrally, and implemented locally, whose job is to publish and facilitate easy access to a broad and consistently comparable range of objective information and open data.

This data and its constant evolution could significantly shape and inform policy making as well as enabling health and care organisations and clinicians to provide better, safer, and more responsive services. The presence of live trusted data would shift the perennial national debate that hovers around the NHS. It could genuinely and intelligently inform the front pages of the press and change our conversations down the pub. It would mean minister's and their acolytes would find it harder to indulge in the luxury of creating short-term vote winning harmful ideologically driven policies based on hearsay and false flags. The NHS is uniquely placed amongst the world's healthcare services to lead the development of a shared evidence base that could have global impact, helping the UK and other countries provide and refine their healthcare systems and services. Precisely what this data and information might be, should be the subject of a continuous discussion. The dataset could start its life with simple information such as treatment waiting times, outcomes, mortality, average length of stay, ward capacity, clinical staff per patient, before building into a more comprehensive consistent and comparable dashboard that GPs, patients, carers, patient groups, and others could readily access.

Leah Binder is the archetypal American Executive. She has been the power dressed broad smiling polished gleaming toothed Chief Executive Officer and President of an influential healthcare oversight and improvement organisation in the USA called the Leapfrog Group, for over fifteen years. The Leapfrog Group is a force for patient safety and describes itself as a national non-profit organisation driving a movement for giant leaps forward in the quality and safety of American health care. The group was set up in 2000 in the wake of increasing and worrying levels of incidents of clinical harm occurring in America's health and care services. Their key approach to improving health and care services is to create greater transparency regarding the performance of hospitals and health services. They collect, analyse, and then openly publish data relating to the quality and safety of over three thousand hospitals and their related services. The service they are seeking to provide is in some respects still a work in progress, not all the data is available for each of the hospitals listed. Naturally, they have their critics, after all the provision of health and care services in the USA is hugely competitive and highly commercialised, and not everyone in the sector is happy to have their services independently rated by an organisation over which they have no control. The Leapfrog Group is akin to something between Trust Pilot, Trip Advisor, and the Care Quality Commission. In its 23yrs of existence, the Leapfrog Group has faced litigation from hospitals who have been unhappy with their rating. Strangely, they have never faced a lawsuit from a hospital that believed it had been over-rated.

The hospital safety scoring grades that the Leapfrog Group apply to each hospital might initially seem a touch simplistic. Each hospital is graded from A to F, and their grade is reassessed twice each year. However, behind each rating is a bank of easily accessible online data and history relating to everything from infection levels, which are rated under six different types of infection, problems with surgery such as blood leakage and wounds left open, safety problems including falls causing broken hips, practices in place to prevent errors, and the responsiveness of doctors, nurses, and hospital staff.

Of course, data in itself can never provide the full picture. Context will always be key. A hospital in a certain location may deal with specific issues and injuries arising from the presence of certain types of industries in the vicinity, which may in turn impact on its ratings. Would you rather have heart surgery in a hospital where more people die because the surgeon specialises in complex cases, or where fewer people die because they undertake such procedures far less often? Even if the data only provides a partial picture, it at least starts a conversation both within and around the organisation and it provides potential patients, their carers, families, and referring GPs, with a basis for asking relevant questions and seeking the most appropriate care.

We here in the UK have no such influential independent and respected organisation. There are pockets of information and data tucked away in places that are accessible if you know where to look for it. There are the National General Practice Profile pages on the UK Gov Website. There are some quality indicators on the NHS England website for NHS Trusts including ambulance services, there are the NHS staff survey results also held on the NHS England website. Then there are the ratings given to health and care providers by the Care Quality Commission, which are generally publicised front and centre by health and care organisations when they have been rated favourably, less prominently when they have not. As for the online presences and websites of each NHS Trust and GP practice and Social Care provider, these are so inconsistent in their content and formats that they offer extraordinarily little in terms of useful data and information and are essentially incomparable in any meaningful sense. We do have a range of initiatives that are attempting to do on a shoestring what the Leapfrog Group appears to be doing reasonably successfully in America. My own view is that a Leapfrog equivalent should be established and funded centrally as part of the drive to implement a single technology platform across all publicly funded health and care services. The information that patients, service users, and other stakeholders within the system would benefit from having access to, is the same information that will help health and care services understand their own performance and improve. I can see no valid reason why each part of the NHS does not have a prominent consistent page on its website entitled, *information and data*.

Epilogue: Can Britain be a model for a better world?

"What is now proved was once only imagined."

William Blake

It would be entirely fair to say we humans don't have a fabulous track-record of thinking ahead, we excel at creating situations that quickly become unmanageable, it's perhaps more accurate to say we are simply unaware of the significance and longer-term consequences of our actions. We are not the best at consequential thinking because our ability and need to innovate remains way ahead of our ability to predict. Debbie and I visited Iceland a few years ago and were at once struck by the absence of trees. We counted the few trees we saw during our time there on less than both hands. When we looked up a bit of the island's history, we were staggered to learn that part of Iceland's original attraction to the Norsemen who first settled there was its sheer abundance of woodland, over a third of the island was once blanketed under a thick canopy of trees. Now Iceland is set to remain a rocky if ruggedly beautiful place, having lost the topsoil needed to ever enable the growth of trees again. Actions have consequences and some things that are lost can never be regained.

In April 2018 the Manic Street Preachers released their thirteenth studio album, *Resistance is Futile*. Its cover featured a striking remastered photo of a samurai warrior, a poignant symbol of a lost era, of a lifetime committed to a code of skilled and courageous if not always selfless sacrifice. The album was a mix of social, political, and personal tracks including a song devoted to the victims of Hillsborough and another on the less than noble ambitions of the world's social media platforms. It reached number two in what old people like me still refer to as the charts. It was only kept from the top spot by the soundtrack of songs from the hit show, *The Greatest Showman* featuring a popular track entitled *This Is Me*. The track is held together with a catchy chorus hook line, *"Look out cause here I come",* a rallying call to the social media obsessed generation to impose their authentic selves and their abilities, perceived or real, upon the world in search of fame and adulation. Irrespective of their quite different musical styles, the ideological contrast between the two albums could not have been greater. Nelson Mandela named one of his daughters Zenani, which means *what have you brought to the world* in the Xhosa language. For *look out here I come* to be anything more than a mantra for a celebrity obsessed generation to seek fame and material gain for its own sake, it needs preceding by the question, *what does the world need*. The answer to which will be shaped by context and perception. Poor countries need wealth and wisdom in inverse proportions to their wealthy counterparts.

Far too many of us are not flourishing and far too many will never even get the opportunity to flourish. It is society and we that need fixing before we attempt to fix our healthcare system. The dream of a better world the NHS represents is dying in front the eyes of any in our era who are prepared to see. The homely blue and white flag of humane collective interdependence we stand under is fraying at the edges. The threads unwind above us in a storm of neoliberal ideology and human frailty as we desperately rally round and try to keep the flagpole upright. The certainty that pervaded the United Kingdom's national psyche about the purpose, character, and enduring capacity of itself and its National Health Service, has been replaced with wilfully blind baseless and ultimately self-defeating optimism. The shaking structures of the NHS are more than merely a reflection of the erosion of our society and the ascendency of self. The presence of a functioning publicly funded health and care system is a litmus test for the presence of civilization. A societal structural institutional indicator species that bodes well for the environment it exists within.

But whatever the challenge facing us it's important we don't fall into the trap of thinking we imagined the present we have or the organisations and institutions that are in it or the way they work. The present we live in is the future we and others created and is largely the result of unintended outcomes. There is no reason a different future can't be created and a great many reasons why it should be. Can Britain become one of the healthiest most fair nations on earth? Could our National Health and Care Service become the largest closely coordinated learning organisation in the world?

Britain, Albion, Pritani, Blighty, the United Kingdom, whatever you prefer to call it, has had a hugely disproportionate impact on our planet, for better and worse. Britain was the first large nation in the world to create a national health service that was publicly funded and free at the point of use for all who needed it. Only New Zealand preceded the UK when it introduced free universal healthcare under the terms of its 1938 Social Security Act. The influences the genies of enterprise Britain released from the bottle of human ambition are still very present in every part of our lives and our planet. The global shadow this country has cast will always far exceed its small relative size. Perhaps the next stage on this unique and strangely influential nations journey through history is as a beacon of human and social development. The answer to the question can Britain be a model for a better world, lies to a great degree with each of us as well as those we elect to govern us. Can you, and I, each become models for a better world and encourage others to do so, and to what degree should we expect and hold government to account for creating the conditions in which we can do so? Land of hope and glory, make thee wiser yet.

Acknowledgements

To the great many people who made time to meet me, speak with me, who I have spoken to in person and virtually exchanged views with during the last few years, and who have been generous with their knowledge and candid in sharing their experiences, and to their colleagues who shuffled diaries to accommodate me, I offer my sincere and heartfelt gratitude and thanks. These include:

Adam Brimelow; NHS Providers | Andra Vlaicu; Friend and Sense-Checker | Andy Bell; Centre for Mental Health | Andy Brogan; Easier inc. | Andy Pow; Specialist Primary Care Accountant | Bev Fitzsimons; Point of Care Foundation | Brendan Martin; Buurtzorg | Cat Duncan-Rees | David Kwo; Healthcare Technology Consultant | David Rowlands; Centre for Health and the Public Interest | David Willis; Clinical Information Manager HSE Ireland | Deborah Coles; INQUEST | Della Reynolds | Dominic Harrison | Dr Alison Schafer; World Health Organisation | Dr Liz Mear; former Chair National Academic Health Science Network | Dr Steve Taylor; GP & NHS Facts and Stats | Emma Wadey; NHS | Evan Kontopantelis; Professor of Date Science & Health Services Research University of Manchester | Farhan Amin; GP | Gemma Clay; NHS | Helen Hughes; Patient Safety Learning | Henry Stewart; Author & Consultant | Ida Hvitved; Healthcare Denmark | Jade Maloney; Institute of Healthcare Management | James Titcombe; Patient Safety Advocate | Jane Chidgey-Clark (Dr); National Guardian for the NHS | Jeff Prescott; Welsh Ambulance Service | Jim Mackey (Sir); NHS | Joanne Hughes; Mothers Instinct | Joe Field | John Walsh; NHS Freedom to Speak Up Guardian | Jon Wilks; Institute of Healthcare Management | Jonathan Sammut; North West Ambulance Service | Karl Roberts; NHS | Lisa Drake; Primary Care Consultant | Liz Ashall-Payne (ORCHA) | Matt Gaskell; NHS | Martin Orton; Professional Records Standards Body | Matthew Taylor; NHS Confederation | Melanie Hodson; Hospice UK | Melanie Leahy | Mike Chitty; Leadership and Organisational Culture Consultant | Morten Mathieson; Sekoia | Nicholas Gruen | Pascale Robinson; We Own It | Paul Whiteing; Association against Medical Accidents (AVMA) | Peter Walsh; former Chief Executive AVMA | Phillip Greenup; Queensland Health | Professor Mary Dixon-Woods; The Health Improvement Institute | Professor Sir Nick Black; London School of Hygiene and Tropical Medicine | Rachel Holiday; Time to Change West Cumbria | Rob Behrens; PHSO |

Roger Kline; Research Fellow Middlesex University | Rory Sutherland | Roy Lilley | Russell Parkinson; The Guardian Service | Sir Robert Francis | Shaun Lintern; Sunday Times | Shayna Jadeja | Sue Allison | Sue Pike; NHS | Sue Wheeler; NHS | Tim Farron MP | Tony Martignetti.

Thank you to the very many inspirational advocates for patient safety I have met over the years and the numerous serving and retired healthcare professionals who took the time to share their experiences and views. Not everyone who did so wanted to be named.

I would also like to thank Healthcare Improvement Scotland; Hospice UK; Keep Our NHS Public; Lincoln University; Mental Health Foundation; NHS England; NHS Resolution; Open Democracy; PULSE; Saint Anselm College Center for Ethics in Society; Save Our NHS; TaxWatch UK; The Centre for Public Impact; The Danish Chamber of Commerce; The Good Law Project; The Money and Mental Health Institute, The National Health Action Party; The National Institute for Health and Care Excellence; The National Ombudsman's Office Netherlands; The Nursing Times; The Open Data Institute; The Open Government Network; The Public Health functions of England, Ireland, Scotland and Wales; The Scottish Public Health Ombudsman; We Own It; numerous Royal Colleges and various NHS Trusts.

Special thanks go to John Seddon of Vanguard Consulting whose insights and writing on the importance of systems thinking were a revelation. You have a lot to answer for John!

In the course of writing this book, I reached out to very many individuals and organisations and spoke with a great number of people. I purposefully made many attempts to engage with bodies and the people within them that I felt would have opposite views to my own. Unfortunately, it appears Upton Sinclair was right, there is little appetite for discussion and dialogue from within most of the unelected unaccountable organisations and bodies that we as taxpayers seem obliged to fund. Many whose nebulous efforts and expensive activity would barely be missed if they were not here and some whose absence would have a substantially positive effect. I believe every publicly funded organisation has a duty to look squarely into the mirror on a regular basis and ask itself, what difference are we making and would anyone other than ourselves mourn our passing. The Care Quality Commission wouldn't engage, but that wasn't a great surprise. And Healthwatch UK, whose former chair Sir Robert Francis described them to me as a *"challenged organisation"*, proved him right.

Various private sector healthcare providers were approached for their views and thoughts, but I think they felt unable or unwise to comment on matters pertaining to publicly funded healthcare services.

Please accept my sincere apologies if I neglected to mention you and feel free to email or ring and harangue me.

Lastly, I should say that any perceived excess of cynicism, use of overly colourful language, or expressing of inappropriate humour, should be attributed to the author alone.

About the author

I think this is where I'm supposed to tell you how relatable and generally fabulous I am; *"Tom embraces Buddhist philosophy, enjoys walks in the country with his wife Debbie, likes to read about Eastern cultures, he works tirelessly on behalf of those he sees as less fortunate than himself, and loves animals."* The truth about me is that I am as fallible, flawed, and perfectly imperfect as the next person. I drive my wife Debbie nuts when I point and shout at the telly without warning.

This is the second of two books I have authored. I was originally driven to write out of necessity as therapy for depression; I've not looked back since! My first book, *Lions, Liars, Donkeys and Penguins - The Killing of Alison* (2020), is the critically acclaimed true story of the events surrounding the suicide of my sister who took her life after being sexually exploited by a nurse in an NHS mental health hospital. I spent decades seeking justice for Alison, but in March 2023 at the High Court in London, I failed in my quest to achieve it. I've come to realise the journey itself was my real victory. I've known the Black Dog well and as I get older I find myself increasingly allergic to fuckwittery, especially when undertaken with public money.

I'm an escapee from radical religion, a former homeless teenage punk who was expelled from school, and a public sector manager who lost my job after whistleblowing. I'm a Fellow of the Institute of Management, I have an MBA and an MSc. What my experiences have taught me is far more valuable than my master's degrees and as well as a budding author I'm a business consultant and trainer using my unique mix of learned, lived, and professional experience and knowledge to help healthcare organisations provide safe services. I'm a regular speaker at the annual Patient Safety Congress and in the wake of the Lucy Letby case I was invited to comment on NHS culture for Newsnight and LBC. I've sat on numerous steering groups contributing to nationally significant topics including Open Government, the Justice System, and NHS leadership. I believe improvement begins with understanding and our ignorance is the greatest enemy we face.

I love good music, especially when heard at Glastonbury. The Clash, Foo Fighters, and the Manic Street Preachers are among the many bands that float my boat. If I could invite any guests for a meal and the craic, at the time of writing this they would be, William Blake, Aldous Huxley, Margaret Mead, Joe Strummer, and my wife Debbie. She is my rock.

If you would like to get in touch you can find me on LinkedIn (tomcumbria), on Twitter @TominCumbria, my website is www.cormetis.com, I can be emailed at tom@cormetis.com

"What is the price of Experience? do men buy it for a song? Or wisdom for a dance in the street? No, it is bought with the price of all that a man hath, his house, his wife, his children. Wisdom is sold in the desolate market where none come to buy, And in the wither'd field where the farmer plows for bread in vain.

William Blake; The Four Zoas

Printed in Great Britain
by Amazon